CW00673268

England, This England

J. G. RAMSAY

England, This England

In the Steps of J. B. Priestley

SINCLAIR-STEVENSON

First published in Great Britain in 1993
by Sinclair-Stevenson
an imprint of Reed Consumer Books Ltd
Michelin House, 81 Fulham Road, London SW3 6RB
and Auckland, Melbourne, Singapore and Toronto

A CIP catalogue record for this book
is available at the British Library
ISBN 1 85619 329 2

Typeset by Falcon Graphic Art Ltd
Wallington, Surrey
Printed in England by Clays Ltd, St Ives plc

for Julie and Edward; and for the evening
light that fell across Pwllheli beach

Contents

Prologue 1
Greater Manchester and Merseyside 5
East Lancashire 45
Tyneside and Cleveland 66
West and South Yorkshire 104
East Midlands and the Potteries 138
The West Midlands 180
Norfolk and Suffolk 206
East Kent and Sussex 236
Hampshire 263
The West Country 285
Gloucestershire and the Journey Home 316
Index 338

Idealists, however, never listen to wiser counsel;
only to the dictates of their own consciences.

SIR PEREGRINE WORSTHORNE

prologue

When I arrived at Basingstoke Station, I asked the ticket collector if there was a source of tourist information anywhere in the town. I seriously expected to be laughed at, in spite of the fact that these days nearly everywhere you go, no matter how mundane the town, no matter how trivial its historical associations, you can usually find a tourist information centre. Everywhere has its source of accommodation and historic facts pleasantly related by smiling femininity, its promotional leaflets and books, its souvenir mugs and key-rings, its supplanting of the fashionable word 'heritage' to the description of incumbent areas, to add bogus sentimental appeal in this crazy mixed-up late-twentieth-century England, where Victorian slums have suddenly become fashionable.

Though I was by no means a tourist in the typical sense of the word, I was still a traveller, and the most direct way of locating accommodation, other than walking the streets, which can waste valuable time, is to find a tourist information centre. I can only assume the ticket collector had not taken much trouble to evaluate the town expanding around his little plastic booth. Perhaps he did not live there. Either way, he did not respond to my question about the location of the tourist information centre very eloquently. He did not laugh, as I expected. In fact, he did not respond to me at all. He merely looked at me vacantly and askance, his mouth noticeably askew, his face slightly puffy-eyed, and proceeded to carry on as if the person standing in front of him simply wasn't there. I might as well have been a sheet of glass. I repeated my question and this time he had the audacity to lift his head on its shoulders, so that he could see if there were any more people coming up behind me from beneath the subway. Then he turned his back and began gloating over page three of a tabloid newspaper.

Why he should have ignored me baffled me. I was as polite to him as we have been assured recently British Rail staff are making a determined effort to be to us. I walked away and stared dumbly at a map on the ticket office wall, but I was not really taking anything in. The map was a place to rest my eyes while I tried to collect myself and decide what I had done wrong. I cannot be the only person who from time to time becomes so immersed in thought as he is walking around that a few seconds after he has said something, he cannot remember what it was. I was still wondering if I had inadvertently uttered an insult, when a young chap appeared alongside me, made some unrepeatable remarks about the emotional credibility of the ticket collector, pointed outside to a familiar brown-and-white sign bolted to a pole – brown-and-white: the corporate colours of Heritage Britain – grinned, then marched away through the station entrance. I noticed that the doors to the building were automated. The young man's remarks had about them a rather falsified, rehearsed air of delivery, like John Cleese playing a hotel owner at his most nonchalant. His words seemed to act as a sort of verbal punch-line to the atmosphere I had inhaled of much of modern England so far. They were instantly evocative of the feel of the country today, far more revealing than the endless wandering of neat suburban streets, the sight of copies of *Reader's Digest* still piled on coffee tables in waiting rooms, or the talk with company directors in a rash of new post-Modernist office buildings with the trendy overhanging eaves. His words were part of the unofficial pattern superimposed on the flavour of English life by mass popular culture, embellishing the country's every thought and move. Since the beginning of October I had been, and still was, in search of England. But all I could find was a blank stare and a mouthful of bad language uttered in a modern south country town.

As I emerged from the station and looked at the architectural hotch-potch arranged before me, that I was in Basingstoke in 1991 was obvious enough. But I was also in the world of *Viz* magazine and lewd chewing-gum advertisements ('Chew on this, dog breath!'); scruffy mongrels mating on patches of municipal grass while our grandparents play bowls in the background; the jokes exchanged routinely between *Daily Telegraph* readers about Ian Hislop's quiz show appearances, which they caught when flicking channels over the weekend while simultaneously thinking about smiling pumpkins; timeless thatched cottages in Suffolk; Keith Waterhouse's latest novel; John Junor's unspoken suspicions about Edward Heath's unmentionable operation; and a million other small idiosyncrasies you could care to mention. A few hours' flight from nearby Heathrow, the Serbs' and Croats' slaughter of one another would just be getting under way, the United Nations soon preparing to go in.

But I was safely in England. England, England, where the glory of the garden does indeed lie in more than meets the eye. England, where I could comfortably switch on to *Newsnight* that evening, as I did in my small Basingstoke room, and listen to Jeremy Paxman, somehow not quite as earnest or as jeering since his coughing fit live on air a couple of years back, diligently informing us about the bloody Yugoslav events. Not long after, on another television network, I would be able to hear Tony Slattery, fresh from his Labatts lager commercials, with his arm back to normal length and his eyeballs back in their sockets, saying, on a light-hearted musical quiz show, that Richard Vranch the pianist has just finished him off by hand, and receiving a burst of mellow tin-can laughter from his audience accordingly. The Los Angeles riots that shook the United States to its foundations and gave England a powerful glimpse of the post-industrial society it has coming, where brutalized hordes are genuinely chastised for not conforming to the moral values of the civilized and the wealthy, and everywhere is in danger of becoming one vast frightening South Africa, had not yet happened. Instead, the England of residential suburbs was moving ever sleepily forward, like all those I had so far seen; like the comfortable suburb where I live, where we smile at each other, allow our children to play with each other, where we count each other's cars, but where we don't really know one another. Even the suet puddings were still being steamed somewhere. The Gulf War was a diminishing memory. John Major would soon be safely ensconced back in number ten. The Labour Party would face another constitutional crisis. Mrs Thatcher would continue to ruffle feathers, having been stabbed in the back by her party in the meantime. Andrew Morton would be a notorious household name, showing us how easy it is to make money writing books if you can only lower yourself to becoming a skunk (that is, releasing an unpleasant smell into the air). Neil Kinnock would be a fading legend, and *The Sunday Telegraph* would have brought back Peregrine Worsthorne, thank God. And so sleepy old England would go.

It would also soon be spring. The economics of the madhouse would finally be upon us. It would be that time of year when we untangle the knot from the lawnmower cable and plan our holidays anew. I would be revisiting all the places described in this book at the screen of a word processor, the sequence already receding into memory and beginning to sparkle with the uneasy glow of nostalgia. When I arrived that afternoon in Hampshire after more than two months of travelling, however, it was still the depths of a particularly uneventful winter.

Meanwhile, Basingstoke and the rest of England, here I came.

I

Greater Manchester and Merseyside

The Journey North

If you are an English person, if you can describe yourself seriously as such a thing these days without inviting a chorus of canned laughter from some of our more enlightened circles, you cannot avoid becoming aware of the north-south antithesis, of the regional snobberies peculiar to the atmosphere of England, as soon as you begin moving through it. It is perhaps symptomatic of the staid, backward-looking atmosphere of a country like ours that one should begin a journey round England by thinking thoughts so predictable as these at all.

They had been turning over in my mind throughout the morning, since I had climbed into the taxi outside my publisher's office and it had moved with the traffic through the early autumn sunshine across London and deposited me at Euston Station, and I'd tried to gear myself up mentally for the three months of travelling that lay ahead. Even the modern interior of Euston Station, with its low corrugated ceiling, its shiny platform surfaces, and its rows of fluorescent light tubes curving toward daylight somewhere beyond the approach lines, where I boarded the northbound express, raised questions. Somehow, it was not the likeliest of settings from which to begin a journey round modern England. For months I had contemplated the undertaking and assumed I should be starting out from a place resembling the kind of big old-fashioned railway terminus as it exists in the popular imagination. Preferably a cavernous interior held up by an embroidery of muscular Victorian cast-iron (as in Euston's neighbour Kings Cross), not something that resembles the functional interiors of those huge distribution warehouses that are gathering alongside the country's motorways. Naturally I was disappointed. But then, my assumptions and my disappointment are part of the problem, if indeed it is a problem, of being English. We are a tremendously preconceived people, something which is merely a reflection of the fact that we are a deeply conservative nation, as a number of our political commentators, and the odd party, realized after the result of the 1992 General Election. Consequently, a journey round modern England will almost certainly include, as a major part of its atmosphere, a contemplation of tradition, but more especially of the past. It hangs like a mill-stone round the country's neck. It is impossible to avoid getting caught up in it, in the great wave of nostalgia sweeping England at the present time, where we seem to be retreating into the safe romanticism of the past because of the uncertainty we feel about the future.

No sooner had the train left the north London suburbs behind, picked up the beginnings of the Home Counties, and roared through a section of countryside between Leighton Buzzard and Bletchley that was pure green and pleasant cliché, than I began thinking about this uncertainty more than ever. I also thought about those irritating prejudices that exist between north and south – more especially in my experience between south and north – prejudices that have shaped the attitude of a nation for generations, so many stubbornly ill-conceived and born of simple ignorance. Again, you see, if you are English you cannot help but be aware of them, and that morning I became enormously irritated with myself for becoming ensnared in the same old trap. I assume this happened because I was aware of the job I had to do and was absurdly conscious of a sort of detached perspective of myself, like a roving documentary camera, for the first few days of the journey, till the novelty began to wear off nearer the weekend. I was heading north at more than a hundred miles an hour, through a dripping dewy landscape glowing gold beneath the most brilliant of blue skies, to Manchester. North to a region that is the butt of an abundance of national stock jokes. North to a region that is host to a plethora of inaccurate social generalizations as well as a lot of Labour Party supporters. I had not been away long enough to develop the kind of jaundiced eye that might distort the perceptions of someone arriving for the first time who is shocked to find that the sun actually shines up there. The sun shone all the way from London to Manchester, and it is perhaps worth remembering it was the same sun hanging in the same sky in the same corner of the same universe.

But on that last day of September it so happened that I was also travelling north to my home. It was a home where I knew there lived a lot of people who were very poor, but also plenty who were very rich, particularly where the south Manchester suburbs blend into Cheshire, where they have long talked about the number of millionaires per square acre in an area that grew originally from the desire of the city's bourgeoisie to move upwind to escape the industrial smog. I was sitting inside a gleaming metal projectile slicing through much the same sort of English countryside and beneath the same fluffy white clouds scudding overhead all the way. All around me was a landscape punctuated with distant church steeples lost in the pearly ambience of an autumnal haze. All around me were the tiny hay bales, the farmhouses, the sheep, the cows, the velvety golf courses raked by the elongated blue-black shadows of poplar trees, the overgrown railway sidings, the gleaming branch lines suddenly sweeping away and blending with the hedgerows, the country church yards, the fans of sombre gravestones sulking beneath the elms, the distant undulating villages, the remaining red telephone boxes scattered far and wide, the great marching pylons, and the synthetic skyline of Milton Keynes. It was a landscape and an England from which John Schlesinger could have selected any number of images perfect for a Conservative Party Political Broadcast; symbolic snapshots which were to recur constantly throughout my travels, asserting themselves so frequently I gradually began to search for them and even found them superimposed over my dreams. That morning I saw it all, including the bypasses and the motorways, the distant blocks of flats, and a handful of derelict bottle kilns on the outskirts of the Potteries, an industrial area to which I would be returning a month or two afterwards. On the seat next to me was the premiere issue of *The Modern Review* and that day's edition of *The Guardian*, which I had picked up chiefly because it was running a profile describing the 'total selfishness of Auberon Waugh'. I had noted with interest, as Mr Waugh might well have noted with interest, that since last I had travelled inter-city, British Rail had become politically correct by prescribing second-class passengers to be 'standard-class' passengers, rather as those self-righteous equal opportunities simpletons who attempt to subvert plain language by designating people of ethnic origin as being of 'alternative skin colour', instead of simply being black. Perhaps one day I shall be bound on a train from London not to Manchester but to Personchester, standing confusedly outside the city's public toilets, looking this way and that, once I have arrived.

But heading north I was aware too of a creeping sense of apprehension. When the train eventually made its way through the outer- then the inner-urban ring of Manchester, and I saw numerous cobbled back alleys bisecting the embankment at right angles, and kids in garish-coloured shellsuits kicked balls about on filthy patches of grass before a backdrop of grey tower blocks when presumably they ought to have been at school, the same old generalizations began to surface. Huge billboard posters depicting a leather-clad Arnold Schwarzenegger sitting atop a chromed motorcycle wielding an oversized shotgun from *Terminator 2* came into view. His sunglassed features scowling over the city, the gleaming muzzle of the projecting gun-barrel, seemed a perfect allegory to the brutalized emotions increasingly permeating some of those wretched streets, where buses and traffic flashed intermittently between the buildings about as frequently as those shellsuited youngsters' chances of not getting a job. It put me into the appropriate mood. During its years of vigorous industrial expansion in the mid-nineteenth century, when the term *laissez-faire* was associated with this part of the world more than it was with anywhere else, Manchester was the only provincial city impudent enough to challenge the commercial supremacy of London, because its principle industry, cotton, was vital to the prosperity of the entire nation. In the process, however, the city developed something of a reputation for harbouring lawlessness and being not much more than a colossal industrial slum; one where the young Frederick Engels conducted the fieldwork among sulphuric fumes and smog that would lead him to socialism and inspire the writings of Karl Marx; one where the poor dug up the corpses of cholera victims to grind up the bones and sell them as fertilizer. Because it lacked adequate municipal administration – a throwback to it having retained the status of a village as recently as 1765 – in those days Manchester was a rough, frontier sort of place, swilling with putrid industrial effluent. It was considered as unsafe to walk the streets of the city after dark as it is today. Conditions in some sectors of the city were so desperate, in fact, they ruled out civilized living altogether. Today Manchester's brash nineteenth-century confidence and former cotton spinning supremacy might only be a memory celebrated in the city's Museum of Science and Industry and the name of a bar in one of its premier hotels, the industrial effluent long since drained away. But if my frequent perusals of the *Manchester Evening News* were anything to go by, I fear the wheel might be once again turning full circle. This is what is unnerving, for the brutality of those Dickensian slums *is* being recast in concrete and barbed-wire, with pump-action robbery and drugs-related violence taking on epidemic proportions, and as an awareness it overshadowed much that I saw and thought throughout this journey.

As the train ran into the city centre beneath a confusion of overhead wires, I thought about this as I looked down into the gloomy streets running adjacent to the viaduct that leads into Piccadilly Station, just as I used to think about it when I spent many an uneasy hour roaming them when I was a student at the city's polytechnic ten years ago. It used to strike me then, as it struck me again that morning, how unfortunate it is that people coming to Manchester from the south by train should arrive at Piccadilly Station and see that part of the city first. Though there are some good buildings remaining, and though the new tram system is being brought through and a huge marina development has begun that will transform the area, it is that bit too far from the main shopping area to avoid the fine coating of shabbiness that penetrates the outskirts of big city centres, once you are away from the hub of activity. Of course I would not wish to emphasise this aspect of Manchester and give an unfair impression of the place before I have arrived or begun talking about it. It is an illusion to believe that rows of boarded-up shops and the smearing of bill posters over large dusty windows can only be found in the north of England, for you find this big city decrepitude, this darkening of neglected architecture, colouring your vision wherever you go. I would not wish to emphasise it in Manchester because I think Manchester is the best city in the country, bearing in mind that in saying these things you need to keep a sensible perspective on the things you observe going on around you, and clearly remember, each time you feel that cosy tug of sentiment when you come upon a nice old town or building, that all English policemen are not a sort of everlasting squad of smiling Jack Warners populating a never-ending rerun of *The Blue Lamp*; that nothing, and nobody, is ever what it seems; and that coming to terms with the truth propping up reality is rather like waking up to discover your favourite childhood film star has been exposed as something rather unpleasant, despite his fictitious public persona being the role model of perfect family man.

As a consequence, I am here to describe what I believe will turn out to be not much more than a series of personal impressions; how one person's moods and responses were stimulated by seeing different parts of the country in a certain sequence or coming upon them in a particular way. And as I emerged from the station into the Manchester sunshine, and made my way past the pile of office blocks grouped around the green oasis called Piccadilly Gardens, observing with interest, as has been observed before, that the statue of Queen Victoria faces the opposite way, I can only assume my thoughts had adjusted themselves to take account of the fact that I was gathering material for a book. My senses were probably working overtime, I knew the north of England better than anywhere, but having spent the better part of the morning in Kensington, walking now into a city that seemed rather more threadbare just there than I remembered, for the first time in my life I was returning to the north wondering what on earth I was going to find.

Manchester

What I found in Manchester was a provincial city with the subtle air of modern English prosperity blowing comfortably along many of its pedestrianized thoroughfares. Whatever the compilers of those current affairs programmes continue to think when they persist in playing a tune by the Brighouse and Rastrick Brass Band when they cut to a report from Lancashire or Yorkshire, go to Manchester and you find a city moving confidently toward the beginning of the next century and virtually unrecognizable from the blackened north country stereotype of old. It is a far cry indeed from the city's position fifteen or twenty years ago, when, soot-blackened and neglected, it was still struggling to come to terms with itself and gain its commercial footing because the trade that built it had finally abandoned it between the wars, and was still on the receiving end of the kind of barbed comments uttered by A.J.P Taylor, who a few years previously had compared Manchester famously to a compost heap. Fortunately, Manchester has since discovered its rich architectural inheritance, even if not so very long ago, when flared trousers were just beginning to flap ridiculously in strong winds above feet perched atop the clumsiest platform heels, the City Planning Department could claim with seriousness that 'although the task of removing the physical legacy of the Industrial Revolution is immense, Manchester is able and determined to accept the challenge'. How quickly attitudes change.

It is true that you can find that air of prosperity coursing through almost any substantial city in modern England, even in central Liverpool, and if you were a foreigner who concentrated on this aspect of the country, and leafed through the odd copy of *Surrey Occasions Magazine* at the expense of everything else, you could come away with entirely the wrong impression. Manchester is still surrounded to the north and east by an almost unbroken ring of former industrial textile towns, which really form a vast sprawling suburb of red brick that appears as though it will go on forever. The huge silent mills float mournfully above the chimney pots like abandoned ships, often right alongside brand-new supermarkets and at the edge of ring roads or overshadowing shiny new industrial units, though many of them are now enormous distribution warehouses owned by mail order catalogue companies and are packed full of advanced technology. The closest mill towns are Rochdale and Oldham, both of which I spent some time exploring, on foot and from the windows of a train. I noted with interest that since I had made a meticulous, almost obsessive photographic study of Oldham six or seven years previously, still more of the old cotton mills had gone; yet more of the old rows of terraced houses and shops – some of which I used to get into when they were boarded up and remove old bakelite light switches and door handles – had been obliterated. I watched some steeplejacks demolishing a mill chimney and listened to the comments of a small crowd of spectators who despised the fact the enormous phallus had risen toward the heavens at all. I suppose their parents having worked in the mill beneath it, and the wages they drew having perhaps played a part in determining their entry into the world when that chimney was still belching black smoke, never really occurred to them. Habitual prejudice of this kind is hardly surprising, though. There can be no other place in England that has been as ashamed of its own image over recent years, and in particular of the quantity of mill chimneys striking from its skyline, than the town of Oldham in Greater Manchester, even if the younger generation living within its boundaries can become bundles of contradiction and turn into mini nationalists the moment comparisons are made between it and the old industrial slums.

Manchester does still have its inner city slums, albeit if the occupants these days tend not to be housed in squat Victorian terraces, have decent sanitation, and no longer share living quarters with livestock or pigs. One of the first things I did when I arrived in Manchester was to look at several of these inner city areas, rather warily at times I admit, because of the air of crime and violence to which they are permanently attached, causing you to feel continually uneasy when you are there. In particular I had another look at that vast run-down wasteland constituting the bulk of Hulme – no visit to Manchester can be complete without it – where the huge and notorious Crescents, enormous horse-shoe shaped system-built deck tenements, form the city's most famous and embarrassing civic landmarks. I was genuinely startled at how much more derelict and overgrown the Crescents had become since I was a student at the nearby polytechnic ten years earlier. They were bad enough back then. One of them was now surrounded by so much vegetation and trees-in-all-the-wrong-places it was difficult to believe there were people actually living there. But there were. Among the blank pieces of chipboard covering hundreds of broken windows, some surrounded by scorch marks from arson attacks, there were sad little lines of washing suspended above the tiny balconies. Pathetic little footpaths meandered between the shrubs and saplings, along which a number of people were actually walking, mainly flat-capped old men in training shoes and Hilda Ogden lookalikes wrapped up in headscarves, and greying West Indians wearing pork-pie hats, all of whom seemed to be carrying well-worn supermarket carrier bags. The significant point to observe is that the grounds to the flats had been overgrown for so long the illicit footpaths had worn into grooves and bedded themselves in, making a mockery of the abandoned thoroughfares designated for pedestrian use by the middle class Utopianists that inspired these places. It is not enough to say, as numerous television and newspaper reports have said, that Hulme was a dismal failure socially and architecturally on a monumental scale: that it was the biggest concrete nuclear fallout shelter of its kind masquerading as human habitation built in Europe: that the whole place reeks of post-apocalyptic analogies and automatically suggests metaphors connected to the after-effects of nuclear war, when as a fate for the human race such a calamity was still considered fashionable. When J.B. Priestley travelled through England, he observed that the dole places reeked of stinking and defeated humanity, and indicated nothing but a shambling, dull-eyed poor imitation of life. The crucial factor today is that nothing much has changed, except the building materials and the failed architectural styles. The faces I encountered walking between those hideous tenements were certainly shambling and dull-eyed. The minor fact that some of the younger residents blast one another in the chest with shotguns to sort out occasional local difficulties, usually concerning the distribution of drugs, is now largely incidental. One man had been found murdered in Moss Side, across the road from the Hulme Crescents, when I was there; his skull and jaw smashed so violently he could not be identified from his dental records. Another was almost hacked to death by several men wielding machetes outside a pub. But then, this is part of the atmosphere and emerging pattern of modern English inner city life, busily turning itself into a sort of down market Soweto, and the more frequently we hear about it in the news, the more we slide over it and remain oblivious to the social changes that are slowly being worked deep within our civilization.

A man I spoke to on a street corner when I was in Hulme blamed the compulsive headbutting behaviour and shotgun delinquency of many modern inner city areas entirely on Margaret Thatcher. Something he did not mention and that suggested he did not actually live there, as we stared across empty car parks glittering with fragments of glass catching the rays of the rising sun, and countless stacks of municipal tenements materialized ghostlike through the early morning mist beyond, was that this anti-social behaviour is only the effect of a very small minority. There is a tendency also to assume that these places are not much more than havens of white working-class delinquency, whereas in fact – and rather surprisingly – in Hulme there are large numbers of students and single black people living in the Crescents. For years families with children have been either settled elsewhere or allocated housing on ground floors only. These places are probably now not just as bad as is commonly believed, at any rate not during the day. Hulme has some eight or nine tenant associations, all attempting to improve the quality of life in the area and liaising with the city council over projected improvements about which they have been promised continuous consultation, though it goes without saying that they remain supremely sceptical of that. There can be little doubt that if the whole of Hulme were refurbished and turned into a vast student hall of residence, rather as happened for the student world games fiasco in Sheffield, the social complexion of the area would change considerably, the air of deprivation and violence probably disappearing more or less overnight (and reappearing elsewhere). As it happens, only a few weeks after I was there at the beginning of this journey, the transformation of Hulme began anew. A two-hundred million pound redevelopment programme lasting five years got under way in November when one of the estate's oldest residents, seventy-six-year-old Marie Blinkhorn, sent a two-ton steel ball crashing into one of the blocks of tenements, so that by the time they are published, these words and my observations when I was in Manchester will already be receding into history.

Some of the problems associated with inner city deprivation seem to be connected to the bottom layer of the working class becoming victims of a welfare system that encourages them to have children to be eligible for council accommodation. The reasons behind the rising tide of violence that is emerging as a marked characteristic of the flavour of modern life are also, of course, many and varied. There have always been slums, just as there have always been a number of half-witted people populating slums and half-witted people in positions of authority. But the notion that modern slums are entirely a product of the renaissance of free market economics has always struck me as something of a nonsense; an easy scapegoat for socialists searching blindfolded for a socio-economic donkey upon which to pin the tail of blame. The subtly brutalizing, opportunistic nature of market forces has doubtless filtered through to influence the unpleasant bearing suspended over these inner urban places; but it is not the entire story by any means, and there is not the space or time to go into what the rest of that story might be just here. To select only the briefest of examples to make an important point, however, it is interesting to observe that some years back *The Economist* referred to modern corporate housing disasters such as Hulme, how they had encased in concrete the problems of social deprivation, alienation, crime, family breakdown, and moral delinquency. It referred to the sport known as 'bombing', whereby youngsters living in Hulme dropped dustbin lids from the upper walkways of deck tenements onto the heads of people passing beneath. This paragraph could have been taken from any newspaper over the past ten years. And yet it was written in 1978, when Margaret Thatcher was an opposition leader associated with clumsy hand-bags, old-fashioned pleated skirts, and with snatching away bottles of school milk, and Britain was being run by a Labour government – by a party that has since blamed social deprivation, crime, and family breakdown entirely on Margaret Thatcher and the Conservative Party, just as that elderly man did on a street corner in Hulme at the beginning of the 1990s.

But it is Manchester the changing city I am determined to concern myself with here, for to me it has the edge over virtually everywhere else, even if we are at the beginning of what will prove to be a lengthy period of austerity and a further commercial contraction due to our inexorable economic decline. Quite how the present changing pattern of trade and tightening of monetary belts and curtailing of public sector borrowing requirements will affect Manchester (and the future of Hulme) this time round is difficult to say. Mingling with the bustling crowds in the central part of the city a day or so after I arrived, the buckles on those monetary belts appeared still to be loosened. The deep streets of the banking quarter, crowned by Sir Edward Lutyens's magnificent Midland Bank, were great canyons of dusty shadow glistening with parked executive cars. Like the subtle veneer of opulence and expense-account embellished laughter circulating self-importantly across prestigious St Ann's Square and along Deansgate, they looked as far away from recession as ever. I ascended an escalator inside a large glass tube and ate a plate of fresh salad sitting by the window of the new food hall that has been opened above the Arndale Centre, a dominating structure that on a number of occasions I have heard described by Mancunians as the largest public lavatory in the world. Staring down at the crowds it was easy to be absorbed by the wholesomeness and vitality of the entire scene, basking as it was beneath crisp sunshine, even if it is worth remembering that the recession had yet to peak when I was there and Norman Lamont was still making feeble prophecies and being laughed at by *The Sunday Times*. All along the main piazzas and avenues the office workers and young dark-stockinged secretaries were emerging from the tower blocks and sitting eating sandwiches or baked potatoes, surrounded by modern herringbone-patterned brick paviour sets (if present trends are anything to go by, these seem destined to cover half the surface of England, if not the whole of Europe), and plenty of reproduction Victorian street furniture. With the leaves of early autumn chasing in circles round their ankles; with the salubrious peal of the town hall clock booming lazily in the background; with the sound of pop music blaring from the dashboard of the occasional Asian exhibitionist displaying himself in a bottom-of-the-range all-white Mercedes at the nearby traffic lights (he is probably a wholesaler of imported clothing from those backstreets of Piccadilly), much of what I saw felt uplifting and rather reassuring. If you kept one eye on the exclusive shops down King Street, and one ear open to the constant bustle and scrape and clacking of shoes, there could be little doubt that here was a city that was an important commercial and financial centre; one where money was being spent and where things of importance happened. Here was a city that had at last got rid of the beleaguered industrial image that tarnished the north of England for so long; a process which got under way in earnest when Castlefield was designated Britain's first Urban Heritage Park back in 1982, and surely culminated in Granada Television finally replacing the gloomy pictures shown over the credits to *Coronation Street* with shots taken in bright sunshine.

Perhaps that is another worthwhile reason to begin a journey such as this in a part of the country that has seen some of the biggest and most far-reaching changes. There has been a lot of noise generated about Manchester's economic changes, and words written about its long period of decline, manifested typically not so very long ago when a newspaper article that pandered to the blackened Mancunian city of old had to create a picture of modern urban-industrial desolation by assembling components from several different photographs into a single montage. I have at times been living in, and commuted to and from, London for the past fifteen years. Apart from a few superficial changes, the Docklands, and Canary Wharf, it does not seem much different to what it was when I first went there, except that in places there is probably a lot more rubbish and men as well as women are getting raped on the Underground. You cannot say the same thing about Manchester, for it has changed enormously. I am certain this impression is something to do with size. London is so vast it rambles and everything soon becomes lost in the blur. In a place the size of Manchester, you can walk from one end of the city centre to the other in less than half-an-hour, which enables its character and its sense of scale to surface more easily, though it maintains the presence of a real city. This also enables its changes to be more easily observed, though you would not think so from the comments that continue to be aimed in the direction of Manchester occasionally today. When Manchester was allocated a considerable amount of public money by central government to enable it to make its bid for the Olympic games not long ago, a number of sniggers could be discerned emanating softly from the all-knowing echelons of Fleet Street – sniggers that are stuck solid at about the year 1965, and based on nothing but secondhand information, grievous bodily reputation, and straightforward lousy prejudice.

It is, you see, almost impossible to find the authentic derelict, soot-blackened Manchester of old, and has been for some time now. The city has undergone a substantial face-lift over the ten or twelve years that I have known it, but what these changes have heralded has been given far less publicity and credence than what was left industrially behind. The city even has its own miniature Docklands – crisp post-Modernist office and apartment blocks, tubular-metal porticoes, trendily-painted chunks of nineteenth-century civil engineering turned into massive ornamental sculptures, multi-screen cinema, science park enshrouded in smoked-glass, and all – down at Salford Quays. There has been much talk and late-night laughter released over glasses of wine about London's Docklands, in particular about its light railway and its padlocked fences and gates, but not much reference to Manchester's Docklands, the biggest development of its kind outside London, forming an important part of the city's commercial renaissance and desire to rectify its shortage of office space. It is a far cry indeed from the scene down at Salford Quays ten years ago, which, as I well remember, was a huge wasteland of overgrown railway sidings and rotting brickwork. The transformation from a vast decaying legacy of Manchester's dockland past and former industrial prominence because of the ship canal has been remarkable, the one disconcerting aspect about it being that there is still a terrible silence hanging over the place. The only sounds breaking it the muggy morning I was there during this journey were those from a flock of seagulls being agitated by water bubbling from an outlet pipe in the centre of one of the dock basins, and the forlorn noise of authentic dockland activity way off down the canal at Trafford Park, as though it were muffled sound going on behind a huge closed door concealing Britain's heavy industrial past. Alongside your feet was the ever present sound of lapping water, one of the characteristic noises of post-industrial, service-oriented, marina-embracing England, and one of the most melancholy sounds I have yet heard. The fact that, like its big equivalent in the south of England, Salford Quays appears to be struggling to attract tenants and businesses, and that the environment could really be said to be a symptom of Britain's deep-rooted economic malaise, is, of course, another matter entirely. At least these places look like they are staring the future full in the face, if most of the rest of the country is not. That is a small consolation that offers hope if nothing else.

Is an image of Salford Quays generally associated with the Manchester of the post-industrial era? No, it probably is not. The north continues to be perceived largely as a flat-caps-and-ferrets stereotype, in the same way it is considered obligatory to joke about the region's industrial dereliction, which is a great pity, because economic transformations cannot be achieved overnight, and that is what is going on here. To me Manchester typifies the way major English provincial cities have been altering over the past eight or ten years; how there might at last be a real possibility that our cultural and commercial emphasis could be starting to shift away from London and be distributed more favourably among the regions. As with its redevelopment of Salford Quays, Manchester has been carried along by all the major trends of recent times, and has probably benefited from them more, and pulled them off more convincingly, than anywhere else. In no other provincial place I know does there appear to have been the scale of environmental changes carried out, from road improvements to urban clean-up programmes, to the renewed potential for traditional forms of public transport, than there has been in the city of Manchester. It has been a slow and at times painful process, but it is working. The city has more vitality and probably more going for it commercially and culturally, and is historically of much greater significance, than cities of similar size and importance such as Birmingham and Bristol, which both consider themselves to be rivals. Manchester was, after all, the world's first industrial region. It could arguably claim to be the place that generated the beginnings of the modern world much as we know it today, if one takes it for granted that without the Industrial Revolution everything that followed could not have happened. That to me makes the city vitally important. (Some would consider it not to be the most noteworthy of claims.) Its original free-trading fundamentals might even have influenced Mrs Thatcher's political credentials. And here Manchester was, in bright autumn sunlight, in post-industrial, post-Thatcher Britain, beginning to hold its head high again, having the advantage, like nearby Liverpool, of possessing good street patterns and some wonderful old architecture; perhaps, because of its smaller scale and the ease with which most of it can be taken in, displaying an air of genuine big city dignity. It was reassuring to see it.

Actually, I think what finally convinced me when I was in Manchester this time, more than the new architecture or the veneer of freshly painted industrial ironwork, was the sight of the new transport system being installed. Manchester has brought back the trams, or a rapid transit system as I believe it is termed, and it is difficult to put down convincingly on paper how uplifting a sight it was to see the construction work taking place without sounding like an excited schoolboy. That Manchester should be the first place in the country to operate such a system seems appropriate, bearing in mind that it was served by the first passenger-carrying railway in the world, when its manufacturers and merchants formed an alliance with their counterparts in Liverpool, enlisted the services of one George

Stephenson, and thwarted the owners of the region's canals, who were charging exorbitant prices to transport goods in and out of the city. The trams were not yet operating when I was there, but to stand at the head of one of Manchester's wide streets and watch the lines being laid, as I did toward the end of my final afternoon, as dusk was approaching, the lights in the shop windows were intensifying, and the offices were emptying, it was impossible to escape the powerful sensation, for a few minutes anyway, that not only was the city on the verge of something new, but that the whole of England was finally moving forward again. It would be so easy to stand in a large English city today and spout the kind of sentimental rubbish that is written to put across some feeling for atmosphere, by talking about key historical happenings and listing meaningless dates. Manchester's plethora of strategic dates and important historical firsts, or that, because of poverty, it has a higher incidence of premature deaths under the age of sixty-five than the national average, even if it does possess the largest university campus in Europe, do not concern me here. What concerns me is the essence of the city I saw before me that afternoon. It was a bustling modern city that looked profoundly healthy and smelt *clean*. It had a breezy cosmopolitan air and without doubt was one of the smartest city centres I saw anywhere in the country, one that has suffered less badly from post-war redevelopment than plenty of other places, if nothing else.

Not long after I was in Manchester the new poles holding up the electric wires to power the tram vehicles were criticized by some traditionalist society or other as spoiling the views down some of the city's main thoroughfares. How predictably querulous, narrow-minded and absurd. To my mind the black tracery of tram wires suspended between the tall buildings, and the poles, do nothing but raise the spirits and capture the essence of a city that is moving ahead with the spirit and flavour of the times – and God knows we need our spirits raising at the present time. The tram lines and the plethora of new cobbles and street furniture smartening the feel of the city between them create a sense of uniformity and are starting to bind streets pleasingly together. At last the ground is speaking again. As the architectural journalist Ian Nairn once observed, 'roads, pavements, walls, and fences are not merely utilities but the cement of a town, as important to the total effect as the buildings themselves'. How very true. If Manchester was anything to go by, there is a real possibility that we might finally be making that realization once more.

Perhaps because I originate from this part of the north of England, because my movements felt to be much the same as they usually are when I am in Manchester, I telescoped together some of the city's more favourable qualities when I was there at the beginning of this journey, and consequently my observations were rather weighed in its favour. That may be so, but I can honestly say that nowhere else in England did I experience anything approaching the sense of optimism that I did, or think that the future might not be so horribly frightening and bleak, as when I was in Manchester. This in a world that is capable of being so fundamentally and horribly corrupt.

Liverpool

Some of that optimism was lingering the morning I caught the train from what was once the longest main line station platform in Europe, until half of it was turned into a car park, and made the short journey from Manchester's faded Victoria Station across the south Lancashire plain into Merseyside.

The sunshine had gone and it was a sullen morning heavily pregnant with rain; the sort of weather for which Manchester is unfortunately though not altogether frivolously renowned. The numerous little video surveillance cameras perched atop metal poles and bolted to the corners of buildings overlooking car parks, the chunks of broken glass embedded into the tops of walls, the station seats bolted to platforms, the signs sliding past the windows such as WARNING! INTRUDER ALARM SYSTEM NOW IN OPERATION, or the deliciously detailed DANGER! RAZOR BARBED WIRE, caught the eye repeatedly, and the optimism accompanying me soon disappeared. The continual threat to personal safety or valuables, the understanding that things are forever on the verge of being stolen, is never far from the surface when you are passing through modern big city England. I thought again about Ian Nairn describing street furniture and highways to be the cement of a town, when Britain's crime statistics were not much more than an itch in its collective trousers and could almost appear comely. I tried to think of a similar metaphor applicable to the never-ending parade of defence mechanisms trailing past the windows of the train, how they were the cement of an emerging civilization, but I quickly gave up. The real English journey, the real England, was, I suppose, finally getting under way.

This put me in the necessary frame of mind to tackle Liverpool, for the breaking of timeworn literary tradition formed the loose brief I tried to set myself for the way I approached the city when I arrived. It would have been easy to follow the example set by plenty of previous observers and carry on descending into pessimism about Liverpool, but I was determined to resist it. I was determined because, though my experience of the city was limited, I knew enough about it to realize there was more to it than the strife-stricken stereotype torpedoed politically by a left-wing hoi polloi as exists in the popular media-enhanced imagination. There can, for instance, be few civic panoramas in England as breath-takingly beautiful as that of the St George's Plateau that confronts you when you emerge from Lime Street Station, and before you stretches the mighty many-columned bulk of St George's Hall, a Grecian temple of such impressive proportions only Edinburgh is capable of offering architecture like this on this sort of grand scale. This is the Liverpool that strangers on arriving are shocked to discover goes some way to dispelling negative generalizations, for it is a Liverpool blessed with an abundance of the most magnificent nineteenth-century architecture; some of which you can see embellishing the new opening titles to *Brookside*.

As my taxi blended with the city centre traffic that morning I decided the positive Liverpool passing outside the windows resembled more the Liverpool I wanted to see. I was determined to avoid concentrating on the city's legendary riots, its impoverished black population, its labour troubles, its chronic unemployment, its contribution to popular entertainment, its reputed scruffiness and its notoriety for being a city that has a chip on its shoulder, has not got any money, and has bred an idle and troublesome workforce. I was determined also to avoid talking about its political wranglings with the Thatcher government when it was controlled by Militant, when the talk was always of gangster socialism and jobs for the boys, rate capping, and unmentionable asides about the ludicrous Derek Hatton. This would all have been too easy and too obvious, though it goes without saying that by avoiding unpleasant subjects, such as the drugs rehabilitation centre I passed down one street, from which were issuing several very unfortunate-looking specimens, I am not denying for one moment that they are, or were, a reality. The poor and the disadvantaged populate cities other than Liverpool, and enough television documentaries have described the problems these people face so that we can bring to mind a rough understanding of what they are. I was also only yet at the beginning of my journey, meaning more opportunities to investigate these things lay ahead. These, at any rate, were the thoughts that were in my mind as the taxi passed the recently refurbished Adelphi Hotel and made its way on through the Chinese quarter toward the new hotel where I had arranged to stay, a few minutes' walk from the restored Albert Dock down along the waterfront. Perhaps I wanted to see a different Liverpool too because I feel I ought to have a stronger emotional attachment to the place than I do. I was born in Liverpool, in the general hospital at Sefton Park just over thirty years ago, one of those accidental babies conceived in a rush of juvenile lust before family planning became an industry, when moral values – or was it virtues? Somehow I can never quite remember which – were still stuck at the mother-in-law level of *A Kind of Loving*. I think I can therefore claim that my roots, my temperament, or my blood, are something of a product of the Merseyside area. The young lady who bore me in Liverpool was only sixteen-years-old, and I assume I was a disgrace to the family because a few weeks later I became an adopted child and was brought up in industrial Yorkshire by different parents, hardly setting foot in Liverpool again until fairly recently, when I started seeking out my beginnings. Despite this, and despite being driven past the said hospital and birthplace during this journey, I feel no emotional affiliation to Liverpool whatever. Nor do I recognize myself in the facial characteristics of people living in the area, many of whom are Irish Catholics or like me are very dark.

I have referred already to the way a series of symbolic snapshots continually presented themselves throughout this venture; small scenes synonymous with the atmosphere and changing face of the newly emergent post-industrial England, superimposing themselves selectively over the structure of the journey and embellishing it almost of their own accord. It happened again within minutes of arriving at my hotel in Liverpool. In each place I arrived at, before I was able to get on with anything else, I had to make a number of telephone calls, usually from hotels at exorbitant and outrageous charges. I had already been struck by the penetrating air of melancholy hanging over the refurbished dockland area along this part of the city's waterfront at Wapping, when I had stepped out of the taxi. I had requested a room overlooking the Mersey, and as soon as I dropped my bags on the floor, made a cup of coffee, and opened one of the complimentary packets of biscuits, I sat down in front of the window and began phoning people up. As I stared out across the dock basin at the glimmering expanse of water receding toward the shipyard at Birkenhead at the opposite side of the river, as I talked on the telephone, I was still half consciously registering the emptiness of the scene spread before me; how noticeable was the lack of shipping or much indication of life. A few seconds later a small white sailing dinghy floated into view directly beneath my window and began moving about like some ridiculous parody of a huge forlorn swan. It was a remarkable sight, not because of the spontaneity with which it happened and how it seemed such a marvellous comment on the spirit of the age. Nor was it because of how minuscule the tiny boat appeared set against an empty square of unusually clean water where once great cargo ships of the world would have rubbed cheek to jowl, the produce of nations going this way and that – fruit and tobacco, timber and metal, cotton and wool, and more than a third of British exports, up and down gangplanks, to and from cranes, on and off never-ending columns of lorries queuing beneath clouds of fluttering seagulls.

It was remarkable because it complied perfectly with the ironic concept of de-industrialized England, rediscovering itself amidst trendy quayside apartments fashioned from environments that were once vast havens of trade necessary to the sound progress through life of many of those now put out of work. An England busily adapting to changing economic fortunes, sprouting cottage industries, turning its architectural and industrial heritage into leisure, and pulling in tourists by the million. That is what the bundle of glossy promotional literature I have before me publicizing the new Merseyside intimates, as did the equivalent literature everywhere I went, though as you would imagine it does not quite use the words I have chosen here because I am reading innocently between the lines.

I went back out and had a look at some of that new Merseyside before lunch and spent an hour wandering round the Albert Dock. Whatever your feelings about the deeper causes behind the new age of nostalgia, there is no doubt that the dock, originally completed in the 1850s, has been magnificently restored. As you walk toward it from the south, the massive brick warehouses grouped to the left nicely contrasting against the granite whiteness of the Royal Liver and Cunard Buildings rearing in the background, the scene blurred by a melée of reproduction dockyard bollards and railings, the gleaming expanse of the Mersey beyond, and a handful of gulls circling high overhead (it is important to observe it is now only a handful), makes for an impressive sight. Once inside you find craft shops and cafés, museums and offices. The Tate Gallery has some space there and there is a television news studio housed in the old Dock Traffic Office, with its interesting cast-iron columns and portico. The old pumphouse has been turned into a pub. The refurbished dock was opened, not surprisingly, by the Prince of Wales, and has been so perfectly restored there is an illustrative, almost velvety quality about the buildings when you stand back and look at them in sharp sunlight; something tremendously solid and heavy. There are no ships, of course, only a few antique ones. If the whole of Liverpool were refurbished and cleaned up in this manner, it would be one of the most impressive cities in the country, piled as it is so effectively along the very edge of the water, forever battered by winds. Some young Liverpudlians, who stopped me on the main road to ask why I was staring so philosophically across the basin, thought the warehouse buildings resembled prisons. I said that was a fair enough comment, until it was remembered that some of the most impressive structures put up by the Victorians happened to be prisons. What surprised me was how many people were there, plenty of them foreign tourists, a number of whom were staying at my hotel and became conscious of themselves in the dining room later that evening. Certainly the Albert Dock is attracting the tourists to Liverpool, though it is difficult to imagine them spending much time in other parts of the city, the coaches lined up in the car parks suggesting there was more than a grain of truth to this. There seemed to be as many French and German accents and inquisitive Japanese faces brandishing cameras, staring down at the square of water glistening in the sunshine around which the old dock warehouses are grouped, as you encounter when you are in the cathedral cities in the south-west of England. Now they are coming to take pictures of England's defunct industrial relics from its age of great commercial prosperity at its premier port in the north; one that never quite got over the day the liners were diverted to Southampton and the Adelphi lost the clientele for which it was supposedly built. The thinking behind the refurbishment of the Albert Dock originally rolled into motion after Michael Heseltine had tea at the Adelphi with a number of industrialists ten or twelve years ago, when the Toxteth riots swivelled the spotlight onto Liverpool. The idea was to create a focal point from which prosperity and employment would follow, or more accurately to which it would be attracted. Conservatism might be something of a dirty word in Liverpool, the voting habits of some of the city's famous working class entertainers and sportsmen a vile joke, particularly in the pubs down the old Dock Road. But at least Heseltine did something positive for Liverpool. Whether or not he was possessed of ulterior political motives, or whether things have turned out quite how he or everyone expected, is another matter, though before this is interpreted as criticism, I should repeat what I said in the previous chapter: economic transformations cannot be achieved overnight.

The Albert Dock is not indicative of Liverpool's seafaring position today by any means. The casual visitor who walks about the city's regenerated waterfront just here at Pier Head where everything tumbles gently down the hill, who peruses the Albert Dock – the largest and most robust group of grade one listed buildings in the country – who mingles with the hum of tourists, who glances across at the muddle of masts constituting the new marina and the inevitable maritime museum, and who squints toward the concrete basins scraped clean of buildings further down river, could be forgiven for assuming this is, or was, the sum total of the docks. For a time I half believed this to be the case myself. In fact, Liverpool's docks were once vast, stretching for more than seven miles along the city's waterfront. The Albert Dock merely happened to be conveniently sited when heritage suddenly became a fashionable word. To stand before the Albert Dock today and watch the tourists milling aimlessly, even if you are aware there is considerable dockland activity still carrying on out in the direction of Bootle and Sefton, it is truly astonishing to consider that as recently as the early 1950s these docks employed just over twenty-thousand people. As recently as the 1960s, across that huge expanse of water before me, now being touched by a sun breaking between the clouds, the golden emptiness of the Atlantic winking beyond for the benefit of all we romantic sightseers leaning against the railings contemplating the long lost Liverpool of the past, it was common to see ships queuing at the mouth of the Mersey ready to berth, sometimes remaining at anchor for more than a week awaiting their turn. But that was before the effects of the loss of Empire, the shifting pattern of world trade, the industrializing countries of the East rising to manufacturing prominence, and the serious decline that finally set in to the British economy toward the end of the 1960s. It was before the massive reduction in Britain's merchant sailing fleet, too, which fell from over three-thousand registered vessels after the war to the several hundred or so we have today. It was also before there emerged different methods of transportation and loading, both nationally and internationally. Cargo that would once have been carried around by men and stored in those vast musky Liverpool warehouses, so quaint now as they are transformed into luxury apartment blocks and art galleries, began to be craned around in containers or on aeroplanes instead. Where ten or twenty pairs of hands were once needed, now were needed only two. And, finally, it was before the effects of labour troubles and the slothful outlook fostered in the mind of a workforce by the National Dock Labour Scheme, guaranteeing dockers a job for life on full pay regardless of trading conditions, filtered through, as they inevitably would. In conjunction with unions' restrictive practices, childish work-to-rules, and Liverpool dockers' stubborn unwillingness to move with the times and handle the new containers (a stubbornness you soon gather was connected to the rampant theft of goods the pre-container age permitted), it was hardly surprising that incoming cargo showed a reluctance to queue up any more at the mouth of the Mersey, but preferred to divert itself to expanding ports on the south and east coasts instead. The consequence of this process, in conjunction with Britain's industries inland upon which Liverpool depended for much of its trade being in decline, was contraction and the drifting of what little trade remained irredeemably away. The world was changing, and Liverpool looked like it was going to lose.

Most of this is obvious when considering the story of Liverpool and its chronic decline, all of it picked up easily enough when you spend some time in the city and talk to its people. So why bother to repeat it? Because, in the same way it is not very widely reported that Liverpool's sectarian political problems of the 1980s are largely a thing of the past, the left-wing rabble that nearly bankrupted it having been marginalized, the council finely balanced and progressing via consensus, it is not so very widely known that in tonnage terms the Liverpool seaport now handles almost as much cargo as it did during the halcyon days of the Empire. Perhaps it has not been so widely reported because the only news the country seems to want to hear about Liverpool these days is bad news. Well, here is some good news. Nearly ten years ago the government let its major share in the Mersey Dock and Harbour Company go, denationalized it so to speak, wrote off its debts, and granted Liverpool freeport status. A few years later it abolished the National Dock Labour

Scheme, meaning investment that had stayed away because of the labour problems associated with it could now flow freely and less warily. Management could at last do its job properly and the private sector could expand. Liverpool began to look interesting again. The result of privatization, rationalization, the reduction in overmanning, and the shaking loose of socialist-inspired shackles has been that the port's annual tonnage handled has quadrupled in ten years from just over nine million tonnes to over twenty-five million tonnes, and it is still rising. In less than a decade, Liverpool docks have been brought back from oblivion to become the country's most successful freeport; one comparable to the very best in Europe. When I was there new container terminals were under construction, and a major railhead was being expanded and upgraded, turning the Royal Seaforth Dock into a Eurofreight Terminal in readiness for the opening of the Channel Tunnel. The idea is that the new terminal will become a gateway for Irish and North American sea traffic, enabling it to be loaded straight onto trains then sent down through England and through the tunnel and on into Europe. There is, however, a crucial difference, or it might be described as a catch, between Liverpool the English seaport of old and the revitalized, expanding freeport of new. Where twenty-thousand men were once needed, and even six-thousand only a decade ago, now are employed a mere *five-hundred*. That to handle what in tonnage terms is claimed to be a comparable amount of traffic as when the workforce was forty times larger (no doubt most of it now imports), means there are probably more shop assistants working in Liverpool today than there are dockers. Clearly, there have been significant improvements in performance and productivity if a fraction of men can handle the same amount of traffic as was once handled by so many, but there is also about such rationalization something rather disturbing.

What *has* been happening economically over the past ten or fifteen years that has resulted in massive redundancies such as those on the docks at Liverpool, or the loss of hundreds of thousands of jobs in other industries elsewhere? What, if one comes to think about it, has been happening over the past thirty years? Now that the fatuous euphoria of the Thatcher years has died away it is possible to step back and see that, if present trading conditions are anything to go by, the supposed economic transformation the 1980s was meant to portend, the new Liverpool – the new England – that was supposed to be in the process of rising phoenix-like from the ashes of the old, might be rather longer in coming than was first expected. True, the old industries have been slimmed down and overmanning problems obliterated more or less at a stroke. They had to be slimmed down to prevent themselves from ultimately imploding. Former unprofitable nationalized industries are now profitable, albeit with hugely reduced workforces, their productivity improved, never mind that they ought still to be in the public sector because their monopoly position enables them to countermand the government's supposed strategy against inflation. But, though it has played an important part, it is doubtful if it has been a question only of the reduction in overmanning. In spite of the noise generated over the past few years about political and economic transformations, after all the hype about the changing of attitudes and the working of economic miracles, it could be said that what has actually taken place in this country is a vast economic contraction for the benefit of the fifteen million or so part of the working population that was never industrially inclined anyway. Manufacturing industry might have been streamlined, but it has also been contained at the expense of the expanding service and high-finance sector. Because of the structural weaknesses this has created within the economy, the stability of the service sector is now in jeopardy. Wherever I went during this journey I was told that high technology would have to replace more and more jobs in the service sector – in banking, office work, and various other administrative occupations – as it has done in various fields of manufacturing and would continue to do so.

That sounds fine, until one examines some of the processes at work deep within our civilization. It is obvious that what is actually happening, roughly speaking over ten or twenty year cycles, but in cycles that are going to become shorter and faster as high-technology influence intensifies, is that international capital is restructuring itself by jettisoning the need for human labour and replacing more and more jobs with machines. What is more, it is being forced to do so all the time to remain competitive. There are now sixteen million people unemployed in European Community countries alone. It does not take a very intelligent mind to calculate what the nett result of this contracting process, taken to its logical conclusion, might be. Every time another contraction occurs – and we are experiencing one at the moment: because of it British industry expects productivity and output to rise, but to be employing fewer people to support it when there is an upturn – the economy does not so much shrink as throb a generation tighter. The conventional wisdom is that the main body of the economy will become healthier each time it slims itself down and eliminates waste in this way, but I seriously doubt whether it will. There is insufficient investment in the industrial infrastructure to fill the gap being left behind. Fat dieted away by an organism becomes released from the main body as water and can easily be flushed away: fat released from an economy generally produces piles of unemployed people. A temporary respite might be accommodated by an artificial boom, such as we experienced five or six years ago, but the deeper malaise continues. Few of our reputable economists appear to possess the imagination to contemplate the dreadful consequences of this tightening process, or more importantly, its social consequences on the potential stability of our society and our civilization. They are adept when it comes to spouting facts and figures, predictions about the alterations to GDP, the effect of economic shifts on the workings of stocks and bonds. But when it comes to the human cost and the workings of fiscal vicissitudes on the human mind they generally seem to be left wanting.

And it is always worth remembering that it is the economics and financial vicissitudes which are a direct product of the workings of the human mind.

The Shape of Things to Come

I was taken for a drive round Liverpool the following morning, rather ironically by a successful young financial advisor I know working in the city, and found myself contemplating something of that human cost; what this relentless economic contraction is capable of doing to the human mind.

I was driven out along the southern part of the waterfront corridor to begin with, out in the direction of the airport, past miles and miles of derelict dockland, abandoned railway land, refurbished warehousing, car showrooms, and the ambiguously landscaped, lumpy grassy site of the Garden Festival. But it was when we made our way back through the inner suburbs that my honourable intentions for the positive picture I wanted to paint of Liverpool took something of a nose-dive. For I was taken, perhaps inevitably, up into Toxteth. Toxteth, battleground of the riots ten years ago, and still showing scars of that tragedy today. But Toxteth, or at any rate the section of Toxteth I saw that bright morning, does not look anywhere near as dangerous or as derelict as the photographs reproduced in the newspapers might have led you to believe. But then, these places rarely do, because some of the domestic architecture to be found in them was built when it was considered fashionable for the prosperous classes to live within the city, and it acts as a disinfectant. Some of the wide tree-lined avenues we passed along in Toxteth, with the big maroon-and-cream Merseybuses tearing along them, dragging up cascades of brilliant yellow sycamore leaves in the downdraught from the central reservations, where they were piled like ploughed snow, looked positively residential. Almost immediately we were passing along another impressive residential avenue with wide pavements facing onto the huge expanse of undulating greenery called Sefton Park; then I was looking for the first time at the hospital where I was born, not feeling any emotion whatever, but only wondering how much smaller the trees might have been thirty years ago. In Sefton Park there is a boating lake, tennis courts, and gardens, and that morning there opened up before us a scintillating explosion of the colours of autumn, thrown across a vivid canvas of the most intense luminous green. Thick black tree trunks stood out against the misty sunshine, crowned by great overhanging bonnets of dewy gold that were peeling away in tiny glittering fragments all the time. I have never seen leaves so thickly piled at the sides of roads and being carried so perfectly down from branches on the breeze as I did that morning at Sefton Park on the border of Toxteth. It was like passing through the opening sequence to one of those sentimental American films set in New England. But when I remarked on the apparent serenity of the scene, I was not surprised to be told that, though it might look innocent enough in crisp sunshine, with a few dogs lolloping and fetching sticks on the sparkling grass, you would not make it your business to walk round there on your own at night, unless you happened to be a fool. On closer inspection we could now see that some of those grand houses were actually boarded up or vandalized, some of them harbouring God knows what clandestine goings-on. Only when you are off the main streets, where the brutality of social deprivation is really nurtured, does Toxteth become noticeably run-down and beset by scorch-marks, or begin to resemble some of those shell-shocked back streets in Ulster.

There is a particular area, centred round a couple of streets notorious for being the place where the young dump stolen cars, where it has been known for criminals to lie in wait for the owners of vehicles and mug them when they arrive to retrieve them. That, I suppose, could be termed a real double whammy. (This was not related to me by my financial advisor friend, but by a successful Liverpool businessman who thought it very funny, indicative of the Scouser's sharp character and ironic humour forged in the harshness of the back street ghettoes.) I was assured on several occasions when I was in Liverpool that there are places in Toxteth that are no-go areas, where the police would be attacked the moment they appeared. Perhaps that is why the buses were driving through Toxteth so fast. To talk seriously about walking into certain streets to take photographs was tantamount to having cracked a very amusing joke, though I am sure there was evidence of exaggeration at work for the benefit of a gullible visitor. My financial advisor friend also had a story to tell. Some years previously he'd had his car stolen from the city's nearby Chinatown district when he was out one evening for dinner, along with some of his personal belongings and his briefcase and papers. The police telephoned to say a number of personal effects had been found scattered across the grass surrounding a municipal housing development, they fitted his description, and he might like to go along and see whether or not they belonged to him. As soon as he arrived a gang of youths began to gather, almost as though they were spectral apparitions materializing from thin-air, to use his description. The word had gone out that someone wearing a suit was in the street, sticks and chains started to appear, and the rest you can imagine. He got out fast, just in the nick of time.

Again, a fairly routine sort of story associated with a modern city such as Liverpool, with the fabric of modern life. But *why* cities such as Liverpool? Why Liverpool? There have, of course, been all kinds of reasons brought forward to justify the rise in crime and the squalid, malevolent texture of many of these inner urban areas. Conservatives blame the deterioration in the social fabric on the failure of socialism and a welfare state breeding a dependency mentality, stripping away personal initiative and self-discipline, and eroding moral responsibility, though it sometimes strikes me as being a peculiar kind of moral responsibility to which they are referring. The Labour Party, the front bench of which now appears to be comprised almost entirely of Scottish accents in spite of being in favour of devolution, blames it on unemployment and poverty, even if, by having embraced market theories, it is careful to avoid mentioning what the causes of unemployment and poverty sometimes are. Jeremy Seabrook, who somewhat improbably has been compared to George Orwell, blames everything, probably a man's desire to sharpen a pencil, probably a man's desire to *use* a pencil, on the influence of market forces. Who is right and who is wrong?

The truth is that they are all right and they are all wrong, for it is a mixture of all these factors interacting against one another. Whatever your political predilections, it strikes me to be elementary common sense that if you nurture a body of people who have no serious hope of participating in the mainstream organization of society and are not much more than jumble stored out of sight in society's attic, people who have little hope of escaping their mean predicament and for whom life is an endless drudgery, then by denying them their common humanity the more adventurous among them will become brutalized, react against their circumstances, begin to behave like animals, and take what they have been conditioned into desiring by the society around them by force. It is the height of naivety to believe that unemployed young men living in a society that continually sensationalizes the power of money, elevates frivolous individuals into figures of public admiration in the entertainment world, jams it down people's throats that blatant exhibitionism in cars, clothes, and what-not is the way to achieve social credibility, will sit peaceably at home reading books like schoolboys on their best behaviour in an old fashioned Presbyterian chapel, or turn themselves into cultured individuals quoting Trollope to one another from the dole queues. In a society that has evolved in such a way that the aggressive playing upon human beings' acquisitive instincts is part of the very fabric of life, then it seems to me to be the height of pig-ignorance to be surprised when a minority of emotionally underdeveloped individuals who cannot obtain the fruits of life we all take so easily for granted will, if their dignity and pride and personal expression is denied them, become frustrated enough to adopt more serious measures to inject some semblance of excitement into their lives. The Right talks about human beings being naturally competitive, which is quite correct. But the moment that competitiveness becomes frustrated in the minds of the poor and results in anti-social behaviour, then to a bigoted element of the Right it becomes unacceptable and the poor are condemned as scum, heathen, moronic, and so on, which is quite stupid and reactionary.

What that bigoted element of the Right means, of course, is that the tyrannical streak that lurks at the very centre of its mind is frustrated because the behaviour of the poor is not conforming to its own narrow aesthetic view. It talks about the social causes but fails to appreciate the economic causes and therefore becomes irritated about the untidiness of society – an irritation which is derived purely from that element of the Right's sentimental outlook and its strong psychological need to feel socially superior to other people to retain a sense of mental composure. (All out-and-out arrogant right-wingers are motivated at bottom by deference and the need to see themselves admired obsequiously.) It is typical of our woolly-minded complacency, of how prosperity blinds our perceptiveness and manipulates our expectations from life – and in this respect 'our' generally means the opinion-forming middle classes who are often the very least qualified to make these kinds of moral judgements – that we should expect those that cannot participate in the mainstream organization of society to conform innocently to our own scale of bourgeois moral values. There is a layer of society being created beneath the very bottom level of the working class, generally described as the 'underclass', for whom there is no hope of ever obtaining a job or leading anything approaching a satisfying or in some cases even a civilized life. There are sectors of cities bringing children into the world that will grow up and never perform a normal day's work in their lives; children that will never learn the sort of moral code you and I take for granted and never become involved constructively in society. What is going to be done with these people? Like everybody else, they are continually exposed to dramatically presented advertisements that play upon their emotions and their desires. They are continually stimulated by the blend of physical aggression and eroticism populating the commercial images in the world around them, tapping into their basic instincts and arousing feelings of lust and envy. Like everyone who is prosperous and at whom these images are really aimed, the poor are also conditioned into believing it is emotionally satisfying to possess modern consumer items such as fast cars, that these things are necessary to the leading of a rewarding life, that they are closely linked up to promiscuity and sex, that not much of a life is possible without them. Like the prosperous, the poor see asinine quiz shows where half-drunk contestants begin to go into orgasm at the prospect of winning money! money! money! probably because they were inebriated before the cameras rolled to begin with. (I was once told that a well-known quiz show allowed the audience free drinks in the studio bar all afternoon before the programme was recorded. It was the only way to Americanize it and overcome the English people's natural aversion to making fools of themselves in public.) Like the prosperous they listen to the same high-powered, foot-stomping, adrenalin-inducing music. They hear a barrage of four-letter monosyllabic language and exciting sound effects and the relentless hammering of gunfire during violent videos.

But, unlike the prosperous, the poor have not much chance of obtaining any serious money so they can get at the things society says they should desire. Unlike the prosperous, a number of the poor find that during their exposure to video delinquency, for example, their pulse beat quickens, that slowly, inexorably, they are expressing themselves more and more violently, more and more physically, though of course they are not aware of it in the objectively subjective sense at all. They become acclimatized to the need to think in terms of exhibitionistic display to achieve personal satisfaction. They find that by thinking physically and hiding behind bravado, they are more easily stimulated, more easily noticed and respected within their own social grouping, where force means survival and survival often means force, but without the gentlemanly veneer obscuring the same impulses at work out in the wider world of economics. Deep in their minds, the frustrations of these people, their lack of opportunity, their lack of purpose, their aimlessness, their degeneracy, the dull monotony of their existence, begin to do strange things to the workings of their psychology and their emotions. More especially, they help to prevent them from rising above a certain level, a fact which never occurs to the intolerant right-wingers who rail indignantly against yobland our yobland because they are too naïve to comprehend the economic causes at the root of it. The preoccupation they have with their own values prevents much chance of them realizing that. And so it goes. A growing sector of society is caught between the influence of flabby-mouthed liberals on the one hand saying that censorship is no way to avert social decay (oh dear), and mealy-mouthed reactionaries extolling the virtues of untrammelled market forces on the other, frothing at the mouth when bishops say that inner city violence is connected to unemployment, and preferring instead to blame it purely on the poor's wretched 'moral values'. It is no use believing that then pulling down the shutters: you have got to analyse the circumstances that have put those moral values in place. But there is, I fear, hardly any likelihood of that, for the most consistent behavioural characteristic of the fascist crowd is their fantastic inability to come to terms with the economic factors that shape our 'moral values', how they can result in the kind of social disintegration, the increase in violence and stupidity, the transformations slowly taking place deep within wretched minds, that is actually going on all around us. So I say again: What is going to be done with these people? Are we truly serious when we show surprise that parts of our cities are descending into a squalid pit of lawlessness? Surely to God we cannot be serious either when we blame the causes entirely on the miserable failure of socialism. And what does that tiny handful of ignorant right-wingers that bullshits in the papers from time to time propose to do about the situation? Erect high-voltage electric fences to cage the people in? Enforce birth control so that the species eventually dies out? Round them up and systematically exterminate them in gas ovens, I wonder?

Liverpool, which throughout its long maritime history depended on a sizeable pool of unskilled or very low-skilled workers and had a history of violent behaviour among its poorer classes chiefly because of this, is nurturing a sizeable underclass and seems to me to be the paradigm of the emerging post-industrial urban society. Because of its weak economic base, it sketches before us the social pattern of the emerging city England, of Britain, because that weak economic base is gradually being transmuted to the rest of the country. I am not picking on Liverpool simply because it has the highest male unemployment rates in the country and is beset with crime and vandalism; nor am I denying that it has not been diversifying its weak economic structure and making considerable progress in recent years. So why do I believe what I say? First of all erase from your mind a picture of the modern Liverpool as a battle-scarred wasteland with armoured-cars patrolling the infamous Kirkby or Netherley council estates. Contrary to popular belief, Liverpool is not much different to anywhere else. In places it is a very beautiful city, populated by prosperous and upstanding citizens. It has the same trendy new Victorian-style shopping arcades, shiny new cars, and modern residential housing estates that you see everywhere. When I was in the city people were going about their daily business in the pleasant sunshine, as I saw them going about their daily business throughout England. Yet the media, which had recently fastened onto another fracas concerning the city's refuse collection service, continued to portray a Liverpool that somehow contained none of this prosperity but was a decrepit city racked by public sector disputes and manned by political racketeers. But wake up from a deep sleep in the pedestrianized piazza in the centre of Liverpool, with the wind from the Atlantic pleasantly disturbing the yellowing leaves of the trees and keeping the air fresh and invigorating, and you could almost have been anywhere. Actually, you could not almost have been anywhere, because town centres still as striking and dignified as this begin to peter out the further into the south of England that you descend. So again, why Liverpool?

Because the indications are that the transition from an industrial manufacturing-based economy to a post-industrial service-orientated economy will produce a more divided, more violent, more intolerant society, of which the doubling of crime statistics over the past ten years are something of a portent. Central to Liverpool's dilemma over the years has been the fact that it was mainly a trading centre rather than an industrial manufacturing centre. Its rough atmosphere was not altogether unconnected to it having nurtured that substantial body of unskilled, rather brutish labourers. But, I repeat, this is very much the pattern of the emerging late-twentieth-century England, where we are all supposed to aspire to become hoteliers and low-paid laundry delivery boys, not skilled machine-operators or chemists who need to increase their brainpower and develop methods of concentration. Of course, that will work very much to the advantage of a choice number of intellectual self-abusers who like still to include dated phraseology such as 'lower orders', etc., in the structure of their vocabulary. This is why I see Liverpool as a sort of paradigm of the future shape of English society. On the surface that society will appear to be quite comfortable and at ease with itself. But out of sight in the background, well out of mind, sometimes only five or ten minutes' walk away from the enticing shop window displays in the busy city centres, a minority element of the subjugated underclass will be sitting at arm's length from all of this, increasingly unable to participate in it and becoming more and more angry. Having been the victims of a failed educational system to begin with, which is not part of a social infrastructure geared toward sensible industrial cohesion, an educational system that still caters primarily for the relatively useless professions, some of this suppressed minority, whose energies and creativity might have been put to a more constructive use in a society that had room for them, will become frustrated and resentful with themselves.

In addition to the aggressive, increasingly sensationalist atmosphere of the post-industrial society that is emerging, it is unquestionable that the deterioration of the social fabric is directly linked to the processes of economic contraction I described above. For what is also happening is that as the use of high-technology intensifies and more and more skilled manufacturing jobs become obsolete, large numbers of people are becoming economically obsolete too. It is no longer necessary for them to become even poorly skilled, to learn a trade, or to have any useful connection to the rest of society at all. The growing brutality of modern society *is* connected to the workings of capitalist economics, and it seems to me that nobody except an idiot – and a very remote, well-padded kind of idiot at that – would claim it was otherwise. Western capitalism is metamorphosing into a different stage: one where millions of unskilled young men who would once have been absorbed by low-skilled employment have simply become superfluous to the workings of international capital, now that much of the work they would have done has been transferred to the industrializing Third World, whom we appear quite happy to see do much of our manufacturing for us. That contracting process is gathering momentum. Of course, it is very easy, if you are prosperous and middle class and able to move freely among refurbished nineteenth-century England, if you can afford to pay a stiff price for a lunch in one of the fashionable heritage cafés instead of grubbing around in some back street hovel, to glance appreciatively at the bright new post-Modernist architecture springing up and believe that the transition from the heavy-industrial to a post-industrial era will herald something better; very easy to believe that everything is proceeding quite smoothly. On the contrary, the ending of the heavy-industrial era, as brutish and physical and degrading as much of it was, leaves some very serious questions unresolved; most notably that of what to do with the growing body of the hardcore unemployed. The 'underclass' is being left to fend very much for itself, and it is not surprising that a small proportion of it is cultivating a brutalized sub-culture very much of its own, where violence and lawlessness are simply extensions of that culture and part of the way of life.

Meanwhile, the vast majority of society continues to prosper and lead fruitful and fairly rewarding lives. The only trouble is, as the end of each afternoon draws close, those bright shop window displays full of desirable goods, like those I saw over several warm afternoons in Liverpool, now have to be protected by steel shutters, as they do throughout Britain and the Western world. At night, more and more shop windows are becoming obscured, in direct response to brutalized men and women being conditioned by, among other things, violent films, some of them sold from the same shops in the same streets behind the very same shutters. Blank rectangles of silver glint in the moonlight, a moonlight which for centuries influenced poets and exuded romantic ambience when it was still safe to walk city streets. Bundles of five and ten pound notes are exchanged down dirty back alleys for small polythene bags full of white powder. The steel shutters become heavier and more substantial to prevent the wares behind them from being stolen to pay for those bags of white powder, so that some wreck of an organism that might once have been a human being – an organism that from early childhood has seen the words NO JOB, NO FUTURE, NO HOPE, NO LIFE superimposed over its destiny – can now pump a bit of excitement into its life through a needle jammed into a projecting blood vessel in its forearm. It is important to remember that statistically it is still a very small minority of people that is perpetuating this kind of behaviour. Society is not falling apart at the seams. Nor am I justifying for one moment the outlook of these people, or implying that crime is forgivable if it is the product of an unjust society. I am no naïve Lord Longford acolyte. We live in a society that is still relatively stable and has much to commend it, make no mistake of that. But there is enough of a process at work beneath the surface of modern England, enough of a social revolution taking place quietly in the background, to make us want to alarm our cars, be fearful of walking the streets after dark, worry about our children when they are playing out with their friends, switch the burglar alarm on and arm the downstairs of the house each night before we retire to bed, above all to make ourselves want to feel *safe* and to reinforce our perceived feeling of security. That is why I want to draw attention to these matters and ask us to perhaps consider the reasons behind them. I do not want to live in a society where I have to constantly be on my guard as I would if I were passing close to wild animals on African bushland, feel anxious throughout the time I am sitting in the theatre if my car is parked down a side street at night, have to worry if my children want to go blackberrying in nearby woodland, listen to an infantile body of intellectual opinion that rails against all of these things but has no understanding of its causes and enjoys such influence it actually perpetuates them. I do not want this kind of future. Do you?

I spent my last day in Liverpool with the businessman who told me that young car thieves sometimes mugged the vehicles' owners when they returned to fetch them. His company is a substantial one. He runs an extensive wholesale fruit-and-vegetable operation from a factory complex out on one of the city's industrial estates. Late in the afternoon I donned a white smock and hat and was shown by his wife over the plant, which struck me as being essentially an enormous refrigerator split into two halves with a row of offices and a car park grafted onto the front. This was their busiest time of the day. There was much frenetic activity as the fresh produce was being unloaded as it came in from Lincolnshire and from growers all over the country. It was being packed and sorted and wheeled onto dozens of articulated lorries so that it could be delivered overnight and be on supermarket shelves throughout the region early the next morning. Both the businessman and his wife live quite close to where the *Brookside* television series is filmed, in a pleasant, prosperous suburb of Liverpool. They were kind enough to invite me to stay with them and after dinner that evening we fell to talking about the kinds of things I have been discussing over the preceding pages. The businessman was quick to respond. He said the Toxteth riots had been in his opinion greatly exaggerated. He knew this because he lived on the edge of Toxteth when they occurred. He had been into the centre of the city for a meal with some friends the night they began. Normally he would have driven home along his usual route through the centre of Toxteth. But that night when he returned late, he had decided, for no reason he could explain, to drive back a different way. He had entered his flat, sat up for a short while, then gone to bed. The next morning, when he drove to work through the centre of Toxteth he was amazed to see burned-out cars, and the people at work were relieved to find that he was okay. He said the riots were actually confined to a very small area, only a few streets. Make no mistake, he said, they were unpleasant enough where they occurred. But he had been able to work out the riots were happening nearby when he was still awake in his flat. The impression given by the news bulletins on television was that the whole of Liverpool was descending into anarchy and sliding into the Mersey. Yet he heard nothing. He could joke about the incidence of car theft in Liverpool. Everyone in the city seems to do this, because they accept it as a hard fact of life, like people in Newcastle. He loved Liverpool and would not wish to live anywhere else. But he resented the stigma of the riots having tarnished the image of Liverpool for so long. It was wrong, he said, dreadfully wrong.

Perhaps his view is a fitting anecdote upon which to take my leave of Merseyside, for I have a suspicion that, in spite of all those negative reports and misapprehensions about Liverpool to the contrary, the city will win through yet.

2

East Lancashire

Through Wigan to Blackburn

The train from Liverpool to Blackburn made its way across the south Lancashire conurbation for the most part along what I believe is generally termed a secondary route. A shifting mass of stormy clouds piled and twisted above the untidy landscape, pushed along by ferocious winds that kept flinging sheets of rain against the glass and pulling intense sunlight in and out of focus. The trees passing outside that were still green were bent almost double, hunched over at truly alarming angles. They would shake themselves upright for a few moments before keeling over again, as though they were being thumped in the stomach and lurching backwards and exposing the underside of their leaves as a gesture of no resistance; a sight which I believe is a symptom of more general rain to come. At Bryn the station seats were fastened to the platforms again, as they had been bolted to the ground beneath the sombre statues in St John's Gardens in the centre of Liverpool. Here and there busy motorways swept silently beneath the railway, the sound of the traffic drowned out by the clattering of the train.

The most noticeable thing about these secondary routes, and I admit reluctantly that it is very much a characteristic of the north of England, is the scruffiness and desolation of many of the smaller stations. This is sometimes used as ammunition by critics to claim that the eventual intention of British Rail, and of the government, is to reduce the railway network in this country to a few main line routes; that they are moving toward it by stealth in readiness for privatization. Subsidized rural and secondary routes are, it is argued, being deliberately run down, so that once flotation becomes official policy, it will be claimed that the less important routes require too much investment to make them profitable again (having been deliberately allowed to deteriorate so that this announcement can be made), and the only serious alternative is to close them down. Some of the journeys I made by train during the accumulation of material for this book served only to reinforce these rumours, which may or not be true.

The stations along the main lines that morning were not too bad. My train stopped at Wigan North Western, which is lucky enough to be placed on the electrified west coast main line and is therefore modern and tidy, and, before it was rebuilt, might have been where George Orwell alighted when he arrived to make his famous foray into the life of the underclass of his own day – much to the chagrin of Wigan's respectable working class – holing up for a while above the legendary tripe shop, along the main road leading into the town from Bolton. But another quality to many of the small urban stations I passed, in addition to their scruffiness and desolation, was that a marked quantity of the notices pasted to the remnants of buildings and hoardings were personal threats of some kind: threats in connection with fare dodging or vandalism. When I rejoined the main line between Wigan and Preston, because they were often positioned in prosperous suburbs, as are many in London, there was a definite alteration to the look of the stations. Suddenly they seemed to want to associate themselves with pastoral scenes and photographs of children and grandmothers. The pictures of summer scenes with trains curving gracefully through mountain passes in Scotland or Wales were almost entirely evident at stations where you could see by glancing at the housing stock above the bridges, or alongside the track, that the passengers would have money to spend to afford long journeys or feel optimistic enough even to embark upon them. The stations in the more urbanized areas, where they blurred into the old industrial districts, were comprised chiefly of straightforward timetable information or the warnings about fare dodging and vandalism; something you could see at a glance was exemplified by the human stock, rather than by the housing stock, getting on and off the train. Just before the train passed the Pilkington glass factory outside St Helens I noticed with alarm, too, that when the conductor-cum-guard made his way through the train to examine everyone's tickets he checked the toilets routinely, to see whether or not anyone was hiding. But he did not check by squinting discreetly to see if the latch said the toilet was engaged. It was obvious he was ensuring the latch actually said the cubicle was vacant, then he deliberately *kicked* the door open, in such a way that anybody concealed inside would be smashed in the face. I saw him do this several times and it seemed to me to be another marvellous little comment, or more accurately an indictment, on the spirit and confrontational atmosphere of the age.

If there are any major differences at all to be noted between the north and south of England, it is that in the north you find more towns that are entirely working class in complexion, and that the disparity between those who are prosperous and those who are not is more marked. The working-class element is, of course, generally not much different to that to be found in Manchester or Liverpool, or Basildon or Dagenham or Stepney for that matter, except that in the old textile towns there tend to be more extensive Indian or Pakistani populations that became established before the traditional industries went into decline. In Liverpool there is an office and banking quarter, as there is usually in any major city, meaning there is a substantial body of middle-class people shuttling in and out of the town at the beginning and end of each day; whereas in places such as Blackburn there is not. This is not to suggest these towns have bare-footed children lining the streets, or that there are soup kitchens standing on every other corner, and folk still walk around in clogs, shawls, and flat caps. They are noticeably less gentrified, less pluralistic, more abrasive than bigger cities, but because of this there is also about the old industrial towns of the north and Midlands, it should be noted, something less pretentious and less self-conscious. There is not the barrier of contrived etiquette you associate with more genteel towns hanging in the air, more of a directness and an intimacy and people being themselves.

This intimacy became evident the moment I seated myself in a café at the edge of the modern shopping precinct in Blackburn – it makes up the bulk of the centre of the town – settled down to consume a hot jacket-potato draped with baked-beans and cheese, began to thaw myself out after the train journey, and for a long time watched this old mill town going about its business on a cold October afternoon. Unlike the fashionable cafés in tourist venues, or at places such as the Albert Dock, where the patrons are generally sightseers who are passing through and everyone talks in whispers and tries not to clink the cutlery against their plates, the clientele visiting the cafés in these industrial towns are usually regulars, often known to the staff by name. Prominently displayed in this café at Blackburn was a handwritten notice announcing to everyone who entered that one of the girls who worked there – her Christian name only had been used – had recently had a baby, and it weighed such-and-such a number of pounds. The fact that the notice had been displayed at all suggested there was a significant number of customers who would be interested in hearing the good news. Immediately you warmed to this climate and felt at ease; felt relaxed enough to leave your bags unattended when you queued at the counter, though this intimacy, this relaxed atmosphere, should not be taken as an indication that these towns do not have their incumbent social or economic problems, however, or that they are all cosy. On a table within earshot of mine were a couple of unemployed teenage boys. They were smoking like chimneys, dragging deeply on their cigarettes between gulps of tea or coffee, and were asking each other routinely how they were going to pass the time of day. These two were not rough-necks, not criminals or yobs in the making, merely normal working-class youngsters desperate for a job and yearning to do something constructive with their lives. This was obvious from the tone of their conversation. One of them – the one who wished to f—— he could get a bloody job – said he had been watching television the whole of the previous afternoon and most of that morning. The other said he was going to play chess with himself for the rest of the day. Perhaps Britain's unemployment registers will produce a nation of brilliant chess players and sportsmen, though no doubt their benefits would be docked once a determination to attain freedom so irresponsibly became public knowledge. What struck me very powerfully about these two youngsters, as it did with the unemployed men I spoke to later, was how matter-of-fact their conversation was; how desolating it was to overhear, how resigned it was to its unalterable fate.

The manager of Blackburn Chamber of Commerce told me something about the present economic position of the town. For a town that was almost wholly a product of nineteenth-century industrialism, the former centre of cotton weaving (as opposed to its spinning, which was concentrated in and around Oldham), one where three out of every four of the working population used to be involved in the textile trade, it will perhaps come as some surprise to learn that the most important industry in Blackburn today is engineering, which employs nearly a quarter of the registered workforce. Of course, the legacy of Blackburn's former textile prominence lingers in the appearance of the town – as it does in all the small industrial towns of East Lancashire – and to a lesser extent affects its perceived image. A number of mills and row upon row of little brick terraced houses continue to dominate substantial quarters, though the amount of mill chimneys projecting from the skyline can nowadays be counted on one hand. The textile foundations of Blackburn are celebrated in the design of the Borough coat of arms, and also the inscribed Latin motto 'Arte et Labore' which translated means 'By Skill and Labour'. This is appropriate considering Blackburn's symptomatic importance to the weaving trade, but it also acts as a sort of echo to the complexion of the economic infrastructure as it stands today; and it is a pity it is not the motto for the whole of England. Though textiles is still an important industry in the area, it tends now to be concentrated in the manufacture of specialist fabrics for specialist markets rather than connected with cotton. With the decline of the textile industry Blackburn underwent a comprehensive policy of industrial diversification, so that today it can boast a fine variety of trades, from high-technology industries, through to aviation electronics, and the manufacture of arms, aircraft, wallpaper, paint, chemicals, and footwear. ICI produce their Perspex acrylic sheet there, a material I have been making use of professionally at one time or another for nearly half of my working life. Both carpets and carpet-making machinery are manufactured in the town as well, and Philips recently began making compact discs at their factory near Padiham. It is the diverse and thriving manufacturing base, not only of Blackburn but of the whole of East Lancashire, that meant that I could be told confidently when I was passing through that the area was weathering the recession much better than other parts of the country. It is interesting to consider that some 26% of people are involved in manufacturing in this country as a whole. In East Lancashire 47% of the working population are involved in manufacturing, almost twice the national average. Perhaps if Lancashire's economic structure – and, as it happens, much of the north of England's economic philosophy – were reflected in national industrial strategy we might not be in the dire economic mess that we are. When I was travelling through the north-west the flimsy service industries of the south-east were dropping like nine pins, whereas the strong manufacturing base of towns such as Blackburn meant they were hardly being affected, though what the story has been since then I am not quite so sure.

I think it is true to say that the British economy is manipulated largely in favour of the south-east of England rather than the whole of the country, chiefly because the south is where the vast majority of capital is handled and controlled. But it seems to me that when we talk about the north-south divide, in addition to the more obvious social disparities that are being referred to, there is also a profound difference in commercial and business outlook too. Industry has always been something of a dirty word in the south of England, as well as a minor joke among educated persons who snigger at it and come nowhere near it. Whereas in the north, it seems to be much more a part of people's natural outlook on life, part of the psychology right across classes, that to produce something is essentially more desirable because it is felt to be more satisfying. When we were told that the economy needed to be 'cooled down' a year or so back, what was actually implied was that a policy of deflation needed to be pursued for the benefit of the south-east. The north was getting along just fine. It was chiefly the absurd explosion in house values and the propensity of easy credit that was causing the economy to run away with itself. So the policies being presently pursued were instigated primarily to influence the boom in property values and the rise in credit in the south-east of England, meaning that manufacturing industry in the north (and south), where things had been moving more steadily and more fundamentally toward long term stability, had to be made to suffer through high interest rates and a ludicrously overvalued pound, because of the short-term outlook of the financial institutions. Much that is wrong with this country economically boils down to the simple fact that people dealing in finance are desperate to make a fast profit for doing absolutely nothing. Or the dealers and parasites and assorted useless hangers-on who have benefited from the high value of the pound and been able to ship in enormous quantities of foreign goods also want to make a fast profit for doing nothing. We do not want to buy something for a pound and sell it for two any more. We want to buy it for a pound and sell it for ten. I am no economist, but even I understand that the way out of a recession – and the best way to avoid going into one – is to encourage private investment in the industrial infrastructure, and to have a sound export base, otherwise you hit balance of payments problems. And yet high interest rates and an overvalued currency kill both these things stone dead, as they have crippled British manufacturing industry throughout much of the 1980s.

If for no other reason than she made an attempt to dent the legal establishment, I believe Mrs Thatcher's economic philosophy was fairly sound in principle. Where she was wrong was that she was biased in favour of service industries rather than manufacturing. If the economic farce of the later 1980s, and all the money swilling around, in particular from North Sea oil, had been invested in skills training and manufacturing where it ought to have been invested, instead of in speculative office buildings that will probably be demolished before they are ever occupied, our economic predicament might have been substantially different today, less dependent upon nationalist sentiment taking international leads to create the bogus impression of monetary strength. If we cannot support a price or a wages freeze, or enforce credit controls (neither of which would be necessary if we could learn to be sensible), then what we need is some kind of system of regional government that can differentiate between the requirements of industry and the behaviour of the consumer, as much as it can differentiate between the needs of north and south. It is utterly absurd to impose agonies on sound industry primarily to curtail the silly spending habits of the public, to slap them on the wrist and prevent them from buying video recorders and kettles. If you want to stop them buying foreign goods, the best thing you can do is value your currency at such a level that we can start making more of the darned things ourselves again. Sometimes I think it is not only the editors of TV news programmes who do not understand basic economics, but blundering figures in far more influential positions than that.

The Last Spinning Mill in Lancashire

The undersides of those leaves being visible from the train when I travelled across to Blackburn did indeed portend the onset of wet weather: late in the afternoon that same day Lancashire was drenched in torrential rain. The following morning when I came to it, however, the wet had disappeared and Blackburn was blanketed in a cloud of yellowish fog that swirled just above the rooftops and rolled along side streets, like some bizarre caricature of an old north country industrial smog. When I crossed the Boulevard outside the railway station, where the town's main bus station is arranged, buildings and street corners appeared then disappeared as vague silhouettes before my eyes. Indistinct figures were visible for a moment beneath street lamps, holding perilously onto railings, before they melted into a grey background that exuded nothing but a slow chorus of rumbling internal combustion sound. Only the patter of walking feet was discernible from the gloom gathered at the point where the old paving stones receded into the lost grounds of the cathedral. Somewhere the brakes of a bus squealed.

By the time I'd had a cup of coffee and emerged back into the bitter morning, the fog had more or less cleared to leave the day sunlit, crisp, and without a sliver of cloud anywhere in the sky. I walked round the town centre for a while, noticing that since last I had been in Blackburn the council headquarters, housed in an office block towering above the busy shopping centre, had been skinned in plastic laminate, like those blocks of flats outside Euston Station in London. Looking at the bold grey ramparts of the shopping centre rearing in the sunlight, at the old Victorian terraced houses tumbling up and down the hillsides around the edges of the town, at the Larkhill flats and Thwaites' brewery tower still struggling to assert themselves because of a bit of lingering mist, at the buses juddering this way and that, and at the multi-racial complexion of the thickening crowds, it seemed to me then that the Blackburn coming alive and getting on with another working day did not look at all bad. It had some sound commercial activity going on in the background. It might not be the prettiest town in the world, but defined sharply against a crisp sky beneath brilliant sunshine Blackburn looked tidy enough. Things could have been worse. They could have been as bad economically, and as uninspiring visually, as some of the places I was to see later in the south-east. This was certainly a turn up for the books, and had been reflected the day before in the optimism percolating carefully in the offices of the Chamber of Commerce; even if, some months afterwards, nearly a thousand young Asians went on the rampage and engaged in running battles with police in the centre of the town, along some of the very streets I passed along in good spirits that morning.

There was not much optimism to be found that same morning in the office of the works manager at India Mill, a couple of miles outside Blackburn, out past the football ground along the main road to Bolton. True, the sunshine was still streaming in through the gaps between the venetian blind hung in front of the window and throwing an abstract stripy pattern pleasingly over the mill manager's face and across the surface of his desk. It could have been a normal working day in a normal factory office anywhere; any one of at least a dozen I saw during this journey. The only difference was the telephones were not busy, the tannoy was not echoing incessantly in the background, the computers were not chattering. You were conscious only of the solitary sound of traffic passing relentlessly on the road outside. More importantly, though I could not see it to begin with, it was possible to feel the magnanimous presence of a great body of redundant architecture lifting immediately behind us, for India Mill had just closed down. Production had ceased at the end of the preceding week, and because people are handed their cards very quickly in these circumstances, already there was only a skeleton staff awaiting the arrival of the auctioneers, machine-breakers, scrap metal merchants, and assorted scavengers that descend to pick over the carcass of industrial concerns once they have shut down. I realize that by having loosely established the modern industrial base of Blackburn, having separated it from its nineteenth-century beginnings, I shall have caused a groan of dismay to sound across the region by concentrating now on the kind of bleak subject matter everyone associates these towns with, as they probably have done since Priestley was in Blackburn in 1933, when it was in the depths of a terrible industrial depression. What appealed to me about India Mill was that I was told it was the last large-scale spinning operation of its kind left in Lancashire, and, for a book of this type, I felt an opportunity to see it before it finally disappeared was an opportunity not to be missed.

There was another reason I wanted to see it as well, though, for what you cannot avoid talking about wherever you go in this country, when you speak to industrialists, is the mysterious shifting pattern to world trade to which these factory closures are connected. And there was a lot of talk about that shifting pattern that morning. It was not very pleasant to be shown round the mill, and by that I am not referring to the conversation I had with the mill manager. The conversation I had with him was stimulating and satisfying enough, because we saw eye-to-eye about the anti-manufacturing attitudes that lie at the heart of this country's endemic economic problems from the moment we shook hands. It was not very pleasant to be shown round because I have been associated with textile mills before when they are about to shut down. During my teens I worked in one myself, during the holidays when I was a student, at the time it went under. At the same time I lived in an industrial suburb that had its textile infrastructure completely obliterated; where the dust of demolition and the grinding of bulldozers and the sound of crashing walls was, for a few years at least, forever drifting on the air. My whole family worked in the Yorkshire textile industry, and the decline of that industry, and the glum expressions on disbelieving managerial faces when nearly a quarter of British manufacturing was wiped out ten or twelve years ago, was a sight with which I am acutely familiar. At India Mill I saw the same expressions again, listened to the same angry refrains ten or twelve years on, bringing back a flood of memories. It was as though time were going backwards or history was repeating itself all over again.

This mill manager had worked at India Mill for forty years, and a rather bewildered look crept across his face as he cast his mind back and told me something of the history of the firm and the changing fortunes of the town. His bewilderment turned to rage when we entered the mill itself, which might only have been quiet because it was the lunch break. There were bins full of yarn in front of the machinery. The place smelt like it was still alive. Everything looked as though it had been suddenly switched off and everyone had left abruptly. 'There are six floors exactly like this,' said the mill manager despondently, gesturing toward the ceiling, his words trailing away. You felt the weight of the huge building piled above you. The rows of pale-green machinery receded into perspective in either direction, all of it standing out against the pale maple floorboards drenched by shafts of sunlight, all of it surrounded by the grim monotony of idleness and enforced silence, all of it due to be stripped out and shipped across to Turkey; to one of the countries making it impossible for the spinning industry to remain a viable economic proposition in Lancashire or in England any longer. The mill manager kept repeating the same facts over and over again; kept appealing to the forces of sanity about how amazed he was that the mill was shutting down at all. I picked a bit of yarn off one of the machines, wrapped it around my forefinger, and thought about those comfortable educated persons making sweeping statements about how Britain can afford to let go of its 'outdated industries' and transpose itself tidily into an information-based economy where we needn't bother to make anything any more. I would suggest they go and spend some time talking with the victims being economically displaced by such an easy changeover. They might not then come across as being quite so smug-faced or naïve, or sound quite so out of touch, if they could make the mental connection between displaced economic activity and the growing divisions within our society. Perhaps they will then take the trouble to realize there are huge numbers of people out there who do not think the same as they do; that there is a growing body of people who are not being given much of an opportunity to think constructively for themselves at all, and I don't just mean the people standing at the end of Blackburn's lengthening dole queues.

At this point I shall be reminded that these words are amusingly sentimental; that what I saw in Blackburn was merely another instance of antiquated British manufacturing industry speedily becoming obsolete, to which we can afford to say goodbye and good riddance. In that case let me explain a few things about India Mill. Here was a mill that twelve months previously had been refitted with hundreds of thousands of pounds worth of the most sophisticated winding machinery available anywhere in the world; state-of-the-art technology that was the most advanced of its kind. Here was a mill that produced so much yarn in an average week the managing director had calculated it could be stretched from the Earth to the moon and back. Here was a mill that had been fully computerized, with a bank of monitors in this manager's office – screens now lifeless and blank – its operation and staff structure streamlined, output and productivity increased as much as it was possible to be, in line with the general improvement in productivity and rationalization of industry throughout the Eighties. But here was a mill that *still* could not compete with Third World prices, where the kind of nineteenth-century industrial exploitation that was railed against in socialist perorations of yesteryear is happening all over again, except that now it is bound up with our own exchange rates, labour costs, and excessive overheads, forever thwarting the committed industrialist or businessman. The electricity bill alone for India Mill was an incredible fifteen-thousand pounds per week. You can streamline your factory and improve your productivity until you are blue in the face; you can talk about as much sophisticated technology as you like; you can employ a workforce comprised entirely of robots and dispense with human beings altogether; but you cannot affect overheads or outgoings when they are beyond your control and continually undermine your profitability. There is something very seriously wrong when manufacturing processes that are modernized and brought up to world-beating standards cannot remain competitive. And with the focus of world trade busily becoming concentrated across in the direction of the Pacific Rim, bringing God knows what horrors for potential conflict in the future stability of the world as the Far East becomes immensely wealthy at our expense, if you are in business in this country it is difficult to avoid becoming caught up in the meantime in the tightening proccss and the desperate scramble to survive. The result is buildings like India Mill being stripped of their machinery and their workforce and being put up for sale. The result is an air of desolation descending over another corner of another industrial town, and frustrated management in stuffy little offices asking why such impeccable modernization can become such a terrible waste so quickly.

Standing in that silent empty mill my guide wondered aloud, as he tried to console himself to the prospect of unemployment, where it was all going to end. We could not go on shutting down industry indefinitely, he said, piling up unemployed people, and not continuing to invest or fill out the cavity being left behind in the economy, even if the vast workforces that generated the wealth of the nineteenth and first half of the twentieth century have now become superfluous to the controllers of modern capital and more and more machines are performing work once performed by people. But, as the traffic sidled to and from Blackburn at the other side of a blur of rooftops rising in the hazy distance through the windows, I pulled on that bit of yarn still wrapped around my forefinger. It snapped, or not so much snapped as broke apart like wet newspaper, and I wondered seriously whether we ought not to have been wondering where it was all going to end, but if it might be only just beginning.

Burnley

I did not stay in Blackburn but instead based myself in the main hotel in the centre of Burnley, a few miles down the road. Burnley looks more like the popular conception of a northern mill town than does Blackburn. Unlike Blackburn it is built almost entirely from stone, a very rough-hewn kind of stone, and in places feels not so much run-down as visibly truncated, where the mills have disappeared and the dual carriageways and a flyover have obliterated everything in their path. It is interesting to consider that some of the recording studio equipment used by zillionaire songwriters and performers such as Phil Collins, Paul McCartney, and Michael Jackson is manufactured in Burnley. Like Blackburn, it has a diverse manufacturing infrastructure backing up its local economy, and makes, among other things, automobile switchgear systems, Michelin tyres, snooker tables, and a famous range of houseware products. The television series *Juliet Bravo* was filmed in and around Burnley. The centre of the town appears to have been scooped out and replaced with a concrete shopping precinct, though it looks noticeably poorer, and is much less substantial, than its equivalent in Blackburn. I would guess this is due to the fact that Burnley is even more an authentic working class town than Blackburn, chiefly because it is smaller and less important. It has a sturdy middle-class quarter up along the wide main road at Reedly Hallow, where there are large Victorian houses and trees. But this is overshadowed by the enormous amount of grid-patterned terraced housing that still comprises the vast bulk of the town, as is the case with nearby Accrington.

If you have never been to this part of the north, but have in your mind a picture of street after street of tiny terraced houses running at angles up gentle slopes, their front doors opening immediately onto pavements and all with little square yards behind them, then that is what much of Burnley, and much of this part of East Lancashire, is still like. You walk to the high points overlooking the towns and before you stretch immensely long furrows of terraced houses, sweeping away into distant perspectives, down toward a few remaining mills or the odd railway viaduct straddling the streets at the bottom. This is especially so at Accrington, where there are more cobbled streets and longer unbroken rows of terraced houses than in any other town in England. There are very few mill chimneys, very few mills looming these days above the streets, or watching over the narrow cobbled back alleys. It has recently become a characteristic of these textile towns, too, that the front walls of many of the little houses are painted beige, cream, pale blue, peach, or even pink, rather as is the tradition in old industrialized parts of South Wales. You stand at the top of streets and do not see rows of grimy facades any more, smeared with the filth of industry. There are still plenty of cobbles, but when you walk up and down these streets now, as I did during my final afternoon in East Lancashire before I moved on, there is an overall sense of brightness to the architecture, instead of the darkness with which these places were once so strongly associated. Recently I watched the old black-and-white film adaptation of Stanley Houghton's play *Hindle Wakes*, made during the early 1950s. The film itself was completely forgettable, but it was set in a Lancashire textile town, and so far as my observations go, the opening shots accompanying the credits were filmed overlooking Burnley. The town looked smoke-blackened. The high angle, almost abstract, views of steep terraced streets, enshrouded in angular black shadows, with cobbles and gas lamps standing starkly on street corners predominant, had a distinct darkness to them. But when you look at Burnley from a distance today, that is not the case any longer. In place of the characterful gas lamps have long been stationed bland concrete posts; and the furrowed rooflines are becoming speckled more and more with the white staring eyes of satellite dishes. Perhaps the change has been a subconscious reaction by the population against the years of dirt and neglect. Or perhaps it has merely been that with the departure of the old industries, so too departed the smog; with both the rain and a concerted programme of stone-cleaning washing away the soot and revealing the towns in their true colours, and the proliferation of DIY superstores giving people the freedom to do with their homes as they wished more than ever before.

That same afternoon I walked up to the Stoneyholme district of Burnley, where I had arranged to be shown round the Jinnah Community Centre. This is in one of Burnley's oldest industrial quarters, one that has incumbent the town's most extensive Asian population, behind what is left of the main railway station. The centre is housed in the front half of the Islamic Central Hall, which is itself established in a converted cinema. It certainly presents an imposing spectacle when viewed from the street. It has been heavily rendered in concrete, all the windows are obscured by wire mesh, the doors are reinforced with steel plate, and graffiti decorates some of the exterior surfaces. The impression is not so much of a centre involved in community relations, coping with unemployment among local Asians of a staggering 45%, as it is of a police station fortified against terrorist attack in Northern Ireland. The sharp contrast when you cross over from the street is surprising. One moment you are standing in bright sunshine, a little hesitant about whether or not you ought to risk opening the main door, then suddenly you are among a hive of warm, rather makeshift-looking fluorescent-lit offices. There are people tapping away at typewriters and telephones are ringing. Voices can be heard talking muffled through the thin walls, and you are realizing just how much parts of these old towns have changed since the heyday of the English working class; before ordinary people deserted them and deteriorated into what the *enfant terrible* Tony Parsons, who writes books about pop stars, describes today as 'white trash'.

Whether the defence shields of the Jinnah Community Centre are intended to protect the building from the criminal aspirations of lively local youngsters, or from people outside the area, I did not manage to ascertain. When I had negotiated a footpath alongside the railway cutting at the top of the street on my way to the community centre I came upon a bit of graffiti daubed across an old mill building which informed me ominously that I was now entering THE NO LAW ZONE. This had seemed rather strange, because I guessed there was probably less breaking of the law here in this largely Asian quarter, more of a sense of community, than in other more prosperous parts of Burnley. For what distinguishes many of these old working-class back-street areas that have become the home to extensive Asian populations in northern towns is the way the people living in them hang together. While I was being shown round the Jinnah centre by the English woman who is the administration officer there, I mentioned this to the Asian community leader, whom we found attending to the central-heating boiler at the end of one of the corridors. I went on to tell him that what had always struck me whenever I had been into an Asian district was that there was a noticeable feeling of community spirit in the air; that as a white person I generally did not feel uneasy walking through them on my own. Asians generally seemed to me to be quite gentle people. There were corresponding parts of towns occupied by rough white or Anglicized West Indian communities, such as Toxteth in Liverpool, that were positively intimidating and that I would purposely avoid. The leader related this to petty social competitiveness, as he squinted into a plug in his hand. He could remember when ordinary English people were more pragmatic and thrifty, as he claimed the majority of Asians are today, and worked within their means. He thought the English now seemed to think it was a virtue to get into debt, so long as they were seen by their neighbours to be prosperous. He could not see the virtue in it. From it develops bubbling resentment, the children suffer, families begin to break down, and society ends up clawing at each others' throats. It was undignified and not the way people ought to behave at all.

I mentioned that when I had been walking round Blackburn that morning I had discovered some streets of abandoned terraced houses that were due to be demolished, not far from the station. Although most of the houses had been bricked up, the streets deserted save for some gipsies looting roof slates and piling them onto a lorry down one of the back alleys, and looking very uneasy when I began taking photographs, there were still a number of children hanging around. I said I had noticed before when taking photographs in the north that gangs of English children tended to leer at the camera, turf abuse, or jump up and down pulling funny faces or making obscene gestures like a parade of monkeys. I have even been stoned by working-class youngsters in the past, when I was taking photographs on a council estate. Asian youngsters, on the other hand, almost without exception, tended to come up and ask intelligent questions. They were full of self-composure and rather inquisitive. They did not display delinquent exhibitionist tendencies as automatically as the English kids, at any rate not when they were below a certain age. As a generalization, it still seemed to have some substance to it when I came upon those derelict cobbled streets in Blackburn, and a handful of Asian youngsters gathered close to me. The community leader believed this was very much to do with Asian culture, in particular its commitment to religion and the way younger members of the community are taught to respect the older generation. They have very strict codes of conduct. It is the duty of Asian youngsters to take care of the old and the infirm when required, which enables them to develop respect for their elders. The English generally are not like that, he said. Some white English youngsters will even mug or rape elderly members of their communities. If a young Asian boy mugged an elderly Asian the consequences for him would be very grave indeed. (I wondered afterwards what the consequences would be if a young Asian mugged a white pensioner.) He believed these attitudes acted as a stabilizing force over peoples' lives, encouraging them to hold together socially and gather round if necessary in the face of hardship. They also encouraged a kind of moral discipline. These were penetrating observations. They stood out because they were not backed up by the ring of sentimentality one normally associates with the native English population reflecting upon the decline in its own moral standards over the years. We both agreed that even in our time we had noticed a change come over English society; that English people now judged each other far too much by their possessions than as people. But I said that this was not yet affecting every sector of society, and was one of the reasons I had been drawn to this part of Burnley.

The competitive undercurrent, the rivalry and the jealousy simmering beneath the surface of much of modern English society, is of course a relatively modern phenomenon. I can just about remember when the community values that are strongly discernible in many Asian quarters today still permeated many white working-class districts. In fact, walking round Stoneyholme again afterwards I was struck, as I often am, by the way the activity going on in the streets – people talking or sitting smoking on doorsteps, children playing ball games and hop-scotch in the road, front doors left ajar, above all the awareness of people going about their daily business – seems to be a parody on how these places were before many of their present inhabitants came anywhere near them. Skip back to those streets forty or fifty years ago, to a warm September evening in 1939, for instance. Consider the people with their Lancashire accents sitting by their radios behind their limp lace curtains with their nice cups of tea, as Chamberlain gloomily announced 'I have to tell you now', and compare these places then with how they are today. Apart from a few superficial details, such as door and window styles, and that some of the cobbles have been tarmacked over, and that there are more cars, the only thing that has radically altered is the appearance and the culture of the majority of people circulating among them. Social life is much the same. These places still look rather poor, the houses appear run-down, as was the whole complex of houses I walked through, street after street of them all identical, further up the hill. But there is not the air of violence and confrontation smouldering in the background that you can perceive infecting desolate concrete wastelands elsewhere. You can still find the same positive values in white English sectors of society, make no mistake of that. But they are not nearly as prevalent or as general as they were, of that I am convinced.

How long the Asian communities will remain immune to Western pressure to conform is difficult to say. How long they will resist the influence of other pressures to conform is perhaps a more pertinent question. Educated English Marxists, habitually contemptuous of their own society and twisting everything around into an attack on the acquisitive values fostered by capitalism, will tell you that the majority population does not encourage the ethnic minorities to integrate. In my experience it is often very much the other way round, probably because at present the generation that came over here in the Fifties to work in the foundries and the mills, with one foot still in India or Pakistan and one eye firmly on the teachings of the Koran, continues to hold the upper hand. It acts as a guiding force and a leaven. But that will not always be the case, for the father-figures are getting old and they will not live forever. There may be processes of change at work already. When I emerged from the Jinnah centre into the dazzling late-afternoon sunshine, the schools had just emptied, and the little streets were alive with scores of Asian children making their way home. Some of the teenage girls, born and reared here, subjected to modern popular English culture, modern popular music, and modern popular advertising, and liking what they see, looked completely Westernized. Some of them were very pretty, with long flowing hair, and they were wearing short skirts, denim jackets, and stiletto heels. The way they composed themselves, the way they were conscious of older males passing them on the street, was entirely Western in character. There is an indication, too, that older teenage Asian males, watching Western films and developing regional accents and nurturing Western values, are showing increasing signs of brutalization as they resign themselves to a lifetime of unemployment, like their English counterparts, now that the industrial jobs their parents came to perform have disappeared. I have already referred to the mob of Asian youngsters that rampaged through the streets of Blackburn months afterwards. Though at present they are fairly buoyant, it is worth remembering that the community infrastructure has been broken down in these places once already. The poorest sectors of the white working-class population had their aspirations manipulated into a new form of emotional submission, as they gradually became exposed to the stimulating appeal of certain market values and were carried away into modern utilitarian environments. I should think the decay in religious belief throughout most of the last hundred years has also played a substantial part in the breakdown in English working class values, as it has played a part in much of the decay of Western civilization in general. There is no reason to doubt seriously that it could not happen again, so that if I were to return to the streets of Stoneyholme in a generation or so's time, there is a distinct possibility that I might not feel quite so safe and secure as I once did.

Before I came away I crouched to take a photograph of the main road running through Stoneyholme when a taxi swung violently round the corner. The Asian driver was probably a few years younger than I was, and he shouted through his open window as he passed, in perfect Lancashire dialect, 'Yer'll wait till ah'm in t'shot, won't yer mate!' I laughed and thought back to George Orwell describing a typical Lancashire working man in 1936 saying 'Ah wur coomin oop street.' It was precisely the same dialect nearly sixty years on. Apart from the more obvious realization that we do indeed live in a funny old world, I realized the important thing to remember today is that, contrary to the outlook of a number of ignorant equal-opportunities apparatchiks, under certain circumstances, in the face of relentless albeit very gradual social change, in the face of a number of quite indiscriminate realities, skin colour does not actually matter a damn.

3

Tyneside and Cleveland

Journey Down the Tyne

I was told when I was in Newcastle that ordinary Geordies cannot always get on with people from further south, but can tolerate Liverpudlians, with whom they feel to have something of a natural affinity. This was put down to the fact that both Newcastle and Liverpool were once great ports that nurtured tough working-class communities, and have each endured long periods of economic decline. For this reason it was suggested the cities' football supporters tended not to fight one another when their respective teams clashed.

If these resemblances are true, and mean the two cities can be regarded as distant relations, then they might go some way to explaining something else that is a feature of them both – their chronic incidence of car theft. It was appropriate that I should be thinking about cars and car theft when I arrived in Newcastle. Though one of the advantages of travelling through densely-populated urban areas in England is the ease with which you can move around on public transport, because my destination when I came away from Burnley had been the north-east, I'd had almost a hundred miles of open country to cross; a significant chunk of it taking me straight through the heart of the Yorkshire Dales via Richmond, much of it devoid of human habitation, and much of it dripping wet when I saw it and obscured by a fog-bank. The use of public transport under the circumstances would not have proved easy, so I'd changed to travelling in my own car. In addition to this, when I turned my attention toward Newcastle, joyriders, along with pit-bull terriers, were very much on the nation's lips. The Meadowell riots had only just happened, and Kenneth Baker was pushing through a number of parliamentary bills. When I had driven past Darlington on my way up to Tyneside, I had tuned into the local radio station, which was carrying as its main story the killing of a baby by joyriders in the Scotswood district of Newcastle. I was aware, too, that joyriding was supposed to be very much a social phenomenon of modern Tyneside, and if as a phenomenon in the media its appeal has receded somewhat today, whatever else one thought about Newcastle at that time, one associated it with car crime and joyriding. But what truly amazed me, in spite of all these negative preconceptions – no matter how much I knew exaggeration could prevent there being a sensible perspective placed on things and on Newcastle – was how quickly I came upon an incidence of car crime, how promptly the problem of car security raised itself, once I arrived in the city.

No sooner had I booked into the big Victorian hotel alongside Newcastle railway station, parked my car adjacent to the platforms round the back, and transported some of my baggage inside, than I went back out to fetch the rest and saw two policemen rushing between the cars. They ran across to another man who was waving at them several hundred yards from my vehicle, and together they all bent down and began examining a sports car. A Geordie business-type who had parked close enough to see what was happening told me that a couple of kids had just been attempting to steal a Golf GTI, but they had been disturbed and made their escape. I said I was amazed because I had just arrived in Newcastle for the first time and had not managed to take my coat off before car theft presented itself. It was highly likely it was pure coincidence I should see it, but it wasn't exactly doing my impression of the city much good. He laughed and welcomed me to the city of car crime, then immediately launched into an abusive tirade against the social deterioration affecting modern society. He thought joyriders, along with hardened criminals, should be rounded up and exterminated. We lived in a society that was far too bloody liberal, he said. If the human body became diseased we took the necessary measures to remove whatever it was that was threatening the part of it that was still healthy and functioning normally. If a vicious dog stepped over the mark and savaged somebody, it was immediately destroyed. We didn't try and coerce it with do-gooding sentimentalist claptrap, as a way of hedging round whatever expediencies might need to be taken. We were pragmatic and simply got rid of it. And so we should be with crime, he said. It was a disease threatening the main body of society, and it had to be regarded as a gangrene that must be isolated and ruthlessly annihilated. Why should he pay his bloody taxes to keep the shit that was destroying society alive in prisons? What purpose did it serve? The government took his taxes to keep these people comfortable, and failed to address the problem fundamentally or take the necessary moral action, with the result he also had to spend thousands more pounds making his business premises secure. There were, he continued, certain human beings that resembled him and me in that they walked around on two legs and could articulate sounds in their throats, but there the resemblance ended. One had to regard them as one regarded dangerous animals in the wild. They did not conform to normal civilized values. They could not be reasoned with. And the social or economic causes for them being how they were were largely irrelevant. *Ipso facto* these people were there, and they were not going to go away. This had to be accepted as the starting point for any subsequent action or discussion. I managed to splutter out that society's inability to face up to these things had probably got something to do with liberal society being too cowardly, and trying to appease its own miserable conscience by failing to face up to social truths and realities. It couldn't come to terms with the mental condition of many of the people perpetrating violent crime, and so it removed them from society and pushed them away out of sight instead, believing it was doing society a favour. Special prisons for violent offenders were a perfect example. He nodded but said that quarantining criminals in prison was no good. There was no soft option. Before long, unless we took a tough stance, the disease would have advanced so far it would prove terminal. He demanded I look at Newcastle, at which a train across in the station emitted a tremendous burst of flatulence and rumbled frantically out of the platform, adding a note of farce to everything he had just said and enabling me to get away.

I was horrified to come across a complete stranger and plunge into a discussion of such gravity. What unnerved me about his frankness and his fascist demeanour, as we stood there in the damp darkness, was that he looked like every young school child's favourite uncle, and he was carrying a bunch of flowers. I suspect his anger was a gut reaction to his feeling vulnerable at having been so close to crime. Nevertheless, when I had carried all my belongings into the hotel, I took the precaution of stripping my vehicle of everything thievable, except the carpets and the vast accumulation of newspapers that always travels with me wherever I go, then, on the advice of the hotel receptionist, drove it down to an NCP car park at the opposite end of the station. It was a roofed compound manned twenty-four hours a day and protected by video surveillance cameras, and for a fairly stiff price your vehicle was secure overnight. Then I returned to my hotel and locked myself in my room until it was time to go down to dinner. When I did go down to dinner, I found myself leaving the television switched on, just in case.

The subject of Tyneside car crime did not finish there. My publisher had put me in touch with a producer at Tyne Tees Television. He is a producer of current affairs programmes, and so was able to show me something of the unofficial, as opposed to the marketed official, face of the Tyne. The following morning he picked me up in his car to take me on a sort of guided tour of the Tyne, and we had not been driving for more that fifteen minutes before we saw two young joyriders along the outskirts of Jarrow. A red sports car had come up close behind at great speed and lurched past us. Suddenly, it swerved across all three lanes on the carriageway at an angle of nearly ninety degrees, with the severity of the notorious handbrake turn. I had my window down and so heard the long slithering of tyres over the wet road surface as the vehicle corrected itself and screeched to a halt in a lay-by. Immediately, two animalistic, almost

Neanderthal-looking youths leapt out, left the doors wide open and the engine running, and fled as fast as they could across a scruffy patch of municipal grass. What had caused them to do this was the sight of a couple of council workers dressed in uniforms and luminescent-green vests who were supervising the installation of a new street lamp on a traffic island further along the road. From that distance they looked exactly like highway policemen. In these parts they have nicknamed this car thieving activity 'twocking' – Taking WithOut Consent. Ram-raiding was invented on Tyneside, and is one of the area's more dubious if notorious exports. So much for sentimental thoughts about the old Tyneside working class, I said, as violent images of riot police and news bulletins from South Africa, not to mention the sales figures of Catherine Cookson's novels, slid into my mind.

Whenever you visit a town or city you come away carrying an impression of the place environmentally, and afterwards find yourself making generalizations whereupon you search for nods of approval from people who know the place in question. My initial impression of Newcastle had not been good. I had arrived there when it was dark and had come close to witnessing crime. During that funny hour between six and seven in the evening when you are in a strange city, when I had pottered out onto the streets to search for a local newspaper, the place had seemed black and somehow steaming and misty and rather murky. (This was due entirely, I should think, to the after-effects of the wet weather.) It was almost as though smoke were drifting from manhole-covers and drains throughout the city, as is supposed to be the case in downtown New York. Newcastle almost felt intimidating, and had done from the moment it materialized rather fortress-like, clinging to the face of, and piled upon, its hundred foot gorge when I first approached it by car in the gathering dusk late in the afternoon. The first most noticeable quality that struck me about the Tyne by daylight – apart from the splendour of Newcastle city centre, of which more later – was the enormous quantity of council estates. I do not mean high-rise blocks of flats or deck tenements. The area seemed to me to have comparatively few of these. I mean pre-war, and probably just post-war, semi-detached houses that became the fashion when working-class slums were pulled down and communities began to be dispersed around the edges of towns and cities. I have never seen so many of these council houses as I did when I was shown Gateshead, Jarrow, Hebburn, South Shields, North Shields, and Wallsend that day. Soon after we crossed the magnificent Tyne Bridge (prototype for the Sydney Harbour Bridge in Australia) and headed away from Newcastle, we travelled along a wide dual carriageway and stared across an absolutely immense expanse of municipal rooftops, all of which were of that grey semi-detached mining community variety, all of which appeared identical, and all of which receded, row after furrowed row, to some unfathomable misty distance. The tremendous sense of perspective was emphasised because of the flatness of the landscape. Apparently what we were looking at was two different estates that blended together somewhere in the middle of the blur of chimney-pots, but it was impossible to decide where that middle was. I have never seen anything quite like it. These council estates were everywhere. They seemed to be separated only by expanses of waste ground covered in a parched straw-coloured grass, bisected by long-abandoned railway cuttings dotted with bent supermarket trolleys and rubbish, and joined together by a succession of dual carriageways and roundabouts teeming with articulated lorries and traffic. The impression left behind, though I am sure it was not entirely accurate and must have been heavily subjective because I was a casual visitor passing through, was of an immense bleakness; a vast working class landscape coloured buff-and-concrete, with hardly any patches of green, hardly any trees, entirely without character or charm, not a decent civic building in sight, and no real substance or much indication of life. It all looked so bland and so utterly functionless. Street after street of little semi-detached houses all exactly the same: a few figures crossing the roads carrying shopping bags as the side roads flickered past one by one: boarded-up windows: a few video shops, some washeterias and newsagents, doubtless struggling to survive. The calender suggested this was autumn in England. Although during my travels up to press I had only seen a limited indication visually that this was in fact true, even when I had passed through the damp and dismal Dales, the theory was that trees were turning vigorous colours of yellow and brown and red throughout the land. There was supposed to be the exquisite smell of woodsmoke in the air. Young school children were being taken on their first nature rambles, were learning about the sycamore, the elm, the horse-chestnut, and pressing leaves flat in little paper folders. But the change of the seasons did not appear to be registering very eloquently here on this south bank of the Tyne. Nature's visual sonnet of the fall had been more or less banished from these dolescapes, except when it settled to lay waste to great patches of urban decay down along the waterfront, across which you half expected to see tumbleweed rolling and hear strong superlatives sounding.

The inspiration for this book came from J.B. Priestley's journey through England in the autumn of 1933. I did not retrace his original footsteps, did not visit the same factories or stand on the same street corners and compare the scenery then and now; and when I set off I was intending to cover more ground in the south of England than he did. Though his book describing an urban ride through England is the only one of its type that in my opinion is still worth reading, I wanted to avoid referring to it, except when I felt it was absolutely necessary. But when I was in Newcastle, it was impossible to avoid making comparisons between some of the things he saw and said, and some of the things I saw and thought, particularly when I was taken down the Tyne that overcast morning. I had left myself in the capable hands of my guide, but there was something of an unintended resemblance in the way I was driven down the Tyne in a saloon car by someone who was a native of the area, starting out along the old Quayside, and being shown all the towns, just as Priestley had been by his antiquarian bookseller friend. And as I passed those gigantic housing estates, it was impossible to avoid feeling that these environments were not places where people really lived, but places where they were stored. I do not know why I should have responded like this to these houses. They were supposed to be a major improvement over their dank Victorian forerunners. They had their bit of space between them. They had gardens and would have rooms of a reasonable size, and had long had kitchens and bathrooms. I spent some time in similar houses when I was young. We had some relatives who lived on a council estate of this type. (They still do, and have since bought their house.) I could, if pushed, feel about them a certain amount of nostalgia, especially about the metal window frames to the little boxroom overlooking the garden at the back of the house where I occasionally used to stay. There was a seven- or eight-year waiting list for council houses in the industrial area where I lived when I was a teenager. Our name was at the end of that list, and a little postcard dropped through the letterbox one day, long after both my parents were dead, saying we could finally have one, by which time it no longer mattered. But I had never experienced municipal housing developments on anything approaching the scale I saw down the Tyne. Though they were strongly regimented, these houses were not crammed together, not tiny house after tiny house, not row after narrow row, as the nineteenth-century industrial housing had been back in East Lancashire. People could, in a modest kind of way, spread themselves out in these newer places. I can imagine how idealistic they must have appeared on those old black-and-white newsreels when they were built, with Standard English patronizingly informing us that Bob and Judy and Jackie and Dave, and little baby Nigel, and not forgetting dog Ted and cat Tiddles, were coming to make a new life for themselves as the great working-class exodus from slummy slumland began. There was plenty of daylight and air came into these new environments, filling the gaps between the gables, and I could see this was still the case that morning. There was no longer the eternal twilight of closely packed terraces spread beneath a pother of tepid industrial smog. Narrow streets – the ones being so artfully romanticized, now that they have gone – no longer became shallow brick canyons permanently divided down the middle of the road by straight shadows whenever the sun was in the sky. But in them something was also missing, for what heritage trail will these modern council estates follow? What nostalgia is flowering here?

When he described Gateshead, Priestley said it was nothing better than a huge dingy working-class dormitory. He said Jarrow was 'a barracks cynically put together so that shipbuilding workers could get some food and sleep between shifts'. The best thing they could have done with these places was pull them down and start again. Well, they did that, because the Gateshead and the Jarrow he saw have almost completely disappeared. But I could not help feeling that the same description applied when I gazed across those immense carpets of misty municipal rooftops today. One vast dingy dormitory had simply been replaced by another, with a few basic amenities lifting them up a notch or two on the scale of civilized living. It must have been the overwhelming vastness of the scale, the dreary monotony of the overall urban scene, but you could not escape the powerful conviction that the people living there lacked a certain amount of individual liberty and direct control over their own lives. These were passive lives that were organized largely at the convenience of bureaucratic bodies and public institutions. That is the language the layout of the environment spoke. The army of unemployed among them provided economic stability and employment for the local unemployment industry. The populace was herded together, not living together. That is the crucial difference between these places and the modern residential housing estates to which they are related. These, too, can be dull and horribly monotonous, soulless and stifling. But there is about them some indivisible quality, a whiff of freedom in the air, something in the way curtains are hung in windows and cars are washed on drives, that says the owners are still in charge; that governments are still dependent upon their taxes and have an interest in attracting their votes; that these are the people that really matter. No doubt the flatness of tone I perceived to that urban wasteland outside Newcastle, the lack of colour, was emphasised by the ceiling of low cloud cover that was now hanging stubbornly over the country. But it was a flatness that persisted, and it was noticeable wherever we went, and it did not go away.

As it happened, we saw a bit of sun that morning after all, though it was the only time I saw decent sunlight when I was in Tyneside, or when I was in Cleveland further down the coast several days later. It managed to squeeze out for us from between the clouds, which parted to reveal a small patch of blue sky for about ten minutes, when we stopped and descended a flight of concrete steps at a promontory of land beneath a railway bridge, somewhere near South Shields. There we looked solemnly down the great silent length of the Tyne in one direction, and toward the yawning expanse of the ocean beckoning in the other. Perhaps I was full of sentimental preconceptions as I stood there, but I could not help feeling that staring out at that glistening grey estuary was like looking across the silent aftermath of some great and recent battle. Again I thought back to Priestley standing by the edge of the Tyne, among the piles of coal dust and mud. He described the air of nearby Jarrow as being thick with the enforced idleness of poverty and misery. Some of that air is still there, stale with the stink of the decades. He mentioned, as a thousand guidebooks have mentioned, that the Venerable Bede was associated with this region. Though he did not go into detail, what was behind the depressed condition of the Jarrow he saw, and at the root afterwards of the hunger march to London by unemployed workers, was the closure of the Palmer Shipbuilding and Iron Company's works. Palmer's had launched their final ship in 1932, the year before Priestley was there, gone into liquidation the following year when Priestley made his journey through England, and had been sold to a controversial organization set up by the shipbuilding industry called the National Shipbuilders Security, and shut down completely, the year after that. The reason for the controversy surrounding the National Shipbuilders Security was that it bought up and deliberately closed down shipyards to reduce shipbuilding capacity, to leave some semblance of an industry that was lean and healthy. These were the 'surgical operations' Priestley mentioned in passing as he looked down at the river from Wallsend, near to a collection of broken-down ruins of working-mens' allotments which are still there, clinging to the hillside above the Tyne, after all these years. It was a sort of asset-stripping operation, streamlining the industry in the way British Coal has been pruned back since the miners' strike, to make it ripe for privatization. The result, then as now, was a necessary pyramid of unemployed people, misery, and despair. The source of much loathing and suffering among Geordies sixty years ago was that the owners of the redundant shipyards were compensated with levies, whereas the yard workers were thrown on the social scrapheap and received absolutely nothing. Like the abandoned yards they were left to rot. At least the look of decomposition visible on some of the ashen faces I saw milling around Tyneside had not quite progressed to the stage of rigor-mortis; probably because in the majority of places marginally improved state benefits, and a body of unemployed with relatively high standards and expectations from life, whatever its dire economic predicament, keeps resentment just below the necessary flashpoint. At least, that is the case at present.

In a way, the economic contraction Priestley saw had come full circle not long before I was on Tyneside, because it was difficult to avoid thinking about the industrial battle that had raged down there among the shipyards over more recent years. That piece of land upon which we were standing overlooking the river had been turned into a sort of viewing station, and to me it resembled a wretched little bandstand without a roof. There had been some attempt made to landscape it, and the path leading toward it. The viewing area had been surfaced with the proverbial herringbone-patterned brick paviours, but what it was there to view neither of us could really understand. Perhaps there was a greater philosophical meaning behind it than first met the eye, or maybe it was something to do with the Geordies' ironic sense of humour. I suspect it was meant to be a kind of pulpit so that people – not tourists: it could not possibly be meant for tourists – could overlook an imaginary past now gone, as we are busy overlooking what is dangerously close to becoming an imaginary England that has gone, instead of picturing the definitive England there might be. A rusty, overgrown railway siding came almost up to where we were standing, and finished suddenly behind a rather lethal-looking spiked metal fence. Directly beneath us, over a thick black stone retaining wall, were the smashed concrete foundations and rubble-strewn remnants of a shipyard, and some empty loading jetties or landing-slips bobbing with rubbish. Up river we could see a vestige of shipping and a tangle of tall cranes, now painted bright primary colours of blue and yellow, injecting a bit of life into the dreary desolation of the overall scene. The rest was silence, a tremendous all-consuming misty silence, except for the incessant screeching of seagulls drifting high overhead.

There is still some shipbuilding along the Tyne, and it is important to remember this. There is also some vigorous and supportive voluntary community work going on in these places; and what I saw of the people when I was there again the following day suggests there is a sharp sense of humour coursing throughout these Tyneside towns, despite seemingly insurmountable odds for a growing percentage of their populations. But both the positive face of the region's old industries as they stand today, and the favourable qualities of the majority of its people, are overshadowed by the story of decline and the maelstrom of rising crime and social disintegration. The transition from an age when coal and traditional heavy-manufacturing industries totally dominated the area has, of course, been swift and decisive. As recently as the mid-1970s, coal, steel, and shipbuilding accounted for 35% of economic activity on Tyneside. That figure has now been reduced to a mere 3%. During the 1960s there were hundreds of coal pits in the area. Now there are about half a dozen, and the rumours are that in a few years' time there will probably be none at all. At the same time we are putting enormous amounts of money into the building of huge terminals at some of our ports to cope with a massive increase in cheap imported coal, despite many of our own seams remaining sound for decades to come and being one of our greatest national assets. And we have the audacity to call this sense. The story of Tyneside shipbuilding is the story of Britain's heavy industry you hear wherever you go – immense contraction, but profitability and stability for the fortunate few still in work, like the five-hundred lucky stevedores at Liverpool docks. I should add that I do not know what the economic or political answer for these butchered industrial heartlands is. I think the social malaise is becoming so deeply ingrained it would take generations to put things right. We might already have reached the point of no return, whereby a vast chunk of the British population will simply exist outside the workings of mainstream economic activity and never participate constructively in society again; dependent on a welfare industry supported by the taxes of those able to take part in the motions of a civilized lifestyle elsewhere. This, I repeat, as I shall repeat it again throughout this book, is the terrifying danger which I believe as a comfortable proportion of society we ignore at our peril. And it is no excuse for a sort of social or intellectual moratorium to be imposed on any sensible discussion taking place about these devastated urban populations. Nor should it mean that to speak about these things sympathetically should have you denigrated as 'left-wing'. And why should drawing attention to these things have you habitually dismissed as being anti-your-own-country? These places are a miserable testimony to the failure of human beings to organize themselves sensibly, nothing more. Whatever your politics, Left or Right, blue, pink, or red, they are there and they cannot be ignored, for the sake of history and the truth.

Of course, the truth is that the vast majority of Tynesiders, like most of the British people, lead prosperous and civilized lives. The vast majority of Tynesiders are in work. Sound industry has been investing heavily in the area. New buildings have been going up. Waterside development has flourished. On another occasion I might book into a hotel in central Newcastle, and put myself at the disposal of somebody who shows me something different. There *is* another and different Tyneside, which I glimpsed briefly when I was there; one which results, apparently, in more Porsche motor cars being sold in Newcastle than anywhere else in the country; one where I was told that to attempt to reserve a table at short notice at the city's most expensive restaurant, at around £60 per head, would almost certainly reveal it to be fully booked. Later I was taken out to Ponteland, Newcastle's wealthiest suburb, where I met a very successful maker of video films for rock groups such as Simple Minds, Queen, and the guitarist Eric Clapton. This was no arrogant cigar-smoking prima donna of the kind I had occasionally seen swanning around Soho studios, like Vietnamese pot-bellied pigs, in London. This was a slim north-easterner born and bred; a man who looked more like a businessman than a creative film-maker; a man who despite lucrative offers from Europe and America to poach his talents, cannot leave Tyneside, and cherishes the moment when his aircraft touches down at Newcastle International Airport after the completion of another globe-trotting assignment; a man who started out working in one of the area's coal mines as a teenager, to which he used to make a gruelling journey by bicycle and train from one side of the city to the other, to start work at six a.m. The sight of this man standing before a pair of French windows, pouring several whiskies from a crystal decanter in a room full of antique furniture looking onto a leaf-speckled lawn in a prosperous part of Newcastle, as an autumn afternoon gave way to dusk and we were all engulfed by shadows, was another symbolic snapshot, not only of the Tyneside we rarely hear about, but the north of England we rarely hear about.

But, though I am probably in danger of stirring up a small hornet's nest by focusing on it for the umpteenth time here, the depressed Tyne I have described so far is a reality. So are such places throughout the land. I think one has to acknowledge that this is so, and go and look at them and walk about them and talk to people living in them to keep a reasonable sense of perspective upon oneself, because a growing number of the inhabitants of these places are going to have an ever-increasing connection to the manner in which we prosperous fortunates conduct our own lives. To see what I mean, compare the yellow pages in major urban conurbations from ten years ago to those of today, and look at how security services have increased; or remember the stories that seem to be surfacing with increasing frequency about restaurants that are doing well because the patrons can see the car park from their tables. These are almost throwaway asides, but they are important because they reveal to us, very succinctly, the emerging pattern to society – a society that is continually looking back over its shoulder to protect what it owns. Directly linked to this new pattern are these dole places as they exist at this moment, as I saw them at the beginning of the 1990s, as is the penetrating silence hanging over so many of this country's smashed industrial areas. Standing beneath that railway bridge near South Shields my companion told me it was this silence down the Tyne that spoke historical volumes. For a few seconds he became impassioned. He said he had not been there for some time now. He was only a couple of years older than me, but shaking his head and motioning to the river he said that until comparatively recently, if we had been standing in the same position, we would never have heard the sound of bloody seagulls. The din of working machinery and the noise of the riveters and platers would have drowned everything out. That blank expanse of sky opposite would have been alive with a latticework of manoeuvring cranes. He found the silence eerie. I said I was quite used to it. To me it could only be described as the post-industrial quietness, the sound of silence that is one of the overpowering non-sounds of the economic restructuring of our age.

We were still talking about this when we met up for lunch with a sports journalist in a pub overlooking the river at North Shields. There is still some sea fishing based on this part of the Tyne, and there was the strong smell of fish and the wittering of gulls hanging over the whole area when I was there. Little fishing trawlers were lined up by the quayside. Lobster nets were arranged on the jetty. Beneath us was a pleasing jumble of rooftops and chimney-pots, lumped together at the base of the hillside and not unlike those to be seen in the small fishing villages along the North Yorkshire coast. Down below, men wearing rubber aprons were spraying the pavements with water from hose-pipes. Blue-handed youths were dragging pallets of fresh fish up the centre of roads. Soon a large ferry made its way in from the sea, passing in front of us at a surprising speed, as ferries always do, and I was being told about a controversy some time back when it was discovered one of these vessels was carrying quantities of nuclear waste, in addition to fare paying passengers from Scandinavia; some of whom come across to shop in Newcastle or at the MetroCentre at Gateshead. Back in my hotel room again that evening, the same part of North Shields was featured on the local news programme on television. A new European ruling was dictating that the diamond netting the fishermen used would have to be substantially enlarged to enable young fish to slip through the gaps. A representative of the fishermen said this would seriously damage their livelihoods and the long-term stability of the industry. So the old controversies raged on, I thought, except now the news reports are shot on crystal-clear videotape instead of that fuzzy sixteen millimetre film, which for some strange reason I always associate with images of Tony Benn wearing woolly cardigans, and pickets warming their hands around braziers outside factory gates in sleety weather. It was like a scene from the Cod War of the 1970s all over again.

History does repeat itself, of course, whatever a number of historians might claim to the contrary. So does left-wing hypocrisy, which I suppose is as relative to contemporary Britain as poverty is to contemporary Tyneside. The same news magazine programme was carrying a story about the Labour Party candidate in the impending Langbaurgh by-election. It had been revealed that at the time the Labour Party had fought vigorously against the privatisation of public utilities, the candidate in question held shares in British Telecom. To me this was frivolous and an irrelevancy, but should we have been surprised? We should not. What we should find rather more puzzling than the clownish antics of some sanctimonious political nobody is the fact that substantial numbers of those working-class communities, teeming throughout some of the modern prefabricated shopping precincts I had seen in rebuilt towns along the banks of the Tyne, still put their faith in a party called Labour.

Ferry Across the Tyne

Priestley crossed the estuary from North Shields to South Shields on 'a fat little ferry boat'. When I was taken down the Tyne I made the journey in reverse and crossed from South Shields to North Shields by road, beneath the river courtesy of the Tyne Tunnel. The following day I made an extensive exploration of the area again, this time using the Metro, Tyneside's very own underground train network, to get about. I bought a Day Rover ticket, which enabled me to travel anywhere on Tyne and Wear public transport for one day for a couple of pounds, without having to worry about fares and destinations, and caught the Metro out to South Shields from the centre of Newcastle.

To reach North Shields to continue my ride it was necessary to cross the Tyne again, but this time I managed to do it using the ferry, and here I met a couple of Tyneside characters. At first glance, when I walked the few hundred yards from the market square of a very busy South Shields down to the landing stage, when I saw the boat, I thought I was looking at the same fat little ferry boat from 1933. It was bulbous and dumpy and exuded character, and resembled a tug boat caricature culled from one of my son's story books. To my amazement, despite its antique appearance and its knobbly, many paint-layered quality, it had only been built about twenty years earlier, no doubt in one of the region's defunct shipyards. And it chugged and swung itself out onto the river and moved with what seemed to me to be a remarkable, almost unnatural agility for a boat.

I was standing on the upper deck, staring down at the sluggish grey water, staring downriver at the yellowing sky and the distant remnants of industrial clutter gathered along the waterfront, when a denimed Geordie young man standing near to me by the railings piped up and began saying how wet the water looked. We started talking and it turned out that, of all the things he could have been, he was an unemployed mortician from Gateshead. The way he put it was that he was one of the unfortunate mugs who had to clean people up when they had been shovelled up from the road after accidents before they were buried. 'Somebody has to bloody do ett,' he laughed. Unfortunately he was now on 'extended leave, sick pay courtesy of the bloody DHSS'. I wondered if he ever got blood under his fingernails, or if that pink tinge was grafted into his skin like a butcher's at the end of a day's work. He looked decidedly undernourished, almost emaciated. I used to think the observations made about the physical quality of different parts of the population under different economic circumstances were exaggerated, especially in these days of nutritious junk food and central heating and pop records for all. But I have been into enough of these areas to know that the stunted quality of this man's physical stock is sometimes a characteristic of the poorer parts of the population that have a history of malnourishment and bad diet, in the same way the tallness and the broadness of the English upper-middle-class is a noticeable quality of some of the examples of male human stock you see circulating around Oxford or Cambridge. You see far too many of these shrivelled, pasty-faced young men in the dole areas for it to be anything but a symptom of their, or their parent's and grandparent's, social circumstances. Besides being extremely thin, this Geordie on the ferry was small, almost effeminately so. He must have had bad eyesight, too, because his eyes leered at me constantly from behind a pair of glasses that had such thick lenses they magnified them to enormous proportions, so that the corners disappeared off the edges of the frames. I was aware of a pair of enormous eyeballs waving around in front of me and looking up at me all the way across the river, flashing above a row of teeth that were stained with nicotine, and from between which issued a never-ending barrage of bad language, and a non-stop catalogue of coarse-grained wit. Waiting to meet him, as everybody filed off the boat at the opposite side of the river, was another youth who physically was the exact opposite of this mortician: he was tall, considerably rounded and overweight, and had a sort of acned scabby face, covered in sores. Because his legs were well endowed with flesh, they rubbed together above his knees constantly as he walked, so that there was a rhythmic swishing noise in the air as we moved away from the little landing stage. He had the coarsest, most aggressive Geordie accent I have yet heard. I was amazed – or 'ameerzed' as they would say round there – at how short his hair was. I had not shaved for two or three days, but the stubble on my chin was longer than the hair on this second youth's head, so that from a few feet away you were aware only of a sort of pinkish-grey stain on his scalp. He too was on 'extended sick leave courtesy of the bloody DHSS'. Together these two young men were going to get drunk in one of the pubs in North Shields, and thus pass another aimless afternoon. The large youth was told that I was there because I was writing a book. 'Ay mon, an' I hope yer goanna write about all these f—— yuppy bastards that's movin' into the eareea,' he shouted. His words came out like bullets from a machine-gun, and he laughed to punctuate his own wit. As he did so he pointed to the top of the hill, where there were some new waterside-type apartments under construction that I had seen the previous afternoon, across the road from the riotous Meadowell estate, itself about five minutes' walk from where we were standing, and which in those parts is known as The Ridges. (Originally, it was going to be arranged for me to talk to some youths from the Meadowell estate, but I had decided at the last minute this was too obvious.) The word 'bastard' is an obligatory suffix to the rhythm of much ordinary Geordie speech. No other regional accent pronounces it quite as menacingly or as forcefully (or as humorously), where the first vowel is lengthened to about half a dozen times its proper length.

Walking with them both up a steep grubby back street into the centre of North Shields, the overweight youth lagging behind and forever gasping to us two 'baaastards' to hang on, I was struck by the ease with which you can get into conversation with the more robust element of the working class. What is especially noticeable is the way they are less squeamish about touching or being touched. They are constantly slapping you on the back and thumping your arm to make a point. You are, in fact, not unnerved by close physical contact with such people in the same way you might be with middle class people, for working class expression is almost wholly physical in outlook anyway. It is the intimacy of the physical contact that relates to the intimacy of their communities, such as I had noticed in that café in Blackburn. While we were still on the ferry the first Geordie youth had immediately shaken my hand when we had told each other our names. For a working-class male to shake a complete stranger by the hand in this way is a sign of friendship and an indication that masculine territory is not being defended, and that the conversation can continue quite freely. Educated middle-class men would find it difficult to get into conversation with each other under similar circumstances so spontaneously, probably because they would be on their guard due to trying to judge one another's intellectual or emotional credibility, and striving, as always, not to reveal their true feelings. You might even wonder if there was a seedy sexual motive behind a forthright public approach, such as I experienced from that Geordie, from a middle-class man. And if a middle-class man were to grip your hand after only a couple of minutes as a gesture of friendship, you would begin to feel very uneasy indeed. Behind the gutsy bravado and boisterous bad language of the working-class male that will suddenly stand a stranger a drink there is usually humour and a no-nonsense genuine honesty that is sometimes so sincere it is embarrassing. This has sometimes struck me so powerfully I have thought afterwards that those educated persons, who squirm at the uncouthness and directness of working-class expression, might be inadvertently reacting against the controlled precociousness a substantial portion of their own class takes for granted as necessary to normal social behaviour.

This much admitted, I cannot deny that as we made our way up that quiet back street it was to the forefront of my mind that I was carrying two-thousand pounds worth of camera equipment in my rucksack, and if the previous fifteen minutes' conversation had been nothing but elaborate play-acting, and I had been selected on the ferry to be mugged, if they had chosen to attack me I would have stood no chance. I was startled at how quickly everyone who had stepped off the ferry with us appeared to have simply vanished into thin air. There was an uneasy moment when we passed behind a couple of parked removal lorries when the two youths went very quiet while we were out of sight of any windows, and my hands and body were tensed. It is appalling that I should have been thinking these things, and that I should put them down on paper now, but that is the kind of social atmosphere under which we are all beginning to live, and that is why I think it is worth recording it. You expect sincerity to be bogus and manipulative. You half expect friendly strangers to wallop you over the head as soon as you are out of sight round a corner in a rough working class district because you know these things actually happen. While it is certainly no suburb of Kensington, the South Shields we had left behind across the river has long had a more substantial middle class community. Property values there have always remained on an upward curve. When I was there I saw schoolboys wearing smart uniforms, a fair quantity of trees, and the first Christmas decorations slung between buildings I had seen in England so far. (Binns the department store presenting the first Christmas window display I had seen.) The gents' toilets in the market square at South Shields had potted geraniums arranged above the cubicles, even if thinking about this distracted me enough so that I almost slipped flat on my back when I skated across a disgusting crustacea of slimy pigeon droppings, on my way down to board the ferry.

North Shields by contrast felt run-down, hence my smouldering feelings of unease. The dim damp side streets I passed through with these two youths did not suggest the populace might possess the frailty and innocence of the inhabitants of an undiscovered South Sea island. There was a sort of starkness to the place, ingrained into the very make up of the old bricks and mortar, and of the dusty windows of empty or boarded-up shops. To our right was a row of completely derelict Victorian buildings outlined on a hill, devoid of roof slates. And in between my walking up that street and finding my way to the Metro station at the top I passed close to only four more human beings, who were not exactly advertisements for sunshine-and-breakfast-cereal cosy suburban living. The first was a very old lady staggering drunkenly round a corner muttering to herself. She looked like something from the 1930s, and I do not exaggerate when I say that. She had a witch's face, with a turned up hairy chin, emaciated hands, thick stockings gathered round her ankles, and – something I do not think I have seen before in my life – she was actually wearing a shawl, or some kind of hood. The next person I saw was a small old man with an ear that was either deformed or missing. And finally, two tattooed youths, again with five o'clock shadows for haircuts, who stiffened as they nearly walked into me from round a corner, who had faces carved from granite and some of the most fearsome expressions I have come across. Once again, I was probably in the wrong place at the wrong moment and forming inaccurate impressions for which I should be wholeheartedly apologizing to the north-east. But if the things I saw down the Tyne were only the things I wanted to see, or they presented themselves purely by coincidence, then there had certainly been a number of strange coincidences since I had arrived in Newcastle a few days earlier.

Fortunately, those Geordie youths did not attack me, and their warmth and openness as we parted made me feel ashamed for thinking that they might have done. They wanted me to join them for a drink, but I declined because the last time I did such a thing, years ago on a train with a gang of football supporters, on the way back from Skegness, I ended up severely inebriated. We shook hands again and made our fairwells in the bitter cold at the top of that street, stepping stupidly around several piles of dog-dirt smeared disgustingly across the pavement. These were rough streets that not only had the sharp wind of impending winter blowing along them, but the cold gust of genuine poverty. Those youths knew better than I did that they did not have much of a future to look forward to, yet they appeared still able to go out and get plastered and make the best of a bad job. (Perhaps somebody somewhere has calculated that ability very astutely.) Contrary to popular belief, not all unemployed young men are criminals in the making, though how long that will remain so I would not be prepared to say. Together these Tyneside young men slapped me on the back and were gone to some smoky North Shields pub. As I crossed the road to make my way up to the station, they shouted that I must go back there and look them up sometime. Though I made copious notes about them when I returned to my hotel room that evening, notes to which I am referring now, I forgot the most important detail of all, for today I cannot even remember their names.

The Tyne and Wear Metro is the jewel in Newcastle's crown. It has only been running since 1980, but it was a pleasure to use it. I feel I cannot praise it enough. Using a modern rapid-transit system such as this raises the spirits enormously, as had the sight of the new tram system being installed filled the air with optimism back in Manchester. These things bind cities together, and their more widespread introduction seems such elementary common sense it is remarkable that so few of our major conurbations possess them already. The only drawback to the system operating on Tyneside is that nobody checked the tickets. Every time I used the trains, I did not have to present my ticket to a collector at a barrier. I could have travelled free on every occasion and nobody would have been the wiser.

Nevertheless, the trains running round Tyneside, and I used a reasonable number, and peered in through the windows of several that were stationary in sidings, were astonishingly and impeccably clean. I used them to reach South Shields, as I have already described, and when I left those youths in North Shields, travelled from there in a circuitous route through Tynemouth and Whitley Bay, round through Gosforth back into the centre of Newcastle. None of the trains had been vandalized. There was no graffiti, and positively no litter. The underground stations in the centre of the city, though they had light-coloured walls, were free from graffiti too. They were as sparkling as an airport terminal. There was an air of cleanliness and crisp efficiency to the running of the whole operation that in my opinion left the London Underground standing. Admittedly, the further away from the city you go, the more graffiti does begin to become a natural part of the station scenery passing outside the windows. But you would think that in densely-packed urban landscapes such as those to be found on the north and south banks of the Tyne, that in places such as Jarrow and Hebburn with continuous histories of mass unemployment, the stations and trains would have been reduced to smithereens long ago.

There is another jewel in Newcastle's crown, and that is the very central part of the city. Anyone who thinks Newcastle is merely another north country dump should go and stand in front of Grey's Monument and look down Grainger Street, and also down Grey Street, where it blends into Dean Street and falls gracefully toward the railway arch, down toward the Bavarian-influenced Quayside. If you stand in front of Grey's Monument, which rather resembles Nelson's Column and celebrates Charles Earl Grey, who was behind political freedom being granted to Newcastle by the Reform Bill of 1832, and look down the length of Grainger Street toward the Central Station at the bottom, you see something I know of no other major city in England possessing today. And that is wide city centre thoroughfares fronted by solid Victorian architecture that retain a completely nineteenth-century scale. There is not a single modern office building rising above the roofline of Grainger Street breaking the view anywhere along its length. The entire street is three and four storeys in height from one end to the other – a distance of perhaps half a mile – and I spotted only one new building that had been slipped furtively between the others, about half way down. Turn ninety-degrees to your left from looking down Grainger Street, look down Grey

Street, and you see an abundance of classical architecture put up by banks, building societies, and insurance companies, curving majestically away, again completely unbroken. There is an almost overpowering feeling of homogeneity to these streets in Newcastle, which were influenced by parts of Edinburgh in the way they were planned and laid out, and some of Nash's work in London. How they have remained intact on such a scale amidst decades of architectural butchery and fashionable banality is quite remarkable. Over thirty years ago, Ian Nairn said that too few people knew about the city of Newcastle, which had the ability to stop you dead in the street. That remains so today. To my mind these central streets of Newcastle constitute one of the finest civic panoramas anywhere in provincial England, and it only amazes me to think that they are not more widely publicized, if one considers the present climate. The story is not quite so good if you look behind Grey's Monument, and it is a pity the city council does not make a more determined effort to remove some of the appalling modern and rather scruffy shop frontages. Nevertheless, to walk from the impressive arched portico of the railway station at the foot of the city centre, echoing atmospherically to announcements and the roaring of diesel engines; to cross into Grainger Street and walk up to Grey's Monument at the top, and perhaps wander through the lively covered Grainger Market, is a satisfying experience. To turn right down Grey Street, to pass through one of the magnificent restored ceramic arcades, is fascinating. To step across into Dean Street, past a non-stop succession of smooth classical frontages and bold corinthian columns rearing eloquently behind a perspective of reproduction gas lamps, is enormously uplifting. To continue down beneath the railway bridge, where the road suddenly steepens to plunge beneath the green arm of the Tyne Bridge, slicing through the sky above a jumble of medieval roof tops, and to come finally to the waterfront and glance across from the railings to the old Baltic Flour Mill at the other side of the river, is to realize you have just conducted one of the great city walks in Britain, if not Europe.

It seemed fitting as a final glimpse of Newcastle, and a pleasant antidote to some of the less savoury aspects of Tyneside

I had experienced elsewhere, to come away stimulated by efficient public transport, and the realization that Newcastle is one of those cities to which you have simply got to go back.

Middlesbrough

On another day being ferociously lashed by rain I drove away from Newcastle in a southerly direction through Gateshead, along more wet and streaming dual carriageways, until I reached Sunderland. Sunderland is another former prominent shipbuilding centre that has recently endured chronic industrial decline. The part of it I stopped at briefly that morning appeared to be comprised along the waterfront of derelict industrial reclamation schemes and not a great deal more. There was a horrible air of melancholy hanging over the empty side streets just there, that nauseating feeling again that you are witnessing the aftermath to something. The bits of remaining nineteenth-century architecture that were scattered around were being pounded relentlessly by the rain, against a backdrop of what resembled enormous metal aircraft hangars. One of these sad remnants was an old brick railway viaduct that suddenly finished half way across the river and was visible some miles in the distance before you reached the town. No doubt there is a small engraved plaque somewhere telling you where the rest of it used to go. Nearby was a sign saying VERY DANGEROUS DOGS. It was so deserted, Sunderland might have been on holiday, though it wasn't because this was a weekday morning. The detail that sticks most strongly in my mind as I drove through the outskirts, because of its contrast against the air of decay, is the sight of rows of multi-coloured bunting flapping madly in the gales above the wet forecourts of new car showrooms. There is, I believe, still a small amount of shipbuilding carried out there – inside those huge corrugated hangars – though to stare across the wide emptiness of the grey and thrashing Wear that I crossed, you would not believe it for a single moment.

This whole region, from the southern part of Tyneside

downwards, used to be a heavy coal mining area. I had never been to this part of the country before, so I spent most of that day exploring it and drove through a bland and uneventful Wearside and County Durham landscape, criss-crossing slowly from one industrial town to the next, in the general direction of Middlesbrough. I looked at the unusual colliery town of Seaham clinging to the coastline down toward Hartlepool, a place I had wanted to visit for many years, but which was the usual anticlimactic disappointment. I looked at the smaller colliery village of Easington, and at the abysmal prefabricated newtowns of Washington and Peterlee; the former being comprised chiefly of modern carriageways and round-abouts and divided into numbered districts rather than named suburbs, and with a sign telling you, inevitably, how to get to a pit museum and to the Old Hall. I also looked at Shotton, where the legends have it there was once a slag heap as big as a mountain, but where there are now some straggly lengths of housing and a suspiciously undulating, rather unnatural-looking bright-green field, where the man-mountain must once have risen but where I think there is still a mine. Throughout all this the rain never stopped. From the outskirts, Middlesbrough contrived to suggest that it might not be a normal town populated by people, with car parks, nursery schools, houses and televisions, but might actually be one enormous oil refinery. This was the huge ICI plant out at Billingham, and it had about it the air of one of those mysterious government installations that were home to unpleasant goings-on in the old *Quatermass* films. Though the refinery dominates the town, and is a tangle of silver-plated domes and catwalks filling the sky at the end of some of Middlesbrough's central streets, Billingham is technically across the river, and is actually a part of Stockton-on-Tees.

I had arranged to stay with some friends of a friend at the charming village of Great Ayton, a few miles outside Middlesbrough. Their home is several cottages that have been combined to make a single large residence. It was a fascinating den of slightly uneven floors, stripped pine, low ceilings, ticking clocks, decent antiques, piles of grated cheese sitting on chop-ping boards, steamy windows with rain drumming against the glass late at night, and superbly-crafted traditional bespoke furniture. Great Ayton is located in pleasant countryside, vigorously marketed as being associated with the life and times of Captain Cook. Cook's mother is buried in the church yard. The village is watched over by an unusual hill called Roseberry Topping that resembles a small inactive volcano and is visible for miles around. It is one of those places with a manicured green, a small private school established in an old gentleman's residence, large Japanese jeeps parked in effective positions outside rows of lamplit windows, and its little banks and building societies are housed in converted cottages. There is an antiquarian bookshop, where I at last picked up an original copy of Priestley's autobiographical aside *Margin Released.* And running through the centre is a rushing stream populated by constantly-quacking ducks. During my first evening there I walked round the village amidst cascades of fluttering leaves and to the sound of howling winds, and down one isolated lane saw a man smiling to himself, his eyes closed, gently playing a piano through a lighted cottage window. Great Ayton seemed to me then to be the quintessential village England on a wet late autumn evening, the secret place where nearly all English people dream of settling down. It formed the ideal setting from which to conduct operations in Cleveland over the next few days, for, having found myself drawn into a contemplation of the Tyneside dolescapes back in Newcastle, I was determined this time to emphasise some aspect of Middlesbrough that was more positive. At any rate, that was my intention to begin with.

As is fairly widely known, Middlesbrough was the fastest-growing industrial town in the country during the first half of the nineteenth century, concentrating chiefly on the manufacture of iron and steel, and latterly shipbuilding. The fact that it is a fairly new town is obvious when you spend an hour walking round it. It has little character and no charm. It has about it something of the air of a frontier post. The only decent civic building that I saw when I was there was the town hall. Unusually, it was built from stone (Middlesbrough is mostly built from brick), and on a smaller scale resembled the Gothic town hall I was to see the following week in

Bradford. Like Newcastle, Middlesbrough suffered badly when traditional manufacturing industries contracted over recent years, but unlike Newcastle it did not, and does not, have a very substantial middle-class element mitigating the air of decline as sharply, once you are milling with the crowds in the central part of the town. Like Burnley it is much more obviously a working-class town. Like Burnley and some of the other textile towns further down country, Middlesbrough was one of those working places that had most of its economic eggs sitting in a single industrial basket, with the result that when decline did come it was hit, and hit hard. Consequently, it has chronic rates of unemployment of some 20%; a figure that will almost certainly have increased since I was there. That means, I suppose, that a fifth of the population is out of work, though it might mean a fifth of the working population. (It also means that four-fifths of the population are *in* work.) Among men unemployment stands at some 27%. Incomes in the town are generally low. There is a widespread number of people living on housing benefits and income support, with a large quantity of children receiving free school meals; and there are the usual high rates of mortality associated with poverty, and the obligatory high crime figures. The town's political complexion is so left-wing it is often referred to jokingly as East Moscow, or I dare say it was until the Berlin Wall came down. Despite all this, there is a massive industrial and commercial regeneration programme under way on Teesside, an area made up of the boroughs of nearby Stockton-on-Tees – a brief examination of which during one of the most torrential downpours I have ever witnessed suggested it had clearly seen better days – Hartlepool, Langbaurgh-on-Tees and, of course, Middlesbrough. The usual types of leisure, retail, and marina housing schemes are being built across the area, along with a quantity of impressive environmental initiatives, including the construction of a major new barrage across the Tees. These are being funded and overseen by the Teesside Development Corporation, a regional development organization of the kind operating in all the major industrial conurbations I had visited already. It was also said to me that Middlesbrough came out on top as offering a good standard of amenities according to a recent survey of its population. This should be taken into account when considering my casual observations as a passer-through.

To try and manoeuvre myself away from negative subject matter, I got in touch with the local Enterprise Support Programme (ESP) and went to have a look at one of their new business centres. I wanted to see how subsidized new businesses were starting up in Middlesbrough, what the success rates were, and what type of work was being done. I suppose I imagined a new building somewhere, perhaps on an industrial estate close to the centre of the town, with tinted-glass windows and an abundance of flower beds and trilling telephones. As it happened, the complex I visited was situated in the centre of a district called St Hilda's. That sounds innocent enough, but anyone who is familiar with Middlesbrough will know all about St Hilda's. Because I was new to the area I did not know about it, but it happens that St Hilda's is the town's most active red-light district, close to old dockland and the blue Transporter Bridge straddling the Tees. One might just as well have said you were going to look at Whitechapel in the London of the mid-nineteenth century for the reputation St Hilda's has among the population of modern Middlesbrough. They say round there that it is 'over the border', because it is separated from the centre of the town by the main railway line. But this talk of a border is really meant to convey the feeling that if you go there you are entering rather dangerous enemy territory. Though the housing does not look too bad – there are some modern terraced dwellings of the sheltered-and-shrubberied variety, mixed with older semi-detached council houses, but no nineteenth-century terraces, and no 1960s slum tenements – it is a severely depressed area. There are patches of bald waste ground situated between the clumps of houses, smattered with scorch-marks from bonfires, and across which roam gangs of wild-eyed young children. Forming a backdrop in one direction is the great steaming refinery, across the river at Billingham. The male unemployment rates for Middlesbrough as a whole I have described. But in St Hilda's they are proportionally the highest in the town, a staggering 43% according to official statistics collected several months before I arrived. So there I was one cold, blustery afternoon, innocently preparing to emphasise some of the more positive aspects of strife-stricken Middlesbrough, and straight away I was drawn into a contemplation of the very things I wanted to avoid. From that moment on it was downhill all the way.

The Enterprise Centre in St Hilda's is one of four such establishments in Middlesbrough, heavily subsidized by the council. It is housed in a converted biscuit factory, but to see it from the outside you would have thought someone was pulling your leg if they told you the building was once associated with the production of pretty confectionary. The neat little drawing of the centre on a leaflet I have in front of me is a different image to the one that confronts you when you arrive. All you can see again is thick concrete, heavy metal-gauzed windows, and steel shutters – another of those police station lookalikes imported from Northern Ireland, surrounded by fragments of broken glass and barricading itself vigorously against the desires of unwanted scruffy humanity. When I eventually managed to find the centre I drove straight past it. I do not know what I thought it was, but I could not possibly associate the barricaded concrete fortress frowning at the top of that street with fledgling businesses. As I approached, a large hairy dog hurtled out from the entrance to some adjacent industrial premises and began chasing the wheels of my car in a ferocious fit of barking. Because I thought I was lost, I drove round the block, and when I passed down the same street again several minutes later, like clockwork the dog frantically emerged again and actually collided with the front of my vehicle and spun away, ricocheting from the impact across some grass in its snarling desperation and fervour. At least the little drawing of the Enterprise Centre on the leaflet is honest enough to include the metal gauze.

The ESP scheme has superseded the old Enterprise Allowance Scheme, which was centrally controlled by the government, where unemployed people were given £40 per week for twelve months to set up their own businesses. Instead, the new scheme gives people £30 per week for thirty weeks, but provides them with office or workshop space as starter units. Middlesbrough was one of the first such schemes to be set up in the country. Tenants can apply for additional funds to purchase new equipment or to expand, if the merits of the business are considered by the ESP board to warrant it. After about two years the businesses are encouraged to move out of the centre into the real world, though I was told that they sometimes have to be nudged, and I should imagine a fair proportion of them immediately collapse. Nationally, the ESP is supervised by eighty-two Training Enterprise Councils spread across the country that have local business and industrial people sitting on their boards of committee. The idea behind decentralization, and the weaning away of the influence of the Department of Employment, was to enable the new scheme to have the flexibility to devise programmes suitable for the economic requirements of different areas, and for them to have closer links with the existing industrial infrastructure. The St Hilda's complex is concerned almost entirely with promoting manufacturing, with the emphasis at present in the small workshops there being on woodworking and metalworking. I was told there is generally a 50% success rate with businesses in the industrial field in the town, and about 80% with those involved in office and information work elsewhere.

The project manager thought it was unfortunate the Centre had been established in such a depressed area. The idea was for the Enterprise Centre to lift the face of St Hilda's and inject it with a new burst of life, but he could see why the residents in the streets outside had little regard for it. It did not benefit the local community in any way because the people working at the Centre, and utilizing the facilities, came mostly from outside. It had no connection to the chronic number of unemployed living in St Hilda's, and so there was a lack of respect for the premises, resentment had built up among the youngsters, and it was forever under attack. Each night, two or three security guards, and at least one guard dog, now patrolled the building. There is something quite pathetic about such a scene, where a hub of small houses fan out around an isolated industrial structure protected by uniformed men and dogs, like the castle with its moat. Until the security guards arrived the Centre suffered continually from theft and vandalism. The project manager himself had been spat at, stoned, physically harassed, threatened, and all the building's tenants had had their cars vandalized, with tyres slashed, aerials bent, windscreens smashed, and so on. It was unthinkable to work there late in the evenings, he said. Throughout the time he was telling me this I had become aware of the sound of children chirruping louder and louder in the street outside. (Apparently, there is a 30% truancy rate in the area). The next moment, as if on cue (how many spontaneous cues there were, uncannily timed when I conducted this journey!), a man leaned into the office and said the children had barricaded the front door closed 'again'. We all rushed into the entrance hall to find that a gang of very small children had wedged a short plank of wood through the tubular steel handles of the doors on the outside of the building, so they could not be opened. 'See what I mean?' said the project manager, shrugging his shoulders. 'How can we seriously expect kids living in places like this to grow up with an outlook for environmental concern and an interest in wildlife, when it is drummed into them from birth they have no prospect of ever obtaining a job in their lives?' The situation had come to a head recently when the children had absolutely pelted the front entrance to the Enterprise Centre with dozens of eggs stolen from a milk float. As a result of that incident, the building was in the process of being fitted with thousands of pounds worth of infra-red camera equipment, so that it was covered from every angle. When anybody approached within fifty feet or so, the cameras would automatically begin recording, and the project manager could simply hand the police a videotape after any incident and let them get on with their inquiries.

As did numerous people say to me throughout this journey, the project manager reflected on the fact that there had always been poverty and people at the bottom of the social pile. But what was new, he said, was the mindless violence, the loss of self-respect, the utter and complete lack of respect for other people's property and the reneging against authority that was the hallmark of an emerging generation. Looking at the street outside again afterwards, now alive with children running this way and that, pretending to machine-gun each other dead beneath a bit of late afternoon sun that came out and slanted feeble yellow light over the entire scene, you could see perfectly clearly how the slow process of brutalization was already well under way. The image of those swarming scruffy children, darting between cars and vans and leaping over dusty flowerbeds gunning each other down, being conditioned to a life of violent expression with the whining and hissing of the refinery forever in the background, remains in my mind as another symbolic snapshot of modern England; one that filled the air with a horrible, chilled sense of foreboding. I had been assured that not much more than a life of car crime seriously beckoned for those youngsters, though at the same time I had been reminded the people of the area knew how to milk welfare benefits to the full, and there was a thriving black market local economy. One of the kids was running round in the centre of the road screaming, 'Terminator! Terminator! Die! Die! Die!' As I unlocked my car, he paused in front of me and pretended to shoot. I might have said 'Stick 'em up' but there would have been no chance for negotiation with this prospective young brute, whose eyes seemed more like those of a vicious dog than a human being. I would have guessed he was about seven- or eight-years-old. What is a young child like that doing being influenced in his behaviour by such a violent film as *The Terminator*? Bearing in mind that the project manager told me there was a mobile video-rental van that came into St Hilda's, and when it did it was 'like the Pied Piper of bloody Hamlyn driving through the area', one can of course easily guess.

Of Jobclubs and the Necessary Unemployed

My other failed attempt at trying to write positively about the changing circumstances of Middlesbrough took me to one of the town's Jobclubs. It was housed in an old RAF social club down a back street near the polytechnic. On the outside was sprayed some graffiti, a legacy of the Gulf War, stating emphatically to the world NO WAR ONLY CLASS WAR.

I had long been sceptical of such feeble gestures as Jobclubs, thrown at the unemployed like a bone is chucked to a dog. And let me say straight away that I did not visit this unemployed men's centre with the intention of writing moving passages about pasty faces, or piously describing the ashen expressions of people who in some cases have been out of work in this area for an unbelievable fifteen or twenty years. Because I'd had no direct contact with Jobclubs, I wanted to find my worst suspicions groundless and emphasise the stories of some of the Teesside men who had made the scheme work to their advantage. But my suspicions were not groundless. Nobody had made the scheme work to their advantage. I saw as miserable and defeated-looking a crowd of working-class men as I have ever seen anywhere. The whole place had a sordid 1970s-social-club atmosphere. A group of around forty mainly middle-aged men, wearing ill-fitting clothes, flared trousers revealing ankles, and limp threadbare pullovers washed completely out of shape, were sitting quietly round small tables in shafts of smoky sunlight. The only things missing were the pints of beer and a treble-chinned Geordie comedian turfing racist jokes on the stage at the front. And not all these men were dejected figures of humanity crushed by a lack of opportunity over the years, but big strapping broad-shouldered Teessiders, thrown out of work when a major shipyard had shut down a year or so earlier. The majority were unskilled, though there had been an influx of welders from the shipyard, who unfortunately tended to be very set in their ways. They had been plate welders for twenty years, and that is what they wanted to carry on doing. But not many people need plate welders any more on Teesside. These men are rather stubborn in their outlook, and are reluctant to adapt to a changing economic climate, and consequently I was told, off the record so to speak, they had little chance of ever obtaining anything beyond a bit of short-term labouring. According to the notes I made, only one man present who had been a welder had been persuaded to go on a course and improve his skills, and that was only because he had been promised a job that never ultimately materialized.

I had gone to the Jobclub with the intention of speaking to a variety of the people present, but I had no sooner started talking to the woman administrator running the club than most of the men got up and began leaving rather quickly. This was because it was Friday and it was Girocheque day. As they shuffled out, the men queued up at the desk at the front of the room where we were sitting, and quite methodically and silently the administrator began handing them forms to sign and a number of ten pence pieces. This went on for quite a few minutes, and throughout that time I tried to decide what this money was for that was being handed over to them. It was only when nearly everybody had left that I was told, to my horror, that the men were actually being given their bus fares to get home. Now we have all probably heard that patrons of the Jobclubs receive free stationery and postage so that they can apply for jobs, which is a reasonable enough gesture; but to see grown men queuing up to be given bus fares so they can get home, like a bunch of untidy schoolboys, hits you in the stomach with a thump. Surely some arrangement could be made between the companies running the Jobclubs (they are generally put out to tender and run by private sector companies, not by the local authorities) and the local public transport executive, whereby the men could be given some kind of pass and avoid the petty indignity of being forced to queue up to be given a few shillings. It cannot do much for anybody's self-respect. On the other hand, they might be, and probably are, perfectly happy to be given a few bits of silver for their troubles, because it would be naïve and sentimental to assume they honour the gesture and spend the money on bus travel. Most probably they pocket the money and walk home. If I were in their position that is what I would do, and you cannot really blame them otherwise. Nevertheless, there is something tragic and deeply humiliating in sitting next to unemployed men twice your own age and watching them being treated like a group of social misfits. It makes you want to turn away with embarrassment. You do not know where to put your face. But what makes you squirm, and therefore what makes your perceptions despicable and hence creates your sense of unease, is that your feelings are essentially selfish. It is being pushed down your throat that *you* are comfortable. *You* do not have to think in terms of a few Godforsaken lousy shillings, and probably have not done seriously since you were a child. If your own small child comes into the bedroom on Sunday mornings and raids your trouser pockets for his moneybox, while you are ploughing through several pounds worth of newspapers and can only mumble disconsolately because you are too absorbed by an editorial comment to bother responding to his request for cash, it hits you in the face with a smack what different universes people really do inhabit. It is so very easy to take money for granted when you are not poor. Whether or not you have worked hard for that money in your trouser pockets, whether or not these unemployed men screw the social security system for every penny they can and use it to supplement black market economics they take for granted; whether they still spend money on beer and cigarettes, or the fact that some of them spend their dole money on drinking instead of food to keep some semblance of a social life going, becomes irrelevant when you mingle among them. To respond to the sight of other human beings thinking seriously in terms of a few ten pence pieces is to be force-fed on your own superior social position, and unless you are completely blinkered I do not see how you can respond in anything except an unsatisfactory way. Even the analogy with schoolboys is disgusting, because you are generally picturing a group of children wearing decent uniforms (you do this automatically), not distorted and ill-fitting hand-me-downs. That mental process itself is merely a by-product of prosperity and the power and importance of money. Such realities cannot do anything but erode the potential for a peaceful, stable structure to society.

When I was travelling round England I came into contact with a small number of people in positions of considerable regional influence. These were people who had connections with public office and the workings of central government; people who filled me in about the present economic situation in certain areas, and who I have not necessarily written about here in the text. I was told at least once, by a figure not without influence, something anyone possessed of reasonable intelligence will have long since realized already – that a 6 or 7% unemployment rate is considered not only politically acceptable, but is also economically desirable. Though no politician of any colour would ever admit such a thing publicly, he said, it is now acknowledged unofficially as being necessary to curb wage demands and inflationary pressures. The horrifying truth of the matter is that it might well be economically prudent to maintain an unemployed sub-class so that the rest of us can continue to live comfortably. Because of the pitiable workings of the human mind and the corrupting effects of power and prestige, anyone with genuine brain matter positioned between their ears realizes life is a cruel moral dilemma, and whether socialism or capitalism is the economic system applied hardly matters.

Though they were to the front of my mind when I was there, I could not bring myself to repeat these facts to the unemployed people I spoke to at that Middlesbrough Jobclub. And it is an awareness that catches in the throat when you rub shoulders with some of the unfortunate people, these brake-pads and hindrances to the desires of the society realpolitik, who are on the receiving end of such a policy, if it is in fact true. It creates a very funny feeling in your stomach when you look at their deferent expressions, when you see a row of cardboard files lined up on a table with grown men's names scrawled on them like so many school projects. But what I do know is this. Sooner or later if you go on treating a minority of people as so much human produce bagged up for sale and flung about on some crazy wholesale economic market to keep the prices stable higher up the retail pile, if you go on denying them their common humanity, you will eventually shoot yourself in the foot. The whole of human history gives testimony to that. Frustration spreads, gathers momentum, and ultimately explodes. One might just as well say that in today's social climate, violent crime is a necessary expedient to a general stability and prosperity for the bulk of the rest of society. Think like that, and it takes only a small step to arrive at the necessary reintroduction of capital punishment to retain the balance, when the economic cracks really do begin to appear. I am convinced we will see that move within the next generation or two anyway, once the present lot in the House of Lords have died off and been replaced by men brought up in a viciously acquisitive and increasingly reactionary and violent world, regardless of their class, culture, or background.

Before I leave Cleveland, in connection with some of the things I have just written, a story that was related to me by the people with whom I was staying in Great Ayton, illustrating how people can become conditioned by their social circumstances. It is worth repeating because a number of our more enlightened commentators, with noses that rise so high in the air they slip over to touch the nape of their necks, dismiss certain human values at the bottom end of the social pile as a gender symptom of being not much more than useless working-class scum. A friend of this man and woman in Great Ayton is a teacher in a primary school, in one of the downtown areas of Middlesbrough. The juniors at the school in question decided it would be a good idea to invite some of the younger infants to a story-reading class. To get the two groups of children into the habit of giving and receiving letters, it was decided to set up an internal postal system within the school, rather as we used to send Christmas cards to one another at my school years and years ago, using little squares of gummed paper to represent the stamps. But it was soon discovered that some of the infants (children the age of five) had not bothered to open their letters. The teachers could not understand why. After much coercion, it was eventually discovered these youngsters were too *frightened* to open their letters. In the sorts of homes they came from, the receiving of mail was something they perceived as a time of sadness, upset, rage, and despair. Their parents generally only received threats or warnings of some kind, or the notification of court appearances, or that they had been denied welfare benefit. This threw the homes in question into turmoil and perhaps meant the children would be eating beans or tinned tomatoes on toast as the main meal of the day for another week. Their reluctance to open the letters sent by the older schoolchildren was a reaction against what they imagined would prove to be negativity, foreboding, and impending mental pain. They were merely trying to protect themselves.

The essential point to grasp is that the children associated the letters they were handed at school with unhappiness and broke out into a sort of cold sweat accordingly. They wanted to run to a corner and hide. The other thing to observe, particularly if one recollects the kids being desensitized that I had seen leaping about across the waste ground in St Hilda's, is that these Middlesbrough infants were still young enough to *feel*. Each morning my own infant runs downstairs to fetch the mail up proudly for his mummy and daddy. Does yours?

4

West and South Yorkshire

To Bradford via Robin Hood's Bay

When I left Great Ayton my plan was to travel down the eastern flank of the North Yorkshire Moors, through Whitby, until I reached Robin Hood's Bay, where I intended to stay the night. But when I reached Robin Hood's Bay, a tight cluster of pantiles and pebbles arranged picturesquely at the foot of a very steep hillside on the east coast, I was running a day or so behind and so decided to press on and try to reach Bradford before nightfall instead.

I did, however, spend an hour wandering in the blustery sunshine around the perimeter of the little village before I left. The most startling sight at Robin Hood's Bay, and it threw everything I had seen over the previous several days into sharp perspective, as well as being yet another symbolic snapshot, was that a fox-hunt was just about to get under way from the car park at the top. I shall never forget the almost surrealistic moment when I drove into the upper part of the village, with a combination of moody synthesizer and melancholy saxophone music playing loudly on the cassette in my car, suddenly coming upon the pack of hounds and red-and-black-jacketed riders sipping glasses of wine, eating pastries being handed round from a solid silver tray, and everything backlit atmospherically by the lowering rays of the afternoon sun. As obvious as it sounds, it was impossible to avoid considering how this quintessentially English scene, and the depressed urban landscapes I had seen over the previous week, actually existed beneath the same section of the Earth's sky. Where were those two Geordie youths from the ferry across the Tyne now? Where were the muted industrial waterfronts, or the long, high, bulbous thick retaining walls, mottled with the stretching shadows of figures and lamp posts and passing traffic, along the old dock road I had seen in Liverpool? Where were the sunken and cracked paving stones, or for that matter the high-technology business parks and layers of mirror-finished glass and the slinky secretaries? Ours appears ever to be the country of sharp social contrasts.

I stopped for a late lunch at Pickering, a pleasant and quite busy little town at the edge of the moors, some distance past the Fylingdales early warning station. It is one of those small towns – like nearby Malton, where it was market day when I passed through – that you are always stopping at to eat lunch when you are travelling, to which you intend to go back and explore more comprehensively at some future date, but, like the Norfolk villages you are forever coming upon in spring sunshine, when you do go back you inevitably find you are hurrying on to somewhere else, and once again are only passing through. A railway preservation society has its headquarters there, but the town has remained authentically picturesque and generally intact, without the dreadful commercialization and seaside gift-shop mentality of places such as Haworth. Many of the shop fronts are original, so that it is pleasing to observe the way they have sagged naturally with age. The same could not be said about the long rows of shabby Victorian shop fronts I passed late that afternoon, when I eventually made my way with a stream of traffic into the outskirts of Bradford, having reached the city by way of York and Leeds. By then it was raining again and it was almost dark, so that in the blue half-light, with these old sagging terraces strung out on either side, their cheap illuminated signs intensifying against the darkness and stepping down the hill toward an eruption of murky tower blocks rearing at the bottom, the city looked run-down and quite depressing.

I knew there was more to the place than hasty generalizations such as this, of course, because Bradford was the city I knew better than any other that I visited during this journey; more so than Manchester. One of the reasons being that, quite a few years ago now, I began to make a comprehensive photographic study of all the old textile towns in the West Yorkshire area, and Bradford was one of the places with which I became completely absorbed. Strange as it might sound, or perhaps as obvious as it might sound, I was motivated to do this when I moved away from Yorkshire and began working in and around London. I say I moved away, but I maintained a house in my home town and used to return to it most weekends. This was at about the time many of the old mills began to shut down due to the effects of the 1979-81 recession. My house was situated in an industrial suburb of Huddersfield, and there came a point when I was returning at the weekends from the south when more and more of this suburb appeared simply to be disappearing. There was a mill built only a few feet behind the back wall of my house, and when that too started to be pulled down I would walk down the road from the bus stop late on Friday evenings, struggling with my baggage on my way back from London, and despite the darkness, would squint and be aware that the chimney-pots of the row of terraced houses where my own home was situated were beginning to reveal themselves beneath the cool glow of the moonlight, as the different levels of the mill were stripped away. I used to wonder what the daylight would reveal. This process went on for months and months. The whole area was devastated by the carnage of industrial decline. To spend a week away from it would mean to return and find an enormous expanse of sky had suddenly dropped in to fill in the view where once vast stone walls had risen and teetered against the sunlight before a ceiling of moving clouds. The suburb where I lived was one of the most heavily industrialized areas of Huddersfield, and this awareness of the sky beginning to take up more and more of your ground level vision, as high walls disappeared, is the strongest sensation I can remember from that time. To give you some idea of the scale of the annihilation, if it had been possible to place the point of a pair of gigantic draughtsman's compasses on the front doorstep of my house, and scribe a perfect circle with a radius of about half a mile, some thirteen textile mills were demolished inside the line of that circle over a period of only twelve or eighteen months. It was certainly an unlucky number for the economy of the area, though it goes without saying that the demolition contractors, of which Huddersfield has a number who quickly became very rich, as it does scrap-metal merchants, made a fine killing. Those were the days when you could buy full-blown redundant textile mills at virtual giveaway prices, pull them down, ship the stone to building companies on the Continent or to other parts of this country, to be used in the construction of new executive dwellings, and make a pretty pot of money. I watched lorry-loads of Yorkshire textile mills drive in columns in and out of the area, leaving the narrow back lanes dusty and grey from the pother of demolition. Nothing was wasted. The hugely thick greasy pitch-pine beams holding up the floors and roofs of the mills and attached outbuildings were stripped and sold as second-hand timber from new yards that sometimes opened up on the sites of textile buildings still in the process of being demolished. I designed some cupboards and the kitchen I had installed in the house I lived in at the time, and had them completely hand-made by a Huddersfield craftsman. Much of the beautiful wood from which he built them, now planed up and smelling resinous and new, came from the streets where I grew up; where in its previous manifestation it had almost certainly supported dozens of textile machines, or acres of rain-lashed slates, for the better part of a century. And we are not talking here about small quaint buildings, but enormous five or six storeyed monsters that dominated the landscape. Mills that were visible lifting from some dip in the land, or lifting bulkily at the end of nearly every street, or towering alongside railway viaducts wherever you went, so that there were nearly always exclamation marks rearing at the end of your environmental thoughts.

It was with these awarenesses in mind that I became conscious of seeing my native part of the country in a rather different light, when I moved away from it to work and saw it slowly dismantled from a distance. So much so that ironically it made the bond I felt toward it grow stronger than ever, encouraging me to go back there and spend months and months walking the moors and all the towns. Over a period of several years I took photographs in rain, snow, and sunshine, absorbing the feel of the places as they were now. In many ways I became aware of their historical significance for the first time, or at any rate perceived them with a broader depth of appreciation and understanding, and the frame of mind nurtured in me back then has overshadowed almost everything I have thought, and more especially written, since. One of the places I meticulously explored was Bradford, where there can be few streets I have not negotiated at some point or other over recent years. Bradford's textile industry suffered badly at about the same time the industrial area I have outlined above suffered badly. Vast areas of the city have changed shape and been cleared, though I think it is true to say the eventual collapse of textiles had been inevitable for some time. There must be fewer mill chimneys projecting from the skyline of modern Bradford than any other industrial town of comparable size in the north of England. Like its red-brick antithesis at the other side of the Pennines, Oldham, you feel that Bradford has been making a concerted attempt to rigorously remove any association with its once most prominent industry from the skyline. When I was there this time, two more mills were in the process of being demolished. Their half-eaten remains, their exposed interior stairwells, their rows of sturdy cast-iron supporting columns, were lifting morosely behind lengths of wooden hoardings fronting onto the pavements along a couple of the city's main roads. The familiar grind and clatter of bulldozers and demolition lorries, lined up to dispose of the re-usable architectural clumber in an oh-so-familiar pattern, was sounding again noisily in the background, though not with the frenzy of ten years ago because that has long since subsided.

A number of recent studies similar to the subject matter of this book have generally concentrated on race relations when discussing Bradford. Bradford has the largest Asian community concentrated within its boundaries anywhere in Britain. There are more than sixty-thousand of them living in the city and there are parts of it they completely dominate, chiefly because the cramped, often squalid industrial quarters they first settled in were seen as undesirable habitations in the eyes of the existing Bradford population at the time. The Asians first came to work the night shifts in the mills during the late 1950s, when the textile industry was still going strong and there were not enough people available in this country who were prepared to tolerate the then poor working conditions, or accept the low wages. The Asians were fortunate in that Bradford, like Liverpool and a number of other northern cities, had a tradition of accepting immigrants. There was a wealthy German and German-Jewish influence in Bradford for many years during its Victorian heyday. There were so many Germans living and working in Bradford, in fact, that when the First World War broke out it was said half the population did not know which way to turn. After the Second World War a quantity of Poles and Ukrainians arrived, escaping pogroms of the kind that are casting their unpleasant shadow over Eastern European countries again today; and there has long been a substantial quantity of Irish. The people from the Indian sub-continent were part of a continuing tradition that had long denoted Bradford to be one of the most cosmopolitan of provincial cites. But, while the influence of earlier groups of immigrants has more or less evaporated, and during the early 1950s there were a mere three-hundred-and-fifty coloured immigrants living in Bradford, the Asians have consolidated their hold. Among the usual plethora of down-market taxi ranks, take-aways, restaurants, clubs, and cinemas that have been part of the fabric of modern urban ethnic England for some time, in Bradford there are now Asian banks, solicitors, accountancy firms, retail chains, and a number of unobtrusive millionaires. There are even Asian estate agencies operating in the city today, and their signs written in Urdu are scattered throughout the old industrial parts of the city. This sharp contrast created by the influence of a different pair of cultures can produce curious results. There are parts of Bradford where you can pass along shabby cobbled streets lined with small Victorian terraced houses at dusk, full of lingering darkened nineteenth-century atmosphere, and there is the smell of curry drifting in the air. Be they Sikhs, Pakistanis, or Indians, it is impossible to spend five minutes in Bradford without becoming aware strongly of the presence of Asians. For this reason, a mill owner I spoke to when I was there during this journey said that someone had forecast to him that by the mid-twenty-first century Bradford will have become the centre of the Muslim faith in Europe. That you can believe.

But with all of this admitted, as someone who knows Bradford and hopefully retains something of a feel and a sort of gloomy affection for the place, to me Bradford is, and always has been, a place I have pre-eminently associated with textiles. There is more to it than the farcical comments uttered by the Centre for Peace Studies at the city's university during Gulf Wars. There is more to it than the much maligned and misunderstood Ray Honeyford, effigies of Salman Rushdie being burned in the streets, and the Bradford Council for Mosques. Though they are visible on the streets in some profusion, when I think of Bradford I do not think first of Indians and Pakistanis. I think first of the history of the Yorkshire wool textile industry, the legacy of which is stamped right across the face of the city. Then I probably think about Indians and Pakistanis. That more and more of Bradford has been eaten relentlessly away by the march of progress is more or less irrelevant. Whatever social and architectural changes might have accrued over the years, worsted textiles built Bradford, and Bradford built worsted textiles. The industry has of course contracted enormously since Victorian times and is not the major employer that it was. (The city council is Bradford's largest single employer today: a fact that will not come as any surprise to a good number of readers.) But that does not matter. If you stand back and contemplate Bradford from one of the hills rising gently around it, most of what you see laid out before you, chiefly thousands and thousands of stone terraced houses rippling in rows up and down the slopes right around the edge of the city, is there because of the nineteenth-century textile industry and nothing more. A book reviewer in a reputable local newspaper was most perturbed when another writer, who was not a native of the area, passing through Bradford during a study of Britain, made a similar point. This was unfortunate, though I suspect the reviewer's consternation was based on his assumption that the writer in question was making the usual derogatory observation, whereas the writer was doing what anybody with eyes and a brain in their head and a feeling for history could easily see for themselves – he was simply stating a truthful fact. This nineteenth-century enigma, as butchered and battered and decrepit as it might be, to me creates a major focal point to Bradford that is impossible to ignore; a framework to which everything contemporary, including the arrival of the Asians thirty years ago, whose children now swarm and multiply along the back streets, the growth of new industries, and the flood of EC money into the city's recent roadbuilding and urban regeneration programme, is directly and inextricably attached. The legacy of Victorian industrialism is the focal point from which nearly everything else you contemplate when you move about Bradford today naturally evolves, however remote the power and importance of that legacy might now appear to be.

The focal point of my attention when I crawled through the torrential rain into Bradford, late that Saturday afternoon, was the old Midland Hotel in Forster Square. I had never stayed there but felt that now would be as good a time as any. My aspirations remained unfulfilled. When I found the hotel in the very centre of the city, a blank facade of boarded-up windows met me at the opposite side of an abundance of traffic lights and an expanse of glistening darkness flaring with a confusion of headlights. The hotel, a grand building in the finest Bradford nineteenth-century tradition, had closed down since last I was there. There is no worse an initial impression when arriving in a city than to come upon a formerly prestigious hotel, centrally positioned and once of some importance, to find it has been abandoned. It is as disheartening a sight as that of trackless or overgrown railway platforms. I had seen a disused hotel like this already. In Liverpool the huge Great Northern Hotel that backs onto Lime Street Station had been abandoned by the time I arrived. But Liverpool has other hotels of quality and distinction. There were no other hotels I knew about of quality and distinction in Bradford. Tired of driving, I was in no mood at that hour on a miserable early evening to begin casting about in search of anything else in the dark and wet. Because I have a number of friends and former professional associates living well within the boundaries of Bradford, I had made some alternative arrangements in case I encountered difficulties. So I turned round immediately and left the shadowy hulk of the Midland Hotel behind, drove out of the city and stayed at a house high in the hills. I was not as close to Bradford as I would have preferred, but under the circumstances, and because I was travelling in my own car, this did not matter. I was soon being welcomed to a warm fireside and given a hot drink and a meal and wondering why I bothered to endure the insular misery of hotels in the first place; hoping the one I had seen in Bradford would not prove to be an unfortunate portent of the things I was to encounter over the ensuing days.

Millscapes in the Winter

It rained heavily throughout the night and for most of the following day, the Sunday, and for most of the day after that. The rain came down with such steady and unrelenting determination that my first couple of days in Bradford were, in fact, uneventful and rather sluggish.

Under the circumstances there was not a great deal that I could do, so I spent much of my time socializing or driving randomly about the area, looking at Bradford and Halifax and Sowerby Bridge, and at most of the towns along the Calder Valley. I visited my old art school several miles outside Bradford, and had a talk with the best lecturer who ever taught me anywhere. It was the first time we had seen each other for more than ten years, and unfortunately, though some of my best memories are as a student in his class, the story was rather gloomy and despondent, because of what I was told were the detrimental effects of educational reforms since I was there, and their impact on the quality of teaching. I even drove as far across as the Colne Valley on the outskirts of Huddersfield, a superb north country landscape with which I was acutely familiar, and which remained as uniquely distinctive as ever. All the time I was conscious of the feeling that there was so much I wanted to say, but as usual not enough space in which to say it.

Driving through these darkened industrial landscapes again, I was also conscious that the old West Riding was conforming to the stereotyped picture still embedded in many people's imagination. This pleased me enormously. It was as though the weather were deliberately behaving as anyone new to the area, or a stranger conducting a journey through England, would expect it to behave. You could have said it was up to its old tricks. I should add that I am not opposed to these conditions, and I was not opposed to them again when I was there this time. There is something intensely satisfying about driving through these West Yorkshire towns in the rain, then calling at the homes of friends where there are flurries of raindrops humming against the windows and the pleasing smell of food and coffee is emanating from kitchens. These are not sentimental perceptions but sensations that are very real in a landscape where the climate often holds the upper hand. One thing I have often noticed about the vernacular architecture of the area is that when it rains as constantly and as thoroughly as it is capable of doing up there, the wet seems to permeate the very texture of the darkened stone and turn it even darker, almost black. Despite the fact that the architectural countenance of the whole region has been in the process of lightening for some years now, both because of a concentrated programme of stonecleaning, and because of the effects of the rain gradually washing away years of industrial grime, you notice this darkening on the old buildings and you notice it on the old dry-stone walls running along the sides of the roads or disappearing across the fields. It is the same effect as when clothing becomes wet, and I cannot honestly say I have noticed it anywhere else in the country. With heavy grey clouds constantly shifting overhead and hanging in tatters above the chimney-pots, it creates a tremendous sense of atmosphere. When I climbed the hills overlooking the Calder Valley on the Sunday afternoon, for a few moments acres of apparently mirror-finished slates were visible stepping away into the mist far below. This was unusual because such effects are most commonly created by the sudden appearance of the sun, but there was not a glint of sunlight showing anywhere.

When there was a short break in the weather and I stopped at an empty Todmorden Park the same day, some distance from

Bradford, where I walked about in the bitter cold and wet, this tremendous sense of north country atmosphere was suspended thickly in the air. There were footpaths sodden with decaying leaves. There were crows moaning with a funereal enthusiasm among the black dripping branches. A large, brick, former cotton mill – unusual for a predominantly stone-built town, though it may help to explain why it is sometimes said the people of Todmorden are not quite sure whether they live in Lancashire or Yorkshire – rose into the sky, its windows lit up against the gathering dusk. For the most morose of half hours I felt like I was the only person alive in the whole world. A little further on I came upon the greeny-bronze statue of John Fielden MP, standing serenely in the gloom. I stood beneath my umbrella, surrounded by falling leaves that were so yellow they seemed to be glowing in the murky half-light, and read the inscription. It said that the statue had been raised by public subscription by the people of Todmorden over a hundred years previously, as gratitude for Fielden succeeding through perseverance to obtain the ten hours act during the late 1840s. That is the kind of history you find yourself contemplating in this rugged but to my mind most invigorating and unique of landscapes. That it has been substantially destroyed in places; that the wealthy cottage-converters have completely ruined many old properties with hopelessly indecorous extensions and the playing out of their childish social fantasies in gardens; that more and more original windows are being superseded by crass and clumsy uPVC replacements; that more and more rooflines are becoming spattered with satellite dishes, has not yet managed to destroy the authentic atmosphere, provided you experience it during the appropriate weather conditions.

I was still thinking of this when, at what could only be termed the perfectly appropriate moment during a mood of deep contemplation before an old statue, it started to rain again. I ran for cover beneath a somewhat dilapidated Edwardian public shelter that smelt of damp cigarette-ends at the other end of the park, alongside the deserted children's playground. By now it was coming dark. There was an attractive blonde-haired woman and her small son, who seemed to me unusually bright and articulate for his age, also sheltering in there. For about twenty minutes we sat talking, our breath shooting out in cloudy gasps. While the rain thrashed the tarmac outside and dripped off the motionless swings and roundabouts and the painted parrots and horses, and the puddles intensified on the adjacent muddy playing fields, and the steep hillsides rising around the town became indistinct grey silhouettes, she told me about her work with business management in and around the nearby city of Manchester. This was a job for which it appeared she was quite highly paid, and was, I suppose, the very last type of career sceptics would expect to end up discussing with someone in a wet Yorkshire mill town. Then the temperature must have dropped a degree or two further and it actually began to snow. To my astonishment the snow quickly became a raging blizzard. Traffic crawled and slithered along the streets. A few figures were huddled in hoods against the sideways torrent. Those blackened streets and houses, and outbuildings with sagging stone roofs, and dry-stone walls, and serrated weaving sheds running along the sides of main roads, the handful of remaining mills, and the great striding viaducts, now stood out even blacker against the valley sides, the grass of which first turned grey and then rapidly intensified to the purest white. This was the landscape I remembered from my childhood, and it was obliterated in a matter of minutes. It was marvellous to see it behaving like that so unexpectedly. It might be assumed that some of the spontaneous coincidences and occurrences that I have referred to during the writing of this book were in some way fabricated to assist the flow of the narrative. The authenticity of reportage has long been suspect. The atmospheric moments I found myself suddenly experiencing were not fabricated. They really happened how they happened when they happened. And the way the snow came down that afternoon was perfectly appropriate to the conception of such a magnificent and invigorating English industrial landscape as this. When the snow comes like that it works wonders and binds the dullest and most mundane of urban townscapes together. Under those conditions the modern rubbish, the columns of tacky chalet bungalows dithering along the edges of fields, the solemn flat-capped old men shuffling across pedestrian footbridges slung between the prefabricated concrete sides of dual carriageways, the black entrances to underpasses, the dirty grey banality cluttered unevenly that makes up the bulk of the centre of modern Bradford and bears a striking resemblance to photographs you see of parts of Eastern Europe, appear almost comely. The snow that Sunday didn't last, of course. By late evening it had changed back to rain, and by daybreak it had disappeared altogether.

Tuesday morning rose to shine down upon Bradford the most brilliant sunshine and revealed there to be not a single cloud anywhere in the deep blue sky. It was the fifth of November, Guy Fawkes night, and there were the distant sounds of exploding fireworks thudding in the air throughout most of the day and late into the night. The greyness and the rain and the snow had gone but scarf and glove weather had finally arrived, for there was a bitter cold filling the busy early morning streets. Little Germany, a few minutes' walk from the centre of Bradford, where I had arranged to meet an old friend, was a dense network of tall blue-black shadows contrasting perfectly against the sunlit mid-Victorian stonework forming the high gulleys of the streets. Little Germany became known by this name because it was originally built by the German and German-Jewish merchants who came to the city during the nineteenth century to set up in the wool business, a number of whom were already associated with the clothing industry in nearby Leeds. Until their arrival in the 1830s, the old Cloth Halls and Piece Halls had been where finished woollen goods were traded, when textiles was still very much a cottage industry – literally – supported by thousands of small and independent manufacturers based in domestic houses out in the surrounding countryside. But as the industry grew and factory methods intensified and became concentrated in the developing cities, during Bradford's industrial heyday Little Germany quickly expanded and became very much the textile merchants' and yarn storing quarter of the city, where the finished goods were bought and sold. There is only a small amount of textile-related business carrying on there today, and for some years the city council has been cleaning up and renovating the gaunt warehouse buildings, which are distinctive for their simple linear facades and overhanging cornices, as are many of Bradford's old commercial buildings. Some Victorian-style street furniture has been installed, and a number of cultural activities and businesses have been encouraged to settle in the area, including an art gallery in a converted mill. The idea has been to promote Little Germany as a sort of Covent Garden of the north. It was difficult to decide whether or not this undertaking was succeeding when I was there that morning. Little Germany seemed to me to be very quiet, almost dead, though there was the constant hum of traffic in the background from a new section of ring road that has recently been built and now embraces the top side of the quarter. In the past when I have been there at the weekend the streets have never been exactly thriving. There is, however, the small and thriving Bradford Playhouse and Film Theatre situated at the edge of Little Germany near the main Leeds Road. It is housed in an interesting Art Deco-inspired building fitted in among a terrace of Victorian buildings and offices up a sloping side street, and it has claims to be one of the most accomplished arts organizations in the northern part of England. Much of the original impetus behind it, when Bradford was very much a theatrically orientated city, was the work of J.B. Priestley. This was the Civic Theatre of which he happened to be president that he referred to when he was in Bradford in 1933, conducting his English journey, though when he was there it was housed in a different building to the one it is today, because in 1935 the original was burnt down. The theatrical side of things continues to be, as it was during the 1930s, a voluntary organization run and maintained by amateurs. It is interesting to observe that, for a serious arts establishment, it receives no external funding or grants of any kind, but depends entirely on box office receipts, private sponsorship, members' subscriptions, and so on. (The film theatre part of the operation does receive arts funding.) Many visitors to Bradford will be aware of the beautifully refurbished Alhambra Theatre alongside the Museum of Photography and the bronze statue of J.B. Priestley. But I wonder how many are aware of Bradford's other important little theatre?

I do not mention any of this as yet another excuse to bring Priestley's name into the structure of this narrative, but to link it to the Northern Theatre School that at one time was based on the Bradford Playhouse premises, and which has had among its more well known graduates Billie Whitelaw, Thelma Barlow, Gorden Kaye, Bernard Hepton, and Tony Richardson. The old friend I had arranged to meet up with that morning in Little Germany was a student at that drama school during the early 1950s, when she won one of the first arts scholarships to be awarded by Leeds City Fathers after the war. She went on to become a young professional actress working in repertory theatre throughout the country. Though she is no longer an actress (she is now a painter, having reared a family in the meantime) she retains the agreeably silvery-haired tanned good looks and impeccable presentation often associated with women from her old profession. When I first got to know her about ten years ago she spoke such perfect and eloquent English I once asked if she had been to a finishing school when she was a girl. I was laughed at, because her background was about as unlike that of a rich little English schoolgirl as it is possible to be. She was Italian by birth (this probably explains why she has retained her complexion), she was born into poverty, and for the first eight years of her life could not speak a word of English because she was brought up in a convent where the girls were beaten if they were found sleeping with their hands beneath the sheets. When we met up again it was the first time she had been back to Little Germany for nearly forty years.

What was interesting about her recollections of Bradford Playhouse when she was a student, something that is perhaps not so very widely known, is that John Braine almost certainly based the amateur theatricals central to the plot in *Room at the Top* around this very same theatre. In addition to being a functioning theatre it was very much a sort of private club, where a particular stratification of Bradford citizens with intelligence and money would congregate. She remembers quite vividly when she was there during the early-to-mid-1950s that the young Braine used to come in and sit down and scrutinize their performances, both in the theatre and in some rehearsal rooms owned by the drama school nearby, and make copious notes in a little book. She believes that several of the characters that appeared in the novel, and consequently in the film, were directly influenced by some of the people working alongside her. In some respects, the drama school was seen by a quantity of the Bradford industrial elite as being a type of finishing school, and she says it was quite likely the naïve and rather shallow character of Susan in Braine's novel was inspired by a wealthy mill owner's daughter who was a student with her at the school at the time. This girl was the authentic Yorkshire mill owner's daughter who has all but disappeared today: very beautiful – the kind of lithe beauty that can flower comfortably on inherited money – very much a part of the sports-car-and-riviera-holidays, yachting lifestyle, and with a history of several abortions behind her. She used to invite my friend to her house, but being technically a foreigner, and due to the terrific, almost overwhelming contrast in lifestyles, my friend was always too conscious of herself to be able to go. She loathed and detested Bradford in those days. She says that many people accept that Bradford is depressed today, and that, like the entire country, it is beginning to live increasingly on the memories of past glories and the accepted wisdom that things are not the way they were. As we walked the bright clean streets of today's Little Germany she reminded me that the Bradford she remembers was a filthy, horrible city that seemed to exist in a permanent bleak twilight, though she admits that her unpleasant memories, beginning the day she arrived at the station deep in the smoky railway cutting up at Laisterdyke, might have been influenced by the fact that she lodged in a foul attic room down Manningham Lane, where the landlady sometimes used to serve tomato soup for dinner that was made from several spoonfuls of watered-down ketchup.

John Braine was, it is said, a one novel man, and it is sometimes claimed, too, that the success behind *Room at the Top* was that it painted a picture of the north of England as it really was. (In other words, it showed the sharp hierarchical contrasts between rich and poor that you still see today, even if the central portion has widened itself out.) I believe the real appeal of it was the honesty of the Joe Lampton characterization – a manifestation of Braine's own suppressed personality that probably resulted in his eventual clumsy rightward move – whose emotions and desires many people, in particular a crucial body of influential book reviewers, could strongly identify with.

Even into the 1950s, despite the smog and the blackness and the austerity, despite the effects of rationing and the immediate post-war depression, it was possible to feel the influence in Bradford of the tail-end of the old industrial dynasties that had once been a sort of aristocracy within the area. The lasting achievement of Braine's novel is that it depicted something of this rich industrial family and social-ladder-climbing elitist side to the modern north; a side few people in southern English literary circles knew about, when there was still enough of it left to describe.

Yorkshire Textiles Today

When you are in the Bradford area you frequently hear people harkning back nostalgically to the lost Bradford, and claiming that the dilution of family influence lies at the root of the textile industry's general decline, and the deterioration in the quality of the city's public life. They are generally people who have never been connected to the textile industry in a working capacity, it is worth noting, but who warmly remember the atmosphere of the smoky industrial city of gas lamps, dog racing, and trams all too easily. It is true that, though there are still a number of old family firms operating in Huddersfield and neighbouring Halifax – both towns that have always produced finer and more expensive cloth than Bradford – their influence has all but died out in the Bradford textile industry today. One of the main reasons behind this is that the very large Yorkshire mills were mostly centred on Bradford, and when outside interests became involved in the purchase of going concerns some years ago, they tended to go automatically for the bigger companies. Most of the others went out of business altogether when the industry tipped into its final disastrous period of decline.

It is a different story to what these old sentimentalists believe if you speak to some of the mill owners and associated people working in the city today, with their noses very much to the economic grindstone. I met quite a few of them when I was in Bradford, and was shown round their mills. One of them, an executive purchasing director with one of Bradford's more important textile concerns, was the very last in the family line of what I suppose could be termed something of the original Bradford mill-owning stock. I should guess he was only a few years older than me, but he had seen enough to be able to tell me that much of the reason behind the Yorkshire textile industry's eventual decline was that until fairly recently the people running the old firms tended to be more than merely blasé in their attitude toward the changes taking place out in the wider world. Because these mill owners had produced a particular type of cloth or spun a certain yarn for generations, they complacently assumed that was exactly what they would carry on doing. They had got fat on good profits but unfortunately had a poor record for re-investing in the modernization of their factories. As recently as the 1960s and 1970s, they persisted stubbornly in this attitude toward the workings of the market place. Trade had fluctuated in the past but it had always come back, they told themselves. So they sat back behind their broad leather-topped desks in their old panelled offices along Bradford's steep industrial streets and waited for it to come back again.

Well, most people will be aware that the difference this time was that trade had fluctuated for good and it did not come back. A decline in the British textile industry that had been increasing steadily since the end of the war, and almost certainly had its origins as long ago in time as the sunset years of the Victorian era, intensified; the mills that had managed to hang on with their antiquated attitudes finally collapsed. The industry proceeded to suffer horribly from the effects of cut-throat foreign competition. Much of the cheaper end of the trade that had once formed the bedrock of Bradford textiles went to the Italians. The better quality worsted side was hit by the rapidly-industrializing Third World. An industry that had a workforce of a hundred-and-fifty-thousand when the Conservatives came to office in 1951 had dropped to only forty-thousand by the time they came to power again in 1979, when they prompted a massive industrial shake-out, much of it sorely needed it has to be admitted. Unfortunately the government presided over policies that worked very much to the advantage of the spectatorial, parasitical element of society, of dealers in currency and dealers in other countries' wares, crippling the competitiveness of the productive, active element of society, of the hapless makers of goods in this country, and limiting their ability to recover. And yet despite all of this, in the face of overwhelming odds, the textile industry managed to turn itself round. Bearing in mind that almost three quarters of remaining British textile production is concentrated in Bradford and a handful of surrounding Yorkshire towns, it still manages to be our sixth-highest export earner, selling its goods in a hundred-and-sixty countries worldwide, and manufacturing enough cloth each year to be wrapped around the globe one and a half times. We are all familiar with the contraction of the textile industry, but how many of us could honestly say we knew textiles continued to be one of our major export earners? The success of the remaining firms in Yorkshire lies in the fact that they are now very much closer to the market, and that they are willing to respond quickly to changes in the nature of demand. Things are not easy, and you do not need to speak to very many managing directors to realize this. Representatives go out in search of business with a fierce determination to secure it, and everybody I spoke to reminded me of that fact before they said hardly anything else. It is true that large quantities of jobs have vanished. Over a five or six year period, from the end of the 1970s to about the middle of the 1980s, 50% of Bradford's manufacturing jobs in textiles and its other important industry, engineering, were lost. But textile jobs have disappeared not only because of recessions and industrial shake-outs, but because of the shaking loose of those staid attitudes and dated working methods that for so long hung like a ball-and-chain around the industry's ankles. There is still a need for genuine skills in some areas, such as in the setting of spinning machinery for the production of fine yarns – here the industry has specialized and managed to remain strong – but on the weaving side skills have gradually been squeezed out by the relentless onslaught of better and better technology. Where a man could once work four looms, he can now work twelve, and more often than not their performance will be monitored by computers. Management structure has been tightened up and thinned down. The result of this wholesale restructuring, and a massive investment in better machinery, is that productivity has improved significantly, enabling the industry to perform well throughout most of the 1980s, though it does not need to be said here that under the economic circumstances at the time of writing things have rather tailed off. The companies that have survived have survived largely because they have carved their own niches and got their marketing strategies right. I was shown round Drummond's mill up along Lumb Lane, just off the city centre in Bradford, where there are so many Asians congregated that twenty-five years ago it was known locally as the Burma Road. The mill looks like the archetypal Yorkshire mill massively rearing in everyone's imagination. It still has a towering jet black chimney – no longer used, of course – and a jumble of Victorian terraced housing is gathered all around. But 90% of the cloth woven in that mill ends up in the men's suit departments of some of Britain's most well-known high street stores, thank God. I saw some of it being woven in one of the sheds. There was a tremendous hazy perspective of blurring machinery where the only sharply defined shapes visible were the blue-overalled weavers moving slowly up and down the aisles, scanning the looms. You walked into a veritable wall of sound (the weavers I saw were wearing ear-muffs, incidentally, and I was also offered a pair) that was so phenomenal it actually caught in the throat. It was the sound that used to fill the streets, muffled through thick walls or behind closed doors, suddenly intensifying when you passed an open loading bay, in the area where I lived as a teenager. But all that machinery in Drummond's mill was coming out at Christmas and being updated and replaced in readiness for the opening up of the single European market. Elsewhere in England someone told me that he thought this country would continue to become not much more than a vast warehouse for South East Asia, and that Britain's remaining industry would be crucified when the international barriers finally came down. The Drummond Group PLC in Bradford was one of the firms I saw that was intending to make sure the new trading conditions worked very much to its advantage, and I should say it spoke for much of the Yorkshire textile industry.

Many of the other mills in Bradford tend to be concentrated on smaller specialist or emerging markets. For instance, a market that hardly existed at all until comparatively recently was the manufacture of textile fabrics used in the upholstery of new cars. It was not that long ago when cars were still upholstered with leather, and later plastic. Now they are generally upholstered with fabric and that fabric needs to be woven in mills. There are also other industrial applications for specialist modern fabrics that might seem unlikely, that come under the umbrella of the modern textile industry. I know of at least one mill in Huddersfield that experienced phenomenal success during the 1980s and substantially rebuilt and expanded its premises. It might still bear something of a resemblance to the traditional stone-built mill from the outside, or it did until its chimney came down about five years ago. But go inside and you find a ultra-high-technology factory producing the polypropylene fibre used in motorway netting construction, and, when it is blended with other fibres, in the manufacture of a hardwearing carpet. In addition to the vast amount of cloth produced by the industry, some of the more unusual things it makes are the green baize used in the covering of snooker tables, typewriter ribbons, even the cloth that is used to encapsulate tennis balls. I have occasionally listened to arrogant anti-manufacturing persons laughing about the north of England's industrial history during games of tennis on warm summer afternoons. The next time they toss a tennis ball into the air before they serve, they would do well to remember that its hairy surface has probably been woven in British textile mills that are quietly serving them.

This is the kind of frivolous, outdated prejudice that the textile industry has been making strenuous attempts to overcome. It is true that you can still walk through the gates into traditional mill yards that look like they have looked for the last hundred years. Out along Bradford's busy Thornton Road, where there is still a sizeable concentration of textile architecture, is situated Daniel Illingworth's mill, where yarn is spun for the Nottingham and Leicester hosiery trades and where yarn was also being spun to make police uniforms when I was there. This is the mill that was used in the film adaptation of *Room at the Top*. The puddle that Laurence Harvey threw his cigarette-end into, with the tall chimney reflected in the water, is still there in the mill yard after all these years; a detail I include simply because when I remembered it I was taken by the arm to see it. Looking across that expanse of cobbles toward the end of a winter's afternoon, with the sun low in the sky gilding the upper storeys of the mill against the deepening sky, with clouds of your own breath surrounding you in the freezing air, you cannot fail to respond to the awesome sense of presence these old buildings and their great thick chimneys exude, simply as solid objects positioned squarely upon the surface of the Earth. Similarly, you can walk into beautifully panelled foyers that are almost as unchanged as they were the day the last line of mortar was trowelled into position outside during the reign of Queen Victoria. But to keep these observations in perspective, to appreciate that this is far from an antiquated industry propped up by memories of its participation in classic British cinema, you need to keep one eye on the rows of blurred green computer screens flickering through the original ornate etched glass panels of the reception area. You need to listen to the chattering of print-outs coming from behind closed doors. You need to remember that part of everyday phraseology in much of the Yorkshire textile industry today, as it is in many industries, is CADCAM – Computer Aided Design and Computer Aided Manufacture. Textile design used to be a very laborious and time consuming process, but patterns can now be changed on screen in a matter of moments, sometimes with clients watching over the shoulder of the designer and making on-the-spot suggestions so they get precisely what they want.

That the Confederation of British Wool Textiles, with its headquarters in Bradford, where I spent some time talking with the director, states emphatically FIRST THINGS FIRST – FORGET THE PAST in a booklet it recently put out, intended to attract young people to a career in textiles, speaks volumes. It makes for an interesting contrast against the general social atmosphere hanging over the country at the present time, where we are busy idealizing the industry of the past and carefully destroying much of our remaining industry in the present. When you drive past Yorkshire mills today, when you climb high above the suburbs and see them rising in the distance above a confusion of tiny rooftops, it is important to remember this. It is important to realize that these fine old buildings, many of which have their upper floors empty but are maintained at the expense of the firm because they have been listed of architectural or historical importance by some sentimentalist in a remote office, who probably sees them chiefly as objects in the distance rising above a confusion of tiny rooftops, belong to a forward-looking, high-technology industry. Are we generally aware of this as a country? We are not. Do we care? We do not. In the meantime, a typically English paradox asserts itself. An industry that continues to be perceived largely as an odorous nineteenth-century smokestack caricature finds itself struggling to be taken seriously in a culture that prefers to settle back and respond favourably to certain of its aesthetic aspects from a hundred years ago instead.

This topsy-turvy age of burgeoning rose-tinted Victorian-embracing nostalgia, this gruelling obsession with old industrial artifacts we are living through, does not greatly help the stigma that is attached to modern manufacturing industry in this country. By causing us to look back it does not encourage us to seriously look forward, a fact which is itself merely a reflection of the terrible lack of direction there is hanging over our affairs. One of the detrimental effects of this situation on the quality and flavour of national life is that it affects the way industry in general is perceived, not to mention the textile industry and much of the north of England. Nor does it help the perception of cities in transition such as Bradford, or help wipe away old muck crusted around brassy Fleet Street eyes. The principle in the textile industry of changing untreated wool fresh from the sheep's back into fine cloth or yarn might not have altered for centuries. But that does not mean manufacturing methods have stayed the same, or that commercial applications have remained unsophisticated. Examine the textile industry close up today and you see an industry that is far from 'quaint' for heaven's sake. And it is not an industry that is superfluous to our transition into an 'advanced information-based economy', as a number of clever economists with no social dimension to their thinking arrogantly believe in the present intellectual climate. But though we are on the slippery slope and have not yet managed to loose our footing entirely, I fear there is not much likelihood of these realities being seriously comprehended. Our culture is too deeply mired in decline, our clever economists too prosperous and remote from everyday society for that to happen. The scandalous ruination and maltreatment of British industry will doubtless carry on unabated. Meanwhile, a number of respectable public figures with comfortable south country majorities, who genuinely believe that recessions are a result only of inflation getting out of hand, who remain oblivious to our underlying economic and cultural weaknesses that are themselves linked to why inflation gets out of hand, will remain impervious to the fact that their country is slowly degenerating into an unimportant third-rate power living on the sentimental proceeds of past imperialist glories. This should appeal to the economic wisdom of the Machiavellian harbingers of permanent mass unemployment, and its incumbent social problems, who scurry to set up production lines in the cheap labour countries of the East, like the idiots who fell over one another to sell tools and materials to Hitler when he was arming Germany in the 1930s.

Two Faces of Sheffield

I travelled the short distance from Bradford down to Sheffield using the M62 for a little while, then the M1. As I overtook the thundering articulated lorries, it struck me that this was a useful way to approach the capital city of South Yorkshire, for if, during the nineteenth century, industry and population became concentrated around the then new and expanding railways, then much the same processes are at work today with motorways and lorries. At the point where the M1 bisects the lower Don Valley at junction 34, and Sheffield spreads itself in the distance over to the right, the carriageway becomes a double-decker road bridge, and what you see gathered alongside that bridge just there is one of the clearest indicators I know to the deep changes underpinning the social and economic dichotomy of our age. On one side are two giant concrete cooling towers, around which is gathered a clutter of industrial paraphernalia and railway lines spanning a hundred-and-fifty years. In the background at the other side is the extensive factory works of British Steel Stainless, its perimeter fences coming almost up to the northbound hardshoulder, and, with its smokeless countenance, its giant corrugated simplicity, and its acres of perfectly landscaped grass, looking more next century than last. Crawling up from the belly of the valley are Sheffield's great swathes of socialist housing – council estates and dozens and dozens of high-rise tenements seemingly grafted to the hillsides and visible for miles around. Before you, and suddenly roaring up far too close behind you flashing their infernal headlights, teem the articulated lorries to and from the country's, and Sheffield's, neat new industrial estates. But it is when you contemplate what lies immediately adjacent to the bridge on the Sheffield side that you begin to get an inkling of the world that is being shaped around us, not only aesthetically, but culturally and economically and anything else important you can think to include in major social generalizations.

For here, a much-needed splash of brick-and-green domed fantasy against the surrounding grey monotony, where only a very few years ago there were still scum-coated streets crossed by railway lines through which I used to pass by coach to see my friends in London when I was a student, where the very tail-end of Victorian industrialism belched steam and smoke from yards piled high with rusting scrap iron, has been built one of the biggest shopping centres in Europe. It is called Meadowhall. They don't tack on 'shopping centre' to the end of its official title as they do with most places, but describe it simply as 'Meadowhall'. With its own High Street and its fashionable Park Lane the idea is, I suppose, that it is so big they want people to get into the habit of thinking about it as though it were just another suburb, a new sector designate of Sheffield like a small town or village. Indeed, with its palm trees, its tacky Mediterranean facades and plaster columns (they sound hollow when you knock them), with its ambiguous mixture of Art Deco-cum-Victoriana styling, Meadowhall is not so much a shopping complex as a small town within a town, or perhaps more specifically one ought to describe it as a giant retail theme park, superintended with the same calculated commercial intentions as any overblown Disneyworld. It is fascinating to observe the contradiction manipulating the ideological free-marketeers who denounce social planning of any kind, who claim society's structure should be determined entirely by market forces, when much of the way market forces work is contrived to influence society's structure in a way that is anything but natural or spontaneous. In these big shopping malls you have this hypocrisy thrown at you by the bucketful. Nine-million people live within an hour's drive of Meadowhall. It claims to employ seven-thousand people, not many of them ex-steelworkers I should imagine, but passive school leavers versed, no doubt, in knowing how to win friends and influence people, seeing as they are generally no longer required to produce the goods that many of them sell. MacDonalds had their busiest first hour of opening at their Meadowhall unit than anywhere else in the country. The millionth customer entered the centre's temperature-controlled, air-conditioned environment when it had been open for only ten days. It has a full-time Show Director to choreograph an in-house store of entertainment. It has its own TV station offering studio and production facilities, advertisements playing out, along with Warner Brothers cartoons for the munching children, on a gigantic 'vidi-wall' prominently positioned in The Oasis food hall, the biggest restaurant in Europe (actually a number of cafés combined), and cooking up some twelve-thousand meals daily. Meadowhall's Lower High Street is supposed to be one of the busiest high streets in the land. It has its own transport interchange and its own ring road, can accommodate up to four-hundred coaches daily, and has buses and trains arriving every few minutes from a catchment area extending across several regions. It is hardly surprising, then, that with all this hustle and bustle, the colossal number of visitors shuttling to and from Meadowhall on Saturdays (thirty-five-thousand vehicles) prompted one of Sheffield's traffic engineers to claim that it is like dealing with two Wembley Cup Finals on the same day, one in the morning and the other in the afternoon. The place captures in an instant the drive behind the consumer-led energy that ruled in the 1980s, of the continuing de-industrialization of Britain. I had already been near a complex of this type on Tyneside. The MetroCentre at Gateshead began the trend of fantasy land megamalls back in 1987. There are similar structures at Dudley in what used to be described as the Black Country, and at Dartford in Essex. But Meadowhall, which is rather better looking, with its large central dome and spoke-like configuration, and is a little softer on the environment than its predecessor further north, is fairly centrally positioned and presented itself quite conveniently during the course of this English journey, when I was making my way down toward the Midlands.

It is obvious that Meadowhall has been successful. The Christmas-shopping crowds I mixed with that day, which presented a reasonable cross-section of social types, from leather-skirted Harrogate sloanes through to cloth-capped very broad-vowelled pensioners, were ample testimony to that. But it does seem almost statutory for any thinking person these days to dislike modern shopping centres. Most of the people I know rarely have anything favourable to say about them, and in talking about them usually begin by making criticisms that promptly descend into witticisms. I was thinking about this when I parked my car in the largest retail car park in Europe when I arrived at Meadowhall (twelve-thousand spaces), on an area of tarmac big enough, I am certain, to accept light aeroplanes, walked through the House of Fraser where there was a bow-tied young gentleman playing a glass grand piano, and entered the main atrium. If it is the prevalence of artificial light that often disconcerts people about these places, in addition to the emphasis on artificial sensations and fabricated reactions, then I was pleasantly surprised to find inside Meadowhall that the central avenues were lit almost entirely by natural light. What I disliked about it, and this is where shopping malls fail in their attempt to compete with outdoor shopping in a controlled environment, is that you have no landmarks to guide yourself so that you know roughly where you are at any given time. Walking along normal streets there is usually something in the background by which you can place yourself geographically, perhaps a distant hill or a building. But in these giant shopping malls you are forever coming back on yourself and getting lost.

Everything looks the same, and once the avenues are thronged with wall-to-wall bobbing heads a strategy for going about your business efficiently becomes impossible. You find it difficult to know precisely where you are, so that if you want to get back to your car, for instance, never mind go back to a shop you saw earlier, you can spend ten minutes trying to find the entrance where you originally came in. This is hampered by the constantly-shifting morass of figures not being cleaved apart by roads or traffic. I heard one woman that morning, who spoke with a southern accent, say to her husband, from the top of one of the grand marbled staircases, that it 'looked like a bloody football crowd down there'. That was very apt. Amidst that glut of humanity I thought I had taken the correct turning to find a cashpoint, but the next moment I was passing the same shop I had noticed a few minutes earlier when I thought I was walking in an entirely different direction. This happened again and again and was due partly I should think to the underlying proclivity of these malls being to deaden sensation. Like many things in a world of increasing technological perfection, they tend to remove the need for thought or feeling and immunize the need to perceive creatively. The point of moving through a real townscape to me is that you experience changes in shadow and light, you feel the wind or the rain, you see condensation on shop windows, smell pastry and coffee as you pass doorways, observe the pattern of street-lights reflected in wet gutters, all of which serve to remind you that you have faculties and that you are actually alive. The temperature inside shopping complexes is generally controlled, so that you need not bother with scarf and gloves during winter, and therefore need not build up a natural appetite and appreciate more spontaneously the comfort of a hot drink or a meal. In real towns and cities, you can sit and eat your lunch and watch the activity out in the street – one of the most interesting pastimes I know – not merely the shuffling crowds, but passing lorries with names and phone numbers painted on their sides, men arriving to clean windows, aircraft flying overhead, all of which encourage you to contemplate the interconnecting nature of society and of the wider world, that people are going places and things are happening beyond the confines of your own tiny bubble.

But these giant centres never really arouse in you a sense of wonder, perhaps only a sense of unease. I wonder whether or not, by bringing vast crowds of people together beneath their domed roofs for the rather self-indulgent act of leisure shopping, in a curious way they encourage people to become less sociable and to grow mentally further apart by forcing them to think about themselves. They seem to have evolved under the pretext that people visiting them will wander aimlessly, their thoughts occupied with canned music and little electronic voices telling them where to spend their money, instead of going into a shopping area to purchase something for a specific purpose, then getting out as quickly as possible to do something constructive, as many of us do. You simply move from one evenly-heated space to another, upon which nature plays none of its special tricks or works any of its exquisite wonders. Perhaps I am missing something important here and the Meadowhall crowds were all being highly amused at my expense. Perhaps like many people who are ruminative I tend to see virtue only in the sublime and am possessed by the instinctive urge to analyse things instead of merely accepting them as they are. Maybe this synthetic perfection is really all very desirable. Maybe once you have become conditioned it is possible to enter a sort of consumerist stupor that enables you ultimately to evolve to some higher level of consciousness so that in the end you can become truly content by not bothering yourself with such trivialities as the whims of the English weather. But I doubt it. If it is possible to attain a different level of consciousness, I suspect it will be because the mind will have been diverted from the need truly to think constructively for itself and will have degenerated into a sort of pleasure-seeking vegetable on legs. We might not have *1984* totalitarian-style thought control, Big Brother's face staring from a telescreen set into the wall, and everyone wearing the same blue boiler-suits shuffling morosely along dim-lit corridors. But we might have gigantic 'vidi-walls' pushing our thoughts along in a particular direction by encouraging us where to go, what to do, what to wear, and ultimately what to think. We might have television sets in our living rooms, not dictating to us menacingly but titillating us, shaping the culture of what we think we know. We might have the spending power and the freedom to clothe ourselves democratically, and shuffle contentedly up and down brightly-lit shopping malls, whereas subconsciously we might find we are in reality conforming to an overall dreary monotony which is merely boiler-suit standardization in another calculating, if frivolous, disguise. Perhaps that frivolity is in the end more dangerous to the human spirit because having achieved eternal synthetic happiness you are never morose enough to strive toward something better. Of course, consumer society has been the focus of enough suspicion and the butt of plenty of jokes, and no doubt there are astute people who would claim it is harmless and that the confusion of shopping malls adds an element of mystery and adventure to modern leisure shopping. But in Meadowhall I kept arriving back at The Oasis, and began to get slowly infuriated in the process. I do not consider myself especially claustrophobic, but I came as near to feeling it as I have done in a long while when I was inside Meadowhall, and by lunchtime that day my overriding awareness was of the urge to get away.

Meadowhall was built on the site of one of Sheffield's biggest steelworks, and it is this that places it into a wider context when you walk about the car park outside. For in addition to being considered for a long time to be the poorer end of Sheffield socially, still with some very rough quarters indeed around the decayed back streets and old pubs of Attercliffe, this eastern quarter of the city has traditionally been the industrial end too. In the background when you arrive and depart from Meadowhall is the continual basso-profundo wheezing-and-thumping of some kind of huge industrial hammer coming from inside the British Steel works situated just across the way. I had the opportunity of standing next to that hammer when I drove back to the steelworks the following morning, and, after being shown an introductory film and given an introductory drink, was taken right around the plant. The steel industry in this country is now a highly-efficient and competitive business, no longer dogged by the industrial relations problems that threatened to destroy it during the 1970s. The hammer I heard from the car park at Meadowhall was actually stamping flat large steel ingots under enormous pressure, then feeding them between massive computer-controlled rollers that were capable of squeezing the hot material to within thousandths of an inch. But that came later. It was what I saw at the beginning and throughout much of the morning that summed up everything I had always imagined to be the gargantuan forces capable of being harnessed during steel production, of the monumental yet oddly graceful business of steel making itself.

This plant is one of the world's most advanced steel-making facilities, and concentrates on the manufacture of one of several different grades of stainless steel (British Steel manufacture heavier grade steel up in Middlesbrough) that is made chiefly by recycling scrap. It was this operation – what they describe artfully as a 'meltdown' – that summed up the Promethean grandeur of the steel industry when I was in Sheffield. Priestley described shipbuilding on Tyneside, of bending iron and riveting steel against steel, as being 'man's work'. So is steel making, and I don't much care if it sounds dated or sentimental to say it. Advanced technology, robotics, space travel, microchips, all these things astonish and reflect the ingenuity of humankind, but they are nothing compared to the scale and power of heavy industrial processes like steel making, however many computers are keeping their eye on its fabrication today. I suspect it is because the explosive nature of steel making is reminiscent of what we imagine to be the forces that created the Earth itself, that from time to time are capable of rending the planet asunder, and hence they awaken in us some deep empathy toward cosmic powers that remains buried at most normal times. So that it can be melted down, the scrap stainless steel is loaded into a huge bin called an electric arc furnace, which has a lid like an old fashioned pressure-cooker that swings out of the way until the container is filled. Though my guide described the great bins carrying the scrap to the furnace every few minutes politely as 'ladles', these were no mere oversized caricatures of kitchen utensils suspended from quaint wooden beams in authentic farmhouse kitchens. They were massive bucket-shaped bins a couple of storeys in height that weighed upwards of fifty tonnes. Protected by asbestos-type clothing, safety helmets, and goggles, the two of us walked along narrow catwalks above tiny figures and diggers flickering stroboscopically in shafts of daylight slanting through open doorways far below, and watched these bins being hoisted to and fro. Everything was shimmering from the heat. There were enormous dark objects, momentarily touched by a rim of fire, forever moving through the smoke in the background and suspended on the end of awesome crane hooks fashioned from layer upon layer of steel plate several inches thick. In another direction, through the vast opening of an adjoining shed, the great hardened ingots were suspended beneath gantries, moving vertically at the same time as they were moving horizontally, computerized LEDs measuring the weight in tens of tonnes and superimposing themselves vividly against the brown darkness. Nearer to us, molten metal – somewhere in intensity between molten lava and liquid gold, with the surface of black clinker bubbling from the heat as though it had only lately gushed down from the mountain – was being poured, as effortlessly as one bowl of soup into the next, from one gigantic ladle into another. It was this constant feeling you had that enormous vague shapes were moving continually on the end of thick cables, their perspectives forever shifting and overlaying one another, that gave everything a tremendous sense of energy. Running throughout was a relentless thundering of sound that somehow got beneath the fillings in your teeth. The blackness would suddenly explode, and showers of sparks would chase one another across the floor of the factory and men would dance out of the way. We watched the giant bins full of scrap hoisted with a lumbering dinosaur-like motion into position by a crane operated from a tiny control-bubble somewhere beneath the ceiling, then, with an ear-shattering clatter, tens of tonnes of scrap stainless steel was shot into the empty container. The sound was fantastic, like the noise of church bells falling down heaven's distant stairs, and you were only left wondering how close you could stand to such a racket without suffering some kind of permanent damage.

To generate the 'meltdown', colossal graphite prongs several feet in diameter are slid vertically through holes in the lid of the closed furnace. They resemble the oversized bars of a giant electric fire, and as they are lowered into position, the scrap steel screams and rends in agony as the prongs bury themselves in the bowels of the container beneath. There is a pause and then it begins. Thunder and lightening slowly surrounds you. The graphite prongs start to turn molten orange and have enough power put through them to power a town the size of nearby Doncaster. Again the fillings in your teeth are disturbed as molten electricity grinds and crackles and turns more than a hundred tonnes of solid metal back into liquid. Nothing impressed me during this journey more than the sight of steel being made in that giant smelting plant in Sheffield. The thick electric cables powering the graphite prongs jumped and twisted and thrashed as the power surged through them. Sparks and smoke and flames licked out from beneath the closed lid of the furnace, turning from red to purple as they found their way between the gap and suddenly touched the air. Miniature bolts of fork lightening crackled upwards. That was the moment when you felt like you really were staring at something that verged on the phantasmagoric. The sound was unbelievable, easily the loudest I have ever heard, and so powerful that in an odd way it began to bring a lump to your throat as you stood there and stared. There must have been something close to atomic fusion, to the act of universal creation itself, going on inside that blazing cauldron during those pandemonious minutes. It was as if an immense ball of energy were straining to be free. Never have I felt so near such a colossal harnessing of energy, of such raw inestimable power.

Just as you wonder if you have been staring into the depths of an active volcano, into the gaping maw of molten hellfire, as if that were not impressive enough, alongside the furnace the extraction chamber comes into life, and into that are blasted the fumes built up during the meltdown. As I try to convey the feeling of this steel making spectacle, it occurs to me how words are such feeble things. I say that this fume extraction looks exactly the same – and sounds just as loud – as a rocket erupting into life moments before it leaves the pad. But how can that awesome sight be seriously conveyed upon the two-dimensional restriction of a sheet of paper? These fumes are filtered and recycled, which explains why, when you are driven onto the British Steel Stainless site, there are no chimneys pumping filth into the Sheffield sky and clogging the lungs of slum children any more. Concentrate on that solid column of fire thrusting sideways into the extraction chamber and you are looking at the close up shots of one of the space shuttle engines on *Tomorrow's World*. There seemed little to distinguish one blast of energy from the other, and it is only astonishing that the whole smelting apparatus bolted to the concrete floor of that steel plant, perhaps the entire Shepcote Lane works, did not lift off as well, so awesome was that immense crescendo of power.

These steelworks are so big that you do not walk from building to building, you drive between them. We went back out into the sunlight again, back into the twitter of birdsong on a dazzling late-autumn morning. When I was shown the rolls of finished stainless steel gleaming innocently in the storage sheds, waiting to be despatched and transformed into sinks and cutlery and buildings and a hundred other industrial applications, the surroundings seemed almost peaceful. No doubt my ears were numbed.

5

East Midlands and the Potteries

Nottingham by Night

Some months before I commenced this journey I spoke to a journalist acquaintance of mine, whom I first met when he was working in Bradford. I telephoned him with a view to meeting up with him when I arrived in West Yorkshire, only to discover he had since left Bradford and was now working in Nottingham. Because we had got on so well together originally, when he interviewed me in connection with a book I had published, and because more than anyone I think he had understood what I had been trying to say when I wrote it, I felt I owed him one and was determined to get together with him again and give him a bit of space in this book.

He is yet another person I know who originates from the south of England, who has settled in the north, prefers the quality and the pace of life to be found there, and would not wish to live anywhere else. Although his home is still in West Yorkshire – he lives in an impressively converted farm-cum-barn, high on a patch of bleak wind-battered moorland, a mile or so up a dirt-track – he commutes down to Nottingham to work during the week, and returns home to his family at the weekends. His daughters are settled at their school and his wife is a lecturer at Manchester University, so for the present time they are coping with a certain amount of family disorientation, chiefly because none of them wishes to settle permanently in the

Midlands. When I used to commute to London every week to work, and travel back to my home in the north at the weekends, it was bad enough coping with the arrangement when I was still single. But I do not think I could cope with it today. For this I admire my journalist friend enormously. However, there is something else I admire him for as well, and this was why I was looking forward to meeting up with him, after he had kindly invited me to stay with him when I asked if he could show me something briefly of his Nottingham. Not wanting the burden of a second mortgage in a place where he did not intend to remain in the long term, not wanting to inject dead money into the renting of a flat (he had done this briefly to begin with), he had decided to invest the money in a cheaper form of housing that he could take home with him during the holidays, and from which the rest of the family could benefit. He had bought himself a narrow boat and was now living on it during the week down at Nottingham's refurbished city marina. If there is an aspect of the modern English social scene that has enjoyed something of a renaissance during recent years, it is the Continental-style redevelopment of many of our inland waterways, docklands, and marinas. A veritable sub-culture is evolving around them. The passing of a lazy couple of weeks on a narrow boat over a holiday is something I have wanted to experience ever since I read a story in a children's book when I was a boy, but the thought of living on one permanently is not my idea of domestic contentment. My journalist friend was doing precisely this and, from what I could gather, coping with it quite admirably. This I had to see.

It was pouring with rain again when I came down the road from Sheffield and Mansfield into Nottingham toward the end of the afternoon. The city, which seemed not as dreary as I had expected, was being thrashed by a torrential downpour of some considerable ferocity; one that looked like it was bedding itself in for the duration. As I wound my way round the one-way system into the multi-storey car park I had been told to aim for in the centre, it was refreshing for once not to become entangled in lane after lane of more or less stationary traffic. This was because the streets themselves were almost deserted, and seemed to be practically running with water, though the rush-hour was but a short time away. A few delivery vans were half cocked on the pavements, and only a few figures or a handful of cars occasionally dashed across my vision. There is something very definitely exhilarating about arriving in a city at a moment such as this, during heavy rain, when it is nearly dark and neon signs are beginning to superimpose themselves brilliantly over the surrounding blue-grey distortion of lighted tower blocks and department store windows. The city, it seems, is in a state of near panic. An air raid siren might just have sounded. You are caught in a pocket of time quite unlike any other. You are lost between dimensions in a continuum of deepening shadow and sheets of swirling rain that suddenly double back, loop-the-loop, and fling themselves haphazardly against acres of rippling glass. If such a city existed all the time, as a real space of concrete and brick and stone and steel, I think I could be quite happy living there. You would always be in a hurry to get to the other side of the street because of the inclement weather conditions, which would inject your movements with spontaneity and deliberation, and keep everyone on their toes. Cities should be invigorating places, and this kind of invigoration is the stuff from which imagination and inspiration really are made. Unfortunately, real cities rarely retain this sense of composure for long. They are often too busy pretending they are something they are not to try and generate a sense of vitality or to excite the imagination, instead of getting on with the business of simply being what they are.

My stay in Nottingham was only going to be brief. We spent the first hour reacquainting ourselves and filling each other in about the past couple of years of our lives in the staff canteen of the Nottingham *Evening Post*. After another hour, talking in the pub across the road with some journalists and an income tax inspector, who had travelled up from London to deliver a lecture at the city university (there was plenty of humorous badinage being exchanged about the big news story of the day: the first Asian Sheriff of Nottingham had just resigned because the Fraud Squad had been called in to investigate the embezzling of public funds for ethnic arts groups), we found ourselves walking among a huddle of boats bobbing in the water down at the marina, not far from the city castle. I noted with interest the level of security surrounding the boats: padlocked gates, barbed-wire fences, and searchlights which had infra-red scanners built into them so they flashed immediately into life when flesh and blood organisms approached. I noticed with even greater interest how reassured I felt at the sight of all this security, and the fact that, being so close to the city centre, I needn't worry about leaving my car unattended overnight. By this time it was pitch black. The rain had stopped and the air smelt marvellously sharp and fresh, though it had turned bitterly cold. Because of the amount of time it was going to take for the boat to decently warm up, after we had eaten and filled the stove with coal, at something approaching ten o'clock it was suggested we don our coats and gloves and walk along the canal tow-path back into the city centre, to see how Nottingham was behaving during an evening in the middle of the week. At first I was none too keen at this prospect – I am rather wary of being in city centres at night, and I dislike the smoky atmosphere of pubs – but I was reminded, quite rightly, that this was a journey round contemporary England I was supposed to be conducting, and it might be a good idea to go and have a look at contemporary Nottingham after dark.

Actually, my initial doubts were based on the assumption that I knew precisely what to expect, having spent enough time on town and city centre streets at night, and in rough pubs and nightclubs, when I was a teenager. Though I never came across them with the frequency I am assured these things happen today, I remember all too well steering clear of groups of animalistic youths kicking one another senseless in the street, arguing over somebody else's girl, or incidents in packed bars where a crowd would suddenly scatter and scream as a brawl ensued near the doorway, and beer glasses would begin to fly. There was a quantity of Nottingham working-class youth assembled in some profusion around the Old Market Square that night, the large open space that forms the focal point to the centre of the city, and where, many years ago, the Goose Fair used to be staged annually until it was moved out to the forest recreation ground. Watching over them was the huge grey columned bulk of the Council House, like a miniature St Paul's Cathedral, bonging lugubriously the increments of the hour, and which the following day I discovered had a number of pleasantly restored shopping arcades situated immediately behind it. What surprised me was how many people there were hanging about in the square, jeering noisily in groups in and out of pubs beating with muffled music, with an average age, I should say, of about seventeen. It could have been my imagination or my frame of mind, but the subtle thread of confrontation which I clearly remembered from when I was young seemed still to be running just beneath the surface of those crowds, crowds that were only a hair's breadth from becoming ugly, after all these years. Only the fashions and the kids' appearance had changed. Step back into Priestley's day, and you would probably have found much the same sort of thing, in different clothes and conforming to different fashions. To my surprise, my journalist friend said he often walked back into the city centre at night to take some air and some exercise. I told him there was no way I would walk along that shadowy canal bank on my own at night. The possible threat to personal safety did, however, seem not to bother him. We walked right round the centre of the city, round the castle, looked at The Trip to Jerusalem, supposedly the oldest pub in England, and built, it seemed, into the very rock-face supporting the castle battlements above it, and then ended up in the dark streets of St Mary's Gate, known locally as the Lace Market, at that hour as quiet as a graveyard. In the middle, a deep black outline rising toward the stars scattered across the night sky high above, was St Mary's Church, another solid lump of ecclesiastical architecture I came across in England that was more or less obscured by scaffolding. Throughout the autumn of 1991 one got the feeling that the whole country was restoring its religious buildings, an observation that was probably entirely correct. The Lace Market is where the nineteenth-century lace merchants of Nottingham built their warehouses and offices and is almost identical in arrangement to Little Germany in Bradford, except that it is made from brick. In Nottingham, as in Bradford, an attempt has been made to renovate the buildings and encourage new businesses to locate themselves there, though with what degree of success at that time of night I could not tell.

It was late by the time we made our way back to the boat. The city periphery, with its shuttered shops and silent car showrooms and its rows of staring street lamps, was quiet and deserted. A sharp wind was beginning to disturb the clumps of leaves running along the pavements in front of the Unemployment Benefit Office. The interior of the boat was by now roasting hot. We settled down with a pot of freshly ground coffee, and had some talk about politics – to be truthful, the subject had formed much of the talk throughout the evening – until well after midnight. Because I was the guest, I was allowed to sleep in the living quarters where the stove was located, and my journalist friend retreated to the kitchen area at the opposite end of the boat. I can usually manage to sleep almost anywhere, provided it is quiet enough. What I did not realize was how stifled the space had become due to the intensity of the heat being generated by the stove while we were out, until I tried to get some sleep during the early hours. At first I was merely warm, but then I was very warm, and then I felt like I was roasting. If you projected your arm into the air, it was possible to feel a body of heat gathered near the ceiling, so I tried to get beneath it by laying on the bottom of the boat, which then began rocking gently as I fumbled about in the darkness and tried to reposition myself comfortably. This proved to have no effect, and so, at about two-thirty in the morning, I unbolted the tiny wooden doors at the front of the boat and stepped out onto the deck. I was stark naked, and the temperatures out there were well below freezing, but for a few minutes the sense of relief was overwhelming. At the precise moment I unlocked the doors, a fox loping silently past on the canal bank looked at me, then bolted. I am not surprised. Somewhat fitfully, I managed to sleep, until six o'clock the following morning when I had to get up and let my journalist friend out through the marina gates. (He was on the early shift at the office.) I had to do this because he only had one key, which I needed so that I could let myself and my vehicle out at a more respectable hour later. The cold outside was truly horrific, as it always is at such a Godforsaken time in the morning in winter. Only half-awake, I stood for a couple of minutes in the freezing marina toilets, my teeth chattering, then staggered blearily through the darkness back to the boat, fell back into my sleeping bag, and slept until I was woken by an express train thundering past on the adjacent railway embankment, at something shortly before nine.

Nottingham by day appeared not as unpleasant or as ugly as I expected. In the centre it seemed presentable and clean, as major modern cities go. It tends to sprawl a bit, leaving the impression in the mind's eye that it is fairly big. There appeared to be a more noticeable quantity of trees sunk into the pavements right across the face of the city, and out into the suburbs; so much so I would venture to say it is a minor visual characteristic of Nottingham. (I was told afterwards that at the beginning of the eighteenth century, Nottingham was sometimes described as a 'garden city': perhaps it is attempting to capture something of that essence anew.) Much of the central shopping area has also been progressively pedestrianized and resurfaced with modern herringbone sets, and in that respect it is following the trend of the times. Even the concrete buildings and tower blocks did not look as grubby or as mouldering or as ashen-faced as is the case in most places – this despite the fact that the city has been carved up to accommodate the proverbial network of dual carriageways and underpasses. There might have been a subjective element influencing my perceptions here, because the morning and afternoon I spent walking around Nottingham were among the few occasions during the journey when the sun was actually shining brilliantly throughout. After a week or two of more or less continuous overcast gloom this might have encouraged something of a false sense of relief, making tower blocks look less inhospitable than they actually were.

Nevertheless, beneath that high, pale autumnal sky, streaked with a few wispy white curls, bisected by the occasional drifting vapour-trail, Nottingham seemed bright, quite colourful, and to be reasonably at ease with itself. I was eating breakfast in a café in the centre of the city early, so that I saw the streets from when they were only sparsely populated, with street cleaners picking up the previous night's rubbish, shopkeepers still rolling up shutters surrounded by flocks of pigeons that would suddenly explode and scatter above the young trees onto the adjacent rooftops when they were disturbed, through to when the central thoroughfares were bustling – something that happened very quickly, implying there was money being spent there. I walked for a while again around the quiet streets of the Lace Market, then sat in the sun in the St Mary's churchyard among the mottled shadows and the pleasant birds-twittering quietness, and went over my notebook. By day, the Lace Market seemed to have been more outwardly successful in its refurbished guise than Little Germany had been in Bradford. There were a number of solicitors' offices and design studios and consultants housed in the quiet confines of those tall, shadowy paved streets. There were some important-looking people walking about, probably barristers, and the polished brass name-plates bolted to the walls outside doors and at the foot of dark staircases were glinting agreeably in the midday sun. That the area felt more lived in and worked in than Little Germany is something which probably derives from the fact that Nottingham is undoubtedly more prosperous today than Bradford, and is a more convincing centre for cultural excursions. I spent another hour wandering round the nearby Lace Hall, an interesting museum which celebrates Nottingham's history as the centre of lace manufacture, in a converted Unitarian Chapel. The trade, which is Nottingham's oldest and most famous, is still operating in a marked capacity within the city, though I was not at all surprised to learn that the revolutionary Jacquardtronic lace machine, which replaced the traditional paper method of pattern changing by substituting it with magnetic tape, bringing lace-making up into the computer age, was actually developed in Germany.

It was just along the outskirts of the Lace Market where I entered a very old fashioned cobbler's shop. My beige-coloured boots were beginning to become soiled due to the amount of walking I was doing. I had been toying with the idea of having them dyed black, but to be honest I really went into the shop because the building's interior, which I caught out of the corner of my eye as I loped past it earlier, looked like it had not changed since the middle of the nineteenth century. The cobbler, an old man with a blithesome face that fitted as perfectly the feel of the interior as a foot would fit the shoes on his shelves, who kept putting his hands in his overall pockets and bobbing backwards and forwards as he spoke with a smile that never vanished from his face, who kept looking up to the ceiling to pluck the words from decades of wisdom born of simple cobbling down a Nottingham back street, emerged from a nest of antiquated belt-driven machinery at the back of the shop and laughed at me for buying cheap footwear. He said the boots would not take the dye correctly. They were, he suggested, the kind of shoes – like most shoes today, I suppose: like the texture of modern life, in fact – that are intended to be disposable. He then pointed to his own black shoes, which were real shoes, and said, not without an air of deliberate satisfaction, that they had actually been brown up until only the previous afternoon.

To claim the shop had not changed for the better part of a century was, I assure you, no exaggeration. It struck me as an interesting paradox that a few yards further along the street, in the Lace Market, the feeling of nineteenth-century England was being tidied up and celebrated and assessed anew. Yet here, at the edge of it, was a piece of nineteenth-century England still functioning. Even the shop's proprietor looked like he belonged deep in the pages of a dusty nineteenth-century novel. The point is, the atmosphere of the place was *genuine*, not contrived. It was not being placed on a pedestal and put on show. It had the informality, the necessary clutter in the background binding everything together. It smelt alive – smelt of leather and polish and wax that was still scraped from tins kept in ancient compartments in tiny mahogany drawers – and the panelled woodwork of the long counter was blurred and dented with fifty layers of paint and the knocks and bumps of decades. I was amazed to find such a place in the middle of a city in which there are air-conditioned shopping precincts and cars with electronic windows. What I was not amazed to discover, when I commented on the elderly quality of the interior, was that this old cobbler was the last in the family line, and when he retired very soon the business and the shop would close for good. He was not the first person to have said such words to me over the previous weeks. I am glad I met him. By the time this book is on the shelves, quite likely shelves in that cobbler's own city, the shop will probably have gone. No doubt by then, too, the interior will have been carefully stripped out and put on display in a warehouse among a myriad other architectural antiques – before being put back into another shop somewhere else, all those dints and scratches now hidden by filler, all those layers of paint chemically removed, to capture the essence of Old England elsewhere anew.

When I left Nottingham I intended finding a route away from the city that would enable me to drive across the bottom part of the Derbyshire Peak District, possibly touching Matlock, in order to reach the Potteries obliquely from the north. I half fancied experiencing some rural bed-and-breakfast along the way, where you can usually obtain a decent night's sleep and sometimes find rewarding conversation over breakfast. In addition to this, the pleasant town of Leek, which I had found interesting on at least one occasion in the past, lay at what from my direction would form the western exit of the Peak District. Because I had only ever seen Leek from the back seat of a car, and because my map indicated the road from Derbyshire would take me straight through the centre of the town, I was hoping to stop and have a brief look at the place during the course of this journey. As it was, I did not manage to see Leek from the front seat of a car, never mind the back. I got nowhere near it, in fact. No matter how hard I tried, I seemed unable to negotiate my way successfully away from the outskirts of Nottingham and find the most direct route out to Derbyshire. This completely destroyed my time schedule. When I should have been well on my way toward the Potteries I was still driving around in circles and getting caught up among a confusion of roundabouts and flyovers. I could not get high enough above the city to the west, so that when I eventually took the nearest route I could find across toward Stoke-on-Trent, with the light fading by the minute, I had to go instead via Derby. Except when a brilliant shaft of sunlight poked out momentarily from the underbelly of a heap of cloud piled in the distance and scanned the landscape, feeling its way determinedly across the cooling towers of a tiny power station silhouetted eerily on the horizon, before blinking abruptly out of existence again, this journey through the East Midlands was quite unremarkable. The dual carriageway simply stretched from one remote vanishing point to another, an observation it is possible to make wherever you are in the country. It looked and felt, like the creeping ruination of the countryside and the gradual bowdlerization of England going on all around it, as though it were going to go on forever, even at a steady seventy miles an hour. The nearer I drew toward the Potteries and Stoke-on-Trent, the more abysmal the weather became. By the time I came into the outskirts of the city the daylight had disappeared and it was raining heavily yet again. That I should be approaching another industrial conurbation in the pouring rain was now becoming something of a recurrent theme, perhaps even a dubious portent. I crawled through the early evening traffic into the outskirts of Longton along the main road from Uttoxeter, my windscreen wipers working furiously against the rain, just as a pottery or a factory of some description was disgorging a horde of anoraked workers out onto the black streets. As they fanned out from the entrance gates and abruptly encountered the sheets of pounding rain, they were suddenly running for cover toward bus shelters like soldiers scattered by a grenade blast. Here was a characteristic glimpse of modern England at the end of another working day, I thought, as people boarded buses, a pelican green man flashed vividly against the blackness, and a chiaroscuro of approaching headlights distorted against glass. Then I was swallowed up by the chronic and quite unbearable traffic congestion that is such a striking characteristic of the pottery towns – this quite apart from their noticeably Victorian, sooty, red-brick complexion – and that in my experience grips them so persistently during the rush-hour periods. (Perhaps I have always arrived in the Potteries at the wrong moment.) Further on, through tiny living-room windows I caught sight of the computer graphics and opening titles to early evening news bulletins, twisting vividly onto television screens and spilling into numerous homes before the curtains were drawn to shut them off from the world, to allow a winter's evening of quiz shows and soap opera finally to set in, set in, set in.

I looked at this jumble of old architecture crowding in upon the worn streets glistening with wet in the darkness. I contemplated the temperature gauge on my dashboard moving dangerously near to the boiling point in the stationary traffic. I considered the present recessionary crisis, and contemplated the newspaper headlines suggesting the country was on the verge of economic collapse. I imagined the murders, the bombings, the child molestations, the rapes, the political corruptions and gazumpings and sex scandals and back-stabbings and pension embezzlings, the piles of festering corpses that would accumulate internationally before this book was put on the shelves, the Michael Buerks and the Anna Fords of the world preparing to smile their courteous good evenings and report the rottenness of the world on *The Six O'Clock News* from the BBC, in vivid satellite-pictured technicolour. I remembered the pictures I had seen of the Potteries during their industrial, smog-enshrouded, potbank-ridden heyday. I remembered the property crisis and all those empty offices surrounding Canary Wharf, upon which Mrs Thatcher had pinned so many of her economic hopes, and which would have faced ruin by the time I came to consider these thoughts again months afterwards.

And I realized how out of touch with reality the people must be who generalize so piously about the essential decency and democracy of the human race.

Dirty Old Towns?

The Potteries lie in a part of North Staffordshire I have been getting to know extremely well over the past few years. My wife originates from the region, having been brought up in Bucknall, just outside Hanley, and latterly on the outskirts of the industrial district, to the north between Tunstall and Congleton, before her education then her career took her away from the area altogether. When I was preparing to head toward the Potteries during this journey, it appealed to me to stay in Burslem. I had arranged to visit a couple of pottery manufacturers based there, and because Burslem tends still to be considered the capital of the region by people from outside, it seemed a likely focal point from which to conduct operations. But for reasons I shall explain presently, by the time I had crawled through that early evening traffic on my way in from Nottingham, I had already decided to stay with my parents-in-law in their bungalow instead. I carried on driving, through Tunstall, out to the opposite end of the Potteries, to the foot of the Staffordshire Moorlands. This is a region of superb hill country a few miles to the north of the industrial towns (one easily missed by visitors new to the area), where the lumpy pinkish-blackened stone, the look of the old houses, and the feel of the dry stone walls running between the fields and along the edges of the roads is so much like that to be found in parts of West Yorkshire, if you had been taken there blindfolded, until you had refocussed your eyes you would swear you had been deposited on the hillsides above Haworth. I was looking forward to spending some time in the Potteries, not only because I would be leaving hotel accommodation behind and staying in an atmosphere that was at once congenial and where I felt at home, but because my wife and son were taking the opportunity to travel down a couple of days after I arrived, to meet up with me for the weekend. Because my stay in the Potteries fell approximately halfway through the journey, the idea was that the weekend would form for me a kind of break, though I would still be working.

The Potteries are, I suppose, something of a geographical and economic oddity. Though they could technically still be considered part of the Midlands, they look as though they ought to belong much further north, possibly in the red-brick triangle formed by Oldham, Rochdale, and Bolton in Lancashire. Even the accent traditional to the region sounds distinctly northern (this is curious considering the closeness of nasally Birmingham) though it is true that it sounds more Yorkshire than it does Lancashire. People travelling north from the south by rail for the first time sometimes assume the Potteries are where the North Country really begins. They then proceed to be confused further as their train pulls out of Stoke station and slides into a mild landscape that might easily be mistaken for the Home Counties, because between the Potteries and the old industrial areas proper there lies some excellent countryside, along with some of the wealthiest and snootiest suburbs in England.

As a region which for hundreds of years has been the centre for manufacture of our cups and saucers and dishes and plates, as well as our ceramic tiles, most of our bathroom furniture, our toilet-pots, our bidets and our sinks, the Potteries retain the unique distinction of being the only industrial region in England to have been named informally after the industry that built them, so that the description has passed into the language and become a by-word. There are no corresponding parts of the country called the Textiles or the Minings. The official name for the region is, of course, the city of Stoke-on-Trent, but what also distinguishes it is that it is not a city in the normal sense of the word at all. There is no huge clutter of suburbs gathered around a single body of weighty municipal and ecclesiastical architecture, mixed in with a number of massive tower blocks and flyovers, rearing somewhere in the middle. Stoke-on-Trent is actually a group of half a dozen small towns which run into one another, rather as the suburbs of London or Manchester blend together, but with each one having a more marked resemblance to an individual industrial town than the last. It is the close proximity the towns bear to one another, and the benefits it was assumed federation would clearly bring, that resulted many years ago in them being brought together into a single municipal entity, the mythical city of Stoke-on-Trent. Arnold Bennett probably did more to bring the Potteries to prominence through the pages of his novels than the products that were manufactured there ever managed. It was Bennett who coined the famous term the Five Towns, which though designed with a fictitious usage in mind, may or may not have had some influence on the decision ultimately to integrate the genuine towns officially into a single corporate whole. As it happens, there are in fact six towns, or if one wants to be technically correct and report accurately what the very amicable local people tell you, there are arguably seven or even eight. But Bennett had an eye and an ear for words. He knew that aesthetically, for the purposes of establishing an imaginary locality for a series of novels, because it was a common multiple, five sounded better on paper than six.

One of the qualities which struck J.B. Priestley most strongly when he was in the Potteries was that the towns felt to have a distinctive self-contained atmosphere of their own. He found this peculiar, because of the almost central position in the country they occupied and how it meant they could communicate easily with nearly every part of England. He thought the towns conveyed an unusual impression of provincial remoteness, something that was emphasised by their littleness and their shabbiness, something which in turn was probably connected to the peculiar intimacy of the earthenware industry and its cosy family atmosphere. Having married into a large family in the area, and consequently having begun to spend some time there, the subtle feeling of insularity that hangs over the Potteries is something I have noticed time and time again. The first time I noticed it was independent of remembering what Priestley had written. It struck me as being so unusual it was a quality which after I had travelled round England, of all the regions of it that I saw, the one I could imagine had probably changed least of all in essence since the 1930s was the Potteries.

Priestley was also struck by what he described as the region's universal littleness; its compactness. He found it 'Lilliputian', not only because of the smallness of the towns themselves, and the paradox of them being designated to be part of a city, but because of the diminutiveness of most of the industrial architecture from which they were originally built. He was more familiar with the 'huge dark boxes of factories and the immensely tall chimneys' glowering at the end of every thoroughfare in his native Bradford. The pottery factories had nothing large or substantial about them at all, he said, with the exception of the 'potbanks', the distinctive bottle shaped ovens that used to characterize the look of the region, where the articles of pottery were stacked in little plaster containers before they were fired, and which looked as if they had been dropped in between the buildings and sunk into the soil. Bizarre brick structures, the potbanks were either short and dumpy like monstrous burgundy bottles, or taller and slimmer with necks so slender they looked like colossal champagne bottles. Because it is still possible to come across a substantial number of mill chimneys projecting from skylines further north, it is tempting to believe there might be a corresponding number of bottle ovens to be found protruding from the skylines of the Potteries. I half expected this to be the case before I ever went there. But, though you will occasionally find the odd one poking solemnly above a yard fence or a dilapidated outbuilding tucked away down a back street, adorned with saplings swaying gently in the breezes, nearly all the potbanks have long since disappeared. Nowadays, most of the pottery is fired in kilns that look exactly like the corrugated containers you see being loaded on and off ships onto articulated lorries or trains. The temperature can be controlled as easily as a cooker in a normal domestic kitchen, and in most places the firing process itself is fully automated. In some of the bigger places that I was shown around in the Potteries, the firing process is in the course of becoming entirely computer controlled. It is the reduction in the huge number of potbanks that probably makes the pottery towns feel smaller and lower on the eye than ever, and why it is possible to say the relative smallness of the architecture and the compact feel of the individual towns remains a salient characteristic of the area today, in spite of there having been the kind of environmental and architectural changes affecting it that have affected everywhere.

Something Priestley did not mention when he was in the Potteries, but which I believe relates strongly to their self-containedness, is the quite extraordinary courtesy and friendliness of the people living there. It is impossible not to be aware of this, and it is doubtful if a book of this kind would be complete without a reference to it. Of course, when making observations such as these it is easy to be dragged down by some of our more enlightened souls, formulating tidy intellectual opinions safely behind desks in distant rooms instead of mixing with people on streets across the land, into dreary accusations about sentimentality. To be honest, I do not normally go in for making these kinds of sweeping generalizations about the different emotional qualities to be found in people living in different parts of the country myself. As a rule, I am sceptical about so-called regional differentiations in popular character. Ordinary people seem to me to be very much the same wherever you go. (Here I shall be reminded that this has not always been the case.) The essential friendliness of Potteries people, who all call you 'duck', is no mere sentimentality, however, it is fact. Anyone who assumes it is another instance of the fallaciousness associated with national folk memory should spend some time in the area and talk to the people. Nowhere else in England, perhaps with the exception of parts of East Lancashire between Accrington and Colne, where people still stand on the doorsteps of grid-patterned terraced houses along some of the steep side streets on warm afternoons, smile at you, and actually bid you hello, do you encounter such gentle humility from ordinary people out in the street. When I walked around one of the towns a couple of days after I arrived in the Potteries, searching for photographic opportunities, because of the slightly perturbed expression you tend to adopt at such times as you scan the streets with your eye, I was startled to find that people would occasionally step out of shop doorways, or stop me in the street, and ask whether or not I was lost. Nowhere but in the Potteries did this happen with anything approaching consistency. In a public situation, most English people respond to a man brandishing a camera by pretending he simply isn't there, and you can observe this most acutely if you bring out a camera in a tube train on the London Underground.

When one thinks of the Potteries one tends to think of Burslem, and certainly one tends to think of it as the mother town. I had heard of Burslem long before I heard of any of the other towns, or knew where or what the region was. For years I passed through Stoke on the train on the main line from Manchester, to and from London, assessed the bigness of the railway station there, saw the Staffordshire Polytechnic buildings coming almost up to the southbound platform, and assumed it was a normal town or city of substantial size, and that the tower blocks and the bulky outline of the place proper must have been hidden out of sight, somewhere in the background. (As it is, the station is one of the biggest buildings in Stoke, and it is said that the fact the main line passes through there is all that gives the town an immediate sense of prominence any more.) Stoke, which is the political administration centre of the Potteries, did not even register in my mind as being associated with the manufacture of earthenware, though I did always loosely associate this process with Burslem. For a long time, all I knew about Stoke was that it had a football team that played in red-and-white striped jerseys. And I had certainly not heard of Hanley, or at any rate, Hanley had not registered mentally as a place of any size or significance. This might have been something to do with the sound of the names of the other places, and the way they rolled off the tongue. Burslem, Stoke, Tunstall, Fenton, and Longton somehow have a ring about them that brings to mind an image of industrial landscapes. They sound hard-edged and grimy; places that probably have a hundred years of industrial toil and the hard effects of traditional manufacture etched into the very substance of their brick.

Hanley, on the other hand, sounds quite mild and pleasant. It might be a market town at the heart of a spiral of pretty villages tucked away somewhere in the Wiltshire countryside. And yet Hanley, which is built on the south-eastern slope of the hills which lift gradually around the rim of the Potteries, is by far the biggest and most important of the old pottery towns. It was never quite as important a manufacturing centre as nearby Burslem, and that remains so today. There is a story as to why Burslem, which, with its famous town hall and its immortalization by Arnold Bennett as mythical Bursley, was originally the most important and the busiest of the pottery towns, and why it was eventually left behind by the expanding Hanley. Around the turn of this century, the civic fathers of Burslem decided they wanted to clean up the town's image by moving its busy street market indoors. But the farmers and street traders refused to go along with this, preferring to relocate their activities in the open air elsewhere instead. The market was moved across to Hanley, the consequence being that Burslem stagnated while Hanley prospered. You can certainly believe this story when you look round either of these places now. Hanley has developed throughout most of this century into the important shopping centre it has become today; to the extent that it is now considered to be the heart and soul of the Potteries, and is described by road signs as the city centre. This process culminated recently with the town following modern retailing fashion by erecting a large covered shopping complex, somewhat ironically if rather predictably named The Potteries Centre, the most significant architectural development to have materialized in the Potteries in recent years, other than the Garden Festival held at Stoke some time ago. There was some controversy both before and after the new centre opened. Not because of the effect it had on Hanley's traditional covered market that had already been demolished to make way for the new structure, and which, after much discussion and debate, was finally rehoused in the basement of the Potteries Centre. Nor was the controversy centred around the new building's distinctive post-Modernist style of design, or its domination of the landscape from miles around. It was because the open food hall central to the development, as is the fashion nowadays selling a variety of different types of meals from pizzas through to baked potatoes and fried fish, had the audacity to serve up all its produce from disposable plastic plates and cups. The reason given for this was that it allowed more economic staffing levels, to cut down on the amount of washing-up, because of the rapid turnover of customers. This, in the Potteries, where most of the country's crockery and its tableware is manufactured! The howls of laughter, and the heads being shaken in dismay, continued long after that fiasco first came to light, and can still be found reverberating across plenty of domestic dinner tables today.

By contrast, Burslem appears to have been in the process of fading away for a very long time. Today it does not have the bustle or vitality of Longton, the town in the Potteries which to me is the most surprising, is the most vigorously working class, and is the easiest to miss. I tend to continually doubt my observations about places when I am walking around, never quite believing them until I hear them confirmed incidentally by something or somebody else afterwards. Even then I am never entirely sure. But the impression of Burslem I had been carrying around with me since last I had seen it was heightened as soon as I spent a morning walking round it when I was in the Potteries during this journey. Plenty of the shops were of the discount variety, and there seemed to be a more noticeable quantity that were empty than I remembered. The retail heart of the place had about it that slightly soiled, fly-blown quality you associate with rows of sombre shops and launderettes clinging to the scrag ends of life in the centre of big council estates. Whenever I have walked around Burslem, I have always thought that, more than any other place I know, it epitomises in a single instance the picture so many people in the south of England have lodged in their minds of what they mistakenly believe to be the semi-derelict industrial towns making up the bulk of the north. It looks run down, and there does not look to be much money or colour in the place; not much suggestion of colour, in fact, at all. What finally did it for me when I saw it this time was that the most substantial hotel in the town, The George, a fine curved building enjoying a prominent position on a corner close to the centre, had closed down. (It was this that prompted me to stay with my parents-in-law several miles outside the industrial district.) It was boarded up with chipboard. I have already remarked about how this sort of thing leaves a bad impression on your reaction to a place, when I arrived in Bradford, and here it was again in Burslem. There was testimony to decline and decay if ever one was needed, bringing with it the sad implication that not many business orientated people need to come to the town and stay in it any longer.

That the hotel should have shut down at all only emphasised the creeping air of decomposition that appeared to have taken hold of Burslem, a quality of the town's complexion which was itself doubtless a reflection of the wider economic depression, the creeping air of decomposition that is the scion of our times, as much as it is a reflection of how much it has been left behind commercially by neighbouring Hanley. Recently, a small cast-iron fountain was erected in the centre of the town's little sloping square, to commemorate the site of a similar structure there many years ago, long since lost. But when I stood in front of it, it was difficult to ignore the air of despondency the town positively exuded, hanging thickly in the background. The last time I had stood and looked across to the George Hotel, several months previously in the pouring rain, I wondered in passing how dim and strangely Victorian and other-worldly the lights appeared behind the old windows; how subdued and limp were the old lace curtains when seen from the street. The hotel seemed to have something about it which was dusty and faded and not quite of our age. I remember wondering distinctly how much longer it was going to last. It must have been a premonition. Since I stood in the same position during this journey, the hotel has, I am pleased to say, been sold and is in the process of being renovated. The open air market that used to be held at the nearby Port Vale football ground has been moved to the centre of Burslem and, I am assured, breathed new life into the heart of the town. And it is perhaps worth remembering, too, that less than two minutes walk from the centre of Burslem, and less than that from the dusty deserted portico of the George Hotel I saw, are the headquarters of Royal Doulton, probably the most prestigious name associated with the Potteries, and one of the most prestigious and instantly recognizable names in the country, if not the world.

Thus there are, as Priestley observed about Bradford sixty years ago, nearly always compensations. The pottery towns might be untidy places, with a curious underlying, timeless, greasy-road-surfaced industrial feeling hanging over them. There might not be what by south-eastern standards would be considered much real prosperity circulating among many of the inhabitants. And they have their chronic unemployment, their crime statistics, and the kind of incumbent social problems that can be found anywhere that has assembled a substantial body of working-class people, make no mistake of that. But this becomes a contradiction in terms when it is set against the sense of vitality the region manages to retain economically, and it is this that relates strongly to the intimacy that Priestley noticed when he passed through the area, still discernible after all these years. To the sensibilities of the average sentimental traveller in search of an idealized green and pleasant land, the Potteries might simply appear to be a collection of scruffy towns, thankfully at a sufficient enough distance north to keep them out of sight and out of civilized mind. That would be most unfortunate, for it is so terribly easy, if you have little or no understanding of the deeper social framework propping these places up, to glide casually through them, glance at the boarded-up windows, look at the arthritic old ladies bent against the prevailing winds, scan the profusion of junk shops, stare up at the huge landscaped slag-heaps flecked with tiny figures walking tiny dogs (this used to be an important coal mining area too), and dismiss them as irrelevant. But though the Potteries have been affected by the decline in traditional manufacturing industry in recent years, they do not appear to have been carpet-bombed into the ground quite as badly as some other areas further north; an observation that is reinforced by a glance through the local yellow pages. There are still several pages in the Stoke-on-Trent directory given over to pottery manufacturers, suppliers, and associated industries such as the production of bathroom furniture, and services such as artwork separation and moulding. Today the Bradford directory can only just manage a full page for its textile manufacturers and its wool merchants alone, and it takes in several important towns from a wide area with a combined population that is much greater than that of Stoke-on-Trent.

Of the hundreds of companies listed in the Stoke-on-Trent directory, by far the biggest concentration of pottery factories is situated in Fenton and Longton, interspersed with long rows of dusty terraced houses lining the main roads. I had noticed the proliferation of factories there before, but it was not until I spent an afternoon walking round the back streets of Longton with my father-in-law, on the Saturday, that I was finally struck by the high number of working potteries there were remaining at that end of the industrial district. Some of the pottery factories are fairly modern, simple, square-faced structures, put up during the 1930s – the kind with metal window frames and curved concrete porticoes – but it is the older ones that are most interesting. Grimy-fronted buildings, often facing onto the main roads, soiled not from years of smog or neglect, but due to their proximity to the spray and splash of passing traffic, they are two or three stories in height, with the company crest engraved into the keystone above a central arched passageway leading into an old cobbled loading yard behind. They certainly do not bring to mind the popular image of the huge dark factories more commonly associated with the industrial north of England. This, however, can be deceptive, for unlike textile mills, which were originally built upwards to five or six stories in height so that a high quantity of machinery on each floor could be operated centrally by a single belt-driven mechanism, pottery factories extended backwards from the road for some distance instead. This reduced their impact on the eye, but often disguised a comparable amount of floor space to the average mill, stretching out somewhere in the background. Around Longton the potteries seem to be everywhere. It is clear that some of them are the premises of suppliers, and for all I know, some of them might be suppliers of earthenware imported from the Far East. But there is definitely some substance to the underlying emphasis on manufacture. You feel to be coming upon factory shops and showrooms at every turn; seem forever to be glimpsing blurred stacks of crockery fresh from the kilns, piled behind frosted glass windows along nearly every other side street.

There also appear to be more derelict bottle ovens protruding from the skyline in Longton than in any other town in the Potteries. There are not many, but there are enough of them for it to become a minor characteristic. There is a cluster perfectly restored, grouped tightly around the Gladstone Museum in Longton, and which, as you look toward them from the scruffy little bus station in the town centre, look like a collection of empty wine bottles pushed to the middle of a huge dining table, somewhere behind the rooftops. But it is the decaying ovens projecting above and among some of the surrounding housing that more directly appeal to me. That afternoon, inevitably, we paid our entrance fee and spent an hour wandering around the inside of the Gladstone Museum, a complete pottery that has been restored to how it would have looked around the turn of this century. There were the usual kinds of well-presented exhibits, audio-visual shows, working machinery, live demonstrations in throwing and ceramic flower-making, and painted wooden carts were parked in the cobbled yard between the bottle ovens outside. But I soon become lethargic in industrial museums. After only a short while I find them tedious, almost embarrassing. Though I can appreciate their historical importance, and the use they have in enlightening parties of school children, I find it difficult to relate to, or generate much interest in, prints of seventeenth-century factory owners, or to become enchanted by the rudiments of pottery manufacture before the Industrial Revolution, much less read the typed blurbs beneath each cased exhibit. What interested me much more than the interior of the Gladstone Museum was the contemporary pottery industry as it was carrying on outside in those attached frosty streets. If we must reflect upon nineteenth-century history as passionately as we are beginning to do, then much better to stand on a street corner with a sharp wind or the rain hitting your face; much better to reflect upon the story over the years of a genuine fragment of history, one that might still be functioning before you; much better for your senses to be stimulated by the imagination, to feel living history and rough brickwork in the flesh, than stare blankly at a small model or an illustration. For it is *feeling* that really matters, and nothing can compare with the feeling of walking real streets and staring up at real buildings and thinking about the real world.

I mentioned this to a man inside the museum who was hand-painting some tiny ceramic articles in an ancient workshop, surrounded by the characteristic Potteries aroma of the oil of cloves. (It is said you can still sit on a bus when the pottery factories finish at five, and smell oil of cloves as the work people climb on board.) He directed us to what he described as the oldest street in the Potteries. It was only a few minutes' walk from the museum. It was a tiny cobbled lane, looked onto by a row of little boarded-up terraced houses, several crumbling bottle ovens, and an overgrown and completely derelict pottery. Recently I was asked by a television company to advise on locations for a drama series to be set in one of the old textile towns further north. If they had asked me to advise for a series to be set in the Potteries, that battered old street would have been a perfect start. Standing outside the little houses, each exactly the same size as the one I spent most of my formative years growing up in, you could truly believe how once the smoke from the bottle ovens, which hung menacingly just above the rooftops when they were all still in use, would have virtually blown into your face as you walked out of your front door. Not only did literary celebrities notice this when they passed through the Potteries during their industrial heyday: the older people still living there tell you about it as well, and how, from the surrounding hills, the towns appeared forever to be lost in a smog-bank in the bottom, and your washing was forever peppered with smuts. The pottery down this lane was so derelict it was literally falling to pieces. Its window frames were dangling open, every pane long since smashed. A few pigeons kept circling the necks of the bottle ovens, which had so many weeds growing out of them they almost looked stubbled. Staring up at those ruptured buildings, almost lost to history and the smoky enclosing dusk, the musty smell of decomposing brick percolating in the air, there was no question that there was more of the authentic atmosphere of bottle-ovened pottery manufacture discernible after five minutes standing in that street than all the perfectly preserved potbanks and working exhibits in the nearby museum put together. Because of their natural sense of decomposition, those ruins encouraged the mind to see for *itself* what was no longer actually there. As a consequence they stimulated the creative faculties into considering the meaning of the past in a way a film show in a museum never can or ever will. I suspect that in our voracious appetite for industrial history and the building of award winning museums, we have all of us really missed the point. Museums fill in too many of the gaps from which the sparkle of imagination flickers. Standing there I felt chilled, but I also felt enormously satisfied. As we walked back to the car, as we walked past another sequence of potteries shut down for the weekend, the last few customers driving away from the factory shops and leaving the car parks sombre and empty beneath a distant aircraft from Manchester Airport thundering high overhead, I began talking about the underlying sense of purpose I am convinced this compact area of England still manages to generate. You have to look beyond the scruffy veneer to appreciate it, of course; to comprehend what the ripple of industry does for the soul of the environment. It is an environment that has taken a hammering, but the pulse of life is still there. Just. My father-in-law knows the Potteries like the back of his hand. He has lived there nearly all his life. He was a teacher then an educational advisor in a string of northern schools, some in the Potteries, until the clownish antics of the left-wing rabble running one of the councils with which he was involved caused him to despair so much he decided he was fighting an uphill battle and took early retirement. He has an open mind. But I think he probably thought it a strange observation to make to say that the Potteries still came across as being alive, having just walked through one of their derelict industrial back streets.

The thing is, that street threw the museum and the dreary snobbishness of those feeble-minded literary sentimentalists who have no grasp of the social importance of manufacturing industry into a sharp perspective. Even with hardly a soul about late on that freezing cold Saturday afternoon, with the roof slates and the pavements and the cars now beginning to turn white with frost, the sky fading from a deep orange to an indigo night where it was lowering thickly above the muddle of black chimney-pots, the remaining factories exuded a noticeable sense of stability, knitting together the little network of streets and houses, making the place feel as though it were still economically alive instead of faded and half dead. How easy to glance down one of these squalid side streets during the week, alive to the noise of function, to the clatter of machinery and living people hard at work, and miss such a minor yet crucial detail. How easy to miss it in our arrogant fulminations against uncivilized aesthetics and the ugliness of these drivelling little corners of Britain, irrelevant to the overall social scene. But then we should not be surprised at such blindness, for it is the history of much of our unofficial national outlook really, never mind our official literature.

Made in Staffordshire

Consider, then, why it is that when you go into a café or a restaurant, nine times out of ten when you examine the cutlery it is invariably made in Japan or Korea. Yet nine times out of ten, when you turn over and examine the earthenware from which you are eating and drinking, even in the basest lorry-driver's café, it is invariably still manufactured in England – almost without exception, in one of these little industrial towns in Stoke-on-Trent.

This to me is a very uplifting thought. It means the artificially high value of the pound that has crippled the export and investment potential of British manufacturers, but worked to the advantage of international money dealers and people sitting on warehouses stacked full of imported goods along back streets and on industrial estates everywhere, has not had quite as significant an impact on the pottery manufacturing industry as it has on many others. Throughout much of the 1980s, the high value of the pound and an abundance of revenue from North Sea oil artificially stimulated an ailing British economy and sucked in foreign stocks, with the result that the only people who really benefited were the people who dealt in things, be it money, property, or imported goods – the people of least use, and with the least amount to offer creatively, to the growth in the mind of a people. It seems to me that you are either someone who is productively orientated, or more specifically, someone who is positive and has something to offer society, or you are not. I should say this difference has as much to do with social background, mental development, and emotional maturity – and above all the British class system – as it has to do with basic animal instinct or anything else. There is no question that the latter of these two broad groups has held this country in its grip for generations. It is unquestionable that the economic weaknesses underpinning our industrial performance, the doubtful intellectual abilities of a substantial number of our governing class, and their remarkable knack of misjudging public opinion and making the wrong economic decision, only reflect the continuing situation where the people that go into politics tend to be the people who are furthest away from understanding what it takes to stimulate a modern industrial economy, to comprehend the human framework necessary to make it work. This really explains why the better part of an elected politician's life in this country is spent making excuses. The people who 'go in to politics' generally continue to be the takers rather than the givers; the suppliers and the dealers, the advisers rather than the *de*visers. Unfortunately, it is often the committed manufacturer who suffers most at the behest of policies initiated by people who have little understanding of the requirements of industry – policies initiated by former lawyers and ex-stockbrokers and property speculators and junk-bond accumulators. The more distasteful aspects of the 1980s, the essential childishness of the yuppie syndrome, the sunglassed clowns driving the open-topped cars, the arrogant sun-bathing on cruisers in the middle of the Thames, the hike in house prices and the gormless blurbs, were merely a by-product of this. As social phenomena, as mental priorities, they started at the top and simply filtered downwards. The problem with this country is that for far too long the non-productive mentality has pulled the strings. For too long the *rentier* outlook has triumphed and always called the shots. Any fool knows that sooner or later this situation will have to change, just as any fool knew that sooner or later we should have to make our exports balance our imports, and that all the blah about the 'economic miracle' during the late 1980s, the fallacy of which Peter Jay has so consistently striven to expose, would be revealed to be the hollow bank overdraft, the huge financial con-trick, it really was.

I aired some of these thoughts in the presence of several manufacturers, when I was shown around their factories at length, when I was in the Potteries. All of them were immediately contemptuous of the present government's attitude toward manufacturing, almost without reservation, though it is worth remembering, before it is assumed these northern factories are run by greasy-haired subscribers to the *Socialist Worker*, that some of them were educated men whom you could take it for granted were true-blue to the core. One managing director of a very old firm, who was as English and as ex-public school in his demeanour and sense of composure as you could possibly hope to find, said he thought the present government had set out with an almost deliberate willingness to make manufacturing industry suffer. I said it was more than likely because the present government didn't understand what manufacturing industry even was. And I was told soberly, more than once, that the pottery industry has never really recovered from the recession at the beginning of the 1980s. I listened to the sort of clear-headed economic counselling that made you truly comprehend the breadth of the gulf that exists between some of our humanities dons and literary pontificators, mistaking common sense and common feeling for 'naïvety' with the usual depressing pig-ignorance, who think they know how society ought to be organized, and these modern industrialists who could solve our country's economic problems if the proper business climate was created and they were given a real chance.

It was while I was being shown round the firm of Wood

and Sons by the managing director's son, on the outskirts of Burslem one clear sunny morning, that another reason for the relative economic stability of the pottery industry in Stoke-on-Trent became known to me. As we walked through room after room of crockery and clattering and buzzing and steaming and whirring and a constant blur of activity, we began talking about the region's curiously underlying sense of insularity – to be honest, because of the din, we spent most our time shouting about it – and also about the friendliness of local people, which soon cropped up again. Because the pottery industry *had* remained relatively buoyant, I was told this meant there was a fairly stable workforce, with the consequence, as we have heard so many times before, for generations of families to go into the same occupation, even into the same factories, one after the other, year after year. (In that one pottery alone, there were several generations of the same families, all at work under the same roof.) We spoke to some of that stable workforce that morning, many of whom you could see were concentrating with the urgency of people whose hands are behaving with the skill and endeavour of the genuine craftsman – and, one should remember, craftswoman – people whose hands were relaying skills and sensitivity to brains, and who were only too pleased to stop and explain to us what it was they were doing. As we came into a room where a couple of dozen women were applying transfer papers to some recently fired crockery, and throughout whom a hint of wit rippled before they abruptly fell silent at the presence of a couple of males, I was told that fewer new people had moved into the area, but by the same token, fewer people had moved away in search of other work, as many had been forced into doing elsewhere, once the old industries went into decline. Communities had not been broken up in the Potteries quite as substantially, or been as devastated economically, as much as they had in other parts of the country. These women, I suppose, belonged to one of those communities, and upstairs in another room a little further on, where some young lads were being trained in the art of mould-making, I thought about this again as I glanced through a window and saw, running diagonally to the main wall of the pottery straight across the street, row upon row of little brick terraced houses. They were shining brilliantly in the early morning sunshine, and the spaces between them were filled in with dense black November shadow, so that the effect was like looking across a freshly ploughed field. We were just high enough above the houses to be level with the chimney pots, so that we could see acres of glistening roof slates steaming from the previous night's melting frost, beneath a tangle of television aerials picked out against the clear blue sky. I do not know, and I should doubt very much, if the pottery I was standing in still drew many of its workers from those houses and attached streets. But you can take it for granted that on a rough scale, you are witnessing there an easy intimacy between human beings and their environment, between housing and industry, that is as broadly stable as it has ever been. It is a satisfying intimacy I would like to imagine resembles that which I remember clearly from my own childhood, even if plenty of the people beneath the factory roof behind us come into Burslem from some of the surrounding towns in cars or on buses, rather than walking along the nearby alleyways as they would once have done.

If some of that traditional interaction between industry, environment, and people can still be found in the Potteries, then much of the traditional way earthenware is made has not changed a great deal either. In fact, the essential methods of pottery manufacture have, apart from the introduction of a few superficial pieces of new machinery, some of which is not as sophisticated-looking as you might expect, barely altered for centuries. I do not mean to imply that if you visit the industrial museums that have sprung up across North Staffordshire, such as the Gladstone Museum, or home in on the working demonstrations in the traditional art of hand-throwing some of the bigger firms stage for the benefit of tourists, you come across an antiquated industry that is inflexible, or has failed to move with the times. One of the strengths of the industry today, as is the case with the British textile industry and even the steel industry, is its diversity and its readiness to adapt quickly to smaller, new and changing markets. What I mean is that the way pottery is manufactured on a mass-production scale has remained much the same as it always has, just as the clay from which it is made still comes in its ground form from Cornwall, where it is still mined. It is still mixed with water in large underground vats, then piped through a system of muslin filters under immense hydraulic pressure to relieve it of most of its moisture, before it is squeezed out of a machine in a continuous length, like toothpaste from a tube, ready to be made into cups and saucers and dishes and plates, and another hundred thousand pairs of Staffordshire Dogs. The industry has, of course, suffered from the effects of foreign competition, particularly from Germany and the Far East. The Japanese who, as we all know, are masters at marketing, have made significant inroads into the North American bone china market, for instance, where a substantial chunk of our exports went. But there are still important areas of the earthenware industry which rely on real skill of eye and hand. Mr Edmund Yorke, the owner of Wood and Sons, described this as 'ancillary work', activity that is so labour intensive the finished result cannot be automated and achieved in any other way, and traditional methods cannot really be improved upon.

The theme of genuine talent or lack of it, the influence of family dynasties and their impact or otherwise on Britain's supposed industrial greatness during the Victorian era that had been raised in Bradford, and the roots of our present economic difficulties, recurred constantly during my travels round England. This was especially so during my stay in the Potteries. Not only were some of the old industrialists of North Staffordshire superb businessmen, who knew how to go out and market their products, who amassed power and fortune, and who held considerable influence, they were equally as able to roll up their shirt-sleeves and sculpt a piece of earthenware. They had a genuine eye for design and could go down onto the factory floor and lend a hand to any part of the process, because they were aware of all the processes inside out, having built up their businesses and devised some of those processes from scratch. So I was told.

It was a subject which returned the morning I went down to Twyfords' administration and product development complex, between the main London railway line and the new Queensway bypass at Cliffe Vale. My guide for the better part of the day, which was absolutely pounded with rain throughout, was Mr Gibson, the company's Public Relations Manager, and I have to say he is one of the most charismatic, jovial, and instantly likeable men I have yet met. He was, as we used to say before we all became serious and tried to deny the eccentricities of our common well of Englishness, a real character, an engaging old fashioned character at that, with a slightly drooping face stored up with humorous anecdote, wearing an immaculate grey chequered suit and a black bow-tie. In the firm's museum upstairs I mentioned I was originally from Huddersfield. I was then ushered toward an extremely weighty-looking nineteenth-century ceramic bath, which my guide slapped heartily to emphasise its stolidity. It was so cumbersome it would have been more at home in the palace of an ancient Egyptian pharaoh. The bath was, I was told, once popular among Huddersfield mill owners, at which I projected a picture in my mind of a number of large salubrious houses still brooding in copses around the edges of the town, where these single-cast ceramic vessels would presumably once have been despatched specially to order, and in the dining rooms of which fat would no doubt once have dribbled down chins after stupendous Victorian meals. We examined closely the bath and a variety of sanitaryware going back hundreds of years. Looking at the ornate floral patterns applied to some of the toilet-pots, or 'closet pans' as they are more politely termed, raising your eyebrow at the fine blue roses disappearing into the knee-bends, through which the contents were expelled, it is difficult to believe the Victorians were being anything but sardonic when they decorated ceramics so flamboyantly for the simple act of 'plucking a rose'. I have a rather perverse interest in the design of toilets and bathroom furniture, at the revelation of which I was immediately given a copy of the book which tied in with Lucinda Lambton's television series about public conveniences from a few years ago, to which my guide had been one of many original advisors. He then pointed to a very old oil painting, encased in a heavy gilt frame. It was a portrait of Thomas William Twyford, one of the accepted pioneers in the application of the principles of hygiene to bathroom sanitaryware, and one of the firm's great innovators. 'Now there,' said my guide, eyeing me sternly over the top of his glasses, daring me to look away from the commanding face attached to the wall, 'there was a brilliant man.' You looked at the terse expression staring back at you from the turn of the century and you believed it. 'So often these men built up their empires,' he went on, reflecting upon the wider Potteries, 'they died, and passed their fortunes on to their offspring, who proved to be imbeciles, and who subsequently reduced their father's and a fair chunk of this industrial area's empire to ruins.'

This was not a new story, I said. I had been told the same thing about the children of mill owners in Bradford, and could think of a couple of minor instances myself, having worked in the film industry and come into contact with the offspring of one or two successful names, who otherwise were more or less talentless non-entities. My own theory behind this is that if you are born into a life of moneyed ease, you never have to struggle, never have to hone your brain, or enlarge your mind, with the strength and determination you do if you are not born into a life of ease but strain constantly to achieve anything you desire from birth. (This may or may not be an indication that only in hierarchical societies will the richness of human endeavour increase.) The imbeciles who ruined industrial empires, like the imbeciles who ruin national economies, ruined them simply because they were born complacent and never had to sharpen their perceptions to learn the meaning of common sense. Under such easy circumstances, in such secure social positions, it is easy to grow up arrogant and to remain oblivious to your own pig-headedness; easy to avoid developing a respect for one's fellow human beings, and consequently to descend into stupidity and cultivate a preoccupation with social posturing and the living of a high life. Money can easily make people believe they are something they are not. An abundance of money can blunt the sensibilities of the rich in the same way a shortage of money can destroy the sensibilities of the poor. The decay in the mental ability of the English ruling class, and our economic performance for the better part of a century, has had much to do with this. Whatever her shortcomings, and whatever the more unpleasant social side effects of her policies might have proved to be, at least Mrs Thatcher made an attempt to break the hold of a small body of the English governing class, and its grip on the ebb and flow of modern society. Because she came to grips with the way ordinary people really thought and behaved, she probably got closer to stimulating the potential equality of people in Britain socially – equality of opportunity, that is – than the Labour Party managed in a hundred years. I am not altogether certain if she articulated the thought objectively, because of her nationalist temperament, but Mrs Thatcher did have the wherewithal to understand that the best hope for this country economically was to create a business climate where anybody, irrespective of social background or how they spoke, could conceivably succeed if they had the talent and were prepared to try hard enough. What a pity that she created the wrong kind of business climate and in the process damaged this country's economy for decades to come.

I was driven out through the mist and wet along a succession of dual carriageways to a large industrial estate some eight or nine miles outside the industrial district, to Twyfords' main manufacturing complex at Alsager, where I was taken from one end of the plant to the other. The processes were much the same as those I had seen at Wood and Sons and elsewhere, except that at Twyfords everything was on a much grander scale, and was, of course, concerned with the manufacture of bathroom furniture as opposed to tableware or ornamental fancies. The plant, which has been increased in size gradually over the years since it was opened in 1957, is actually the biggest single factory of its type anywhere in the Western world. This I could believe. There seemed to be miles and miles of buildings, with fluorescent light tubes and a tangle of ducting and metal girders hanging from the ceiling vanishing into an interminable perspective. There was a tremendous and constant bustle of activity, despite the workforce being on a four day week due to the crippling effects of the recession. It was also extremely hot in there. This was winter, and outside it was very cold. But inside the temperature was tropically-inspired, and most of the men were walking about stripped to the waist, or wearing running shorts, or both. In one room a potter was 'fettling' dozens of bathroom sinks, still soft and pliable because they were fresh from the mould – he was scraping away any loose residue with a blade, then wiping them over with a damp sponge – before they were fired. He was handling the grey sinks with tender yet confident dexterity, like a mother handles a baby. Because he had learned to feel the amount of give in the raw clay, he knew precisely how to hold each unit; knew how much pressure each corner could take, and I was told that if I tried to pick one up myself it would almost certainly have collapsed in my hands. In another room we watched dozens of moulds being cracked open. In another we watched men tapping the finished sinks and pedestals with little hammers, then listening to the sound to see if they could detect imperfections. In another we stood and stared at a bank of computer screens linked to the long kilns running through the centre of the factory, toward which computer-guided 'slave cars' were continually driving trolleys loaded with articles waiting to be fired, under the scrutiny of a series of video cameras hanging and blinking from the ceiling. In another room we passed bank after bank of battery moulds that looked like parodies of spinning machines in cotton mills, connected to overhead pipes through which the liquid clay was pumped and found its way from the mixing vats into the casting chambers. Interspersed throughout were miles and miles of little metal trays hanging from a continuously moving conveyor system. These conveyor cars passed round and round, were forever moving in front and behind you, would suddenly lift up, turn corners, cross over each other, then pass directly above your head as they forked and went off in opposite directions, the people working beneath protected by a cage of metal gauze. The trays had a couple of feet between them and looked like miniature ski-lifts, except that where the skier would sit was sat a piece of bathroom furniture on its way through the factory, on its way to be collected by one of the slave cars, en-route to or from the kilns. This was mass-production on a huge scale, so huge thirty-thousand items are produced in that factory each week, every one of them passing through the factory on one of these amusing little conveyor cars. It was an astonishing sight, overwhelming in its intricacy and complexity.

The subject of output returned when I was taken into a quiet room that had about it the air of being away from the general hub of activity. In it we watched a rather awesome new piece of machinery at work. All ceramic bathroom furniture is formed in moulds, usually in the battery moulds I have referred to above. But this new method, called pressure casting, is set to revolutionize productivity, and, inevitably, is a process dependent upon a machine invented by the Japanese. The most labour-intensive aspect of pottery manufacture is the reduction of moisture in the clay prior to firing, and the retention of a stable shape. In the Twyfords plant, this normally takes just over an hour per article. Pressure casting reduces the time down to a mere eight minutes. Straightaway you could see how the machine was affecting the need for man-power, of the need to use *people*, because there was only one man in control of the entire operation and the scale of that operation made him look and no doubt feel diminutive. That was why the room felt so quiet and so empty and away from the run of things. Because it was devoid of people there was no atmosphere. Basically, an immensely powerful hydraulic press extends slowly from the bowels of the machine and crushes the life out of a body of clay, as would a car crusher, pushing it into a mould at the opposite end. As we stood, feebly watching the monster at work, the gleaming chrome hydraulic-ram revealing itself amidst a background of darkened metal casing, I was told that the prospects of such machinery and its effect on labour (in other words, its effect on jobs) and productivity are not merely astonishing, but actually quite terrifying. There was something deeply disturbing, almost revolting, in the way that muscular chrome ram gradually revealed itself, surrounded by the subtle yet awesome gasping of raw mechanical power, like giant air-brakes being released. Fortunately, pressure casting is not easily adaptable to every product, due to the complexity of some of the shapes, so it might not have such a significant impact on Twyfords' seven-hundred employees (over half of whom, from secretaries through to senior management, became shareholders in the company when it was floated five years ago) after all. Even so, we cannot go on replacing human beings with machines like this forever, that is for certain. I suspect that though we are bound to hit major problems, economic as well as social, sometime soon, society will in the end not allow itself to self-destruct, even if it has already lit the fuse.

Afterwards, I was taken for a late lunch in a very good wine bar across the road from the museum back in the centre of Hanley. My guide throughout the day, Mr Gibson the Public Relations Manager with Twyfords, had at one time been very much connected to this museum, which, as one would expect due to its location, houses an immense collection of pottery. Before we ate, we made a whistle-stop tour of the museum, which is an ugly purpose-built building and was the baby of one Arnold Mountford CBE. I had been into the museum a few days previously, and felt to have been staring at so much anonymous earthenware. Much of it is extremely valuable, is superbly crafted, and has interesting history behind it, but the vast majority did not appeal to my own tastes. There was not enough modern pottery on display for my liking. However, when I was whisked around the museum by Mr Gibson I was altogether more impressed. History rolled from his tongue. He spoke about these pieces of pottery as though he were one of the knowledgeable experts on the *Antiques Roadshow*, and parried deftly my criticism about the lack of modern design evident by reminding me, as everyone does in the Potteries who talks about the Hanley museum, that what is on display is only a fraction of the complete collection stored elsewhere. Millions of homes throughout Britain will have small ceramic animals standing on their mantlepieces or on top of their television sets. Perhaps with the slight exception of the pale-green or blue pieces – usually caricatured rabbits, or dogs – produced by the now defunct firm of Sylvac, I would not display such things in my own home. But when you are shown round a museum by someone bursting with enthusiasm for a part of England where he has grown up and made a life in this most traditional of industries, when you are shown a collection of perhaps several hundred ceramic dogs, all of them proudly donated from a single collection for the benefit of the Potteries and our national heritage, all of them produced in the little towns spreading out from the epicentre of that spotlit gallery in a museum, frankly you cannot fail but be impressed. You look at those dogs and mentally you project a sort of newsreel in the mind's eye of the history of these little pottery towns. You see their narrow streets, their back alleys, the old bottle ovens being detonated, the new corrugated sheds going up, the cobbles shining in the wet, in a flash. Most of the cobbles have now gone. A number of young kids break into the tiny brick houses up and down the sloping streets to steal valuable Royal Doulton figures displayed on windowsills by unsuspecting old ladies, to barter them for drugs money. Some of the youths even take the trouble to travel down from Liverpool to enjoy the privilege of stealing a small segment of North Staffordshire history. You see the little corner shops selling oatcakes – a delicious local delicacy – which are a sort of cross between a pancake and a chapatti, and which astonished me by their cheapness when I first bought some at an oatcake stall in Burslem market. I have said it once but I will say it again so that the point is driven home: if you look deeply enough you see something more to these old industrial towns than first meets the eye.

I think the reason I took so strongly and so easily to the Potteries is that they reminded me of the industrial suburbs where I spent the better part of my life growing up. I found myself saying to a number of people, as I found myself saying again in that wine bar over lunch in front of a roaring coal fire, that if I had to describe the Potteries in a phrase, it would be to say that they seem to have stood still somewhere at about the year 1975. I do not mean to imply anything negative by saying that, or that everyone still staggers about in platform shoes and wears bell-bottomed jeans and listens to Bay City Rollers records. What I mean is there seemed to me to be a sense of stability remaining there; a stability that has completely vanished in so many other areas; a process that began to accelerate toward the end of the 1970s. I do not think I exaggerate when I say there is still something of a working relationship between people and industry in the Potteries, imbuing the environment with what to me is an all-important sense of purpose and of life. I am no longer a part of such an environment myself. The one I experienced during my youth was devastated ten or fifteen years ago and has changed forever. Several days ago, I walked through it again for the first time in a long while, and was aware once more of the dreadful silence hanging in the air above the patches of waste ground scraped clean of industry and covered in weeds. I was aware of the almost unnatural sound of leaves and trees rustling in the fresh summer breeze, where once they would have blended with the hum of looms. But here, here in North Staffordshire, something of the sound and smell of that original essence remains. The ordinary people there have not yet been completely defeated by the illogical workings of an economic system they do not understand. The women I talked to in the pottery factories laughed the same catty laughter, and exchanged the same coarse-grained jokes, as the women who worked in the textile mills I used to go into as a youngster. It is the humour and laughter of fairly stable industry, of people living in a community that has not yet had the life irrevocably stamped out of it. It is laughter still embellished by the ring of hope.

And here, I think, one gets to the heart of why the essential friendliness of ordinary people is such a marked characteristic of the Potteries. Throughout the time I was there, I was aware of a curious feeling of *déjà vu*, not only because of the comparisons I have made with my own beginnings above. I should be more precise and say that I became aware of this feeling much later, when I read through what J.B. Priestley had written about the area when he was there sixty years before on his own *English Journey*, having purposefully avoided doing so until I was away from the region altogether. He said that nowhere else in England did he see people working in factories that looked more contented than these Potteries folk. Neither did I. They were, and they still are, enlarging their personalities through a craft requiring skill and personal judgement, not leaving their personalities behind and clocking confrontationally in to a job of drudgery and boredom, manipulated by tired union officials. They are still, to my amazement, on piece-work after all this time, which probably has the effect of keeping them alert and preventing them falling 'asleep at the switch'. Because it is a traditional manufacturing industry, it might amuse the likes of Norman Macrae, but because these people have found an outlet for their productive, and to a substantial extent, their creative energies, they do not regard their work as so much toil exchanged for a wage at the end of a week, but an expression of themselves. In Priestley's day, the pottery factories were mainly small family concerns, where the employers knew their workforces by their

Christian names. From what I saw and heard, they still are and they still do. As a result of all these things, I was told confidently by more than one managing director that labour troubles in the pottery industry were rare – something Priestley was told, to my amazement, when he was there. No doubt the picture I have painted of the Potteries is rather more rosy than it ought to be, and I have avoided discussing the unemployed. It is probably ludicrous to suggest that a trade, which before the war had over eight-hundred pottery firms registered in Stoke-on-Trent and today has less than two-hundred, is anywhere near as buoyant as it was. But I am told that many of these smaller firms were swallowed up in takeovers and the management of some of those that remain assured me they were fairly optimistic about the future. And it is plain to see that, though the Potteries have suffered, the chief industry there is still such an integral part of the region's compound structure as to have a profound impact on the look and feel of the area. So much so that it is possible to make generalizations about it that are almost impossible to make convincingly anywhere else in the country today.

To me it is vitally important to grasp the positive aspects of the Potteries and get them into the proper perspective, rather than moan on familiarly about the blight of dereliction and decay, or talk to the nearest unemployed person moping in a corner in a pub. It is the positive aspects of the area which remain that manage to suggest the Potteries are now a unique region of England from which we could learn a great deal. To people who appreciate that there is more to the purpose of human existence than indulging in a sort of lazy art gallery urchin's pious contemplation of life, laced with smug-faced bluster – and I met people who could appreciate it, dozens of them, when I made this journey – these small towns represent more than piles of freshly packed earthenware, account books, and invoices. They indicate the sense of cohesion and purpose manufacturing industry is capable of imbuing into a society, when people are united in a common productive enterprise, working to the betterment of the common ground, if their minds are being allowed to work, once the confrontational attitudes – the 'them and us' syndrome – between workforce and employer have been eliminated. I am not dragging up socialist ideals here. The educated Marxists who perceive working-class people to be pawns ruthlessly manipulated by scheming capitalists are simply naïve people who probably have some kind of neurotic grudge against society, linked to their own failures, and do not understand how ordinary mortals really think, react, and behave. Though they may be strongly independent and often reactionary in outlook, ordinary people are not interested in controlling their own destiny politically through workers' dictatorships. The scruffy fools who blather through megaphones outside bus stations about obliterating the capitalist dictatorship really mean that they want to control the working class through their own dictatorship, and force society to conform to their own narrow aesthetic view, just as a ridiculous minority of sexual deviants try to convince themselves their own way of life is superior to everybody else's. Without ever turning the thought consciously over in their minds, most ordinary people know by instinct that all a workers' revolution would lead to ultimately would be the replacement of one ruling elite by another. They know that any political power unit will always end up defending its own vested interests, and that the corrupting effect of power means that political solutions will always be about the playing off of one bunch of inadequates against another; about the measuring of the material advantages proffered by one as opposed to the other. It seems to me that more than a fair sprinkling of ordinary people have a shrewd understanding that the terminal economic problems festering away at the heart of this country's affairs are a result of incompetency and plain bad management, not predetermined scheming by the English upper classes. This is why many of them have the ability to laugh at extremists and to appreciate the crudity of jokes too offensive to be aired on television, yet manage to retain affection for the Royal Family. What they want is a secure job, a decent roof over their heads, and a bit of spare cash to enjoy a reasonable amount of recreational activity. Millions of them are proud enough to feel they would like to obtain this through their own independent efforts. And before a number of our more enlightened souls express horror at such patronizing words, remember that, in the name of moderation, in the name of

God, and in the name of sanity, if one thinks about it, these things are all that most people want, irrespective of social background.

If we must have capitalism, then give us the kind of capitalism that creates a business climate that enables the most able minds to surface and exert the strongest influence; where there is pride put back into productivity and inventing; where the banks and industry and the colleges and universities work together intelligently instead of against one another cynically; where the economic benefits filter down rather than filter through tax-fiddles away; where once and for all there is a restoration of proper national pride, instead of a useless wheeler-dealing attitude to life that implodes the moment it becomes clear the impetus behind it is so much bloated nationalistic flatulence, ringing to the hollow sound of financial jiggery-pokery, when the economic *fatwa* comes back like a boomerang and everything begins to collapse likc a pack of cards.

6

The West Midlands

Motorway City

I came away from the Potteries early one very frosty morning and made my way down the old A34, for about fifty miles, toward Birmingham. The road was surprisingly though agreeably traffic free, to say it was a weekday morning. This seemed strange, even at nine o'clock. It could almost have been a Sunday. The A34 was once the main artery from Staffordshire down to Birmingham, before the M6 was built during the 1960s. I suppose the reason it was as deserted as it was when I drove over it was that most of the traffic had abandoned it and was today congesting the M6 several miles away, at the opposite side of rolling fields, speckled appealingly with farmhouses and spreading out in typical Midlands fashion over to my right.

Once I was through Stafford, then the disjointed accumulation of tower blocks, cubes, and squares scattered haphazardly around a circumnavigatory road system describing themselves as the town of Walsall, it did not take me long to reach the outskirts of Birmingham. For some time, the main body of the city was outlined mistily on the horizon several miles distant, lifting beyond a seemingly interminable expanse of suburban roof and tree tops spread out up ahead. The traffic remained quite light, even when I had broken through the outer ring of the city limits and started to negotiate the long dual carriageway plunging through a succession of underpasses and flyovers

– at one point, I passed the Saddam Hussein mosque (the construction of the building was financed by Iraq), which during the Gulf War remained surprisingly graffiti-free – right up into the city centre itself. The reason the traffic remained light was that most of it which was homing in towards the city from the north would be in the process of being swung round and funnelled into the centre from the south, courtesy of Birmingham's legendary motorway network; an aspect of the city I am usually anxious to avoid.

Birmingham is not my favourite city. It would not be an exaggeration to say that Birmingham is not many people's favourite city, chiefly because of the sheer, astonishing ugliness of the city centre, and also because of its notorious inner ring-road system. They tell you when you are in Birmingham that if you know where you are going, then the ring-road system works extremely well (they say the same thing in Leeds); but if you don't know where you are going, then that is probably the foundation of why you take such an instant dislike to the place. This seems to me to be a realistic supposition, for in no other city in England have I ended up wasting so much time taking the wrong turning or the wrong exit from roundabouts, and arriving late for meetings, as I have done when using these multi-lane carriageways in Birmingham. They are a dominating feature of the Birmingham city landscape. Wherever you are the roads seem to be of an unusually large width, an observation which you might pass off as being a touch psychological in origin, were it not linked to the speed you feel you have to move along at mentally to keep up with the flow of traffic that is forever coursing along them. Whichever direction you approach Birmingham from, you soon come into contact with these horrendous eight lane roads that have four lanes aimed in one direction, and four lanes aimed in the other. What is especially unnerving, particularly when the traffic is busy (in its own way this is also darkly amusing) is that if you are on one side of one of these carriageways, the traffic from the inner two lanes is invariably trying to cross over to the outer two lanes, the traffic from the outer two lanes invariably trying to cross over to the inner. You feel like you are caught up in some madhouse of lunatic drivers, an awareness that is probably not as far from the truth as it might at first sound. We have most of us had our hearts in our mouths at one time or another, when driving along a normal stretch of motorway, when comes the uneasy moment where you are travelling at speed in the outside lane, and the cars gushing down the slip road merely indicate as they accelerate toward the main flow, expecting you to move over to enable them to join the stream of traffic without them having to slow down at the white dotted line. If the motorway is busy, and you cannot immediately move over, there can be a tense few seconds when you are afraid to brake because of the vehicles driving too close behind, and are unable to move over to the middle lane because of the cars speeding alongside.

This sort of thing seems to be happening constantly on the multi-lane carriageways in Birmingham. What makes it worse is the frequency of the junctions, so that there is a steady stream of vehicles constantly jostling for space. Normal busy motorways feel civilized in comparison. At times, especially during the Birmingham rush-hour periods, the speed of the traffic becomes so fast-paced it actually becomes farcical. There can be no serious justification behind such absurd race-track behaviour, except that drivers are simply brutalized beyond reproach. You wonder not only what on earth you are caught up in, but on a more philosophical scale, what on earth the human race is doing with itself, struggling like this, haggling for territorial rights, all in the name of social mobility and the supposed functioning of a modern economy. What prompts the fierce clashing of territories much of the time on the ring road in Birmingham is the way the outer two lanes will suddenly rise up to enable traffic to leave the carriageway at the next roundabout, beneath which the inner two lanes continue their forward plunge, into an underpass and the seeming abyss. Then, as the ribbed-concrete and pebble-dash retaining walls that are holding the roundabout up above you are blurring past, you are no sooner out the other side into daylight again than the outer two lanes bringing the traffic down from the roundabout are trailing in at speed to meet you, like something from a child's Scalextric track. If you do not know where you are going, and you are being forced to travel at speed to keep up with the flow and not collide with the traffic filing in toward the jetstream alongside, you can easily overshoot the point where the outer two lanes rise up again to deposit vehicles at the next elevated roundabout, and miss your exit entirely. This is especially so when the vehicles surging up behind you *do* know where they are going, and they immediately jump into the space you were hoping to fill.

All of this happened on my very first day in Birmingham when I was there for the purposes of writing this book, so that I was aggravated before I had decently settled into a hotel. I completely lost my bearings at one point, in the midst of an unspeakable morass of converging and diverging traffic. The next moment I was heading away from the city through a hideous prefabricated concrete cutting, beneath an array of blue overhead destination gantries flickering stroboscopically overhead, which informed me I was now heading out toward the motorways. This happened so quickly, with such finality, there was a stupid moment when it felt as though I had finished my business in the city and was actually leaving, when I was supposed to be only just arriving. Then, sooner than it was possible to think, travelling at that velocity amidst such a dangerous surge of traffic, I was being raised up on concrete pillars and swung round, inevitably, onto the preposterous tangle of elevated tarmac known as Spaghetti Junction, laid out up ahead against the pale afternoon sky. From that angle, as I tore in toward it, it looked more like some kind of children's play-track slotted together than a construction seriously instigated by municipal committees and a Department of Transport. Seen in the flesh, seen down at eye level, Spaghetti Junction never seems quite as ominous as the legends that grew up around it during the 1970s made it out to be. It is also smaller than you would expect. The aerial photographs you see of it on the postcards on sale in the souvenir shops in Birmingham, and the aerial shots that appear from time to time on television news bulletins, suggest it covers a much larger area than it actually does. Spaghetti Junction seems to me to be not so much an appalling sight as an utterly ridiculous one. Perhaps to appreciate its true significance aesthetically, it has to be remembered that it was a product of the same cultural atmosphere that gave us the disgusting sense of design masquerading as popular taste in this country around twenty years ago.

Nevertheless, one thing is for certain: if you are coming to Birmingham for the first time, and you negotiate Spaghetti Junction because you are approaching from the south instead of the north, as I did, and you see up ahead the swaggering jumble of tower blocks making up the bulk of the city centre standing sharply against the sky, you are definitely prepared for the air of the place, of that there can be little doubt. Birmingham has long marketed itself as the motorway city, and the implication from this is that it considers the reputation that has followed with considerable pride. But an off-shoot of this has been the ugly, big city, slightly mad, Greco-Spanish sort of automobile jostling that has become such a hallmark of the character of the city today. This seems to suit the feel of modern Birmingham, for it feels to me like no other city in the country; something that would not be such a bad thing were it not that so often it is for all the wrong reasons. When you approach it from Spaghetti Junction, especially if you have just been forced to turn round and contemplate it from that angle completely against your will as I had, you know you are being drawn into the swirling vortex of big city tension, just as you do in certain areas of London. There is something big and noisy and substantial about Birmingham; something mean and abrasive and inhuman and slightly uncivilized, like the bloated faces, glistening with sweat, one associates with stock-market haggling. The city looks assertive. It is ugly, but ugly in a boisterous way that is manifestly *arrogant*. When you are up in the thick of it you can feel it crowding in upon you. It is completely lacking in charm, of course. But to me what is so distinctive about Birmingham architecturally – and by saying this, I am not saying for one moment that I approve of it – is that you cannot deny that the place looks *impressive*, if one interprets the word 'impressive' as it is defined in the *Oxford English Dictionary* (to mean something that is powerful or exciting), instead of the way it is usually applied inaccurately in everyday English speech – to indicate that one is responding to something favourably.

There is no mistaking that Birmingham is an important

St George's Hall, Liverpool

Back Streets of Blackburn

above: No Pictures Please. Burnley *below:* Pennine Moors

left:
Yorkshire Dales

below:
Colne, Lancashire

Quayside, Newcastle-upon-Tyne

left:
Grainger Street,
Newcastle

below:
View Down the Tyne

Little Germany, Bradford

Bradford Textile Mills

Bradford Textile Workers

Halifax

Industrial Stoke-on-Trent

Rural Stoke-on-Trent

The Oasis,
Meadowhall

Birmingham Skyscraper

Sheffield Patriot

left:
Royal Pavilion,
Brighton

below:
Village Lane
near Norwich

Basingstoke

left:
Cirencester

below:
Lavenham,
Suffolk

city, no mistaking it at all. What is more mystifying is your understanding that, theoretically, it was the same species of creature that built it as built our twelfth-century cathedrals and much of our best classical architecture, when the closest thing we had to mechanical automation was a simple block-and-tackle.

This is Birmingham

I had been to Birmingham before, several times in fact. I had done a small amount of business with a firm in one of the city's industrial suburbs that is connected to the electro-plating trade, for which Birmingham is known (chromium plating was invented there), and was on speaking terms with the two proprietors. I had also enjoyed a bird's-eye view of the city from the top floor of the Birmingham office belonging to the company for which my wife once worked, and had time to consider on more than one occasion that it possessed one of the ugliest panoramas to be found anywhere. From the top floor of an office block, Birmingham looked to be a rambling mass of grey, prefabricated non-descriptiveness, just as it appeared to be when you were a dozen or so stories down below on the ground, hemmed in among the crush of buses and traffic. So many places can be dismissed as ugly, and there is nothing much else that can be said about them. Not much follows in the way of thought process or evaluation. The ugliness of Sheffield, for instance, is simply an ugliness, a compendium of architectural disjointedness and bad planning that appears in places to have been scattered across the surface of the city like chicken-feed strewn across a farmyard. But the impact of its unevenness tends to be mitigated by the Pennine hills rising gently around it. Birmingham does not have this kind of elevated background scenery to soften the blandness of its urban contour-line. This enables another quality to surface, the one that is really responsible for the air of architectural vulgarity many people find offensive when contemplating Birmingham. Because the central part of the city is spread across the face of a shallow hill, it is lifted up slightly and is more starkly outlined against the sky. There is no clutter of distant suburbs filling in the gaps between the buildings. As a consequence, Birmingham has always seemed to me to resemble more than any other English city I know the long distance shots you used to see on the opening credits to those dreadful American soap-operas that were popular several years back, where a jumble of skyscrapers elbowed one another for attention on the skyline, the clouds reflected across acres of mirror-finished glass; and the great freeways, swirling with traffic, swept toward them as perspective lines sweep toward a vanishing point. Birmingham, in its modest English way, is rather like this. It may be scattered piecemeal and conform to no controlled sense of pattern, unlike some of those much vaster American cities. But you find it difficult to escape the interesting feeling that the essential haphazardness of it all, has somehow not been deliberately *planned*.

Much has been said and written about the architecture of Birmingham, of course. The architecture of Birmingham is, in fact, considered to be something of a national stock joke, and was so long before the Prince of Wales made his famous attack on the Bull Ring Centre and the appalling Central Library, putting the city on the defensive, some years back. It is, however, not enough merely to talk negatively about the Bull Ring Centre, dismiss Birmingham as being ugly and be done with it. You have to look deeper. For something I cannot recall having heard mentioned about the feel of the city is the underlying sense of energy you perceive bound up with the slabs of dirty concrete straining skywards, if you stand back and look hard enough. To an extent, you can perceive the same sort of thing in nearly any major city in the country. But in Birmingham, as an essence, it feels to be uniquely concentrated. When you stand and look at Birmingham, you seem to perceive tower blocks and nothing else. From only a mile or two distant, it is possible to take in the whole of the city centre in a single glance, something you cannot do with London, for instance, because of its size and the way it sprawls. Wherever you are situated on the outskirts of Birmingham, whichever direction along whichever main road or railway line you approach it from, whether you catch sight of it between trees, or through the gaps between buildings as you climb into your car out in the suburbs, whether you are up in front of it among the crowds circulating around New Street Station and the Bull Ring Centre, that distinctive jumble of closely grouped modern high-rise is piled powerfully and dominatingly on the horizon-line, like a string of huge prefabricated concrete exclamation marks at the end of another great architectural sentence. The brashness seems so absolute it is almost stifling. This is the secret to Birmingham's architectural and aesthetic distinction.

Notwithstanding Birmingham's intensely self-conscious aesthetic reputation, or its attempt to seemingly burlesque and sanctify the meaning of modernism by once deliberately bulldozing itself wholesale architecturally, there are some good buildings remaining. After I had booked into The Grand on Colmore Row, I went back out and walked to the top of the street, to the point where it opens out into Victoria Square, now free of traffic, in the central part of the city, and had a look at some of them. As you walk down the side of the Town Hall, more or less a Roman temple mounted on a rugged Corinthian-columned podium, and which holds the unusual distinction of having been designed by the same man who invented the hansom cab, you capture something of the strong spirit of independence for which the city was always known, and of its nineteenth-century reputation for pioneering achievements in municipal administration; one that produced the first town planning scheme in Britain. (This is strangely ironic, considering the hash it was to make of its own planning years hence.) Adjacent is the dominating bulk of the Council House and the adjoining Art Gallery and Museum, distinguished for its collection of Pre-Raphaelite paintings, and which that afternoon I did not linger over because it was alive with parties of noisy school children who appeared to think they had been let loose in a gymnasium. Running all the way up from The Grand to the old Post Office building at the top is a long and impressive line of elderly architecture which, while I was there, like the impressive portico of the council headquarters, was in the process of being sandblasted and restored behind a tangle of scaffolding and tarpaulins, sometimes issuing banging and drilling till quite late at night. This grandiose impression was, unfortunately, rather short-lived when I found myself guided round the front of the Council House by a series of protective hoardings into the adjoining Chamberlain Square. It was so long since I had examined the notes I made during the Prince of Wales' television documentary about architecture that I had completely forgotten his attack on Birmingham's Central Library, or indeed what the building looked like at all. Chamberlain Square is also pedestrianized. Central to it is the Chamberlain Memorial Fountain, a structure that, if you have tears blurring your eyes from the wind as I had when you stand and stare at it, resembles the top half of a Gothic church tower that has been set into concrete. Behind it curves a steady gradient of shallow concrete steps, so that the entire space forms a natural amphitheatre. Backing on to it is the rear section of the Town Hall, and at the other side, the Council House and Art Gallery. Behind the steps sits a bulging concrete monstrosity resembling a short flight of giant concrete stairs tipped upside down, breathtaking in its simple vulgarity. The contrast it creates against the small oasis of the nineteenth century loosely grouped around it is so violent, as you look at it you begin to doubt your own convictions. Good sense tells you it is a ridiculous spectacle. But because the clashing created is as pronounced as it is, you could misinterpret your reactions and begin to believe there is actually something anarchically appealing about it.

Because of its proximity to a gathering of weighty Victorian civic building, at first I assumed the building was another incidence of municipal architecture gone desperately wrong. I walked inside it, having not the slightest idea what purpose it served, mainly because of the volume of people who looked to be walking innocently in and out of the entrance, suggesting that it might be some kind of public place, perhaps a Hayward Gallery-type exhibition hall. To my amazement I discovered, when I inquired, that I was standing inside the Central Library. This was not obvious, not obvious at all, and at first I assumed a cryptic inference to the shallow architectural merit of much of modern Birmingham was being aired, as opposed to what one normally expects to derive from the content of intelligent books. Opening up before me was a large open area, not unlike the central atrium to a modern shopping mall, called 'Paradise Forum'. Placed at strategic intervals throughout, creating a ludicrous contrast to the building's utilitarian fabrication, were a number of mock-Greek columns and crumbling porticoes, alongside which were standing what remain in my memory as papier-mache statues. Surrounding them were craft stalls, people selling little artifacts from brightly-painted market barrows, and one man drawing charcoal portraits, so that the space gave a vague implication it might have been another of those places that have had a brief glance at Covent Garden. The Prince of Wales, describing the building, I take it, from the outside, said it resembled an incinerator in which to burn books, rather than a place in which to house them. That is an observation which is entirely accurate. (Or at any rate it is so externally and aesthetically: ergonomically, the building might function very well indeed.) You cannot see a single book in the place when you are down in the atrium of the 'Paradise Forum'. You do not feel that ache for information and knowledge welling inside you that the sight of row upon row of books in libraries – not in bookshops: never in bookshops – normally evokes. It is the constant sense of clutter, of things continually obtruding into your vision, that is such a striking characteristic of Birmingham. If there is any characteristic about the place to be highlighted at all, it is that it seems to be completely unco-ordinated.

And so it was in here, inside one of its buildings as well as out. Everything clashed in this outlandish interior, this theatre of the tasteless and the absurd. There was the concrete building, filled with tubular hi-tech Pompidou Centre-type girders, the essence of ancient Greece, traditional hand-painted wooden barrows straight from the Portobello Road, and to top it all, an ultra-modern American-style ice-cream parlour-cum-sandwich bar. I ate my lunch in that café, and the wiry youth who waited on me approached brandishing something I had not seen before; something which perhaps illustrates clearer than anything the at times hilarious, though behind the comical aspect the deadly serious, way advanced technology is gnawing away at the most elementary of human tasks – he was holding an electronic note-pad. It would appear that very soon it will not be necessary for the human organism to master the art of holding a pen any more. Rather than taking my order down by hand in the usual way, the youth stroked an electronic instrument over a device that resembled an office calculator, which he detached from his belt. I asked him what on earth he was doing. He told me that the pen relayed an electronic signal across to the cash register, where the customer's invoice was printed out automatically, presumably to reduce the potential for error. It was difficult not to laugh at such electronic gimmickry, though to be honest I had already been highly amused ever since I had walked into the 'Paradise Forum', if not since I had driven into the entire city.

I was brought back down to earth that afternoon when I crossed over from one English social reality straight into another: I drove out to talk with the leader of the Birmingham Baptist Inner City Project (BBICP), at its headquarters in a beautiful little brick church down at Balsall Heath, where there is some good work being done to help some of the poorest people in the city. Balsall Heath sounds as though it might be a pleasant enough quarter. Though the feel of the area is the feel of inner city areas everywhere, with busy main roads, a muddle of disjointed architectural Victoriana, cheap shops, and looming perpetually as a backcloth, the canvas of tower blocks and industrial estates surrounded by a saturnine scribble of searchlights and video-surveillance cameras, there was an abundance of mature trees lining the main road I drove along to reach it, softening the approach. Some of the older housing stock, its brickwork glowing beautifully in the afternoon sun, looked very good indeed; and along the main street there was a handful of magnificent nineteenth-century buildings, admittedly fraying now, one of them housing, in a dingy back room, an Afro-Caribbean association where I stopped to ask for directions. But Balsall Heath is actually a very deprived area, and throughout most of the past ten years, the city's Baptist denomination has been attempting to boost community relations there, alleviate some of the more unpleasant social consequences of impoverishment in inner urban areas, and attract greater numbers of people to join the faith. There are a dozen churches involved in the project – I saw a handful scattered right across Birmingham – and they are all situated in the poorest quarters of the city, some designated as being among the most impoverished in the country. There are the usual social problems associated with these areas, high unemployment, drug addiction, homelessness, domestic violence, and sub-standard housing. Crime is commonplace, part of the social fabric. When I arrived, and said I had made a brief exploration of the area on foot, there seemed to be a moment of genuine surprise when I said that, no, I had not been stopped in the street and offered drugs. That is the kind of place that Balsall Heath is. It seems to be accepted as fairly routine that you should encounter vice, rather as you would notice the sun shining outside during a heatwave. At night the shops are armour-plated, and, in addition to the other social problems the area has, as if those were not enough, it happens to be one of the city's busiest red-light districts. On the way there, I stopped off at the electro-plating firm I have already referred to, to see how the owners were keeping (business was terrible), and to ask for directions to Balsall Heath. When I mentioned the name of a particular road it had been recommended I head for over the telephone by the Urban Missioner at the BBICP, my electro-plating friends instantly erupted into bittersweet laughter, nearly spilling their cups of tea. That road, it seems – to someone as unfamiliar with the city as I was, as had already happened to me up in Middlesbrough – is generally acknowledged to be *the* place to search for girls offering themselves for hire. If only it were possible to find such streets and such social realities and an assortment of people renting out their sexual organs by the hour truly so amusing.

It is bodies such as the Baptist Union that have been making a serious attempt to break the social deadlock hanging over these places and give the poor people assembled there encouragement and hope. There is a tendency to assume that anything with the words 'inner city' in its official title must automatically be council or government funded, as had been the case with the Asian community centre I had visited in Burnley. This is often not the case at all, which is why the activities of a number of secular religious groups (here I suppose one can include the Salvation Army, which has generally kept its hands free of the dirt of politics and done much good work for the disadvantaged of Britain), are often vastly worthier causes than the squalid little petitions established by left-wing councils and a crowd of jeering pressure groups, that have as their real motivation the thumbing of noses at the philosophy of the current government. What I found remarkable about the BBICP – this is why I want to give it some space – is that the project's funding is derived almost entirely from congregational donations. They have obviously liaised with the city council, in particular over the projected site of a new community, training, and rehabilitation centre across the road, that has not advanced beyond the discussion stage for five years because there is not the money available to purchase the land. It is very difficult for independent organizations to work successfully with councils unless they possess substantial resources to begin with, which the Baptists unfortunately do not. Broader funding has been provided by the West Midlands Baptist Association, and, I believe, the selling of church property; but the majority injected into the establishment I saw had been raised through the offertory after services in some of the more prosperous parts of the city. I am not a religious man in any way, but I have to say that if I ever found myself developing a theological compunction, I would be more than happy to think that it might enable me to join up with people such as these Birmingham Baptists. There is something rather humiliating in coming upon such people – humiliating in that it forces you to come to terms with the feebleness of your own selfish preoccupations – something almost moving when you contemplate the work they do and their outlook on life. I couldn't help becoming aware that I was a fairly comfortable human being who would find it difficult to get involved in such schemes because I am always too busy, as are most of the people I mix with, even when we think we have a realistic social awareness and shrewd understanding of life. That is really only another way of saying we are too much concerned with ourselves. Yet these church people make the time, something that must surely entail a certain amount of devotion and self-sacrifice and genuine response to the plight of the less fortunate imposing on their private lives and aspirations, not just the dropping of a few coppers into an envelope when the woman calls from Christian Aid.

How many of us are seriously prepared to do this? I am intensely sceptical of many charities. Because they generally play on the sentimental feelings of the fortunate, though they do obvious good, I do wonder if many of them sometimes exacerbate the problems they set out to solve and continually diffuse the flashpoint that might be reached necessitating political intervention, thereby indirectly ensuring genuine solutions will never materialize at all. But the most immediately striking thing about people such as these I met in the inner city landscape of Birmingham, quite apart from their straightforward decency, is the obvious lack of political motivation in what they have set themselves up to do. They simply wish to help people less fortunate than themselves. Think what you think about religion: the benevolent nature of their activities is humanitarian and entirely voluntary. It takes courage and determination, and as usual with anything voluntary that attempts to make inroads into the tragedy of human suffering, it suffers from a chronic shortage of funding and gives the impression that it is only just managing to make ends meet. Not many people are interested in what is going on, because there is no immediately obvious commercial gain to be had, only longer term social gain (from which sound commercial gain would come), which is generally not worth tuppence. When I was there some young unemployed lads were playing pool in a small youth club housed in an annex at the side of the church. There were some shelves lined with worn paperback books of the popular sort, some posters, and a few old chairs, but you could see at a glance that everything in the room had probably been scraped together with difficulty. But it was working. As I left, a number of youngsters, all of whom were black, were homing in toward it along the street outside, beneath a ruler-straight row of terraced houses plunging now toward the deepest winter dusk. What kind of Birmingham would they be growing up to inherit? One where social accomplishment for the dispossessed is measured primarily in terms of drug pushing and ram-raiding? I think what truly startled me about the outlook these young people had on life, though in reality it was beginning to startle me less and less because of the frequency with which I was encountering it, was the way in which they take it for granted that unemployment is part of the natural scheme of things, as though it were just another piece of furniture sitting in the corner of a room.

Are the positive efforts being made by groups like the Birmingham Baptists the kind of thing the official Birmingham is keen to associate itself with? Are the organizers likely to feature in news year's honours lists? This is not a frivolous question. Elsewhere, I spoke to a smart young woman working in an executive capacity within one of the city's development agencies, when I spent a morning looking over Aston's ultra-modern science park. That was a very different environment indeed from the traditional heavy metal-bashing industry Birmingham I had purposefully avoided; the Birmingham which, to cite one of the creakiest guidebook cliches of them all, was always regarded as the 'city of a thousand trades', where it was claimed you could have anything made, from cars to bicycles to jewellery to screws. (That claim will soon be transferred via our exploitation to China, while our own dole queues lengthen and a number of our comfortable economic commentators damn the social and international consequences.) The woman I talked to is highly-qualified, educated, well-paid, and in no position to harbour left-wing grudges. She lives with her husband in one of the area's more affluent suburbs. But she profoundly believed that the city was publicizing only the image it wanted people to see. She thought such a philosophy could in the longer run generate adverse reactions. Some friends of hers had visited the city, having become familiar with the 'Big Heart of England' Birmingham emphasised in its promotional literature; the Birmingham marketing itself as a centre for international excursions; the up and coming Birmingham that enticed the Royal Ballet to establish its base of operations there; the Birmingham of the National Exhibition Centre, vast pop concerts, and Cadbury World; the Birmingham cocking a snook at London. But her friends baulked at the place when they arrived. They were shocked and revolted at the run-down nature of the vast ring of suburbs clinging to the hub of the much publicized city of commercial opportunity, all of them carefully deleted from its glossy publicity material. As a criticism, this was general, I said, and had formed the hook upon which I had disseminated much of the emerging post-industrial nostalgia in a book I had already written about the north of England. It is not only race horses that sometimes wear blinkers. But if this compartmentalization of Birmingham by the people running it is true, then I do not think one can really believe it is deliberate. Birmingham, like nearly everywhere provincially, is trying, and trying damned hard. If there are failings to be observed then that is because the dynamo behind the noisy renaissance of Birmingham, after it lost nearly a quarter of a million jobs when its heavy-industrial manufacturing base was devastated, is the modern prosperous outlook of comfortable English people, closing themselves unconsciously off from unpleasant realities, not necessarily because they do not want to be shoved up against realities that might throw into question the foundation of much that they hold precious as a culture, but because they are simply too busy getting on with the business of running their own affairs. The prosperity they are capable of generating ought to work to the city's advantage as a whole. At least that is the dubious theory. Unfortunately, the side effect of the compartmentalization of our perceptions and of reality is that it does help to promote a false, almost fanciful picture of society, one of the results of which is bogus publicity material popularizing cities. It obscures truth, which each and every one of us should struggle against if we value our individual liberties, because if we do not, sooner or later it might not only catch up with us, but catch up with a vengeance. The more I saw as I travelled around the country, the more I became aware of the festering seeds of corruption, municipal, political, societal, and mental; and of the importance organized crime is going to play, American-style, in the running of our municipal affairs, once it buys its way into council chambers as more and more services are put out to tender. But by the same token, the more I became aware of this, the more I felt it is probably true to say that in our kind of democracy, as fantastic as it sounds, truth is the enemy of freedom – or at any rate, of our kind of freedom. That is the kind of warped indictment few appear to possess the intellectual stamina to comprehend, perhaps with the exception, I suspect, of someone such as Peregrine Worsthorne.

This Sporting Life

The next day I went back again to the 'Paradise Forum'. I did not do this because I thought I might have been imagining things when I was there the previous morning, but to eat my lunch again in that American-style café, before entering the Library Exhibition Hall next door, where the Design Council and the Chartered Institute of Patent Agents had staged a magnificent celebration of *100 Years of British Invention.*

This was altogether more worthy as a topic of serious consideration than bad architecture and frivolous interior decoration, mainly because the failing of the one is probably linked to the lack of initiative in the other. It was also to Birmingham's credit, and it was appropriate, that the exhibition was being held there at all. The city was at the heart of the Industrial Revolution, markets itself as being situated in the very heart of England, and fell more or less exactly midway during the course of my journey. It was pure coincidence that I came across the exhibition how I did when I did. I had no idea it was being staged, and only discovered it when I glanced through a locally-produced magazine outlining cultural-happenings in my hotel room when I arrived. When I went round that exhibition I quickly became disenchanted, however, because I knew I was getting to the heart not only of the country I had been commissioned to write about, in the physical sense of the term, or of what makes me think how I do, but what it is that lies at the root of our social and economic misgivings. For what must strike anyone walking into such an exhibition, where a century of important British inventions are displayed before them, from the first stainless steel pans in 1913 through to Clive Sinclair's first pocket calculator and beyond (the British invented the pocket calculator, not the Japanese, as is commonly believed), is the sheer quantity and quality of things which first saw the light of day in this country. And yet, how many of us could name more than half a dozen? We could probably most of us bring to mind the hovercraft, Concord, or the Harrier jump-jet, or if we were in nostalgic mode the Mini, both car and skirt, but not many more.

What struck me as worrying was the number of important innovations developed in this country in recent years that probably very few of us know about at all. I studied Industrial Design to degree level, so walking around that exhibition I did feel to be in something of my element. But even I was ashamed to be unaware of the nature of some of our latest inventions. This only reflects the lack of importance science and industry play within our culture. The exhibition was not staged in a very large room, but it took me two hours to work my way slowly and meticulously around it. I was depressed at how few people joined me throughout the whole of that time. Those that did looked like bored pensioners getting out of the cold. If I had to define patriotism, if I had to define that clutching sensation in the centre of the chest each time I contemplate my country and what I believe it represents, and is capable of representing creatively and intellectually, I would not polish up little golden buttons depicting embossed lions and unicorns and begin talking about pageantry. I would lead anyone firmly by the arm into that exhibition and tell them to look, absorb, appreciate, and above all *understand*. Unfortunately, there is not the space to go into our attitudes toward industry and manufacturing to any great depth here. However, the anti-manufacturing attitudes deeply ingrained within the culture of this country – attitudes that continually suppress people of genuine foresight and have both feet embedded firmly in a dated social structure: attitudes which, in the words of the Design Council, propagate a deep 'resistance to progress and change, and . . . limit Britain's potential to channel inventiveness, knowledge and creativity into successful new product development', can best be exemplified by the story of Alan Brazier.

Brazier devised the Vax 3-in-1 vacuum cleaner, a machine which is currently featuring in a new television advertising campaign as I write these words, and which was prominently displayed in the exhibition. During the early-1970s, he was a dairy farmer and milkman who ran a contract cleaning business as a sideline. He thought the industrial cleaning appliances available at the time were unsatisfactory, so he devised a prototype replacement machine of his own. One thing which often strikes you as fascinating in the story of product development, and it struck me again that afternoon in Birmingham, is the Heath-Robinson nature of the way some of our greatest inventions and industrial breakthroughs began. Sir Christopher Cockerell, the inventor of that undervalued machine the hovercraft, made his first model prototype using a coffee pot and a hair-dryer. And so it was with Alan Brazier. He wanted to construct a cleaning machine that would combine a vacuum cleaner and carpet cleaner together, and his prototype was made using a milk churn, a shower head, and an egg crate. From these crude beginnings he developed the machine successfully and manufactured it for industrial use. However, it was in the domestic market where he felt the greatest potential resided, so in 1977 he designed a domestic version of the cleaner, and launched it a couple of years later. Unfortunately, his partnership with a leading industrial company, and also with a venture capital organization upon whom he had depended for investment, proved unsuccessful, and sales of the Vax 3-in-1 remained minimal. But Brazier knew instinctively and frustratedly that the product would sell, if only the necessary level of cash and commitment were injected into it. He had the flair and the eye to know his idea would work. The problem was he did not have full control over the marketing or the manufacturing of the product, and its capabilities were not being realized. So he bought the company himself, invested the small amount of profits in a television advertising campaign – one which I clearly remember when I was a student – gambled, and launched the cleaner anew. The results, now that he was in control, were miraculous. Sales boomed. Today, one in ten homes own a Vax 3-in-1, and it is exported to some forty-three countries. As Brazier has admitted himself, he was treated as the mad inventor who possessed a bit of marketing flair, but was not really supposed to know about anything else. The crucial factor is that he looked to the longer term in his business projections. And look where it has got him now. Recently, he was included in *The Sunday Times* top three-hundred richest people in Britain, worth, if I remember correctly, some twenty-five to thirty million pounds. Amplify the moral of his story many times, and consider the impact to the quality and capability of our economy.

Why is it worth telling the story of Alan Brazier's struggle to manufacture a British product? Because the difficulties he faced are really the story of Britain's, but more specifically of England's, attitude toward science, technology, and manufacturing industry embodied in miniature. The people of real foresight, the people who have something positive and constructive to offer society and their country, who could get this nation back on its industrial feet, get it functioning and push it in the direction of becoming genuinely prosperous again, who could inject it with stable long-term instead of facile short-term wealth, are crushed by the lords of finance, a social structure, and a hopeless stop-go economic philosophy devoid of industrial strategy that works continually against them. As a culture, we identify ourselves strongly with, among other things, the somewhat overrated writings of William Shakespeare. But do we identify ourselves with design engineering? The moment someone comes along living on the surface of the actual planet Earth, someone bursting with inventiveness and a practical solution to modern practical problems, they are dismissed as being intellectually insignificant or irrelevant, and are suppressed by the dead hand of an Establishment social structure manipulated in favour of the *rentier* and hordes of attached professional parasites. I can think of a number of choice conservative souls who extol the virtues of anything traditional, anything old, anything rural, anything ancient, anything past; people who during the course of their ignorant rantings do not much more than justify their emotional outlook on the world unto themselves. There is much platitudinous talk about literature, philosophy, history, religion, politics, but little about science, technology, industry, design, or the philosophy of *making*. And why? Because these people have usually been educated in literature, philosophy, history, religion or politics, but rarely in science, technology, industry, design, or the philosophy of *making*. They are given a certain amount of public credence and rationalize their sentimental feelings by making a number of physical realities conform to their political beliefs through continually harping on about the past. But where are the penetrating references to the broader economic framework holding together everything they so dearly cherish? Do they have any comprehension of the industrial structure that supports their fox-hunting antics and their love of the Cotswold countryside? Nowhere do you encounter much awareness of research or development, or, heaven forbid, manufacturing and industrial performance out in the real world of exports and imports and profits and loss. And yet, consider the relative intellectual significance these people enjoy, which is modest but considerable. Then contrast their 'beliefs' against the value of intelligent industrialists to the actual English society of job creation and repressed industrial potential. A hundred years from now, these 'thinkers' writings, and what they ate for breakfast, will be mulled over in university theses and agonized over in profiles in television documentaries incidentally and as a matter of course. But who will be able to remember the names of committed industrialists, much less the wealth generated by a million vacuum cleaners churned out from a factory somewhere in the Shropshire countryside, or the products of thousands of other factories exactly like it?

Vacuum Cleaners? Why, you can hear the laughter beginning to break out already, when we still, as amusing as it might be to waistcoated and bespectacled philosophers, as they sip their glasses of sherry in shiny leather armchairs in ancient book-lined studies, retain some semblance of that long-suffering entity called a manufacturing infrastructure.

The general mood of pessimism I appeared to be descending into in Birmingham intensified during my final evening in the city. For a good number of weeks I had been loosely aware that at some point or other it might be necessary to observe a sporting spectacle being patronized by ordinary people. In Birmingham there was not much to choose from. Football was out because there were no matches being played, it was too obvious, and it had already been done. So I ended up sitting through, of all things, a tedious several hours of greyhound racing in a stadium a couple of miles outside the centre of the city. The evening did not begin too badly. Once inside the stadium, the crowd, the behaviour of which was altogether more interesting as a topic of study than the tedium of the racing itself, quickly settled down to split itself into two distinct halves. One half, sitting inside the stand on wooden pews arranged in tier formation that could not have been more basic if they had still been stacked in piles in a timber yard, consulted little paper programmes and wrote things studiously onto betting slips as the commentator's voice mumbled continually from a speaker somewhere in the background, before each race. Above them flickered a battery of television monitors, shuffling constantly a procession of computerized numbers and snapping abruptly into video close-ups of individual dogs out on the track, then flicking back again, so that you felt half the time that you were watching the thing in your living room at home. This part of the crowd had about it a civilized and formal composure, was quite mild in complexion and character, debated the proceedings unfolding before it assiduously, bandying the names of individual dogs around as though they were grandparents' favourite children, and was innocent enough. It was only when, sufficiently bored, I turned my attention to the other part of the crowd assembled through the windows outside, every single component of which was male, and rumbustiously male at that, that the evening shifted very abruptly into second gear, revealing a very different breed of punter indeed.

As with serious horse race betting, the idea with dog racing is to place your bet as late as possible. Because of the competitiveness this encourages between people, one minute the men seemed to be attempting to give the impression they were whistling innocently, so to speak, and looking the other way; then, just before the race was about to begin – literally seconds before – there would be a sudden rush to place last-minute bets, a frantic babble of greedy voices, clamouring for attention, would erupt into life, and the proceedings became very ugly very quickly. All the time I was there, never once did the men appear to show much interest in the dogs. Most of the time they hung about near the place where the bookies were stationed, talking among themselves and stamping their feet to keep warm (it was horribly cold); or they spent the time between races in a smoke-filled bar built beneath the stadium, emerging only a few minutes before each race to place their bets. This they seemed to have timed with clockwork precision. Each time the commentator's mechanical voice announced the next race, booming out across the night air from echoing loudspeakers positioned at intervals right around the stadium, the swing doors of the bar would open and the men would barge out as one and pace about on a patch of concrete in front of the bookies, like a pack of pit-bull terriers waiting for a fight. This happened throughout the evening, and though the betting was boisterous enough, most of the time it passed off without incident.

This was not the case when an important race cropped up about halfway through the programme that offered the biggest potential winnings so far. Because I had been trying to keep my eye on the state of the betting (I thought I had better actively participate in at least one race, so the experience was complete), as well as observe what was happening to the structure and feel of the crowd, as I paced up and down, stamping my feet and blowing into my hands to try and keep warm, I was lucky enough to be tensed in anticipation. If I hadn't been, I am almost certain I would have been slack enough in my composure to be surprised, and to have fallen over and been trampled. For the movement of figures toward the bookies that came just before the race started was not so much a mild surge, as had been the case hitherto, as a combined lunge by the entire crowd. I have never experienced anything quite like it. The scramble of bodies was so violent it remains in my mind for a confusing few seconds as an image of distorted faces skewed at crazy angles, being buffeted in a shifting mass by elbows and shoulders jammed against cheeks. (It probably seemed worse than it really was because I was right in the midst of it.) Everywhere could be heard the ridiculous sound of heavy exhaling and muffled grunting and the gasping of breath and the incessant rustling of anoraks. There were people who actually, physically *threw* themselves on top of the people immediately in front, so that a small pyramid of figures began to build beneath each bookie. The crowd shrieked and shouted obscenities and thrust handfuls of ten and twenty pound notes into the air. Not since the mass play-fights and rugby scrums I remember participating in when I was at school, which were just as dangerous and humiliating, have I been involved in such an ugly stampede, where people are so tightly packed bowel to bowel they cannot move and you feel like the blood is going to explode from your ears. I was carried a good seven or eight feet across the concrete completely against my will. There was a horrifying moment when everyone seemed to become locked together, and I found myself clutching a handful of somebody else's jacket to remain on my feet so tightly I broke a fingernail. Locked solid, the crowd seemed unable to shift either one way or the other. If I had lifted my feet off the ground I would have remained precisely where I was. That was the most frightening moment. You felt like you were going to suffocate, but then the crowd swayed, gave a huge unanimous groan and heaved violently sideways, releasing itself from a sort of mass gridlock.

As I managed to extricate myself from the seething scrum of bodies, the bit of fur stapled crudely to a short wooden pole representing the hapless hare had begun its tremulous run around the perimeter of the track and tripped open the cages. The commentator had announced, with the seemingly stifled desire to shriek the information aloud like a mischievous schoolboy, that 'the hare is on the move, the hare is on the move'. The ridiculous rush of dogs – a jostle of flailing legs and struggling paws and flattened ears and lolloping tongues as they began their desperate scramble – had shot past. The sand had been left jumping in the air. And I'd thought that if the men comprising that surge of odorous masculinity were the descendants of the same essentially decent Birmingham working class Priestley observed one Saturday night gathered at a whist drive (the same working class that used to enjoy its weekly shilling at the betting shop, in the hope of escaping a life of drudgery while it anticipated a world of socialism, the football pools, and equal opportunity) then it had certainly come up in the world. In addition to what I can only describe as a handful of ridiculously cliched back street gangster types strutting importantly about, sporting spiv moustaches and pork-pie hats and reeking sharply of unfiltered nicotine, a couple of them actually flanked by oversized halfwits, I saw rough working-class men, with faces that looked like they were chiselled from stone, with hands the size of a bunch of bananas, stuffing wads of banknotes into the faces of the bookies that the average sophisticated person would think twice about handing over to an antiques dealer in exchange for a rare piece of pottery. All of this in the name of money and the power it has to manipulate the pattern of human behaviour. All of this in a city where there are people giving their damnedest for no financial remuneration whatever, to help ameliorate the suffering of other human beings, one in five of whom are without a job and do not hold much hope of ever obtaining one in their lives. Perhaps some of them were at that race meeting. God knows, nothing surprises me any more in this corrupt topsy-turvy world, where men's desires can be dictated by the remorseless power contained in a five or a ten pound note.

Not surprised at what I had witnessed, beginning to feel distinctly faint due to the relentless icy winds that never stopped gusting all night, I decided I'd had enough and caught a bus through a bleak West Midlands inner city landscape studded with high-rise flats, back into the city centre. On its way in, the bus filled up with youngsters heading out for a night on the town. I was amazed, as I used to be amazed when I mingled with such people when I was a teenager and was one of them myself, at how scantily dressed the majority of them were, despite the sub-zero temperatures. Back in the city centre, Birmingham was warming up for the nightshift. The streets were alive with jeering teenagers who had money in their pockets and were emerging noisily onto their nocturnal parading ground ready to spend it. The girls piled off the bus and giggled like chickens and had curly hair-dos and scraped along in clumsy stilettoes and had pink legs and wore skirts so short you wondered seriously why they had bothered to squeeze into them at all. The lads, lanky and ape-like, with short hair-cuts, some with little trendy patterns ploughed into the sides of their heads, exploded into peals of Brummie laughter and lolloped across the roads, spreadeagled defiantly in the path of oncoming headlights. The Christmas lights were slung across Corporation Street above them from one side to the other. The doorways to some of the building societies and the banks, with their glitzy enticements and big percentage signs and smiles and pictures of children and teddy bears and Christmas stockings and fireplaces and puppies and more beckoning dreams, along with some of the department store porticoes, were becoming the station for a number of homeless youngsters bedding themselves down for the night. I paused at the entrance to a famous chain store, but before I could open my mouth to ask the incumbent if he was prepared to talk, he silently and spontaneously aimed an obscene two-fingered gesture straight in my direction, a few miles from a sports stadium where for a couple of quid you could stand and observe basic animal instinct scrabbling around among itself in a way nothing short of disgusting.

And in the background to it all were the huge neon signs imprinted on the night sky, the tower blocks lifting massively into darkness, and the distant police sirens screaming, screaming, across the night air.

7

Norfolk and Suffolk

Across the Fens to Ely

With most of the places visited so far, I had arranged to talk to people, or visit a number of industrial premises, before I arrived. This was as inevitable as it was practical. You cannot simply arrive in a city, where you intend to remain for several days, and seriously expect to see people at short notice when their diaries might be booked up weeks in advance. Some of the visits to factories I made were organized months beforehand, and had to be, otherwise there would have been no chance of getting to see the things I wanted to see at all.

With Birmingham it was different. Although I had attempted to arrange a couple of visits through my publisher before I set off at the beginning of October, for some peculiar reason none of the letters we sent to Birmingham were responded to. The consequence was that I arrived there with nothing officially arranged at all. I had not worried unduly about this, but had deliberately left my timetable open because it appealed to me to see how a city of that size could take hold of the imagination, when I was under pressure to gather material under a somewhat limited time schedule. This had worked very well. So much so that before I left Birmingham, I decided to make a significant change to my itinerary. I had originally intended to travel from Birmingham down through the Cotswolds into Bristol and the West Country, before skirting back along the south coast, up into Kent and finally into East Anglia. But because of how well Birmingham had turned out I decided instead to plunge into something of the unknown, cut across country to Norwich, passing through a good half dozen counties en-route, and complete the second half of the journey the opposite way round to the path I originally projected.

It was after dark when I left Birmingham late one Sunday afternoon. I headed out from the southern side of the city toward the airport and the exhibition centre, and picked up the main dual carriageway across in the direction of Coventry. My destination was Ely in Cambridgeshire, where I had arranged to stay at a boarding-house owned by a retired master from the King Edward public school that is situated in the centre of the little city. I did not stop at Coventry, or drive through it, but skirted around the periphery courtesy of yet another ring road. I have only ever been into Coventry once, during the middle of an horrendous heatwave, and it struck me then, though this is not especially obvious when you are driving through the city suburbs, to be one of the most charmless and thoroughly ruined places I had ever seen. It was once a very old and historical place, a city famous for its spires; but it was bombed heavily during the war. Quite how much of the new Coventry was a result of the designs of the Luftwaffe, and how much of it was a result of the influence of municipal planning or the effect of corruption afterwards, is difficult to say. Either way Coventry is a mess, more noticeably so, because of its smaller size, than Birmingham. In the very heart of the city there sits marooned a tight enclave of ancient buildings, the famous derelict cathedral, a clutch of timber-and-lath, a few narrow passageways, and some neat signs inevitably commemorating the legend of Lady Godiva. When I first saw it, Coventry was basking beneath seamless heat, the shadows from the grand old trees framing the cathedral casting patterns across large numbers of students sunning themselves lazily on the grass. It is remarkable how that little sanctum of peace and tranquillity has survived, for it is surrounded entirely by a ring – perhaps in reality it is choked by a noose – of concrete and trendy post-war marble, more so than Birmingham, which is equally as famous for its ring of concrete as it is for its immense quantity of windy subways. Down one street in Coventry, which I believe had the unlikely name of Greyfriars Way, there was a lone, ancient, half-timbered building; the sort that would have appealed to H.V. Morton in his halcyon days, when Coventry was still Coventry. This was Ford's Hospital, stranded among a mêlée of grooved concrete and the most unalluring modern brick facades imaginable. It looked hopelessly lost and seemed to harmonize perfectly with the aimless crowds thronging the adjacent precincts, licking ice-creams beneath boiling sunshine, where you had the distinct sensation, as you do in some modern southern English towns, that nothing has ever happened there, and probably never will. What is more remarkable still, and I thought so again when I negotiated its flyovers and underpasses and read the direction signs when I passed round it again this time, is that Coventry is less than a quarter of an hour (down another stretch of dual carriageway, of course) from Shakespeare country, and some of the most famous and historic towns in the land. Is there no end to these ridiculous contrasts, these blatant juxtapositions?

One of the reasons I decided to head toward Ely, in addition to it being ideally situated to break the long drive from the West Midlands across into Norfolk, was that it had been strongly recommended I see the cathedral by night. I had been told that when you approached Ely across the fens in the darkness the cathedral was magnificently floodlit, a great thrusting of ecclesiastical architecture sailing majestically above the rooftops of the city; a vast structure boiling in a cauldron of light like an explosion of magic cascading through a child's imagination. However, after a couple of hours of that satisfying sense of preternatural vagueness you associate with driving through the English countryside at night, after travelling along the A1 for a little while – once the Great North Road until the M1 stole its thunder – and having skirted the outskirts of Huntingdon, which showed no indication of being in the heart of the English Shires but lost only in the heart of impenetrable darkness, when I eventually approached Ely and squinted at the blackness up ahead, I could not detect the presence of the cathedral anywhere. The only soaring lights were clusters of tall lamp standards that drew gradually nearer and revealed themselves to be illuminating sombre empty roundabouts, before I plunged on again into the blackness. This was strange. The cathedral was supposed to be raised up on its famous floating Isle, and yet I saw nothing. I reached the centre of the city – because of its small size, it would be easier to be able to describe Ely as a town, if not merely a large village – performed a u-turn at some traffic lights, and pulled over down a side street, adjacent to a small modern shopping precinct, and wound down my window. (Even historic Ely has its concrete and pebbledash: there is, it seems, no escape.) I was confounded and tried to determine my bearings. There was no cathedral anywhere. Was I actually in Ely, or had I taken a wrong turning some distance back in one of the quiet villages behind me, the ones with deserted little high streets and pubs bulging up to the narrow roadsides that kept materializing Christmas card-like as a scattering of illuminated cottage windows from the depths of the night? I got out of my car, then was astonished to see that there, more or less in front of me, colossal and imposing and stacked upon itself, shooting straight up into the darkness, as cold and as sheer as an Arctic glacier and as silent as a mausoleum, was the mighty cathedral. The streets were deserted, the slates of the little shops and houses touched, as was the outline of the great grey cathedral ramparts, by the blue gaze of the moonlight. It was freezing cold and there was not a single shaft of spotlight anywhere. This was just my luck, I thought. The one evening I chose to arrive, the lights were switched off. But, as I stood there staring, the cathedral flanked by a series of crooked buildings and ancient English walls, its dripping polygonal towers and turrets exuding the magnitude of centuries, I realized that, on second thoughts, to stumble across it like that in the dark was a more satisfying way to discover it after all. I was amazed at how close I had managed to get to it without noticing it, which had suddenly imbued it with the most unbelievable sense of presence. It was immeasurably more powerful an initial impression than any nebulous floodlit spectacle seen rearing across the distant plains. That was because to come upon it like that was more personal and more intimate. See it illuminated from miles away and you see the cathedral as everybody else, even as a camera, can see it. The imagination is not allowed to work, the senses cannot be startled, reactions cannot occur spontaneously. You are forced to look at it against your will. Close up, a towering pillar of darkness suddenly revealing itself, silent and domineering against a spectral array of tiny stars flung against the deeper blackness of the heavens above – heavens one can only assume the builders of such an imposing citadel were in some ways hoping they could reach – the moment belongs to you, and to you alone.

The City of Norwich

Though I had been into Norfolk before I had never been to Norwich. Nevertheless, I had a good idea what to expect when I approached the county's old commercial nucleus. There were several reasons why. Most notable is the simple geographic position of Norwich, out on the rump of England described as East Anglia. As the region's capital, the symmetrical manner in which the major roads lead in to the city from the surrounding areas, and its remoteness from another major commercial centre, is strongly appealing. Norwich sits at the centre of a network of roads like a spider sits at the centre of a web, and you can see how by turning to any map of the British Isles. You can see by glancing at the same map, too, that there is a distinct lack of motorways anywhere in the immediate vicinity; something that not only bodes well for any section of English landscape but these days is very nearly a rarity. (This is, apparently, due to change around Norwich, much to the detriment of East Anglia.) You feel that Norwich must be at the heart of something important, and it helps to contribute to the Norwich mystique.

My anticipation of the city had also played a part in my changing the direction of my itinerary. After so much squalid urban disorder, after so many distorted caricatures of towns and cities masquerading as civilized living, I wanted to see Norwich sooner rather than later. As I drove toward it across a colourless and uninspiring flat landscape situated in a section of country which by night appeared to have had the power to enamour but by day appeared simply to have become dull and monotonous again, I was passing through a Dutch landscape that I remembered as not being renowned for its enervating qualities, particularly during sullen weather, something that happens to be a characteristic of the area and was so that damp, drizzly morning. Such tabletop countryside, held down by a vast canopy of sky, needs interesting cloud formations piled above it to really make it work successfully. But in a curious way the seemingly interminable flatness, though it does little to raise the spirits or enlighten the senses, particularly if you are used to the constantly shifting light and alternating shadows and undulating perspectives of hilly areas, might have helped create the right kind of approach to Norwich that day because in an odd way it served to emphasise its feeling of remoteness; that you were nearing something special. For weeks I had been looking forward to arriving there. For a long time I had been led to believe Norwich was a medieval city largely untouched by the kind of ruinous modernization that has destroyed the character of much of the rest of town and city England; more so, you hear it implied, than York, which aesthetically is interesting but which I dislike chiefly because of its commercialization and its constant congestion from tourists. Norwich was also one of the few important places left in England that I had never visited, and was far enough away from mainstream geography and the clumsiness of mainstream dross to suggest that it might, just might, have something different to offer the weary traveller. I was not, I hasten to add, naïve or unrealistic enough to believe Norwich might have remained in some kind of time-warp; a sort of everlasting montage of photographs cut out of a 1950s edition of *The Country Life Picture Book of Great Britain*, snapped just before the carnage of redevelopment began and the rest of the country moved confidently on. I knew there would probably have been compromises. But it did not seem unreasonable to assume, if the legends were being kind, that the compromises made might be noticeably less marked; that there might be one town or city of substantial size left in England, the pattern of which, like some of the smaller towns I had passed through in North Yorkshire already, could have remained more or less intact, with wide streets and big shops and a genuine old fashioned, ring-road-free, authentic city atmosphere; one where people continued to be civilized and street corners had not been obliterated to accommodate traffic. Encouraged by the marketing of the city, spurred on by comments made by some of the people I spoke to on the telephone before I arrived, I had quite high expectations of Norwich, and it was with more than merely the usual sense of relief after a long drive that I saw the smudge of a city collecting itself and forming a substantial outline in the distance.

It is a curious fact that many of the most beautiful and revered buildings in this part of East Anglia were once the homes of textile weavers and merchants, having survived chiefly because, centuries previously, their economic activities failed and there was not the prosperity left behind creating the need for them to be pulled down and built anew. Though it now seems difficult to believe, Norwich used to be an important textile town, a wealthy and thriving worsted weaving centre exporting cloth to northern Europe as long ago as the fourteenth century. As recently as a couple of hundred years past it was one of the most important and most heavily populated cities in England; even if this was at a time when the population nationally was only between two and three millions, with sheep outnumbering the quantity of people by roughly three to one, and places such as Bradford and Manchester were not much more than villages at the confluence of streams. By the time steam power began to exert its influence on the workings of the textile industry toward the end of the eighteenth century, and a twinkle began to register in the north of England's eye, Norwich was in the unfortunate position of lacking readily accessible sources of coal and running water to enable it to rapidly expand. Its location at the eastern side of England had been advantageous enough for its trading activities with northern Europe. But its remoteness meant it had poor communications links with the rest of its own country, and consequently it was unable to compete with the expanding towns clustered together in the emerging industrial hinterlands elsewhere. The result, as you discover if you delve into the origins of the worsted industry in the West Riding, was that the textile industry of Norfolk moved north. It took with it many of its workers and bred a race of people whom it is sometimes claimed owe their sober qualities to their ancestors from East Anglia – sober qualities it is taken for granted can be found embellishing the psychology of people common to both regions today – the trade itself taking its name after the village of Worstead to the north of Norwich. Norwich missed out on the Industrial Revolution, entered a period of economic decline and took on the appearance and characteristics of a market town, thereby avoiding the excessive industrial expansion that blanketed most of central England and wiped out much of the medieval architecture for which Norwich the city is becoming increasingly renowned. The rest, as they say wearily when contemplating the urban decay visible today in the north of England, is history. To an extent the pendulum could be said to be swinging back again the other way, for Norwich now sits at the centre of the fastest growing region in the country. How strange that the physical differences between a former textile capital such as Norwich and a former textile capital such as Bradford, the latter itself having undergone a period of steady economic decline but lacking the trading background or historical foundations of the former, and which originally expanded at the considerable expense of places such as Norwich, should owe much of their present condition to the workings hundreds of years apart of the very same industry. This is not to say that while the north of England flourished Norwich became a sleepy and antiquated cathedral city lacking entrepreneurial flair, or that it stagnated. Norwich diversified. Insurance and mustard, the manufacture of agricultural implements, brewing, light engineering, paper making and publishing, leather working, in particular the making of children's and women's shoes, banking, even the breeding of canaries, have all been concerns through which the city has prospered at one time or another, and in some cases still does. And, of course, it has for a long time been the centre of an enormous agricultural region, an industry that continues to play a vital role in the economic fortunes of the area today.

All of these things drew me toward Norwich with earnest, though I have to be honest and say that when I passed through the outer residential ring, the first substantial article of the city proper that came into view was a concrete box jutting up above the pleasant tree-lined avenues ahead. My spirits sank, sank so abruptly my initial reaction to Norwich was that I took a vague dislike to the place. This will probably mystify many people as much as it will astound and horrify others. I suspect the reaction was against the irritation I felt at having allowed myself to be taken in by the enigma that has developed favourably concerning the environmental quality of the city over recent years. You go to a place such as Newcastle expecting to be disappointed, so that when you are not disappointed your expectations are flounced and you are surprised and stimulated, even if there is much ugliness and decay and dismal city side streets. Unfortunately the same reaction can work in reverse. This was rather what happened with Norwich, because the growing fame of the city architecturally for having remained substantially intact appears to me to be somewhat exaggerated. This celebrated medieval metropolis is, in fact, riddled with concrete – or at any rate it is around the outskirts of the city centre, through which there ploughs the kind of ring road system, bordered by a shabby dishabille of curtain walls, supermarkets, home DIY stores, and acres and acres of parked cars, as depressing as that to be found anywhere. There is also a preponderance of modern office buildings rising in the direction of the castle and scattered throughout the entire city, which sets a more realistic tone for much of what you see when you are there, reputation or no reputation.

I had the opportunity of surveying the whole of Norwich not long after I arrived, from the top floor of what I gathered to be its highest office block. I was being shown over the site of the new Castle Mall shopping complex that is being built at the top end of the city centre at Timberhill, immediately beneath the castle. My guide was another Public Relations Manager, this time a representative of the firm of contractors that is developing the scheme. Throughout the time I was with him, I felt an awkward, nagging sense of unease. I was being welcomed into the city by someone who, if I remember correctly, had been born and bred there, still lived there, and was taking the trouble to introduce me to a huge construction project about which Norwich is immensely proud. And yet there was I, with these awkward feelings about the city percolating inside my head, becoming increasingly troubled about what I was eventually going to write about it. Still, the Castle Mall project is impressive enough. A massive hole, hundreds of yards across and seemingly as deep, has been scooped out of the earth at the foot of the castle, on the site of the old cattle market that for years after it was vacated by farmers and animals was used as a large car park. Much of the impetus behind the new development is Norwich's growing importance regionally. Apparently it needs a greater variety of shopping, even if it did seem to me to be bursting with retail outlets and a thriving market place already. The reason behind the size of the hole, which we examined from ground level to begin with, is that the complex will be built entirely *underground*, with a man-made park with gardens arranged above it, blending it into the landscaping already embracing the castle. This will enable the economic benefits of modern large-scale, Meadowhall-type indoor shopping to be brought into Norwich, without creating the sort of major blot on the city skyline enormous building projects like these generally entail – and presumably without having any serious effect on the retail pattern in the rest of the city centre, which happens to be very close. It is certainly a novel way of closing ourselves off from major developments environmentally that we find necessary to the pattern of modern life, but which we find increasingly difficult to accommodate sentimentally as a culture. Perhaps we are all busily becoming ostriches at heart. From the ninth floor of the aforementioned office block, where there were some models and computer-generated drawings of the proposed centre arranged in a boardroom, we looked down onto the construction site, down into the great gaping clay chasm, deep inside which the tiny contractors and their dumper trucks swarmed and chugged like toys. We could clearly discern the emerging levels of the complex, seemingly grafted onto the sides of the hole, like the layering of a huge neapolitan ice-cream. We could also clearly see that the reputation for Norwich possessing a high quantity of beautiful churches, a legacy of its wealth and prominence commercially as far back as Anglo-Saxon times, was neatly emphasised by the number of steeples projecting mistily from the city skyline: though I wondered afterwards whether or not a more inspired aphorism could be devised to relate to the number of ugly modern buildings visible from up there as well, including the blocks of flats and the rows of deck tenements straight from Hulme in Manchester, out in the direction of Mousehold Heath, where the tabletop landscape gives way quite abruptly to substantially elevated ground toward the east.

I suspect the growing aesthetic reputation of Norwich is rooted in it having retained much of its original medieval street pattern, and that consequently many excellent old buildings and thoroughfares have survived in the centre. But I cannot for the life in me understand what sends people into pangs of ecstasy about the place environmentally. It makes you realize how blinded and frivolous we can become when we have our heads shoved deep into the nose-bag of sentimentality; how feeble are our emotions and how they can manipulate honesty, clear-sightedness, and objectivity. If you have been drawn into believing Norwich has escaped the more unpleasant side effects of post-war urban redevelopment, and avoided Poulson-like municipal corruption (reputedly because of the stable Labour-controlled council that has been in charge of the city's political affairs for decades), there is a very strange feeling begins to wend its way toward the pit of your stomach. You don't need to be standing on the ninth floor of an office block to become aware of it either. Norwich was recently nominated in a report commissioned by the EEC carried out by Reading University as the most attractive city in Britain, and I was reminded of this several times when I was there. If this was partly, or even wholly, a reference to the look of the city, then it seems to me to be a somewhat dubious accolade, though I should imagine plenty of us are sceptical enough about anything that is a product of the EEC anyway. It does not say much for the perceptiveness of the people behind these findings, much less the uniformity of their standards. What it does say something about is the acute compartmentalization of perception that can be seen infecting national sensibility at the present time; a frame of mind that so irritated that young woman I spoke to in Birmingham, as we struggle to find something positive to fasten onto when we ponder the mess of environmental degradation sprawling around us after years of stupidity and corruption. What a crazy, mixed up, period we are living through. I cannot help feeling that each time we find ourselves being influenced by these romantic notions, each time we pick up a magazine promoting the 'beauties of England', with its cosy cobbled-alley atmosphere and its emphasis on tulips and its lurking tea-room contemplation of life, we are actively participating in the romanticized version the country is painting of itself and effectively making things worse. In the long run we are distancing ourselves from facing up to the real challenges that lie ahead. We are ensuring the anachronisms, and the fanciful illusions generated about cities such as Norwich, will become more sharply defined, our awareness more distorted, than ever. There is hanging over much of our comprehension of contemporary England the air of someone picking for bits of edible flesh over the bones of a half-decomposed dead fish. To imply that Norwich is something totally unique, distinct from the untidy heap making up the rest of modern urban Britain, is no excuse, and makes no allowance, for the damage that has actually been inflicted – damage that is just as important, and takes up as much of the space in your perceptions, as an afternoon spent wandering the city's abundance of medieval passageways, the talk about the Norwich School of Painters, or the guidebooks reminding you for the umpteenth time that it used to have a pub for every day of the week and a church for every week of the year. Norwich *is* a city with variety. Norwich *is* an interesting and beautiful city – in parts. But then the whole of England is interesting and beautiful – in parts.

Before I make an enemy of the city of Norwich forever, to its credit I would say its growing reputation aesthetically seems to be referred to more frequently by people from outside the city than by the people living there, who have a more shrewd understanding of their surroundings (see the *Norwich Discovery Walks*) than one might at first expect. All the same, as I unpacked my things when I arrived, having spent the afternoon acquainting myself with it, the favourable remarks of previous observers fresh in my mind, the obvious conclusion to reach was what on earth all the fuss had been about.

The Window Factory

When I arrived in Norwich I did not book into a hotel in the centre of the city, but managed instead to locate a charming guest-house several miles outside. I describe it as a guest-house but in actual fact it was an isolated cottage, beautifully restored and situated at the edge of one of those remote hamlets surrounded by miles of open countryside where it is so quiet at night, when you stand at the door to take in some air before bed, you hear things rustling occasionally in the undergrowth. Everything about it suggested that I was not only staying in authentic rural English bed-and-breakfast – the first I had lodged in during the journey so far – but that it was a living manifestation of traditional English country taste, if not everything the English hold dear sentimentally as a culture. The marked degree of lace curtain draped deliciously among the shadows, the abundance of stripped pine furniture squatting in darkened corners, the squares of daylight slanting across shiny wooden floors that always creaked at the appropriate moment, and the rag dolls staring vacantly from the pillows of empty four-poster beds, created the impression that you were coming upon a sequence of photographic illustrations cut out of one of the Laura Ashley company's latest off-the-shoulder catalogues. All day long the house was permeated by the most wonderful smells of cooking breakfast, freshly ground coffee, and the acrid yet exquisite smell of a real coal burning fire. After so much urban sound, busy roads, squalid inner city decay, endless anonymous crowds, and fitful nights and inadequate food in big hotels, it came as an enormous relief to wake to the sound of chirruping birds instead of the familiar rumble of early morning traffic, the slamming of hotel room doors, or the muffled whining of lifts. I felt better than I had done for weeks, even if I was reminded confidently, as one would perhaps expect in that part of the world, that this was due entirely to the bracing air blowing onto East Anglia straight from the sea.

I compared the excessive price of good city centre hotels,

and their lack of comeliness to these family-run guest-houses, with the establishment's proprietor one morning over breakfast. We were sitting in a conservatory (wood, not plastic) that had been built onto the rear of the house, and which he himself had installed to his own specification. When he and his wife had moved up some years previously from the south of England to Norfolk, they had bought the house in a severely derelict condition. Between them they had spent several years transforming it from a crumbling shell into what it was when I was there, having lived in a caravan in the garden in the meantime. There must be plenty of people who have done this throughout the past ten years; people at the right age and living at the right moment; people not too young and not too old; people who were able to sell their existing property and bank enough of a difference to make a good profit to provide themselves with a modest but sustainable private income, purchase an old property in need of conversion in another part of the country, free themselves from large overheads, and more or less retire, keeping at arm's length from the rat-race. Perhaps these people will be the forerunner to a new form of landed gentry. Inevitably, we found ourselves commenting on the smallness of the world, because it appeared that at one time, not that many years previously, we had lived within streets of each other in Forest Hill in south London. I commented with interest on the quality and arrangement of the furniture within the conservatory, and the proprietor then went on to make one of those interesting little observations about people that would probably only be discernible to someone who is the owner of a guest-house. Originally, he had installed a single long table in the conservatory, but had noticed that the different groups of guests tended not to speak when they were dining together. They would sit in abject silence consuming their breakfast, pretending to be keeping one ear on the radio in the mornings, or staring solemnly into their dinners in the evenings. The atmosphere created was so stale the proprietor felt he had to do something, so he introduced a number of tables, and spaced everybody out instead. From then on, with only a few feet established between them, he found the guests would turn around to speak to one another enthusiastically, even if it meant they had to twist around in their seats uncomfortably to hold a conversation. He was at a loss to explain this. All he could deduce was that it was another instance of the unpredictable manner in which human beings, but more especially English human beings, behave in a group situation territorially.

Perhaps it has been the willingness of Norwich to adapt quickly to changing economic circumstances that is the secret to its durability, and why the country's largest manufacturer of uPVC doors and windows has been able to successfully establish its headquarters there, and seize a corresponding chunk of the domestic market. UPVC doors and windows are undoubtedly one of the burgeoning environmental textures of our age and in particular of the country I travelled through during the closing months of 1991, where I seemed to be coming upon shops, advertisements, delivery vans, and the sight of them being installed down comfy suburban and narrow industrial back streets at nearly every other glance. Few aesthetic ingredients of the contemporary social scene are, in fact, having quite such an impact on the look and feel of traditional English houses, on the subtle surface texture of modern urban England, than the installation of plastic doors and windows. Most thinking people I know have something to say about them, usually something contemptuous, chiefly because they equate the synthetic imitativeness of many of the designs, and their social desirability, to the shallowness of today's moral values. The manufacture and investiture of uPVC doors and windows, along with plastic conservatories to which they are closely related, is, however, a highly complex and lucrative business. It was one of the boom industries, perhaps one of the inevitable industries, of the Thatcher years. The changing styles of our doors and windows are also one of those minor yet crucial environmental details we forget about until we examine old photographs. Like the substitution of our old 1930s' street furniture with Continental-style replacements in the 1960s (when the character promptly disappeared from British street signs, at the same time as they immediately became more discernible to passing motorists), they are going to have a profound impact on the cosmetic feel of this country over the years to come. So, rather than concentrating on the obvious and more traditional industries of Norwich, which would have been easy, I drove out on the Cromer road to the airport industrial estate and spent the morning with the Production Controller at the modern factory complex of Anglian Windows, to see how they were made.

Both the Production Controller and myself had something in common in that we were both originally from the north of England, and once this became apparent I was told proudly that the uPVC industry really began in this country in the north. He himself had been the first person to extrude uPVC in girder form, or *profile* as it is described technically, in this country. He pressed the first button on the very first machine, having fashioned windows up to that stage from ready-made material imported from Germany, before he was procured by Anglian Windows and sent for three months training across to Bavaria. There is a tendency to assume uPVC doors and windows are a new innovation, whereas in fact they have been around on the Continent since the late-1950s. It is only another instance of this country supposedly lagging behind much of the rest of Europe that they took as long to appear here as they did. The story goes that they started to be introduced after the directors of a well-known firm of double-glazing manufacturers based in Lancashire went across to Germany on a business trip. The windows to the rooms of the hotel where they were staying had been fabricated from uPVC, and they were so impressed they set about finding out what they were and how they were made. Though they began by importing profiles ready made, they soon decided the manufacture of uPVC doors and windows rather than aluminium, which never really caught on, was a potential growth industry, and invested in their own tooling and began to produce their own profiles from scratch. Anglian Windows have done this too and been so successful they are now exporting their product back to both Germany and France. The main reason I was given for this was that the company can beat foreign competition hands-down on delivery, though I suspect it is that we are better at marketing too. Anglian also send out finished windows and doors, manufactured entirely in their Norwich factories from scale drawings, ready to be fitted straight into buildings in the same European countries. They even have their own transporter lorries in which to deliver them. That seemed to me to be a very ironical though at the same time a very agreeable situation. We started by taking the idea from the Germans, and now we are shipping it back to them because it appears we are capable of doing the thing better than they are. So often you hear about things turning out the other way round. In these dismal days of economic despondency, huge balance of trade deficits, general pessimism toward our commitment to manufacturing, and doom-laden editions of *The Money Programme*, it is heartening to hear such success stories; encouraging to come across sophisticated modern English factories clamouring to the noise of machinery and bursting with full order books in the depths of a recession. It is heartening because it shows that with adequate investment and a sensible industrial strategy things can actually be achieved.

For a long time I was sceptical about the way many crude uPVC doors and windows defaced old houses and buildings. With their installation the character is disappearing, once and for all, from the villages, small towns, and old houses of England. But only when you are welcomed into places where these things are made, when you sit down and talk to committed business people to whom the feel, the smell, the warmth, and the sight and sound of newly manufactured plastic profiles being squeezed at length from a confusion of roaring machinery like toothpaste from a tube is a way of life, can you begin to climb over your initial prejudices and look at the situation more objectively. For there is more to the argument for and against uPVC doors and windows than just dismissing them abusively, joining the Victorian Society or frantically absorbing monthly bulletins issued by English Heritage, and beginning to talk despondently about the sad history of moulding-planes. I said as much to the Production Controller when we began a tour of the factory proper. I told him that though I felt the principle of making doors and windows from plastic had nothing especially wrong with it, it was the way in which many of them had been designed and installed that was behind much of my initial scepticism. To my mind, the appeal of plastic material is that, like metal, it can be moulded into almost any shape that is desired. But with doors and windows this had not been taken far enough, probably through inadequate designers and aesthetically illiterate businessmen. If you have a marvellously weathered old stone cottage, its character fashioned by the elements blasting down at it for so long it blends to perfection with the tone and contour of the landscape of which it has become indelibly a part, it is scandalous to install synthetic window frames that do not complement harmoniously the rest of the building. And yet, slowly, surreptitiously this is happening right across the surface of England; for these fittings are becoming a part of the new England and they are not going to go away. In the old West Riding of Yorkshire, near to where I grew up, it is possible to come upon numerous detached eighteenth- or nineteenth-century cottages, huddled high on exposed hillsides, their old stones beaten into hollows by the relentless hammering of inclement weather, completely ruined by some mental incompetent having installed horrible little uPVC windows that look so out of place they are like salt rubbed into the wound of bad taste. And yet plenty of people consider these things socially desirable, the houses themselves sometimes increasing in value, incredibly, by being destroyed in this way. (Perhaps it is the insulating properties of the windows that lie behind their appeal.) It is the lack of charm inherent to the simple synthetic perfection of the material itself that lies at the heart of the problem. The effect on the eye when one comes upon uPVC windows installed in old buildings is nearly always grotesque. Only on newer buildings, such as jerry-built Scandinavian-type bungalows, where the tastelessness of the architecture and the synthetic finish of the material appear to compliment one another for all the wrong reasons, do they actually enhance what is already there. Why the properties of the material have not been exploited to the full remains something of a mystery to me. It has often struck me as strange that in an automated age, when we are capable of shaping synthetic materials as never before, we should have produced so much banality aesthetically, when designers and manufacturers ought to be freer than they ever have been before. Surely, with the state of technology today it takes only a small mental step to imagine perfect reproduction uPVC sashed windows that operate more smoothly, and have the subtlety and delicate relief detail of wooden originals. There are probably complications of which I am not aware, but why is this not being done?

Across in the extrusion plant at Anglian Windows I was shown more than a dozen complicated-looking computer-controlled machines (they reminded you at once of very big lathes), all of which were emitting from one end continuous lengths of different shaped profile, all of them surrounded by the most fantastic tangle of pipes and cables, due to the hot material needing to be cooled continually and the toxic gasses removed. The impression was that you were walking through an enormous bag of knitting. These machines, which are monitored from a control room that resembles the interior of a modern railway signal box, are never switched off. They run on continuous shifts, twenty four hours a day, seven days a week, and as my guide had a few words with one of the operators, I looked around and wondered how the archetypal image of the traditional English manufactory has been fast disappearing over these past few years. If what represented it until comparatively recently was the sight of row upon row of battered Victorian-looking machinery weighing many tons, surrounded by hundreds of greasy-overalled and plastic begoggled Arthur Seatons hunched intently over a never-ending catherine-wheel of sparks, then what is increasingly representing it today is the intensely-lit, computer-dependant, almost hospital environment I walked into out at Anglian Windows, where you feel there is hardly a speck of dust or waste collected anywhere. What strikes you immediately, as it did when I was shown that huge piece of machinery replacing jobs at the Twyfords factory in the Potteries, is the surprising lack of people involved, and also the informal appearance of those that are. The greasy-overalls and the steel toe-capped boots are almost a thing of the past because the machines really are gaining the ascendency.

That window factory certainly set my mind working in relation to the rest of Norwich. The day after, as I mingled with the crowds back in the centre of the city, I thought how unusual a combination it was that this antique capital should be the home to a respectable company making such quintessentially modern architectural accoutrements as replacement plastic doors and windows, when it is situated in a part of the country noted for its remoteness, for occasionally lagging behind the rest of provincial life, and with a growing reputation for having supposedly escaped some of the more unpleasant ravages of 1960s town and city planning. The sun shining onto the busy streets and the multi-coloured, stripy canvas rooftops of the open market stalls, huddled effectively together in the centre of the famous square, raised the spirits straight away. It was not a strong sun, and as the morning progressed it became increasingly strained. The pale blue high in the sky gradually gave way to a swathe of grey gathering menacingly from the west. By the time I came to eat my lunch in a café at the bottom of that famous narrow pebbled lane-cum-medieval alley pitched down a gentle slope called Elm Hill, the sun was only just managing to struggle through a tracery of bare tree branches and throw soft-focus shadows, touched by the most delicate strokes of mellowing amber, onto the flint cobbles undulating appealingly away at the other side of the street. Those patterns were entrancing, and I watched them pull themselves in and out of focus throughout several courses of the most excellent food. Elm Hill is medieval Norwich at its best. It is one of those enchanting slices of authentic England that foreign tourists and home grown sentimentalists find so alluring, and which Marxists often find so amusing. So enchanting, in fact, the council only permits the application of certain pigments of paint to the old buildings that are in keeping with the atmosphere of the fifteenth century. Elm Hill offers an assortment of distorted buildings and darkened passageways, a profusion of tiny gnarled windows and crooked gables, and is so perfectly preserved it is difficult to believe it was derelict as recently as the 1930s, until, after the efforts of the Norwich Society, it was restored to become one of the major tourist attractions of the city. It does not look to have been touched for generations, even if the last surviving tree that gave it its name was killed off, somewhat ironically, if one takes into account the historical associations of the city (an influx of immigrants arrived there from the Netherlands fleeing religious persecution centuries ago), by Dutch elm disease not that many years back.

All of this was a fine contrast to the high technology factory I had seen the previous day, whose brochures were now open before me on the table. If we must have a deluge of plastic windows fitted to our homes, looking at those I saw being manufactured in Norwich, and looking at Elm Hill, it is a pity the same commitment that has been put into the development of the manufacturing technology has not been put into exploiting the working properties of the material to the full by creating an unlimited selection of more subtle and better-designed shapes, as good or better than their wooden predecessors. I suspect, though, this will prove to be an even greater challenge than was the invention of the technology from which they are made, or the devising of a way of manufacturing coloured uPVC doors and windows that do not fade with time. (This has been the problem with producing coloured profile so far, though Anglian are working on it.) The relentless onslaught will proceed accordingly, if the wave of bad taste that is one of the scions of our age is anything to go by. Perhaps, just as they are pioneering coloured profile manufacture today, and are as successful as they are at exporting the product they currently produce from their own splendid factories, Anglian Windows will be at the forefront of the much-needed improvement in profile design. That would be something Norwich really could be proud about, if it wants to be known for having avoided the worst excesses of modern urban and architectural planning.

Through Lavenham and Essex to Kent

Felixstowe appealed to me as worth a visit after Norwich. I knew it was a port that had grown throughout most of the years Liverpool had declined, ostensibly for reasons contrary, and possibly connected to, some of the loss of trade to Merseyside. But Felixstowe was rather more easterly than I preferred to travel, and I wanted to be in Brighton the following weekend.

Even before I had turned the direction of the latter half of the journey on its head, I had intended stopping off at Basildon in Essex. Basildon was strategically positioned between Norfolk and Kent, was a reasonably comprehensive centre of population, and offered the interesting prospect of studying Essex

Man grazing in its natural habitat, out on the saltmarshes east of London. Round the fireside the evening before I left Norwich, however, I was reminded quite correctly that Essex Man exists just about everywhere, or at any rate his aspirations do, and he has risen to prominence as a sort of impending cult figure chiefly because of a southern orientated media assuming its own part of the country is the centre of the universe. It was suggested, if I was intending to sketch a generous portrait of contemporary England, that I really ought to visit some of the ancient textile villages of Suffolk on my journey down into Kent, and not to speak to too many people while I was there either, but simply absorb the atmosphere of the countryside instead. A number of names were reeled off, with Kersey and Lavenham designated as the most interesting, and the most likely to make me question whether or not I was still standing upright once I was in them. This intrigued me. I had heard of them both. I knew vaguely that Kersey was supposed to be one of the prettiest and most photographed villages in Britain, and that Lavenham had a fairly important church. But outside a few references in guidebooks, I knew nothing about either of them, or even exactly where they were. They are not prominent on any map. I was prepared to be open minded about the subject matter for the remainder of the journey, as I suggested earlier. A spell in remote countryside was also an attractive proposition, after so many urban landscapes and the observation of the workings of industrial activity. So I took the advice and took the narrow back lanes away from Norwich late one morning, through a stretch of countryside upon which had descended a fog so dense it was barely possible to see the old oak trees and the piles of recently harvested sugar beet common to that part of East Anglia trailing away from the sides of the road, and headed toward Suffolk.

Although I had never been into Suffolk before, I had seen enough paintings and photographs and guides to the British countryside to know roughly what to expect. All the way down a sort of metamorphosis architecturally gradually took place, the houses themselves becoming prettier and more Constable-looking and more plaster-finished the further south I travelled. Once I had passed through Bury St Edmunds, the familiar spectacle of thatched cottages and clusters of bulging timber-framed frontages joined together by perfect toy-town hedgerows began. The vernacular architecture of west Suffolk has a slightly north European, Laplandish, children's-conception-of-fairyland feel to it. It was poor weather when I arrived, but I can imagine that on a sharp late autumnal day, beneath a fresh high blue sky, with the sound of rooks crooning and clouds of leaves fluttering down the tiny deserted lanes, you really do grasp something of the essence of medieval England. Nowhere else during this journey was I aware of such a penetrating, all-consuming silence, not even in Norfolk. Many of these houses are ancient Flemish weavers' cottages, another legacy of the importance of the woollen industry in East Anglia during the Middle Ages, very different indeed to the more recent woollen industry with which I am familiar, and against which so much prejudice has been fostered. As a consequence many of the buildings in west Suffolk are four- or five-hundred-years-old and have survived for precisely the reasons that much of old Norwich survived – that when industry and prosperity departed with the arrival of the Industrial Revolution, they left behind the emerging paradox of a beauty and a sense of human scale that grew out of neglect; because commercially the towns and villages failed, but failed at just the right moment in time. The cottages are set against the most pleasant rolling scenery, and many of them are painted outlandish colours of pink or blue or mustard or peach or cream or even mauve; those that are wearing bulbous bonnets of thatch having an immensely characterful and top-heavy quality, as perfectly manicured as the fleece of a prizewinning sheep on display at an old fashioned country show.

But nothing had quite prepared me for the bizarre three-dimensional spectacle of Lavenham, which is perhaps the most remarkable and fascinating collection of ancient buildings grouped into a village I have come across anywhere. Since I was there, I have seen it described in a guidebook as containing the most perfect black-and-white timbered houses to be found in Britain; a description I find difficult to improve upon. No amount of clever writing, no string of fancy adjectives, can adequately convey the impression of coming upon the sight of that crooked village for the first time. I had wondered a few days earlier that, when considered as an autonomous entity, the ugliness of Birmingham is so profound it could almost have come from a single mind. And so it is with much of the prettiness of Lavenham, which looks from a distance like one vast theatrical set that was fairly amateurishly and hastily put together, but with enough enthusiasm to imbue it with real charm. In fact, it amazes me to think that you can find villages such as Lavenham only an hour or so's drive from Birmingham at all, and I well understood why that commercial traveller in Norwich had made the comment about feeling inebriated when standing upright once you were there. The houses and shops along the couple of main streets in Lavenham are unbelievably warped. They look as though they are always about to fall over or tumble into the street, and reminded me at once of the strange distorted backgrounds in the early German expressionist cinema, where the buildings were deliberately built in forced perspective to project an air of foreboding and menace. Some of the houses in Lavenham, especially that small cluster around the curve at the top end of the main street going out of the village, were so incredibly gnarled and twisted I would say the front walls facing onto the road were leaning backwards from the pavement to some thirty or forty degrees. I have occasionally seen the effects of mining subsidence on very old workers' cottages in other parts of the country, but nothing as severe as the sagging houses in Lavenham, which look to be in the process of slowly collapsing into the earth. You find it difficult to believe that verticals can seriously be perpendicular to horizontals anywhere in the old part of the village. What also strikes you as remarkable is that the houses are actually lived in, contain furniture and tabletops and cups of tea and lavatory chains and bookshelves and kettles. There must be something of a conspiracy against the innocent laws of gravity going on permanently behind those ancient walls, where floors must be rivalling the notion of becoming slopes. You cannot seriously believe those buildings contain normal household furniture, because to look at their distorted facades and picture a wardrobe placed against a wall is to imagine a cavity above the skirting board in which it would be possible to slide a wedge of cheese, and a very substantial wedge of cheese at that. And what about picture frames? Are they hung in such houses, or are they bolted to the walls? This is not the modern world of MFI fitted-kitchens and Currys electrical and High Speed Trains but some outrageous interpretation of the world of the Brothers Grimm. Some three-hundred buildings in Lavenham are listed as being of architectural or historical importance and as I stood staring at the old Wool Merchants House, which is undoubtedly one of them, I was not in the least surprised when a couple of American tourists appeared and began telling me about a man they had spoken to in a neighbouring village, who was about to hold a garden party to celebrate the five-hundredth birthday of his house.

It was mid-afternoon by the time I came into Kersey. I drove along its single undulating street, on for a further couple of miles, deposited my bags at the farm where I had arranged to stay, and then, while there was still a couple of hours' daylight left, freshened up and went back out to explore the surrounding countryside. As it was, I spent what little amount of day there was left looking at Kersey. According to a caption beneath a photograph of Kersey I read in a bookshop in nearby Hadleigh, even the ducks that live there know how to pose correctly for photographers. That seemed to me a very reasonable assessment of their behaviour. Crossing the narrow street at the foot of the village is a little trickling stream, around which this flight of ducks is stationed permanently, and I had already nudged them out of the way with the front of my car when I passed through earlier. They are curious, lumpy-faced ducks that look as though they have had a streak of turkey bred into them at some point or other years past, which is probably why such creatures are known as turkey ducks. As you walk up and down the narrow street of Kersey, inhaling a strong whiff of the authentic atmosphere of Tudor England, these ducks move bodily and ponderously out of the shadows, like tired stage-hands, and arrange themselves in an appealing formation around the little wooden footbridge, or around the edges of the stream. You stand staring at them and they stand staring expectantly back at you, occasionally shifting their weight from one pink webbed foot to the other, no doubt waiting to be fed. I drove through perhaps fifty or a hundred villages like this during the course of my journey. Some of them had ducks and streams and perfect village greens, and came close to being reasonably untouched, but rarely ever entirely. There was always, *always*, a sprinkling of post-war or mock-Spanish Old English Scandinavian rubbish clinging to the edges, making a mockery of the ancient stocks and red post-boxes embedded into mossy stone walls somewhere in the centre, like the ring of dirt round a bath. Only in the Yorkshire Dales and the Cotswolds did I come across obscure villages that approached being as untampered with and as steadfastly defended from the workings of the outside world as much as these Suffolk villages. Even Lavenham has its architectural banality tacked onto the outside, where you find it difficult to believe such mediocrity was presented for planning permission, never mind actually received it.

But Kersey is in a time warp. It does not even possess street lamps, with the result that at night it is pitch black there, with only lighted windows and the blaze of passing headlights cut out against the darkness. It is impossible to be in the village five minutes without getting caught up in the deep mood, the almost ghostly silence of the place. After my encounter with the village's incumbent wild-fowl, I climbed the small hill that rises at the top of the street, sat on a bench in front of the church, and absorbed the quiet, still marvelling for a long time over the notion that I was actually sitting in late-twentieth-century England. I say there was a silence, but of course, discreetly going on in the background, there were the barely audible sounds of authentic rural England, so at one with the landscape they do not really separate themselves until you begin to concentrate. Only the lowing of cattle, the muffled clucking of chickens, a remote dog bark, the sudden cracking of wings and the cooing of doves becoming agitated around the belfry alongside where I was sitting, and intermittently and somewhat unnervingly, the deep thudding of distant gun-shots, came at me across that overwhelming sombreness, where the rolling meadows stretched up beyond the crooked little village to melt into an enclosing smoky dusk. There was also the occasional moaning of distant crows, always such a morbid and funereal sound, embellishing perfectly the piercing melancholy of authentic rural England on sullen winter afternoons. All that was missing was the calling of the hunt leader's horn and the distant baying of hounds. Kersey seemed to me then the type of village the Germans invaded in Graham Greene's short story set during the war; but there was also something else, some indefinable undercurrent that was vaguely disturbing that I could not and cannot still pinpoint. Perhaps it was the deep melancholy of the weather conditions, which were so profound the air actually felt heavy, as it does before a summer storm. If this was indeed the timeless England that the Germans and the Japanese and the Americans travel so far to see, the lost England we have all been searching for since H.V. Morton for God knows how many years, the timeless Constable countryside of Roger Scruton and his chugging motorcycle, the land of hope and glory spread out beneath the same sky as a National Health Service that, according to Mr Scruton, produces a lot of useless geriatrics, they should go straight to that tiny corner of west Suffolk, where they will find marooned an island of tranquillity floating upon a bigger island of shabbiness and inexorable decay.

The following morning over breakfast I had a long conversation with one of the guests at the farmhouse where I was staying. He was a market researcher in agriculture and was involved with the farming fraternity of the area. I said that all the way down into Suffolk I had seen pile after pile of sugar beet at the sides of the roads, and he then went on to relate a brief outline of the agricultural history of the area; one that is as traditional and as deeply ingrained as the old cottages themselves. I had passed a large sugar refinery on the outskirts of Bury St Edmunds, and it would appear that the industry is fairly well stitched-up, for you cannot grow sugar beet round there except under contract from the particular company in question. So much for tradition, I thought. We began talking about the villages, and I said that, as pretty as most of them were, the quality that struck me about the smaller ones was their lifelessness and their deadness. I suppose that if Kersey had been a real village with a heart, the atmosphere hanging over it might have been rather less morose. The turn-of-the-century photographs I saw of Kersey elsewhere depicted the familiar sight of people standing, staring aimlessly at the camera amongst the piles of horse dung dolloped in the centre of the street. At least there were people, even if they were probably not much more than glorified peasants. Back then these villages were lived in. People did not just sleep there and spend weekends cultivating perfect English rose gardens. Now they seem to be not much more than ornaments arranged on a countryside mantlepiece, immaculately preserved with only a little cracking here and there to the original glazing. But there is no life. If there is a lack of people and interesting incidents in the preceding paragraphs, it is because while I was in those tiny villages in Suffolk I saw hardly anybody at all. There was a shortage even of passing cars. I felt the sound of my own car must have been the first noise to have broken the air for days. Public transport appears to be an obsolete form of life. The width of the roads would barely allow it. I think that if I lived there I should go insane after only a very short time, stranded in the midst of such melancholia, remote from the hub of life. Kersey and some of the other hamlets nearby are probably not much more than expensive and very exclusive dormitory villages, coming alive briefly during the evenings and first thing in the mornings, as are such villages everywhere, north as well as south. And consequently there is hanging over them a lack of spirit, substance, and soul. I could not even find a village shop in Kersey, though there were several pubs, one of which – the one that looked like a house, as pubs used to do – I was told is sometimes frequented by farmers and genuine local characters. But the village shop is the pulse-beat of any small community, and a gathering of people without one cannot be much of a community.

The sense of timelessness was compounded when I went back to Kersey before I left the area and actually saw two men thatching the roof of a cottage set back from the road. That was the moment when I finally shook my head. It was shouted to me that this job has to be done roughly every twenty-five years. And a fairly secure job in those parts it must be too, I thought, as I walked away expecting to bump into a shire horse. I felt like I was floating in some obscure limbo. Was this ancient craft being carried out in the same England where wretched smoky job clubs teetered and tottered down the back streets of Middlesbrough and Birmingham and men queued up to be given coppers and shillings? Where Asian weavers stared solemnly at strangers across a blur of moving spindles in textile mills in Bradford? Where joyriders screeched to a halt along dual carriageways in Newcastle? Where dazzling molten steel was poured like volcanic lava from one fifty ton bin into another? Where people drooled hungrily over illustrations in glossy uPVC door and window catalogues? Where kindred sights and sounds and happenings and industries and trades and people and activities swarmed, thrived, heaved and multiplied?

It was. I began thinking that if we ever reach a new feudal England of old at all, the lords of information and technology conducting their operations from computer terminals plugged in beneath ancient roofs in warped medieval villages like Kersey will be prepared to pay very handsomely indeed to keep their thatched roofs intact. That, if nothing else, might keep a genuine craft alive. I fell when I was in Kersey, fell full length on my back down a flight of slippery moss-covered steps leading away from the church, back to the deserted village street. If I had hurt myself there would have been no one available to help, because there seemed to be nobody alive in the village. The crash and the grunt and the crude double-barrelled expletive I uttered disturbed the doves in the belfry once again with such timing I felt like I had slipped in a scene from a Jacques Tati film. Perhaps the guardian spirit of Kersey was exacting a small revenge for the sceptical remarks I had scribbled in my notebook earlier, on the pulpit of ground rearing above; at the awkward thoughts that had come into my head as I paced about a church yard sparkling magically with hundreds of gossamer spiders' webs covered in dew suspended in the grass, and, still floating on that obscure limbo, I had wondered in which century, in which country, in which dimension, in which continuum, in which corner of which universe I really was. Perhaps twenty-first century English thatchers will drive enormous Japanese jeeps, like the thirty-grand monster I saw standing blatantly outside one of the ancient pubs in a hamlet near South Milford, defying the parking lines alongside an assortment of Jaguars and Range Rovers. Perhaps they already do.

On my way from Essex down into Kent the following day, I crossed the Dartford Bridge. A great expanse of recession-hit warehousing and distribution-predisposed industry opened up and disappeared interminably, fading toward a milky peach-coloured mist draped across the street-patterns far below. After miles and miles of monotonous motorway Kersey and Lavenham were as far away as ever. Whatever the future brings, however many more miles of motorway are laid, it will not make much difference to the timelessness of remote west Suffolk villages. For that matter it will not make much difference to the timelessness of remote villages everywhere; whose lost industries are only quaint memories glozed over in guidebooks, while simultaneously conservationists rail against the vast ugliness descending on the Thames estuary caused by real industry out in the real world, from which the real country and conservationist sentimentality actually makes its living.

Thinking about that, as the juggernauts screamed past with their hideous dinosaur like roar, I looked toward the East and thought about the real world, then felt depressed and horribly cold. But the heater in my car was blowing out what ought to have been only the cosiest warmth.

8

East Kent and Sussex

The Apple Farmer

Staring across the fertile East Kent countryside, now streaked with late afternoon autumn sunshine, I was struck again by how it is that meeting people you might otherwise never come into contact with gradually alters the conventional picture you have carried around in your mind for so long of the country in which you live. As you move from city to city and from one county to the next, though there is an overall similarity, only when you have focused on economic aspects unique to different areas do you begin to understand what different universes different people really do inhabit. Minor aesthetic observations you have made over the years begin to pull themselves together like the missing pieces of a jigsaw finally being slotted into place, meaning you can never reflect on what you see from the train or car window as you rush through the countryside in quite the same way again.

Take fruit growing, for instance. Serious writers pore for hours over their thesauruses in the struggle to craft readable prose, and to avoid using the same word twice in a sentence or a paragraph. Political historians grapple with the past to try and make some sense of the present, and newspaper columnists scratch their heads confusedly because Edward Heath has been awarded the Order of the Garter, in spite of having been a fairly useless prime minister. We each of us take our little universes and our own personal spaces deadly seriously. But, in our ceaseless endeavour to generalize and derive meaning from the complexity of the world, do we stop to think about some of the technical complications inherent to the workings of agriculture? Do we toss an English apple up and down on our palm before we bite into it, and speculate seriously as to how it actually got there? We do not, because we find it difficult as a culture to attach much philosophical or intellectual significance to the growing of food. Because we are a nation moved by a feeling for tradition, we can attach poetic significance to it easily enough, provided it is lumped together sentimentally with the atmosphere of sepia-toned photographs depicting pregnant hay wagons lumbering up and down winding country lanes, the smell of thyme, the whistle of a train on a quiet pre-war branch-line, or the buzzing of bees on warm September afternoons. But I would say such an attitude is essentially a selfish gesture, a knee-jerk reaction by inner sentiment, born of an understandable desire to avoid facing up to the true unpleasantness of the world, and to go on sucking our thumbs. In the real world, many of us, pontificators, proselytizers, and sentimentalists alike, push the produce of agriculture into our mouths with scarcely a moment's thought about where it came from or for the farmers who grew it. Superior persons in book-lined studies could not exercise their pathetic prejudices so assuredly, were it not for a multitude of farmers having as much of an understanding about the workings of the soil and the seasons as superior persons do about the emotional traumas such-and-such a novelist went through, whilst squatting in a pig-sty in southern France in 1815. And, when all is said and done, which is the more crucial to the basic human condition? We have an ingrained knack of remaining oblivious to some of the barest essentials of our existence and the people responsible for them, never mind wondering whether or not they influence our own narrow outlook on life. Beyond the regular contributors to *Farmers Weekly*, who can really be bothered to be interested in the ergonomics of modern agricultural methods, other than the Green Party drawing attention to some of the more dubious aspects, for propaganda reasons, during its pre-election broadcasts?

In the fading light and the lowering temperature of East Kent that afternoon I was walking with an apple farmer through one of his orchards, and I raised some of these questions. Hoovering the ground alongside us was one of the biggest dogs I have ever seen – I believe it was a member of the Saint Bernard family – so wide and so solid you felt you could have safely saddled it up and ridden it back to the half-timbered farmhouse losing itself among the shadows deepening behind us. We had paused to look across row upon row of bare apple trees stretching away from us toward the gathering sunset. Our breath was shooting out in gasps, our hands were shoved deep into our coat pockets, the remnants of the recent harvest were scattered up and down the aisles before us, the white pointed tip of the odd oast-house could still be seen protruding from the folds in the silent Kentish countryside undulating for miles around. This was one of those moments where the things you are being told and the thoughts you are thinking react against the prevailing atmospheric conditions and imbue it with a philosophical resonance you remember for years afterwards. The farmer was telling me that because of our position above the equator, the strength of the light falling onto that part of Kent means he cannot grow trees of more than eight feet in height, without adversely affecting the quality of his fruit. His Spanish competitors, on the other hand, can grow much taller trees because of the more generous levels of Mediterranean sunshine. As a consequence, for him to remain competitive he has to farm greater areas of land with greater technical proficiency. He owns two more farms, similar in size to the one over which I was being shown, and on all three every tree has to be looked at individually and pruned very precisely. This is vital to the success of the following year's crop. The angle at which the branches will grow has to be calculated in advance, to train them to expand in such a way that the fruit hangs properly; otherwise it might fall to the ground too early and ruin the harvest. Taking in an impressive panorama comprised almost as far as the eye could see of nothing but apple trees, the thought of having to attend to each one on that farm alone, to such a degree of detail, was enough to make the mind reel. The prosect of doing it on three seemed to be truly awesome.

It is hardly surprising that throughout the winter months the farmer and his staff of ten are engaged in nothing but pruning.

Then there is the business of cross-pollination, about which we were taught at school but have since probably forgotten. Plant one type of apple on its own and it would not grow properly. Plant several different varieties together, and the bees cross-pollinate them, producing healthy apples of the correct shape with adequate durability. They thrive successfully because they depend on one another communally to retain their individuality. There is something deeply moving about such beautiful natural interaction as that, from which we ought to be able to extract a great deal. Whether it sounds hackneyed to say it or not, to me this is the sort of phenomenon that matters; the kind that helps to keep the Earth spinning successfully around the Sun, but which, in our clever sophistication, and with our marvellous capacity to have noses formed from the hardest toffee, we all too easily dismiss as merely prosaic. It is only when you have spent some time in the presence of such interesting and committed people as that Kentish farmer that your bird's-eye view of the world, with which you felt so comfortable beforehand, begins to pale in significance so that you start to feel inadequate and even pathetic. The reader may be assuming I was being converted by the type of stubbled English farmer populating the evergreen pastures of national folk memory, whose farmyard was an appealing clutter of rusting paraphernalia, and whom, as sophisticated persons, we are all supposed to patronize and pretend to feel inferior to for the sake of English romanticism, as a matter of course. Nothing could be further from the truth. Erase from your mind a wellington-booted country bumpkin wearing a faded grey tanktop, smelling of dried cow dung, harbouring a deep suspicion of outsiders and modern technology. When I was a schoolboy I worked for some time for a Yorkshire farmer who was just such an old fashioned type (this is where I obtained the above description), who still took snuff from the back of his hand, and held his trousers up with a piece of rope. The farmer whose hospitality I enjoyed that afternoon in Kent was wearing very muddy wellington boots when I met him, admittedly. But he also spoke perfect Queen's English, has a degree in horticulture from Reading University, and confessed, as we walked back to the farmhouse while there was still some light left to see by, that the farming fraternity in his part of the country was comfortably middle class – a middle class of which he would not, I am certain, feel in the least bit intimidated if I were to announce publicly he was one of the cornerstones, with holdings of the size that he has.

Back in the warmth of his kitchen, once darkness had finally settled, over a pot of tea we began talking about English sentimentality and the steadily increasing nostalgia we are showing toward the past. It seems the farmer's was only the second generation of a family business begun by his father during the 1920s. (As an industry, apple growing was of no real importance in this country until after the second world war.) Also, largely because of research carried out by the influential East Malling Research Institute in Maidstone, we are now on the verge of developing new apples that have a natural immunity to scab and mildew, the two chief scourges of fruit farming in this country. Apples grown today were, he said, much superior to those grown in the past. And, with the improvement in modern dietary habits, along with the general awareness of leading a healthier lifestyle, the farmer told me that he was very confident indeed about the future of English apple growing. But was this changing any of our fundamental assumptions? I doubted it. I said that as a nation, we seem to be forever looking back over our shoulders for inspiration. We are haunted by the belief that what was accomplished by earlier generations, especially when it comes to our perception of almost anything architectural, is automatically superior to nearly all things modern. This the farmer wholeheartedly endorsed, but then admitted, after he had thought for a moment or two and stirred his tea again, that it probably could be extended to include the growing of apples. The public perception of apples was, he said, still tarnished by the scare story that surfaced some years back claiming allegedly carcinogenic pesticides were being sprayed onto the fruit to control diseases – a controversy which he assured me was blown hopelessly out of all proportion. (I had been told the same thing about the riots on the Meadowell estate in Newcastle, a few weeks earlier.) He himself controls diseases using predatory insects, and could honestly say to the public that apples grown on his farms are not chemically treated. Nevertheless, there are probably people who cannot examine an English apple without taking it for granted that it could not possibly be superior to an apple grown during the age of steam trains. As if it were second nature, we accept nowadays that there is too much high-volume automation at work and not enough copper kettles boiling on open ranges in stone-flagged kitchens. But this cancels out a sensible assessment of the benefits to other areas of our lives modernization has brought; one of the most notable being the physical comfort to be able to idealize the age of steam through the wrong end of a telescope in the first place. Such a profound contradiction in terms appears to be becoming an ever stronger defining characteristic of the English people than it has been. Why?

Because it is one of the symptoms of a nation in economic decline, backed up by the outlook of a political class which, as hard as it tries, is brought up to speak with dignity but is unfortunately imbued with entirely the wrong kind of brainpower. We are unable to project an adequate vision of the future with which we can feel sufficiently comfortable, just as we do not have an adequate understanding of how education, industry, and politicians really have got to work together if we are to remain in the economic big league. Because the socio-economic repercussions would inevitably interfere with our precious – some would say precocious – clinging to tradition, we fasten our sights onto an idealized version of the past instead, to cancel out the uncertainty we feel for the present. I am not saying here that tradition is necessarily a bad thing. There is nobody surrounded by the paraphernalia of tradition more than this particular writer. Tradition creates a framework from which a certain amount of stability and inspiration follows. But it is a question of what degree of emphasis is placed upon that tradition; how much we allow it to dominate the way we conduct our lives and our constitutional affairs. At the present time we cannot make a sensible enough break psychologically with the amount of effort necessary to improve our economic performance. This begins right at the top in our constitutional assembly, with both its feet embedded firmly in the eighteenth century, and filters down through the population to affect the style of plastic coach lamps fastened to the outside of mock-Georgian houses, and our inability to attach social prestige to manufacturing industry. Sooner or later the crunch is going to come, of course – it always does in the end – as it did with the sterling crisis and our inevitable withdrawal from the ERM, because the pound joined the mechanism at an artificially high value. In the meantime, as I suggested earlier, we go on sucking our thumbs. The more technologically advanced we are forced into becoming, the further national sentiment retreats into the security of the past; the more sharply defined become the anachronisms. There is more to the increasing popularity of Victorian-styled uPVC doors and windows, the implications of the 1992 General Election result, and Hugo Young's suggestion during the fallout period afterwards that Britain was indeed a deeply conservative nation, than we care to admit.

I have often heard people, especially old working-class people, claim that food does not taste as good today as it used to. It does not matter whether it is bread or beer or fish and chips; the modern variety is dismissed habitually as being inferior to its predecessor. Though there is undoubtedly some truth in this as a generalization (compare some types of commercially produced tomatoes to those grown in greenhouses in back gardens), I suspect that most of the time what we actually mean, quite apart from the influence of nostalgia, is that the modern methods by which food is farmed are less agreeable to the way we feel it ought still to be farmed. That is to say, the whole atmosphere – and by that we really mean the entire modern world – is romantically less stimulating to the imagination, and therefore less *picturesque*. We cannot, if we are honest with ourselves, expect to produce a school of poetry inspired by the grading of fruit by East Kent Packers, the destination of most of my farmer friend's colossal crop of Cox and Russet apples, once his harvest has been completed. The articulated lorries grinding up and down the M2, which will increase in volume once the Channel Tunnel is opened, will have no place in future English folk memory. There is too much corrugated-tin associated with the atmosphere of modern distribution and not enough pan-tiles for that to happen. I suppose at bottom this is a reaction against machine automation and the dehumanizing effects of speed, as much as it is against crude aesthetics and the passing of the shire horse. In a country such as England, forever clutching its horse-brasses to its breast and gluing mock-Tudor beams incongruously to its ceilings, difficulties were bound to arise once the cost-effective installation of concrete kerbstones bumped up against the nation's burgeoning pre-twentieth century nostalgia. The difficulty we have accommodating modern high-technology manufacturing in our national psychology is that it contrasts against our strong feeling for tradition, and deep love of the countryside. This awareness derives from the understandable conviction that more automation means we are unable to identify romantically with the practical side of the process more easily. We need to be stimulated aesthetically on something approaching a human scale. A greater quantity of hands and more straw baskets we can relate to. The application by machine of computer coded labels we cannot. There is a struggle raging permanently, just beneath the surface of the modern popular English consciousness, between the numbing effect of increasing comfort and a dependability upon push-button technology reducing the need to use our feelings and our senses more creatively. We may feel the need to recreate the look of Victorian doors, but we don't seem to notice that if they are pressed out of plastic, so that they do not require much maintenance, or the use of hands in the forming of simulated panelling – the very things which gave the originals their style and their appeal – this does represent rather a falsification in terms. Sentimentality, as always, rules the day; though ironically, it may yet turn out to be this nation's hidden reserve of strength, finally determining its destiny independent of a federalist Europe, despite the political consequences, the accusations, the denials, the establishment of lucrative reputations, the sceptical editions of *Panorama*, the chuckling of Marxists who lambast capitalism but take for granted all that it offers them materially, the resting of spectacles despondently by Nicholas Ridley on the bridge of his nose, and the slow burning of the flame through the blue touch-paper, has continued unabated.

I went back out into the cold that afternoon and drove

along pitch-black country lanes. After a while, I joined a main road. Yet another rush-hour was just getting under way. Somewhere beyond the hedges the motorway would be preparing itself for another succession of traffic delays due to repairwork and resurfacing. The Channel Tunnel would be approaching completion, the farce of the rail link still unresolved. The petrol station signs would be emblazoned vividly against the blackness. The backlit perspex cut-outs of jolly fat men would be marching above the forecourts toward the Little Chefs, the cars lined up silently outside, the heads nodding animatedly as they fed themselves, and smoked, and drank, and laughed at one another, and stared at newspapers behind the glass. After another while, I joined the motorway. Inevitably, one of the lanes was closed. The traffic bunched up. Thousands of plastic cones filed slowly past. The traffic stretched out, the cones speeded up for a minute or two, the traffic slowed down then bunched up again. Before me in the darkness a cascade of white and orange lights, flung haphazardly across the bottom edge of the huge black canvas of night, pulsated with headlights and drew gradually nearer. Two hundred-and-thirty-thousand miles above, the moon was illuminated by a sun shining on the opposite side of the world. Far below, my tiny vehicle moved microscopically along, beneath that shining disc hanging among a myriad of twinkling specks, disappearing momentarily beneath the bridges. The signs flashing past briefly in the glare, and the map laid open on the seat next to mine, informed me I was heading toward Canterbury. Canterbury tales. Canterbury pilgrims. Canterbury the see of the Primate of All England. Canterbury, once the capital city of Ethelbert's kingdom of Kent. Canterbury, historic city.

My speed reduced. Another sequence of roundabouts and nondescript suburbs and pelican crossings and contrived grass verges began.

Canterbury

Of all the town and city centres I visited during the course of my journey, irrespective of size, the one in which I felt least intimidated or in danger at night was Canterbury. Doubtless, by making public statements such as this someone will be able to produce statistics suggesting that Canterbury has the highest incidence of mugging for a place of its size anywhere in England. It is interesting as a guide to the social atmospherics of our age that it is worth making observations about personal safety in a public place and setting them down on paper like this at all. These days we seem to accept it as part of the natural scheme of things that the darkened doorway we are approaching, as we walk along a city centre street during the hours of darkness, might well contain a masked hoodlum wielding a baseball bat. That assumption might not have become so ingrained if we'd had more articulate and more courageous politicians running our affairs over the years, with a greater accountability to their country instead of themselves.

I did not stay long in Canterbury. I only stayed the one night, in fact, before turning my attention toward thc south coast early the following morning. Before I arrived, I had intended to remain there for several days. What changed my mind was that during the evening, totally unexpectedly, I discovered an evocative Canterbury, pleasantly lubricated with the romantic ambience you find permeating theatrically-antiquated streetscapes at that time of year (late November) anywhere. If I was indeed searching for a series of symbolic snapshots of modern England, I felt there was no reason whatever to stay and see anything more, because I found one in Canterbury before I had even properly begun. But that realization came a little later. First, having booked into my hotel, I went out of a side entrance and immediately became lost. (Canterbury is another of those places that sizewise, if it did not possess a cathedral and have remnants of castle walls interspersed with its ring road, you would more properly describe as a town.) Because I had arrived during the rush-hour, because it was dark and because the place was new to me, I crawled into the city in such a way that I did not gain my bearings adequately. Although I discovered later that I was less than two minutes' walk from the medieval part – the Dickensian set pieces that would have appealed to the young David Lean – inadvertently, I actually walked away from it.

Canterbury was bombed during the war, and assaulted again architecturally in places after it. One part of it, all concrete and 1960s' marble, looks like a prototype for small town redevelopment according to Colin Buchanan; something that is worth remembering, what with the city's exploitation of the enigma of Chaucer and Dickens. The more modern bits were all that I saw to begin with. I wandered for some time along those hollow, nondescript back streets that are an indiscriminate mixture of crudely modernized mews cottages, mysterious buttressed walls that might belong to big post offices or Victorian hospitals, and patches of cobbles showing up beneath the glow of street-lamps at the bottom of darkened alleyways. This was my initial impression of Canterbury, in addition to the glut of traffic I had been caught up with on my way in. After about half and hour of this aimlessness, I ran down a grassy embankment and ended up walking along leaf-encrusted, very frosty, very slippery stone flags. Alongside was a small church nestling among the shadows, surrounded by an array of crooked gravestones, illuminated eerily by the glow of a single cast-iron lamp sunk into the ground at an angle, next to a gate. A sign informed me I was walking, inevitably, along the Canterbury Heritage Trail. It was very dark. I could hear the mumble of traffic and smell car fumes coming through the trees behind me. I could also sense, in a way I cannot describe, that I was very close to the city centre. And yet, throughout the time I was roaming those streets and shadows and small commercial forecourts scattered with cars and the pattern of dim windows, I passed hardly anybody. At times, this sort of experience is not at all unpleasant, provided you are in the right kind of place, in the right mood, and do not feel intimidated by the kind of observation I made at the beginning of this piece.

Sensing a vague trickle of noise in the sharp air I walked in the opposite direction, cut along another narrow side street, then stepped into a scene of pure English sentimentality. This happened so abruptly and so unexpectedly I turned immediately, walked back several hundred yards round the corner, then walked into it again, slowly and very deliberately, to check that I was not imagining things. I can feel the sensation, as though I were opening a door, even now, months afterwards, in broad daylight. For it was Thursday night and it was late-night opening, and the central shopping area was charged with the atmosphere of impending Christmas. All the necessary ingredients were there – the ancient alleyways; the literary associations; the reflections on the age of pilgrims past, old enough to be distorted and the more brutal aspects be suppressed; the huge cathedral touched by floodlights towering above the clutter of darkened rooftops; the sagging windows and the bulging doorways; the shiny cobbles and the gnarled timbers; the muffled laughter from the bistros and the bars. There were coloured lights strung between the gables of the old buildings the entire length of High Street. As with all such cramped medieval townscapes, you feel the buildings are leaning against each other for support, with the odd one nestled tightly in among the others like someone squeezing between figures seated on a crowded park bench, rather than positioned alongside one another for convenience.

Down the narrow side streets, which in Canterbury are carbon copies of The Shambles and attached thoroughfares in York – perhaps it is really the other way round – the buildings are like illustrations to a Gothic poem. They look as though they are confronting one another from opposing pavements, instead of facing one another from opposite sides of a street. Canterbury does this as well as its handful of counterparts elsewhere, at least in the old parts crowded around Mercery Lane and Christchurch Gate, the astonishing carved entrance to the cathedral close in the Buttermarket. Here was one of the country's most famous old cities, preparing itself for Christmas. There was certainly not much evidence of recession, though of course there might have been a greater degree of window shopping going on than I realized. The fancy gift shops I walked in and out of were bursting with chocolate petticoat tails, pure butter shortbread, sugared almonds, cartons of fruit-and-nut mix, assorted toffees packed into London bus tin moneyboxes, and goodness knows what else. The bookshops smelt warmly of new paper, and were giving prominence to the usual depressing rubbish. The Amstrad computers and the Sony hi-fi stacks were piled in the windows, knocked back with a little tinsel, so that they did not look too self-conscious as products of a computer age slipped in among fifteenth-century passageways. The cuddly toys were beckoning to the passers-by – I bought a Winnie the Pooh for my three-year-old son, hand-made, amazingly amidst the imported Taiwanese and Chinese multitudes, in Cheltenham – the spray snow was tucked into the corners of the mock-Georgian bow windows. All that was missing were artificial snow flakes falling gently in the background, and Terry Wogan and Bruce Forsyth dressed as Father Christmases, bridging the gaps between the programmes.

Because this southern part of England was vulnerable historically to invasion, the oldest cities tended to be strongly fortified. Canterbury retains much of its original medieval wall, and at the bottom of St Peter's Street stands the West Gate, a battlemented keep spanning the road, and the city's sole surviving medieval entrance. It was here, near the railway level crossing out the other side, having walked the full length of High Street down into St Peter's Street examining the menus stuck to the windows of Canterbury's vast quantity of restaurants, that I discovered an old vagrant sitting on the pavement. He was unspeakably dirty and had his knees tucked up under his chin and stank so powerfully of urine you could taste the ammonia on the back of your throat. He saluted me when we caught each others' eye as I approached, but when I tried to engage in conversation with him, he merely uncoiled and leered toothlessly, a bundle of decrepit clothing and foul smells. I was fascinated by the condition of his gums. They were a sort of crustacea of blackened-pink flesh, shining in the glare of passing headlights, and twisting into all sorts of obscene contortions. He cackled so throatily that after only a few seconds his inebriated face began to look very strained indeed. Then he erupted into a fit of violent, bronchial coughing, just as a down-and-out I'd met in a subway up in Blackburn had done. As the phlegm dangled loosely from his lips, and he squirmed helplessly on the pavement, I had a horrible premonition he was going to start choking. I felt exposed. People on the opposite pavement began to stare, so that I also felt like a meddling social worker. Worse still, they might have thought I was mugging him. I imagined a crowd gathering and the accusations beginning to fling, and some brutalized halfwit pushing to the front in a shellsuit.

Once I was certain the vagrant was okay, I retreated hastily into a nearby candlelit restaurant, which happened to be serving wholefood and was a fascinating den of darkly painted woodwork and antique teapots, so old it might have been like that for the past three hundred years. There I consumed an exceptionally good meal, along with a small amount of wine, so that when I emerged onto the streets again to attempt a small amount of Christmas shopping, I was more than a little convivial with the bustling early evening atmosphere. The streets had filled up. It felt as though something was afoot. There was a festive feeling in the air; the kind that might still permeate fairy stories when the King is coming to town, if only there were not so many skulls being blown in half by bullets across the face of this misbegotten world. Canterbury was beaming. The air was alive with the scraping and clacking of womens' heels, and the shouting of street vendors selling sheets of Christmas wrapping paper five for a pound. I could feel myself beginning to be drawn into the cosy atmosphere of the scene. I had a sudden longing to have my family there with me; a feeling which, if I had consumed just a glass or two more of wine and truly been able to appreciate the distance between us, would probably have pushed me into another fit of depression. In the background, hanging in the air above the doorways to the shops, was the shaking of jingle bells and the singing of Bing Crosby and the beating rhythm of pop music (I often find that to hear the sound around you most acutely, it is best to stick one finger in one ear), booming from within. Some of the youngsters were dancing jigs to this music as they moved up the street. Definitely not much evidence of recession here amidst the seasonal jollity and the sliding of credit cards between magnetic eyes in an abundance of hungry cash-tills. Here, sink estates were out of sight, out of season, and well out of mind. Here, I suppose, sharply defined beneath the glossy veneer of modern consumer prosperity, looking in places like something wrenched up from Euro Disney and dumped down beneath a ceiling of twinkling stars onto good old English chalk, cheerful with the jocularity of students from the nearby university circulating loudly among the pubs, was J.K. Galbraith's Culture of Contentment.

I found my way to W.H. Smith's, near a multi-storey car park, and tried to locate the latest issues of *Living Marxism* or *The Spectator*. The nearest periodical I could find to either of that name was *Living France*. It is a symptom of your geographic location down in that corner of England, and the construction of the Channel Tunnel half an hour away, that you can find French property magazines on sale in the newsagents. France will soon be as accessible as London. The south-east, it has sometimes been said, is supposed to be the most susceptible to the influence of Continental ideas. I heard plenty of French voices on the streets of Canterbury that evening. Apparently they come over in droves, in search no doubt of the bogus English mystique. If that is so, it is to be hoped it is a scenario that can be exploited to the full. Let us absorb French spending power while we can.

Something of the festive atmosphere remained after nine, when the crowds had gone, the air was quiet, and only a handful of figures could be seen lighting cigarettes in shop doorways. The steel shutters were being pulled down, the young middle-class females went silent then sniggered when they drew alongside males, the fast-food trays were dumped in the concrete flower-bins, the beams of lonesome bicycles weaved this way and that as mysterious hooded figures rode them home along the side streets. Back in my hotel room, I heard more French voices talking animatedly in the corridor outside, like wooden caricatures from *'allo, 'allo*. I remember thinking vaguely, as I eventually began to drift off to sleep, that the quality the English really find so amusing about the French accent is its throaty severity.

Brighton

Coming away from Canterbury I did not take the obvious and most direct route by road down to Brighton. I decided to complete the closing phase of my journey on public transport instead, which, as it turned out, proved to be entirely by train. But I was in the awkward position at that stage of having to find somewhere to leave my car before I could sensibly proceed. I did not want to leave it in Canterbury and have the trouble of retrieving it later. So I drove back along the M2 into London, where I had arranged to have it driven home, caught the tube across to Victoria Station, then the electric train straight down through Croydon and Surrey to Brighton. At first I could not escape the feeling that I was leaving Canterbury and travelling in completely the wrong direction; an awareness influenced by my staring at road maps for weeks on end, and having developed the consciousness that travel felt smoother, and took on a better sense of uniformity in the mind's eye, if you felt to be going in as direct a line as possible. Doubling back on myself would create an awkward blip in the flow of the journey. But I quickly warmed to the idea, because the ensuing train journey carried me through the south London suburbs, and prompted me to think back to some of the squalid places I lodged in when I lived there many years ago, in particular a faded room I once took overlooking Clapham Common. For if there was one type of hotel accommodation I had not experienced by the time I turned toward Brighton during this journey it was the really down-market, cheap boarding-house that can be found in the heart of big town or city centres – the kind which is probably not a great deal more expensive by today's standards than traditional common-lodging-houses were in years past. It was likely that Brighton, with its seedy sexual undertones, its faded look in corners of being a town that has never quite managed to catch up since the end of the war, and its boasts in official handouts about the large number of hotels it possesses, would have more than its fair share to choose from. So, not being the kind of person who becomes unduly fussy about the quality of his surroundings at most normal times, as I emerged from Brighton's impressive vaulted Victorian railway station (somewhere between York and Kings Cross in its sense of scale and grandeur, but much quieter than either), stepped between the taxis and the traffic, then made my way toward the brightening of sky at the foot of the old part of the town, I decided spontaneously to try and locate a cheap boarding-house.

I suppose that at that stage of the proceedings I was possessed by some notion of literary integrity, though it turned out that the chief benefit of the exercise was that I was able to make an obvious comparison between shabbier lodging places and some of the more luxurious hotels I stayed in elsewhere. That I should have been motivated by what seems to me now a rather stupid sense of creative optimism seems all the more unlikely in the comfort of a warm study months afterwards, for not much creative energy had been forthcoming at the prospect of going to Brighton and writing about it during the few hours before I arrived. I was now in the lower right-hand corner of what we poor disadvantaged plebeians from the north consider to be that mysterious entity, traditionally swarming, so the legends went, with sun-bathing lounge-lizards, poncy clergymen, and flimsy businesses that more recently went bust the moment interest rates were adjusted a point or two – the prosperous south-east of England. Many splendid descriptive passages have been written over the years about these pleasant rolling Downs, descending gently toward the Sussex seaboard to embrace Brighton at the foot of their final chalky sweep. As much has been said about the beauty of the mild landscape down there as has been admitted about the reputation for bloated prosperity it has established for itself over recent years – along with cynical rumours about Tory governments tinkering with the economy primarily to keep that sector of the country and its wealthy itinerants happy, and their voting habits consistent.

Apart from the wealthiness of the south-east being in my opinion greatly exaggerated, (most of the 'wealth' in the south is absorbed by inflated mortgage repayments), it is to me a landscape without vitality, character, and clout. The quality that has often struck me most strongly about the area, because it was largely bypassed by the Industrial Revolution, is the lack of a penetrating sense of history stretching back through the last couple of centuries, which to my mind are the ones that really matter. The landscape of the region is often described as mellow, but to me this could be said to be a substitute for uninspiring and bland. Of course, the south-east has its castles and its country estates, its ancient churches and its remote villages, even its fashionable valleys, all of which are interesting and charming enough. No other part of England is able to exhibit such strong medieval connections, and reveal so many half-timbered buildings as you turn sharply into market squares. But, like parts of Cheshire and East Anglia, you tend to encounter either the very old or the very new. Not a great deal appears to have happened in between, except the cultivation of fields and hedgerows. They haven't nicknamed parts of this area '1066 Country' for nothing, whether Hastings is well within its boundaries or not. Ignoring the huge bulk of London, which looms permanently at the back of the mind like the city in the distance in a children's fairy story, the area lacks major focal points, which really means it lacks a clutter of densely populated cities. Hence that feeling that you are moving through a landscape that was not really affected by the nineteenth century. (This the south-east considers to work very much to its advantage.) These things I have said will sound like the most appalling generalizations to the area's inhabitants. Perhaps as someone originally from the north-west of England, I take it too easily for granted that a sense of history must be bound up with rugged factory architecture and blackened Nonconformist chapels, rows of tiny houses disappearing into the golden mists of the autumn mornings, and the legacy of ingrained labour struggles turning chunks of Peter Snow's maps of the British Isles red as the results come in at General Election times. If that is so, I do not have the space here to attempt justifications. I mention it in passing only as a way of suggesting that the very real physical differences that exist between parts of the north and south might be reflected equally as strongly in what are claimed to be the very real differences that exist in the psychology of the two regions' inhabitants as well. Presumably these are linked to social attitudes instilled over generations that cannot be passed off lightly as amusing or irrelevant, as they frequently are by a handful of our snootier Home Counties writers who do not understand the economic foundations of their own prejudices, never mind those of some of the unfortunate masses crushed in among the urban squalor north of the Trent.

Something Brighton had in common with the popular view of much of the north when I was there, something that nicely contradicted information I had come across elsewhere suggesting the town enjoyed a substantial amount of sunshine all year round, was that the weather remained impenetrably overcast. It was also horribly cold, much more so than had been the case further inland, though it was quickly pointed out, once I began criticizing the gloominess of the place, that until a day or so previously conditions had been nearly as good as summer. Having reached one of this country's premier coastal resorts, I did feel that I ought to be filled with a sense of optimism, chiefly because there is supposed to be something about the atmosphere of arriving in a terminus station at the seaside quite unlike that of arriving in any other. Though I am sure most of us try hard to pretend there is something special in travelling to the end of a length of railway track that finishes close to the ocean – no doubt this is a hangover from childhood, when such enthusiasm is very real – I did not have this feeling as I walked away from the station when I arrived in Brighton. When I turned onto the promenade at the bottom of Queens Road and West Street, it was a minute or two before I even registered the presence of the sea. It was visible only as a sort of sluggish grey pus, with a derelict pier cut off from the mainland for some distance plunging straight out into the abyss on one side, and another pier flashing feebly with a few lights and lewd signs on the other. When you come upon a popular English seaside resort like that, brooding beneath the dismal grey of a freezing winter's afternoon, I think you feel that you ought really to be buffeted by lashing gales and encounter thudding waves exploding over the old pebbly-concrete ramparts, sending the few figures foolish enough to be braving the elements cascading to the opposite side of the road in fear and disgust. I was hoping this was what Brighton, the only major coastal resort I was scheduled to visit during my journey (also, I believe, the largest in the country) would be able to offer. My hopes were in vain, though whether this was the fault of the climate or of the town I cannot entirely decide.

They say Brighton is lively. Not in the way that the traditional north country resorts are considered lively, but lively in the sense that socially it has, shall we say, something of a cosmopolitan complexion; an aspect of modern Brighton you can pick up easily if you spend five minutes walking round the Old Steine, or wandering through the older, trendier part of the town around the Gloucester Road quarter, with its plethora of street stalls and effeminate-bohemian undertones. Something of Brighton's modern flavour can be discerned by the fact that the *Gay Times* was prominently displayed on the counters in most of the newsagents I entered when I was there, to catch the eye of customers who might otherwise not go near the magazine racks. The place does not have the vulgar frivolity of a Blackpool. There are no garish funfairs lifting above the rooftops of the residential part of the town, probably because Brighton has never needed to fortify itself against train-loads of rowdy cotton workers descending for a fortnight from Lancashire mills. (No doubt it would have been more than happy to barricade itself against the youths on scooters and motor-cycles who brawled in the town, as they did in Margate some distance away, over Bank Holiday weekends throughout most of the 1960s.) If, as Priestley claimed, Blackpool is the kind of resort that could only have been a product of a virile industrial democracy, then Brighton must surely have been a product of London's stuffy gentlemen of leisure desiring a breath of sea air. Though it seems unlikely – impossible – as a comment on the atmosphere of the place by today's standards, Brighton actually used to be considered dignified. Few people can have failed to have heard Horace Smith's description that it was 'the Queen of Watering Places'. Fewer still can have failed to have heard it described informally, because of its nearness to the capital, as London-by-the-Sea. Because it was once supposed to have thrived on an air of sophistication, a view influenced almost certainly by the wealth of excellent Regency architecture contained within the town and in adjoining Hove, it was said that Brighton retained some of the advantages of London, while eliminating, because of its smaller size, many of the disadvantages. It was a 'breeding ground both of poets and sportsmen, of actors and gentlemen of leisure, of the aristocracy and the proletariat', claimed S.P.B. Mais somewhat ambiguously in 1948. Interestingly enough, this was written at about the time the film adaptation of

Brighton Rock was being shot there, a book that, whatever the limitations of its characterizations, portrayed a more squalid side to Brighton which, in the opinion of someone I spoke to the following morning, has not entirely disappeared today.

It is easy to see why Brighton was considered dignified. No matter the frivolity the London day-trippers brought with them as they came to fill the beach in their droves from the mid-nineteenth century onwards, Brighton can never have been the sort of resort that was concerned merely with people escaping hard work to indulge in riotous, excruciating fun. It has never catered purely for the old sixpenny crowd. It has an abundance of stylish restaurants clustered in the old medieval part of the town around a network of very cramped alleyways called The Lanes, probably linked to its growing importance as a conference venue. I have an interest in early plastics, and nearby I found an excellent antiques shop specializing in these things, which was appropriate, because Brighton has claims to be the antiques centre of Europe. It has its regal associations and, of course, its Royal Pavilion. This is Nash's fascinating structure and the town's most well known: a magnificent chunk of domed Indian pastiche resembling, when I came upon it through the grey semi-mist, a row of giant onions standing behind a tracery of leafless trees. Brighton also has its literary associations. Kipling lived nearby for a time and Dickens wrote *Dombey and Son* and *Bleak House* while he was there. Brighton has all of these things, but if it was said to retain some of the advantages of London in the past, then it has certainly managed to import some of its disadvantages today. The tone of the place was set for me by the grey office blocks that come almost up to the water's edge and lift high above the promenade, an aspect of the town I never really managed to get used to. (You feel that you ought to be coming upon a tall Victorian tower and trams.) I spent a most miserable hour walking up and down the back streets near the seafront when I arrived. Throughout that time the sea behaved as though it might only have been an expanse of water receding into the mist in the Lake District. There were none of the familiar background sounds of breaking waves or screeching seagulls encouraging the air of lofty optimism these places are generally supposed to bring out in the mind of the beholder. The gloom was emphasised by the big hotels, which were all quiet, their lounges empty. They either had bored doormen standing outside, absurdly overdressed in top-hat-and-tails and looking very conscious of themselves, or they were forlornly offering attractive discount rates fastened to sandwich boards standing on the pavements, none of which I was wise enough to take up. The previous week a man in Suffolk told me that the face of Brighton reminded him of a fifty-year-old tart wearing high heels and laddered stockings. The only tarts I saw hanging about the place when I was there were the quarrelsome ageing pansies Richard West had noticed when he had been in Brighton on a similar trip round England some years before me, and who immediately brought dated Dick Emery caricatures to mind as they emerged from those newsagents doorways. Notwithstanding the description of the town as an ageing tart being one that is common, it is the best I have yet heard.

As with any substantially-sized English seaside resort, Brighton has its cramped side streets stacked with bow-fronted, Palladian-styled boarding-houses, some rising characteristically in steep tiers, and all painted white or varying shades of cream. Remembering the task I had set myself on the way down, moving among them it did not take me long to find an establishment that looked suitably dog-eared and tatty. When I was ushered in through the small vestibule, I indicated that I was a traveller carrying the minimum amount of baggage, but as I was taken along a dark corridor and shown to my room I was surprised to be asked by the proprietor whether or not I would 'actually' require a towel. Simultaneously I inhaled the cool, stale stink of the place, a compound mixture part frying food, part babies' nappies, part antiquarian bookseller. As there were no clean towels folded neatly at the foot of the bed already, smelling deliciously of femininity, when I said that I would actually require a towel, I did not add that this was because I was one of those funny people who actually intended to wash. The towel which was then handed to me had had the colour and the life washed completely out of it. It was obviously very old, but more sinister still, had about it an underlying smell that I was convinced afterwards was vaguely faecal in origin. This would not be worth mentioning were it not that it set the tone for the entire place, and for the duration of my stay there, which proved to be exceedingly brief. The general atmosphere became clear the moment the landlord left me alone in my room. It was cramped, dank, and claustrophobic, with very little space available round the sides of the bed. As I contemplated the dismal view beneath the window, it struck me that it could have passed for a sketch of a back yard in an East End slum during the early years of this century. It was framed by old fire-escapes and uneven ridge tiles, and a little square of toneless grey sky. As I stared up the high blank brick walls opposite, what struck me most powerfully was the overwhelming silence. It was a permanent late Sunday-afternoon quiet, broken only by the occasional hollow moan of a distant car – remarkable considering the proximity of the town centre – then nothing. I had breathed in plenty of quiet whilst travelling through East Anglia, but that was a different kind of quiet entirely. There it had been open and airy, bringing with it a strong whiff of freedom and a suggestion of high wispy clouds and the texture of natural things. The quiet surrounding me in that room in Brighton was stifling and oppressive. This was one of those gloomy English boarding-houses that exist permanently between 1950 and 1973 – the kind in which neurotic characters played by John Mills used to lodge in old films, at the top of very dark staircases – with dim light-bulbs, limp net curtains hanging behind dusty old windows, internally-wallpapered cupboards, and one of those little old-fashioned enamel electric fires with the plaster filaments and the worn canvas cable. The detail that sticks most strongly in my mind, as it does in all such places if you are possessed of even the most rudimentary aesthetic sensibility, is the pathetic little pictures that were hanging on the walls. They resembled very badly done painting-by-numbers that had not been hung there for sound aesthetic effect: pictures of boats on beaches and Mediterranean sunsets intended only to break up a monotony of space and divert attention from too serious a contemplation of the squalid surroundings, not only of the room but probably of the entire street. These were living quarters that did not belong to the same slice of time and space that you or I inhabit.

They belonged to that subterranean world, uninfluenced by market trends, largely inhabited by the unemployed and the 'dispossessed'.

For what is remarkable is that there are people who actually *live* in these places, usually only for several weeks at a time, because social security regulations force them to move around so they may continue to claim their benefit. God knows what frustrations they must endure. It is amusing to think that by the time Brighton had become a fashionable watering place, Dr Johnson considered it so desolate that 'if one had a mind to hang oneself for desperation at being obliged to live there, it would be difficult to find a tree on which to fasten the rope'. I suppose these days there are plenty of dismal boarding-houses with an abundance of high staircases that would assist in this action quite adequately, and plenty of hooded balconies with fancy ironwork for that matter. I had hoped to speak with some of the people lodging there with me, to learn what their potted histories might be in this bleak corner of England late in 1991. But, except for a strange-looking middle-aged couple at breakfast, and a Japanese youth who sat as far away from everybody else as he could, I saw nobody when I was there. I only heard them. They seemed deliberately to emerge from their rooms only when they knew the corridor outside was clear, so as not to come face to face with anybody on the landings. As soon as a door closed, another further along would open, a pair of feet would pad softly down the stairs and out into the street; and each time a couple of the wooden steps made one of those repetitive, irritating little squeaks. The only voices I heard were whispers. I became dismayed, not because of the hideous melancholy of the place, but because of the lack of comfort, the difficulty I found in working without a table in my room, and the lousy food. I caved in immediately, and after one of the worst breakfasts I have ever had the misfortune to have placed before me in my life, the following morning booked out, walked across town, and booked straight into Brighton's newest hotel for the remainder of my stay.

No doubt it could be argued that Brighton compensates for the dearth of activity it might endure during the winter months by the surge of business that descends upon it during summer.

Though there are reputed to be some two-million people visiting each year, and though it claims to have more than half the country's population living within a three hour drive, it does not depend entirely upon the tourist trade for its business. The head offices of American Express are based here, and there is some manufacturing industry situated in the town as well. I did not investigate any of this, but the following day walked round the town centre again, which was now very busy; ate a baked-potato in a popular café while writing a couple of postcards, one to my wife and the other to my publisher; went back out and then, when standing alongside the ornamental fountain down in the Steine, decided on the spur of the moment that if I was supposed to be following in the steps of J.B. Priestley, then I would step onto the nearest bus, just as he had climbed onto the nearest tram when he got bored walking round the centre of Birmingham sixty years previously. Just as he had said to the tram conductor I said to the driver that I would go as far as the bus went. Like Priestley, I did not know where it was going. This day, too, was lowering and sullen. I was not offered mile after mile of 'mean dinginess' from the upstairs windows, nor was the confusion of streets and railway bridges through which the bus crept and passed beneath especially decayed. The seediness of Brighton had merely been replaced with the blandness of the suburbs, I too found much of it anaemic, and it was indeed the common stuff out of which most of our big towns are made. Just as Priestley's tram conductor had done in 1933, the bus driver announced the terminus after about half an hour. Just as Priestley did, I got out to find we had climbed to the top of a hill. On one side of me there was not a sports stadium or a high brick wall, but rows of scruffy council dwellings grafted onto the edge of a massive residential housing estate; one that was probably having its foundation stones laid when Priestley was sitting atop his tram, and where now the Downs descended gracefully almost to touch the back gardens. On the other side there was not a patch of waste ground, some allotments, or a scrapyard, but a smooth field with a busy road winding up toward a row of pointed gables and a new bypass under construction running along the top. I walked to the edge of this council estate and did not see beneath me and afar the vast smoky hollow of an industrial city, with innumerable tall chimneys thrusting out of the murk. I saw innumerable television aerials, satellite dishes, incongruous replacement doors and windows, and rooflines interfered with over the years; and in the distance the grey bar of the sea. Here, too, a cold wind was blowing over the summit of this hill, bringing with it dust and grit and the odd filthy bit of paper. Here, too, there was little to raise a man's spirits. Not even an old windmill perched atop a brick-and-flint barn further down the hill, hemmed in by a jumble of dreary architectural hotch-potch and an unlikely HERITAGE OF HOVE sign, and famous in those parts for having being painted by Constable during the early part of the nineteenth century – less the steel mesh protecting the quaint little windows, of course – managed to do that.

I walked round this estate for two hours, realized that council houses are either neglected by their tenants, or ruined by their owners the same north as well as south, caught the bus back to Hove, then walked the couple of miles along the elegant esplanade, past the sweeping Regency crescents and squares, rumoured still to be the haunt of an abundance of retired gentlefolk in addition to the strong winds that blow the topiary beneath the grand terraces into all sorts of crazy shapes. Further along, I descended some steps, inhaled the salty air, crunched along the pebbly beach and stood staring at the derelict pier; then, as the daylight was beginning to fade, I made my way back up to the main road. Here the tone of the Brighton I experienced well out of season was summed up when I saw, through the lounge windows of one of the seafront's premier hotels, an array of frail old faces all putting coffee cups tremulously to their mouths and staring solemnly out to sea. What were they doing there, and what were they thinking? This was an interesting thought. The sea was so lethargic and uninterested in the stretch of beach it was struggling to breast, so similar in colour to the tone of the sky, the sagging grey clouds so sullen and so low, the two simply blurred together in the excuse passing for a near-horizon line and swelled to form a single expanse of murk. And yet here was the familiar sight of a row of English people sitting behind panes of glass (more often than not it will be behind the windscreens of their cars, high on a hillside or a clifftop), staring out vacantly at an uninspiring view. In spite of their reputation for having a suspicion of abstract thinking, perhaps the English are more philosophical than they allow themselves credit for. I can think of at least one travel writer who has sneered discreetly at the characteristic the English possess for sitting inside and looking out: for driving up to a high vantage point to stare solemnly at the view. But most writers would think nothing of doing the same thing, the justification being it promotes the solitary sense of awareness from which the contemplative frame of mind necessary to the flow of creativity stirs. Why shouldn't ordinary people who drive to a high point close to where they live, even if it is to read through some wretched tabloid rag and occasionally look up to the distant cloud formations while they allow a piece of information to sink in, be motivated similarly?

Because the more enlightened mind takes it for granted that its own thought processes are the more virtuous, that is why.

9

Hampshire

The Sussex Coast Railway

The young man who attended to me at the information counter at Brighton Station told me that to reach Basingstoke I would have to travel back in toward London, over the same length of track I had travelled down to the south coast on a few days earlier, and change at Clapham Junction. I told him that I did not want to do that, but wished to travel the more circuitous route via Southampton and Winchester instead. There then followed one of those increasingly tiresome conversations, like haggling with market traders, where I was politely but obstinately advised that it really would be in my best interests to go via Clapham. But I was adamant, so the attendant lifted a very thick timetable directory up from beneath the counter, throughout the consultation of which he sniffed repeatedly and twitched his mouth like a girner. After a few moments he implied that to travel the long way round would be more trouble than it was worth, even though the map in my bag did suggest there were a number of lines operating from Brighton out in the general direction of Hampshire.

Having achieved nothing, I went outside and paced up and down the station concourse, beneath the echoing of train announcements and to the slamming of taxi doors, trying to decide what to do next. I was determined to travel along the south coast, rather than double back on myself again, as I had done after Canterbury. I had considered travelling by bus to Basingstoke, but decided against it because the fare was slightly more expensive than making the journey by train, but more significantly, it took longer. I didn't mind hanging around too long on railway stations, provided this was not due to train delays, so that you could calculate how much time you might have to look around outside before you arrived. So I waited until I could see through the information office windows that the young man was attending to somebody else, went back inside, approached an attractive dark-haired young lady a few positions away from him, and repeated my query. To retain a certain amount of credibility, and to divert suspicion that I might be a railway enthusiast – I saw the young man eyeing me doubtfully – I explained to her that I was writing a book about contemporary England, and that it was necessary for me to cover as much ground as possible, even if it did sound eccentric. Immediately I received the sort of co-operation authors seem mysteriously able to attract wherever they go, and was away without any trouble less than twenty minutes later.

The countryside between Brighton and Southampton is fairly bland, and does not have much redeeming character. For a while the sea is visible over to your left, sprinkled occasionally with motionless yachts, until the train curves slightly inland somewhere past Worthing, and the water disappears. All the time, over to your right, as you clatter through the stations and level crossings, and judder across the points on British Rail's Network South East, the bottom edge of the South Downs accompanies your passage, rolling along at the opposite side of a flat expanse of wide fields. Sometimes the Downs come a little closer, sometimes they lurch further away, but all the time they are there, looking as though they are only playing at being hills. The morning I saw them, they were barely visible much of the time, because the landscape was blanketed in a damp mist. This was an interesting observation to be able to make because only a few days earlier I had read a newspaper article that pandered to the long-held belief that this kind of depressing weather is a characteristic only of the north of England. The writer in question had visited the north-west shortly before his article had been published and he set the scene for his readers (whom one must take it from the tone of the article were assumed only to be Southerners), by slipping in the obligatory generalization about the overcast weather up there at that time of year, as though it were peculiar only to the old industrial areas. I happen to know that the same stretch of cloud cover to which he was referring extended unbroken from the north of England, down through the Midlands and the south, out across the English Channel to the Continent. And yet, how fascinating it is to observe the way prefabricated thought patterns manipulate hack journalists, so that miserable grey cloud ceases to become miserable grey cloud once it forms beneath a certain latitude!

Though there may be strong differences physically between aspects of the English landscape from place to place, the truth is that what you see from the train window is much the same everywhere. Houses had been modernized just as tastelessly, there were satellite dishes protruding from rooflines just as noticeably, when the train slid through Chichester and along the outskirts of Portsmouth Harbour that morning, as between Liverpool and Wigan in the north. However, one very noticeable difference, which strikes you quickly when you move around on trains in the south-east of England, is the seriousness with which rail travel is treated down there. From what I can gather, the standard of service on Network South East is considered to be something of a stock joke. I do not use the service regularly enough to make a sensible enough judgement of it, though my publisher laughed several times when I asked him for his comments on the subject. You become accustomed to anticipating delays wherever you travel on the trains in this country, rather as you would expect to be hit by a large metal projectile on wheels if you stepped out onto a busy main road without looking. Almost without thinking, when I was planning my journeys by train toward the end of this assignment, I found myself allowing substantial margins for delay, if I was arranging to meet someone at the other end. 'I should be there for one o'clock,' I would say to somebody on the telephone, then would add characteristically, 'but in case the train is late, expect me at two.' What kind of answer is that, if someone has asked what time you will be getting there, so they can arrange to meet you? How easily we say these things when planning our lives around the usage of trains, so that we are apologizing for our arrival before we have even set off. If I travel by train to an important meeting in a city centre, I often make sure I am there a good hour beforehand. I would rather sit for an hour somewhere prior to the meeting, than risk the embarrassment of arriving late. Consequently, for people who think like this, there must be a substantial amount of their lives wasted, if all the hours spent sitting around were added together, because of mistrust of a public utility. Scepticism toward British Rail, like the weather is, however, one of the defining characteristics of the flavour of national life, even though the vast majority of trains run on time, and the standard of comfort and the quality of the amenities is reasonably comprehensive. That the scepticism remains, but nothing much is done to alleviate it, is often pinned down to the capacity for tolerance that is said to define the English character. Whereas really, the general tolerance of the English, as with their outward acceptance of foreigners which disguises a subtle racism you come across in any pub, is born simply of a desire not to have to get involved.

My thoughts that morning on the electric train to Southampton were, however, not so much concerned with the quality of the service as with the tidiness of the stations. As the countryside rolled tiresomely by, unappealing except for the large green-and-silver corrugated bulk of The Body Shop's main headquarters which slid past at one point, superimposing itself over the monotony surrounded by a fan of cars, it occurred to me how most of the stations actually looked lived in. They were nearly all immaculately kept. The old wooden knobs on the doors of the station buildings were shiny from the grease of human palms. They looked like they were doors that went somewhere; openings that were in regular use. There were uniformed men sweeping platforms, a sight which hardly any English person can honestly fail to respond to favourably. That nearly all the stations were still staffed was by far and away the most noticeable feature of all, apart from the frequency of stations in general. There were none of those sad processions of sealed up doors, boarded up windows, and awkwardly bald platforms that you see scattered right across the face of the north. No endless streams of semi-ruinous stations, grudgingly kept open, filing sombrely past the windows, occasionally interspersed with a beautifully restored film set, such as Hebden Bridge in West Yorkshire, which is lucky enough to be a tourist town and can therefore pretend that history beyond its boundaries, and the history of British Railways, never actually happened at all.

What reinforces the seriousness with which the railways are treated in the south of England, what gives them their cohesiveness in the mind's eye and illustrates how important they are to the running of peoples' lives, is that the stations and the trains are painted in matching liveries of red and blue and white and grey. This sort of thing is always an uplifting sight, because it helps to create a sense of uniformity and identity. As well as creating continuity, it helps to reduce the impact of the banality of much modern railway architecture on the eye. It softens the sharp division between the traditional country or village station, many of which I passed through that morning (there was a station on average every couple of miles or so), and the corrugated-and-metal accoutrements that have been grafted onto some of the other stations over the years. A flimsy iron bus shelter embedded into a station platform, half-heartedly kidding prospective passengers it is there to be waited in, with not the slightest amount of relief detail or finials, is bad enough. But it is surprising how its crudity can be reduced if it happens to be painted in a combination of Network South East colours. Anyone who believes the running of the railway network in the south is a joke *must* travel between Blackburn and Burnley in East Lancashire, and wait for a connection to Colne at Rose Grove. There is a better quality of trackside surroundings in many Third World countries, where at least there is the sunshine and the scenery to mitigate the air of decomposition. It will be interesting to see what happens after the railways in this country are privatized again because there is a great deal of romanticism bound up with our attitude towards this subject. Each time privatization is mentioned on the news, we are shown shots of steam locomotives resplendent in the liveries of the old big four companies; something that always seems to me rather pointless and stupid. And yet, despite having had diesel traction here for almost forty years, and no steam locomotives running officially for the past twenty-five, a picture of *The Flying Scotsman* rolling pristinely out of an engine shed, surrounded by a horde of photographers, is still to a great extent the way national sentiment responds to the thought of railways. I know people who are violently opposed to the Conservative Party's privatisation of public utilities, but who, because of the itch of romance, can stop short when the privatisation of the railways is mentioned. Secretly, they harbour a hope of returning to the railway scene of those lazy, hazy summer days of yesteryear, when railways were railways, and little boys waved innocently from brick bridges and creosoted fences at passing trains, instead of exposing their bare backsides or throwing boulders. It is surprising how easily this picture has become embedded in the minds of people who are too young to remember steam trains, never mind the pre-war companies, or the brown-and-cream of the GWR, but who take Dolby stereo for granted and could not possibly imagine a world without it.

Meanwhile, if there is any truth to the barrage of criticism for Network South East's mediocre standard of service, it needs pointing out in its favour that, generally speaking, it has a good standard of basic amenities. But, of course, no one really bothers to notice that, least of all the commentators who take them for granted. Perhaps it *is* pointed out to television journalists by Sir Bob Reid, or even Jimmy Knapp, but their comments are simply edited out of the footage before it is broadcast. Or maybe it is that the plausible degree of investment in the railways in the south is at the expense of a seeming lip-service paid to investment in railways in the north, and no one really wants to draw attention to the matter.

Basingstoke

I had about forty minutes to wait for my connection to Basingstoke – the ultra-modern Wessex Electric that immediately brought Continental trains to mind – when I arrived at

Southampton. Because I was laden with bags, I did not leave the station, which was ferociously cold and windy, as stations in this country almost invariably are. What I therefore saw of Southampton did not work much in its favour. Outside, near the approach lines, was a long column of military vehicles, mostly tanks, chained to lowmac wagons in a siding. There was sand collected in some of the grooves, and the names such as *Desert Crusader*, hand-painted onto the side of them, probably meant they were on their way back from the Gulf. The platform was packed with returning, mainly elderly, holidaymakers. There were so many of them they were almost falling over one another's suitcases, and the air was alive with Cockney accents. They were, it seemed, returning to London having first returned to England from the Continent by ferry. If their chirruping conversation was anything to go by, and if the scraps of information I picked up were true, they were on their way home to little modern maisonettes built on the sites of the old flattened terraces in Bethnal Green and Stepney. I felt like I was standing in a scene from one of the old *Huggets* films, updated as the inevitable remake, and it was difficult not to smile at the gratuitous innocence of it all. You felt like you could have settled down to tea and biscuits round a coal fire and had a good natter with the lot of them. I asked one of the pensioners if he knew that Benny Hill originated from Southampton – Hill was still alive then – and that he still kept a house there. No, said the Cockney, he did not know, and he didn't think Benny Hill was at all bloody funny. That was a shame, I thought, because Benny Hill is still the comedian who most recently made me laugh louder and longer than any other, in an unforgettable sketch in one of his shows. At least Hill wasn't revealed to be a homosexual after he died, which I half expected to happen.

The view of Basingstoke from the approaching train does not bode well for the prospective tourist, or purveyor of the traditional English scene. One minute you are hurtling through the mild Hampshire countryside – countryside no different to that which can be found north of Leeds, around Tadcaster and Wetherby – the fields shiny with potatoes and cabbages, studded with occasional cottages connected by hedgerows and a sequence of trees. The next, industrial estates are beginning to trail in alongside the track, then office blocks are crowding together above the rooftops and flora of a small town. It happens as abruptly as some of those cities appear in the middle of the American desert, and is only marginally less startling than the sudden impact of Croydon from the windows of the Brighton express. Basingstoke is what could best be described as a blueprint for the modern service-sector town of the future England – England the new industrial power, according to the atmosphere of the 1980s, Professor Alan Walters, and the failed theories of the Centre for Policy Studies – manifested in three dimensions, though there is manufacturing industry, such as the making of fork lift trucks and aviation electronics, located there as well. Mercantile Credit, Provident Life Assurance, Motorola, IBM Digital, Sun Life of Canada, Johnson and Johnson, Wiggins Teape, and the pharmaceutical company Eli Lily are all names we recognize, and they are pre-eminent among some four-hundred companies that have established their operations in the town over the past thirty years. Forté, which owns the Happy Eater and Little Chef chains, also has its main headquarters there, as does the Automobile Association, with whom the vehicle I conducted much of this journey in is insured, courtesy of Fanum House.

By far the most dominating feature environmentally of Basingstoke is the large prefabricated shopping centre that makes up the bulk of the centre of the town. It confronts you the moment you emerge from the station, and immediately swallows you up. As is the custom nowadays with towns that began destroying themselves internally about twenty-five years ago, only to regret it later, Basingstoke carefully observes in its official literature that this shopping centre was built in an architectural style that is now commonly acknowledged as not having aged very well at all. I take this to be a coded reference intimating that it is bloody awful. I could sense the same thought processes at work – the stating of unequivocal facts, but through teeth that were probably more than a little gritted – varnishing the caption describing the view on a souvenir postcard I found on sale in the tourist information office. The view is down Wote Street, with nineteenth-century shops on one side, and modern architecture lifting boldly on the other. The caption admits that a multi-storey car park and the recently-built fifteen-storey Churchill Plaza office block 'now dominate the skyline'. Alongside the trendily cropped photograph, copperplate handwriting and a coat of arms agonizingly evoke the ambience of Merrie England, condensing once again, this time onto a piece of card six inches by four, the great psychological dichotomy of our age – the battle raging between two powerful historical tensions, forever pulling in opposite directions, yet coming together spontaneously to form a single indeterminate entity somewhere in the middle. A middle we generally accept to be the face of modern England, but a middle we nevertheless find terribly difficult to come to terms with objectively as a people. Hence the proliferation of these wretched little postcards in the tourist information centres in the middle of present day towns.

It was the scene I walked into when I came out of the station, walked beneath a modern, unusually graffiti free pedestrian subway, and up into the shopping precinct teeming with early afternoon crowds, that I experienced a strong feeling of *déjà vu*. Basingstoke is twinned with Alencon in France, Braine l'Alleud in Belgium, and Euskirchen in Germany. I do not know the reasons for this. I do not know the reasons for the twinning of towns anywhere. I always assume it must be something to do with size, or a vague similarity visually and commercially, discernible only to the anaesthetized insight of bureaucrats. Whatever it is, there is in my opinion a fourth town with which Basingstoke ought to be twinned – Blackburn in Lancashire. If you were to describe to someone concisely the impression of arriving in Blackburn via train, you would say that you walked out of a station entrance, down into a pedestrian subway slung beneath a main road, and up into a large, very square, rather austere modern shopping centre. The shopping centre would be on such a large scale the only charitable conclusion you would be able to reach would be that it looks as though, about twenty years ago, a substantial chunk of the original town centre was scooped out by an enormous excavator, in one gigantic stroke, and the new structure was craned in, readily assembled, to fill the available space *en masse*.

But substitute the word 'Basingstoke' for 'Blackburn' in the above description, and there is no question that anyone living in Basingstoke would assume you were talking about their town. Even the brutal, quite sprawling design of the respective shopping centres – very late-Sixties, very rectilinear – is remarkably similar, as is the size of both towns' railway stations. All round the edges of central Basingstoke, bits of the old town cling to the vast bulk of the shopping centre rising somewhere in the middle, like streamers and tin cans to the rear bumper of a departing wedding car. It is just the same up in Blackburn. In both places, a number of the original streets leading to the precinct entrances have recently been pedestrianized with the obligatory herringbone sets, which in Blackburn are coloured red and in Basingstoke are mustard. Both are peppered fashionably throughout with reproduction Victorian street furniture, in spite of the absurd grey contrasts rising in the background. Each has a museum commemorating the history of the town; a number of columned and porticoed nineteenth-century civic buildings, as sturdy as old West Riding chapels; a church brooding beneath vast featureless curtain walling flecked with air vents, forming the rear of the shopping centre; a multi-storey car park connecting with the shops; a number of tower blocks; and knots of youths sitting on the edges of flower-bins flicking cigarette-ends at one another at lunchtimes. The spacial relationship of the rest of the town centre to the shopping complex in both places, the pedestrianisation that has been carried out, their overall size, and their position in relation to surrounding countryside geographically, has about it the same sort of weight on the eye visually; even if the marked resemblance they bear to each other, as a collection of units of architecture placed squarely upon the surface of the Earth, is in rough arrangement only rather than style or types of buildings. Both are also towns that could be said to be very much concerned with the workings of industry, as opposed to the tanning of themselves in the sunshine, like a Bath or a Stratford-upon-Avon. And, finally, the populations in the Boroughs to which both Basingstoke and Blackburn are the administration centres are the same – a hundred-and-forty-thousand each.

These remarkable similarities between the two places at once startled and fascinated me. They were, however, fairly unimportant in comparison to a major *difference* which I began to pick up quickly once I was settled in Basingstoke – a difference which, paradoxically, only meant something because it gave it an even greater historical parity with Blackburn, making some of the physical resemblances I have outlined here all the more interesting. For if Blackburn could be said to symbolize the nineteenth-century mill town, one that for a long time has been coming to terms with major economic shifts in late-twentieth-century England and a steady decline in traditional manufacturing importance, then Basingstoke could be said to be its exact antithesis. It is as symbolic a representation of an English industrial town in the second half of the twentieth century as Blackburn was in the second half of the nineteenth. This contrariety is to me what binds them so strongly together, leading quite naturally onto a very important difference between the two places which I have as yet barely touched upon. And that is the difference in their social atmospherics, and consequently, their political disposition, of which more a little later. When you are walking through central Basingstoke you feel to be walking through a town that has living within its boundaries an indigenous middle-class population. It does have its incumbent working class, make no mistake of that. You are aware of it the moment you arrive, though I should say, almost without reservation, that a significant number of the bull-necked, more exhibitionistic males moving around the centre of the town were probably specimens of genuine Hampshire Man, popular in the region of Essex. Blackburn, on the other hand, has a much bigger indigenous working-class population, so that if anything you feel the entire population is working class – a traditional north country working class that would probably find it easy to trade insults with its bluer-hued contemporaries in Basildon.

Basingstoke is one of those tidy south country towns which are part old-brickwork-glowing-in-autumn-sunlight, part mirrored glass and chrome, part quiet churchyard, concrete balustrade, and almshouses, that became more important around the western edge of London, out toward the Berkshire countryside, after the war. The mental picture I carry around with me of such places is nearly always embellished by railways, for what characterizes them so strongly is that they tend to have four main railway lines, which deviate hardly an inch, plunging straight through the middle, or at any rate along one edge. (The remnant of a railway route running through Blackburn feels distinctly to be in a backwater.) You stand on the platforms at the stations, looking at those lines disappearing into their tiny perspectives, and there is at once something about them that signifies instant importance, with big terminus stations rooted firmly at either end. It is something to do with the shininess of the rails and the solidity of the modern concrete sleepers onto which they are fastened, as opposed to the oily wooden sleepers smelling of creosote still to be found on many quieter routes elsewhere. Those lines are in constant use and they take a constant pounding from the westward-bound expresses. The determination with which they were originally engineered, albeit over fairly easy terrain, seems to have been captured in the very straightness of the tracks, along with a growing nostalgia for the romance of Brunel and God's Wonderful Railway that is so strongly associated with the time when they first strove out toward Bristol.

And yet, like nearby Maidenhead, where I strove to live ten years ago but was more unhappy than I have been anywhere else in my life, Basingstoke is one of those places in the south that does not feel to have much of a sense of history hanging over its head, and certainly not much charm. It does not exude that deep-rooted sense of permanence stretching back down the years, the chief difference, of course, with its counterpart in Lancashire. This is rather unsatisfactory as an observation because Basingstoke is, in fact, a very old market town. It can demonstrate plenty of references to the Romans and to Cromwell, begin talking about prehistoric settlements, the staging of Dane and Saxon battles just beyond its boundaries, the fact that it used to be an important town in coaching days because of its situation on the main road to the south-west of England, and that it was once the centre of woollen manufacture in the area, easily enough, once you start delving into its background. The handful of town guides given to me by a young lady in the council offices are full of the usual historical citation. One which struck me as interesting – one of those useless pieces of information which you catalogue and carry around with you forevermore – is that situated between Basingstoke and nearby Silchester is the first English country house that happened to be built with a portico, now in the care of the National Trust; though I should imagine the guides' reference to the pretty village of Dummer as being the former home of HRH the Duchess of York will be politely deleted from the next edition.

I had not, however, come to Basingstoke in the hope of stumbling across piles of moss-covered stones. After the antiquities of Norwich and Suffolk, the packaged enchantment of Canterbury, and the funny taste in the mouth of Brighton, I was there very much to be propelled into the landscape of modern suburban meat-and-two-veg respectability; of the fairly prosperous southern English variety bordered by DIY superstores, Sainsbury's, and laminated industrial park glass. Throughout the two months I had been travelling through England I had really glimpsed a series of components. The components could be said to integrate to form an overall picture of the country. This, perhaps, is the best such an undertaking as this can hope for. But, although in most cases those components had about them some compelling quality distinctly their own, unique to the history of a given area and bound up with its customs and traditions, I was aware that I had yet to find what would represent for me the true essence of contemporary England. Something else, something that could best be described as process-packed social realism, was missing. By saying social realism, I do not mean the drug dealers blasting one another in the chest with shotguns to sort out local difficulties in the damp slums I had walked through weeks earlier up in Manchester. Nor do I mean I had yet to be set down in a place such as Milton Keynes. I knew without seeing it again that Milton Keynes was at once too sharply defined, too isolated an impression of an idealized England there never was, to relate sensibly to the sprawl of urban ambiguity, the accumulated clutter of centuries, gathered all around it that is much closer in essence to the England there is likely to be.

This was what had drawn me ultimately to Basingstoke. I had never been there, but I knew enough about it to have been drawn to it as though by magnetic attraction. Though I did not finally decide to visit the town till the day before I was due to leave Brighton, I could sense that Basingstoke, with its fragmentary combination of old and especially new, would probably get closer than anything I had so far seen to the broad shape of the England that is coming. One of the reasons for this is that twenty-five years ago, Basingstoke was the fastest growing town in Britain. It became the boom town of the south. It is now considered one of the most affluent places in that part of the country in which to live, no doubt for the more upwardly mobile as opposed to the authentically rich. It is also one of the most important commercial development centres in the whole of southern England, just as, a hundred-and-fifty years ago, Blackburn's part of Lancashire was one of the fastest growing industrial areas in the north.

For, if Basingstoke the old market town can still be found – and it can, toward the top end, where there is still a street market every Wednesday, as there has been since 1214 – then it has proceeded to be stifled by Basingstoke the industrial new town, which over the past twenty years has continued to expand at a phenomenal rate, at the end of the Surrey stockbroker belt. When Priestley conducted his English journey during the 1930s, if he had stopped off at Basingstoke, he would have found a small market town that still had a population of only fourteen-thousand several years after he had been chauffeured away from it in his limousine. Today the population is approaching the hundred-thousand mark, and what is significant is that this has been the result of a policy of deliberate urban expansion rather than natural-unnatural ergonomic growth. We are not talking here about the dumping of vast quantities of working-class people in some post-war socially engineered housing disaster; some rotten high-rise wasteland doomed to failure. Basingstoke claims it was chosen as a natural site for London overspill chiefly because of its excellent geographic position and its emerging communications links. It is three quarters of an hour away from London by train (a remarkable two-hundred-and-fifty stop at Basingstoke each day), and less than that from the docks at Southampton and Portsmouth. Both Heathrow and Gatwick airports are less than an hour's drive away, courtesy of an intersection of the M3 motorway which comes close to the southern part of the town. And yet Basingstoke has strong links with its past and is situated in an area of downland speckled with picturesque villages as solidly conservative as you will find anywhere, its agricultural land well known for the growing of watercress, with Watership Down, ancestral homes and ruins, the training of racehorses, and the enigma of Jane Austen, who was born at nearby Steventon, close at hand. What gives Basingstoke the town its curiously streamlined, almost synthetic feel, is not only that it is largely new. It is the combination of its modern service industry economic base, the factories and warehouses of which, like the modern housing estates, sprawl right around the circumference of the town, and that it is a comfortable Conservative seat, but crucially, that it is a comfortable Conservative seat of the modern 'popular capitalist' kind. This is the reason for its strategic importance to the face of modern England. It was also the reason why I had ultimately been drawn there, and why, more than anywhere else I visited, the town represented for me the emergent face of the future England, even though this face has been in the process of emerging for well over half a century, and exists everywhere.

This *England*

A long walk round the outside of the town revealed how strongly this face has become established already. Basingstoke is very much the England Priestley noticed was moving its newer industries south before the war, into buildings of concrete and glass and chromium-plate, surrounded by beds of tulips and grass verges bristling with daffodils each spring. Environments where it was still understood that a job of work had got to be done, but where it was taken for granted there would no longer be any smoke drifting above factory rooftops. The 1979-81 recession was merely the high apogee of this process, an explosion of dynamite at the end of a trail of economic gunpowder laid some fifty or sixty years previously. Basingstoke is England *with* some semblance of an industrial base, with the corrugated warehouses and the piles of mirror-finish windows bordered by wide lawns, rows of young silver-birch trees, and a preponderance of open spaces: but *without* the densely packed back-to-backs, the striding mill chimneys, or the narrow back alleys teeming with Asian children – without, in fact, the weighty dignity, the accumulated architectural legacy, of the past hundred-and-fifty years, etched into the very substance of its pattern, or its soul.

This enables Basingstoke's essentials, along with its contemporary allusions, to surface more easily, and is where you come back to its most pressing contrast of all against Blackburn. Blackburn is a strong Labour seat. It has a substantial immigrant population, nearly all of whom are housed, as is so often the case in the old northern towns, in nineteenth-century terraced properties down all those steep cobbled backs streets. But you would be hard pressed to find many black faces on the streets of Basingstoke. None of the housing is dingy or old enough. Politically Blackburn used to belong to Barbara Castle, a name I heard bandied about with some amusement when I was there near the beginning of this journey. Now it is the seat of Jack Straw, who, whether he sounds like an old children's game or not, is nevertheless the opposition bench's education spokesman at the time of writing, or perhaps one ought to be politically correct and say spokesperson. I do not know whether the sizeable quantity of the Blackburn working class that votes Labour does so these days out of solidarity or out of tradition. It probably does so out of straightforward self-interest. But Basingstoke, I am quite certain, could be said to be the haunt of the notorious C2s – the skilled manual workers who, throughout the past thirty or forty years, have been in the process of moving up the social hierarchy from traditional working-class environments and easing themselves gradually in among the Tory voting 'new middle classes'. And they, too, will have been doing so out of straightforward self-interest. When you hear the newspapers or television people talking belatedly about the bedrock of skilled working-class votes that are crucial to the Conservatives retaining office, as well as referring to a sizeable chunk of support spread throughout, for instance, West Midlands suburbia, the media is also talking about the strong body of support that exists in places such as Basingstoke.

Which brings me back into the centre of the town on a busy winter afternoon, once I have been very kindly collected from the end of London Street by the landlady of the house where I am staying, and taken in her car out to her home in the suburbs, at the end of a very long stretch of new dual carriageway. The sky is still thickly overcast and it is cold. Before walking the couple of miles back into the town centre, I have had time to notice that the house I am lodging in is a typical semi-detached structure down the kind of leafy southern English side street Geoffrey Palmer inhabits permanently in television sitcoms. It was probably built after the war, but remained near enough to the influence of pre-war designs to retain a certain amount of aesthetic appeal. I have also had chance to note that the landlady – a strongly-built woman with an engaging cherubic face, reminiscent of those Victorian china dolls you see sitting in the corners of antique shops – and her husband have recently added an extension to their house, so they have some additional rooms to let off to lodgers. On the way out to the house, driving through a modern open-plan environment spiked systematically with brutally functional new street lamps, and every so often, passing silhouetted figures hunched at computer terminals behind rows of tinted glass surrounded by sheets of futuristic ribbed-aluminium, I had been told that because of Basingstoke's size and commercial importance, there is a reasonable turnover of skilled workers, along with visiting business people, shuttling permanently to and from the town. This means there is money to be made providing them with modest but comfortable lodgings; one from which I, as a traveller, am benefiting.

But, when we had pulled up at a roundabout and I had caught sight first of a row of tennis courts, then, in the gaps between the trees, a school yard full of pleasant-looking small children throwing balls about and playing hopscotch as only English children should, I was told that Basingstoke had unfortunately begun to feel the unsettling effects of recession, though thankfully not as badly as some places. Both my host and her husband, with whom I had a lengthy conversation that evening – he is occupied in a skilled capacity in the printing trade – spoke with the native accent common to ordinary people in the south-east of England. They might well have been the children of people who moved out to Basingstoke over thirty years ago, when firms relocating there from London were automatically allocated tenancies for their employees on one of the large council estates that were evolving around the edges of the town. If they are descendants of the original settlers, they consider themselves middle class today nevertheless. The car in which we had pulled up on the drive outside the house was the one in which the landlady ran her children to school in the mornings, but was not, I observed later, quite as new as the main family saloon. I had been deposited into the sort of box-room that all teenagers have lived in who come from normal suburban homes in normal suburban England. I had freshened up in a normal family bathroom. And now, as I say, I am surrounded by normal, reasonably affluent-looking caucasian crowds back in the very centre of the town. Some female canvassers wearing lycra ski-pants are gliding gracefully between the shoppers on roller-skates, handing out shiny leaflets. There is the aroma of chlorine from what I take to be some kind of subterranean swimming pool percolating warmly in the air, courtesy of a large corrugated vent. The air is busy with moving feet. The shop assistants are nodding their heads above the cash tills, and smiling at the customers, through the windows. The shopping centre has recently been refurbished, and, I was told the following morning over breakfast, has now been roofed over in a part previously exposed to the air. Suspended above the arcades and between the avenues are the obligatory Christmas decorations, intensifying against the leaden sky now that dusk is finally descending. The bright bulbs present rather an odd contrast against the slabs of prefabricated concrete and the bland featureless walls; and there is none of the party-time atmosphere of Canterbury.

Notwithstanding this minor aesthetic *désaccord*, there is above all a penetrating sense of cleanliness to the texture of the whole scene; a feeling of contentment and of lives being lived. It is rather mundane, it is bland, the shop windows are emblazoned with SALE NOW ON signs, signs which will have been up for many, many months, due to the economic doldrums of the time. But the shopping centre is tidy, it is looked after and maintained, and it is serving its purpose quite adequately, thank-you-very-much. Plenty of Marxists would fall about at the prospect of walking into such a setting and being asked to take it seriously, though among the older ones the utilitarian style of the architecture might awaken some long lost nostalgia for what were once considered collectivist-inspired building methods, especially when it was still fashionable to worship Russia. But plenty of normal Basingstoke people are happy to spend several hours there each Saturday afternoon, and quite content to see the security guards employed by the well-known insurance company that controls a substantial chunk of the town, oust young undesirables that threaten to ruin the continuity of the scene.

By the time I came to seat myself by the window of a restaurant toward the end of my first afternoon, I had already decided that, in spite of its obvious social aspirations, Basingstoke had none of the pretensions of a Guildford or a Wilmslow or an English literary intellectual. Just as it appears to be one huge business park-cum-industrial estate, interwoven with dual carriageways and modern ribbon developed housing, with an old fashioned town hall poking up somewhere in the middle, so it appears too to be a symbolic manifestation of modern English prosperity, of the kind the averagely bookish-inclined would automatically dismiss as populist, tasteless, and complacent. It might be the kind of universe that would be unsettling to serious subscribers to *Traditional Homes*, who would be able to proposition considerable parts of the town for the magazine's Mess of the Month award, never mind individual buildings, without much difficulty. And it is the kind of universe that is a permanent butt of jokes to the average *Daily Telegraph* diarist. But what cannot be denied is that the lives being lived in that universe are, by their very conformity and crisp standards, not only a delineation of the modern popular English ideal, but of modern popular English Conservatism. Or at any rate, they are the reason why Conservatism has taken hold of the kind of mind that fifty years ago would have conformed in another direction and voted Labour as a matter of course.

And here one comes to the social quality Basingstoke clearly represents. Though the town boomed throughout the 1980s, taking the advantages proffered by supply-side reforms in its stride, it is to my mind not so much a town that you would associate instantly as a product of a country governed by a Margaret Thatcher, as one you would associate instantly with one governed by a John Major. Politically it belongs to the Conservatives, but its Conservatism, like Mr Major's pragmatism in comparison to his predecessor's, seems to be rather more restrained. It is, in point of fact, low-key and fairly ordinary, just as Basingstoke itself is what could best be termed low-key and fairly ordinary. But by its very ordinariness and its monotonous human scale, with a minimalist amount of detail and little squares of cropped grass positioned in all the correct places, Basingstoke is likely to outlast the overblown Canary Wharf schemes of this world a thousand times over. When I was in Basingstoke, Mr Major's reserved manner, his bank manager's ordinariness, was considered more of a liability than an asset to his party. He had none of the stature he was to have accrued for himself by April 10 the following spring, when a lot of people laughed on the opposite side of their faces. This is worth noting here, because in the 1992 General Election, in spite of a swing to Labour of nearly four per cent, and in spite of the air of grim resolve hanging over the serious Tory camp, the Conservative majority in Basingstoke actually went *up* by four thousand. That is the significant point. Basingstoke is one of the constituencies that endorsed Mr Major securely for a second term, even though it has suffered the unemployment that has begun to afflict important areas of the south-east. Perhaps the inhabitants of Basingstoke knew something the No Turning Back committee, and all those knowledgeable commentators in Westminster, not to mention the Labour Party public relations hierarchy, and the private enterprise haughtiness that built Canary Wharf and pushed it toward the stars – stars that must now seem a lot further away than they did four or five years ago – clearly did not.

If that was so, then you can clearly see why. Basingstoke

carries steadily on in the background of steady England. It is steady England, but it is an England becoming steadily plasticized. Like many things in a world of standardized sensation, where the influence of the craftsman is being left further and further behind, where the need for human beings to think constructively for themselves is being steadily eroded, Basingstoke is rather like those little plastic fences you can buy from garden centres: the ones that make an effort to appear presentable only from the side facing onto the road. But, when you turn them around and examine them from behind, you find they are hollow and brittle, to cut down on the amount of material involved in their manufacture, something that does not present too much of a problem so long as they are not placed under the wrong kind of sustained pressure. Basingstoke is the kind of town that can only exist in a world where there are Ripons and Castle Combes and steep lanes in Shaftesburys and original red telephone boxes in remote Dales villages that all want to be left quietly alone. Perhaps it is the kind of facile environment in which the passive people will live who Priestley observed in embryonic form sixty years ago, doped up now not only on a liberal supply of cheap luxuries but punch-drunk on television soap opera and violent American cinema as well, and perhaps finally creating a set of people without ambition or any real desire to think or act for themselves – 'the perfect subjects for an iron autocracy'. Perhaps, but I doubt it.

The morning I came away, I walked through a subway beneath a roundabout at one of the intersections on the town's ring-road. There was nowhere any graffiti to be seen on any of the walls. I realized then why I had registered the cleanliness of the walls in the prefabricated concrete tunnel I had walked through, to reach the shopping centre, when I arrived. These days, you expect to be surrounded in public spaces by scrawls of obscenities wherever you go, so that when you are not, it seems strange, almost unnatural. The subways plunging beneath that roundabout (I checked them all) might, for all I know, have been recently repainted, because I did come across small instances of graffiti elsewhere in the town. Nevertheless, those clean pistachio-coloured walls summed up better than anything the modern Basingstoke I thought I had seen – uninteresting aesthetically, but getting on with life and tidy. As the train bore me away, I found myself thinking that whether or not there would be any graffiti sprayed on those subway walls a week or a year later hardly mattered. What was important was that the picture you carry away with you of Basingstoke is that it is the kind of place where you do not *expect* to find much graffiti on subway walls. The town is like an architectural model made real. It is a symbiosis of the modern environmental vernacular. It follows – and I repeat – that it is not in the least bit charming. It is, in fact, one of the most charmless places I have ever visited. I cannot possibly imagine living there. There is more charm to Barnsley, where the rough faces, and the air of debauched mining industry floating permanently in the background, at least generate the feeling that something worthwhile has happened there in the past, besides the disgusting remodelling of the town centre throughout most of the 1960s.

But the charmlessness of Basingstoke, that functional arrangement of the modern urban schematic, is really a polarization of the charmlessness of modern life. It exists everywhere. Love it or hate it, like our dependency on machine technology which we all of us at some point rail against because of its dehumanizing effect on our lives, it is not going to go away.

10

The West Country

On Salisbury Station, of Sleepless Nights

The sight of Salisbury cathedral slicing majestically into the sky in the distance is supposed to be one of the characteristic sights of England. I had never seen it, but it seemed symptomatic of the overcast, anticlimactic atmosphere of much of this journey that by the time I finally did see it, as the train negotiated a wide curve on the outskirts of the town and I waited for the foreshortened carriages to bend out of the way, the slender spire itself was obscured by a tangle of scaffolding erected around it in the distance.

That morning I was running late, not because I had already succeeded again in confusing a British Rail member of staff by asking to travel a more circuitous route to reach Bristol, before I boarded the train at Basingstoke, but because the train had been delayed due to a points failure near Andover. There was nearly an hour to pass before my connection was due to arrive at Salisbury, so after pacing up and down beneath a canopy of curved Victorian awnings exuding the ambient summer's day station-sound of chirruping sparrows (even though this was winter), I entered the platform cafeteria and drank a pot of coffee and ate a chocolate-chip muffin. The next sixty minutes constituted one of those empty sockets of time human beings invariably have to plug themselves into when they are made late between trains. The handful of lethargic-looking people sitting in there with me appeared still to be half asleep. A popular radio programme muttered away in the background, but when the presenter treated us to the gruesome details of a true love story sent in by a listener an air of melancholy descended and several of the people, who looked as though they might have been supporting the rest of the world squarely upon their shoulders, must have decided they'd had enough, abruptly got up, and left. The couple that remained perked up when a semi-articulate girl and a man much older than herself, with bits of skin showing among the tattoos smothering his forearms, suddenly exploded into a violent argument in front of the magazine rack, and a sequence of badly scripted yet authentic kitchen-sink-drama unfolded excruciatingly before our eyes. This was over some trivial domestic issue, fantastic in its tedious predictability, because the girl claimed the man had been looking at somebody else in the pub the previous evening. So much for the success of post-war social engineering, I thought.

Depressed both by this and by the sad story unfolding on the radio, I ventured into the washroom. I can only assume that Salisbury is an important changing place for trains carrying football supporters to and from different parts of the West Country, because the toilet in there was a fascinating testimonial to the animalistic stupidity it is taken for granted, almost at a subconscious level, must accompany the passage through of a combined body of rowdy masculinity wherever it goes. The cisterns in the cubicles had aluminium fastenings riveted securely over the lids, so that no one could get at the workings inside. (What struck me as interesting was the feeble saw marks one of these fastenings had on one end.) More amusing still was the spectacle of the condom-machine fastened to the wall alongside the urinals. If it had been built to withstand the impact of close range artillery fire, it could not have been more armour-plated. It had quarter-inch thick, two-inch wide steel straps clamping the front closed and the whole contraption securely to the wall. Prominently displayed at one corner, in such a way that it must have been put there deliberately by somebody with a very droll sense of humour, was one of the chunkiest padlocks I have ever seen. Looking so exposed the machine appeared to project a personality of its own; as self-consciously fastened on to the wall as those stiff bow-legged mongrels you see strutting importantly in packs around council estates. I went back out onto the station platform where by now there was a young schoolboy scribbling the number of a diesel locomotive feverishly into a little notebook, wished to God we could all retain such innocence, looked stupidly over a wall at the cathedral spire wrapped in its cocoon of metal and tarpaulin, thought about the Middle Ages and Constable's paintings, and wondered what fantastic progress we had really made. For if the sight of Salisbury cathedral coming slowly into view is one of the characteristic sights of England, then surely to goodness the condom-machine clamped to the wall of the gents toilet in the city's railway station is another.

As the train leaves the influence of Salisbury Plain behind, and curves purposefully through the long valley of the Avon and draws closer toward Bath, the countryside gradually becomes more interesting. At about the same time as it begins to become pleated with a succession of small towns and villages, the land begins to wrinkle gently. Then it begins to lift, the hills and the old grey stones rising from the line not quite Cotswold, not quite Yorkshire Dales, yet clearly containing elements of them both. Quaint silk mills for which the region is known – mills that are perceived in rather a different light to their counterparts further north – become visible, tucked in perfectly among the branches that are by now nearly brushing against the carriage windows. The little bouquets of grey architecture group themselves attractively around the train as it finds its way through the stations and curves gracefully between the bends. Ancient slates dappled with fungus tumble into the cuts and hollows, losing themselves among groves of trees that channel between them a fuss of glittering streams. By the time you come upon the charming spectacle of Bradford-on-Avon, stacking itself in terraces up the steep hillsides above its famous arched bridge, the limestone spell is complete, though you are realizing too that you are passing through a sequence of towns on the way to Bristol about as different from the Basingstoke you have only lately left behind as it is possible to be.

A very different and rather unpleasant spell must have

decided to cast itself over my journey at that point. Since I had left the south coast the thought had been nagging away at the back of my mind that I had given in too easily at that shabby boarding-house in Brighton. For reasons which in retrospect I can only sensibly put down to my being fatigued, when I arrived in Bristol I deliberately booked again into what I knew would almost certainly prove to be down-market lodgings. I must assume I was heroic enough to take this course of action to retain some semblance of serious creative composure about what it was I was supposed to be doing, which was to assemble a broadly realistic social picture of contemporary England. I had booked a room over the telephone before I left Basingstoke, but this time I purposely chose somewhere further away from the city centre, in the hope it would improve the quality of the surroundings by at least a notch. That assumption was something of a miscalculation, to say the least. I had my doubts the moment I was deposited by the taxi outside the lodging-house early in the afternoon. The tiny cubicle I was shown into beneath the rafters at the top of the house had cheap distempered walls, and clearly the window had only recently been opened to allow the smell of the previous occupant to clear. In its favour, however, it did provide a decently-sized towel. But this luxury paled into insignificance when I stepped across the landing into a filthy bathroom. It had a useless shower that sprayed water across the grubby linoleum floor because the door to the cubicle was broken, so that you had to have your wits about you to remain on your feet. More disgusting still, the communal bar of soap was matted with a variety of different coloured pubic hairs – hairs that you can only ever really remove effectively by using your fingernails like a pair of tweezers. This was far from an improvement over Brighton. The first night I spent in Brighton was luxurious in comparison. At least there I managed to obtain some sleep, even if I had been woken at five-thirty in the morning by somebody blundering about in the corridor outside my room. The lack of sleep I obtained that night in Bristol meant it was the worst night I had anywhere when I was travelling around England for the purposes of writing this book. The lodging-house was situated on a busy and very noisy main road, something I had noticed when I arrived but which had not bothered me unduly because at that stage my attention had been drawn to Bristol city centre, which I had been able to see rising at the other side of the rooftops outside my window. How unsuspecting in our innocence we can be.

There was a group of fairly boisterous youths staying at this lodging-house. When I got back late that afternoon they were stationed around the telephone at the foot of the stairs, as they were for several hours, bellowing with laughter. It was a really irritating, bus-stop delinquent hinnying, interspersed with liberal expulsions of belching and great tearings of flatulence that ricocheted up the staircase until well after midnight. Though I was jostled when I had to make my way between these youths, and though there was the noise of feet running up and down and doors opening and shutting throughout the evening, what I could not cope with was the noise of the traffic outside on the main road when I climbed into bed. That was when things really began to deteriorate. I switched my light off at about a quarter to eleven, and assumed at first that the cars probably had something to do with the pubs emptying, and would die down presently. But the noise did not die down. It got steadily worse. Even at one o'clock in the morning, not having slept a moment, the volume of traffic passing beneath my window was heavy enough for it to have been a continuation of the early evening rush-hour. I could almost smell the fumes. The swishing this way and that of a constant flurry of cars carried on well into the early hours, when it was promptly replaced by the roar of heavy articulated lorries grinding past one after the other. I tried everything at my disposal to get away from that noise. I made some crude ear-plugs from toilet tissue, which failed miserably, even when I twisted them into damp points and pushed them in as far as they would go. I pushed my bed to the opposite end of the room, to a ridiculous chorus of squeaking castors and groaning floorboards, but gained nothing because the cubicle was not much longer than it was wide, and not much longer than the mattress itself. And then, to prolong the agony, when the lorries and the cars did eventually begin to subside at around four o'clock, the guest house hot-water boiler, situated immediately beneath the point in my room where my head was located after I had shifted the bed, switched itself on, and its sound was funnelled up through the disposal pipe into my washbasin, so that it was like trying to get to sleep next to a small electric generator. I look back now and am amazed to picture myself walking stupidly around this lodging-house in the middle of the night, with a chorus of muffled masculine snoring rumbling from behind an assortment of doors on the landings, trying to locate the boiler so that I could switch it off and damn the consequences, and failing miserably.

There was a nightmarish moment, at God knows what unearthly hour, when a car pulled up in the street outside and disgorged a bundle of jeering youngsters into a nearby house. Then the downdraught from the lorries that thundered past set off the youngsters' car alarm. I could not believe what was happening. The racket just went on and on and on. The roaring of a lorry, then the car alarm. Silence. Another lorry. The alarm again. Silence. Another lorry. The alarm. Then the buzz and tinny rattle of a lightweight motorcycle, the flimsiness of which I have to say, after such a never-ending bombardment, actually made me laugh, though I suspect in reality I was actually beginning to cry. The sequence of events seemed to have been so well scripted and so brilliantly co-ordinated, I would not have been in the least bit surprised if one of those millionaire television personalities that earn their living making fools of the British public, and no doubt inadvertently contributing to the backwardness of our workforce and emphasising how our particular type of social hierarchy works, had stepped out of the tatty little wardrobe standing in the corner of my room, followed by a camera crew, and informed me that the whole evening, perhaps even the entire English journey, had actually been a send-up arranged by my publisher. Anything seemed possible at that Godforsaken hour, for by that time, weary in a way I could not make plain with ordinary useless words, I wondered if the world was going mad. You would have had to have been laid there, damning the insane civilization around you into the ground, damning the foolishness of your literary integrity for putting yourself into these preposterous circumstances, damning the sound of the body at the other side of my flimsy bedroom wall, which had staggered up the staircase after the pubs had closed, fallen into bed muttering to itself bemusedly and was now snoring and grunting, oblivious to the din outside, oblivious to its consciousness having been wiped out by drink, to truly appreciate the helplessness of the situation. I did not sleep all night. I merely drifted in a vile fitfulness. I would feel myself beginning to drift, then would be jerked awake by a passing vehicle, or a lorry activating the car alarm. At that moment I would pick out, at the very edge of my consciousness, the distant bonging of a church clock, so that I found myself struggling to concentrate and count the number of peals, vaguely telling myself how silly this was, but being unable to stop, and hence being unable to make that final escape into sleep. At times, the dreams I began to enter contained car alarms, colossal car alarms blaring in some hellish subterranean world I knew not where. Somewhere in the background, I eventually became aware of the sound of a torrent of passing traffic. Slowly, inexorably, it became more substantial and more real, until I could sense the blackness of the room turning grey, that the morning rush-hour had begun again, and another day had opened for business above the surface of Bristol, south-west England, planet Earth.

After bad experiences like sleepless nights in rotten lodging-houses, it would be the easiest thing in the world to leave the town or city in question, move to the next place on the itinerary, and begin again. But as I sat in the breakfast room the following morning (the food was actually quite good), and listened to the posturing conversation of the youths, who were slurping their cups of tea and now gibbering loudly again – of course they were really broadcasting to the rest of the room – I knew it would be impractical to leave Bristol. I had things to do, but more importantly, there were people that I had arranged to see and who had put themselves out to arrange to see me. In addition to this, that infernal grey cloud cover that had been hanging over the south for days on end, suggesting the whole of England were suspended beneath a pall of gloom that would last forever, had finally broken. I felt optimistic again, even if I did feel fuzzy-headed from acute lack of sleep. All of this had the effect of making one look forward to the approaching day. Through my window Bristol spread itself mistily beneath the crispest of blue winter skies. There was not a cloud visible anywhere. The roads and the pavements and the parked cars, the muddled bare branches of the trees, the tops of post-boxes and railings, the roof slates stretching for miles, the garden paths, the little patches of grass and the dustbin lids and the old tin-cans pressed flat in the gutters, were all suffused with a thick layer of frost. A postman was walking up a garden path whistling. Somewhere there was the sound of milk-crates bumping heavily over uneven tarmac on the back of a passing float. Buses, bright in the early morning sunshine, were flashing past the gaps between buildings. So I walked out into brilliant sunshine, along slippery pavements and footbridges, and made my way back into the city centre, up to College Green. There I booked straight into what must be the best and most luxurious hotel anywhere in the West Country, if not one of the best in the whole country – the Royal Swallow Hotel, right alongside the city's cathedral. As this was the last proper hotel I would be patronizing during my journey, and in view of the previous night's ordeal, I was determined to finish with a bang and damn the cost or the consequences.

At the same time I damned those squalid little semi-doss-houses masquerading as hotels out in the suburbs of large cities everywhere. Hostelries that have as their hallmark cardboard walls and the sound of deafening cisterns and snoring delinquents echoing across threadbare landings deep into the night: hostelries that go on being there because there is a substantial body of people that actually require them.

Blue Chip City

Provided you are under no obligation to reach a meeting, there is something not altogether unpleasant in arriving in a large city you have not visited before, having no bearings whatever, and trying to locate the main shopping area. It is surprising how difficult this can sometimes prove to be. It proved difficult in Bristol because, like Nottingham, the city centre seemed to sprawl and not to have an immediately noticeable focal point drawing you toward it at all. Bristol did, in fact, seem dull and disjointed, with none of the airy dignity of a Leeds or a Manchester. It appeared to offer nothing but the kind of big city environmental muddle, with the familiar staggered hotch-potch of office blocks, street patterns destroyed to accommodate motor vehicles, and pedestrians channelled hastily out of the way, that you expect to find anywhere. This, along with the episode in that bad lodging-house, was a disappointing introduction to a city I had long wanted to visit. Priestley visited Bristol, for the first time, near the beginning of his journey round England, when he admitted he was still in an optimistic mood. He liked the place. He thought that what was admirable about it was that it was both old and alive, not a museum piece living on tourists and the sale of bogus antiques. He thought it had an air. You could wander about it and wonder and admire, he said, and he liked it so much that when he left he hoped soon to renew the acquaintance. I do not know if Priestley did return to Bristol, but ten years after he first went there, much of the city he saw was bombed into rubble; just as some ten years after that, greater damage still was inflicted by city planners and inadequate politicians than the Luftwaffe ever managed.

I experienced Bristol, for the first time, toward the end of my journey round England, when I was feeling drained, irritated, and far from optimistic. I did not much care for the place, at any rate not to begin with. If it retained any qualities that were admirable and still worth emphasising, it was that the cars and figures swirling round it in the centre contrived to suggest it was still alive, that commerce was ticking over, that people were going about their business, but not a great deal more. I certainly did not wonder and admire, for it is a farce, an utter farce, to talk about big, slovenly industrial cities as though they were a characteristic only of the urban landscape north of Watford. (You could make a good start by looking at Watford itself.) Bristol had the same ring of neglected suburbs grafted onto it, the same scruffy Victorian shops petering out where the butchered main roads trailed away from the pull of the commercial nucleus, that are possessed by major provincial cities throughout Britain. It could have been the sunny weather that had suddenly brought them more out into the open, but I also saw more beggars on the streets of Bristol than anywhere else in England, though you do sometimes hear it said that such people congregate where there is more wealth and hence a greater degree of passing trade. Yet Bristol, which is where the popular television series *Casualty* is made, did not feel to me anywhere near as prosperous as Manchester, even if, like Manchester (and Birmingham), it claims to be the second financial capital outside London. The dirty corrugated-shed describing itself as the city's main bus station, carpeted with cigarette-ends and lined with another assortment of vagrants requesting cash from the Bristol working class, is one of the most desolating spectacles I have ever had the misfortune to come across. The bright new bus stations in some of the old South Yorkshire mining towns feel luxurious in comparison. Bristol was, I could quickly see, far from genuinely old, though I should imagine that, like nearly everywhere in the emerging historical theme park called Modern England, it will be increasingly content to live on tourists and the sale of bogus antiques: to promote the notion that once it was actually very old indeed. This is what was so interesting a contrast with what Priestley saw, particularly in view of his observation that back then, when it was still possible to find masts and funnels straddling the central streets where the ships swelled up the floating harbour almost into Broad Quay, he thought it was old but 'not living in the past'. For if Priestley were still alive, and had seen the Bristol I saw, if he had read the opening paragraph to one of the city's most recent official guides, which states confidently that 'without doubt Bristol is fast emerging as one of the most dynamic centres for tourism in the British Isles', then he might well have found himself disliking the city today for the very reasons he once endorsed it.

Though I was not surprised to find myself contemplating any of this, I was surprised at how hilly Bristol was. My impression after a couple of days walking and bussing around it was that it can be split roughly into two distinct shopping areas, with a sort of nondescript section containing banks, the Old Markets, and the huge open traffic island above Broad Quay, pushed somewhere in between. If you walk up the hill from College Green, up to where the road begins to level out onto Queens

Road to form the beginning of Clifton, Bristol's most prestigious suburb, an abundance of impressive nineteenth-century building begins to group itself. Not far beyond that hangs the suspension bridge spanning the grand Avon gorge, its outline described by thousands of small bulbs when it is lit up at night. With the rush of traffic pouring up and down Park Street, with the imposing bulk of the Wills Memorial Building standing monumentally at the top in brilliant winter sunshine, you feel that you are entering a somewhat different Bristol to the shopping centre-and-department-store version simmering in the haze below, as indeed you are. It is at that moment when the observations I made a paragraph or two above this one begin to shift into rather a different perspective. For Clifton has something vaguely Oxford about it, due of course to the presence of the university, which has an excellent reputation. The shops are good. The window displays, bristling with mannequins in commanding postures, and arrays of stylish chrome pans, are catering for people with genuine aesthetic awareness. The further you walk up Park Street, the more exclusive, the less commercialized, Bristol appears to become. There is a selection of decent bookshops, interspersed with a succession of pleasant cafés, bistros, and wine bars. The lunchtime I was there, the pavements were busy, in places congested, far more brisk and assertive in their sense of composure than the ordinary shopping area in the city below, with its slow shuffling crowds and its chorus of bronchial coughs. In Clifton there was Christmas music in the air again, plenty of well-groomed faces, and continental-looking women of the kind you bump into down quiet mews in Kensington, with confident expressions, and swept back hair flowing around distinctive Georgio Armani sunglasses. The streets had a satisfying, vigorous, cosmopolitan air that good city centre universities always generate as their immediate offshoot. The very bone structure of the faces, the mild contemplative quality of the expressions, the long stripy scarves knotted stylishly around the supple necks – all testified quietly to the presence of the educated English middle class. Here was a wide city thoroughfare that could so easily have become neglected and plastered with bill posters had it not been for the presence of the university.

Being a major port, and an ancient city, Bristol used to have a reputation for having an economy based around mixed trade, meaning it could escape the worst effects of recession. During the seventeenth and eighteenth centuries it grew rich on its trade with the West Indies, chiefly in sugar, tobacco, and rum, and more notoriously, its bartering of African slaves. Later came chocolate, shipbuilding, and a hundred other industries. But what is surprising today, considering that Bristol and the south west were largely uninfluenced by the Industrial Revolution, is that for a city situated so far south a considerable amount of manufacturing industry has become established there, chiefly in connection with Defence contracts for the government. Bristol has for some time now been heavily dependent upon the Defence industry for much of its economic stability, and manufacturing growth in the area has supposedly been higher in recent times than anywhere else in the country. There are, or there certainly have been until comparatively recently, a staggering twenty-five-thousand people employed in the city working on Defence contracts in one form or another. This makes up nearly half of Bristol's commercial activity, most notably for the firms of Rolls-Royce and British Aerospace, which is why it is worth remembering that the first Concorde aircraft was built in Bristol. But now, mainly because of the improving international situation, as we are all well aware substantial cuts are being made in Defence spending, and Bristol looks like it is going to suffer as a result. Fortunately, some years back, it began marketing itself vigorously as the Blue Chip City, in an attempt to target more high-technology industry and attract it into the area. That it has had considerable success is perhaps to Bristol's credit rather than it is to the nation's as a whole, for if there is one characteristic that distinguishes our economic record it is our failure to modernize and to come to terms with advanced technology. And I suppose there must be something deeply ironic in that throughout the duration of the Cold War years, massive staple industries could remain buoyant because of the threat of conflict with other nations, and once this threat diminished, something which ought to have been to the relief of everyone, with it should come the sort of impact on peoples' economic stability more normally associated with conflict.

Still, I was assured by the knowledgable young lady I spoke to in the offices of Bristol's Economic Development Unit that the Blue Chip City initiative appeared to be reaping dividends. There were, she said, a quantity of highly-skilled, highly-qualified people beginning to come onto the local labour market from Defence-related occupations; people who are being absorbed quickly into new high-technology concerns – possibly adding substance to the notion that Britain's supposed skills shortage is one of the major contributing factors that lies at the heart of its endemic economic problems, and its chronic unemployment. If that is indeed so, let us hope that some of the money saved in Defence cuts can be redirected into worthwhile training programmes. Or, much better than half-hearted schemes designed to massage the unemployment figures, tax incentives for industry to invest in better training skills and plant machinery, and do the job properly for itself.

The General Practitioner

The subject of Bristol's rich and poor cropped up when I travelled out through one of its less prosperous quarters to speak with a doctor whom I had been recommended to see while still in Norwich. He was about my own age, and his constituency took in people from a residential area in the city, as well as from several run-down council estates, where in recent years there have been a number of riots. He claimed there were disturbances happening in one form or another in Bristol much of the time, but that they are generally not important or dramatic enough to make the headlines. I heard this in a number of cities I visited throughout England, where minor incidents, perhaps a small group of youths turning over a couple of cars and firebombing them on their way home from the pub, are quite routine.

When the last of his patients had left and he pulled down the blinds to shut out the sunshine, we began talking about the changes in the running of the National Health Service, which have been in the process of materializing for a number of years now. Most people will be familiar with the rough form these changes are taking, so there is no need to go into the argument for or against them here. What worried this doctor was that the reforms had meant an increase in his workload. He now had to become distracted by administration work, something he did not train for and did not wish to involve himself with when he made his choice of career. This startled me, not because I thought I shouldn't have to listen to such grievances, but because I heard a repeat run, almost sentence for sentence, of what I had been told by my old art school lecturer when I was in Bradford, when he explained what had been the derogatory effects of educational reforms on the quality of his teaching. Both men were speaking independently of each other, but it was as if they had been referring to the same script, and I am not meaning to imply anything sarcastic by saying that. Just as I was told in Bradford that the effect of educational reforms meant a situation had developed whereby for the college to receive adequate funding it was encouraged to attract greater numbers of students, so the doctor said the chief effect of the health service reforms for him meant that the amount of remuneration he received – his operating budget and his income from the NHS – was now directly dependent upon the number of patients he had on his register. (It is perhaps not as widely recognized as it should be that GPs are not employed directly by the NHS. Unlike doctors working in hospitals, they are self-employed, working for the state under contract, rather as authors work for publishers under contract, and allocated budgets with which they must work accordingly. It follows that if there was one thing about which this doctor was most adamant, it was that the reforms were beginning to undermine the traditional independence of GPs.)

He could appreciate that the government had genuinely believed that in adopting a more businesslike approach to the running of the NHS, making doctors more accountable to their funds by creating internal markets, this would tighten up the system and give better value for money. But once the medical welfare of people becomes mixed up with human instinct, he said, that is not necessarily the way things work out. Because doctors were being encouraged to take on more patients he thought this was starting to undermine the amount of time they spent attending to them. If that is true, then you can see that doctors are probably being placed in positions of moral difficulty with increasing frequency, particularly at their station within society. If they generally are, as this young Bristol doctor certainly is, competent at their jobs, people who are caring and humane and have a degree of social responsibility motivating them in what they do, they may elect to run their surgeries longer, to accommodate everyone sitting in the waiting room. But this may begin to interfere with their personal lives outside surgery hours, something that must surely happen already. What if they have arranged to go out for the evening? Under pressure to finish quicker they might feel obliged to skip the finer points. But though it might hurt to say it, and hurt even more if you happen to be one, doctors are probably being encouraged now to work with greater professional responsibility, to tighten up the competency and the speed with which they work. This Bristol doctor could see the logic in that, but for him it had meant an increase in personal stress because he cares about his patients and detests the feeling that he should be forced to compromise in the way he treats them. The one-to-one relationship was suffering, he said, the very essence of the medical profession, because the needs of one patient are not entirely the same as the next. Just as at my old art school I was told the one-to-one relationship between tutor and students, which I remember so well, had deteriorated since I was there, and consequently the quality of the product coming out at the other end (the students) had suffered, so this doctor told me there was now a real danger that the quality of patient care might begin to suffer as well. If you have the same number of doctors being employed to look after more patients in the same amount of time as before, if they are under pressure to increase productivity, as it were, to retain adequate funding and earn for themselves an adequate salary, the quality of the service will be affected accordingly. In a situation influenced by market practices, a multi-layered, and more often than not, two-tiered system generally develops because the bargaining nature of market forces ensures that you do not so much wish to give better value for money than your competitor as oust your competitor altogether. Obviously, doctors are not trading in a free-market situation, but the same thought processes inevitably begin to apply. While still strapped to an essentially centralist system loosely tacked onto a few market reforms, I was told that the effect of the health service reforms might prove only to be a tightening of the existing system, a holding in of the fat so to speak rather than a getting rid of the fat altogether, with the existing quality of service being the chief casualty. For instance, as a GP's budget begins to run low, he might well be forced to shop around for a cheaper service, if one of his patients requires specialized treatment. Doctor A in Bristol might have a patient that needs such-and-such an operation. But opted-out hospital X just down the road is asking too high a price for the operation because it employs better surgeons who are paid better salaries, although they could get the patient onto the operating table straight away. So Doctor A might have to travel many miles, perhaps all the way up to Newcastle, to hospital Y, where a surgeon can operate more quickly, at a more competitive price, but whose credentials are altogether more dubious. However, because there are already other doctors who are feeling the pinch financially, as is Doctor A, there is already a waiting list. Doctor A has to join the queue. What develops is a two-tier system, with the patients on the receiving end of what amount essentially to cuts in public expenditure, and the people comfortable enough not to be affected going private when it suits them. This doctor in Bristol believed the patients on the receiving end would be concentrated in parts of the country already at a social disadvantage to begin with, which generally means the inner cities. This is the nightmare scenario, of course, one we are assured, what with the talk about safety nets and so forth, will not be allowed to happen. But from what I could gather, it is beginning to happen already.

For a long time it has seemed to me that what we really mean when we say we want to reform the funding of the NHS is that we want to reform the management structure, in other words the way the funding is actually administered. The problems with the NHS lie in the fact that its enormous bureaucracy is not seriously accountable to the profit motive, which still appears to be the best way of getting human beings to operate efficiently.

There is a lack of business flair in the huge health organization as it stands. That is the real issue at stake here, and a market approach makes superficial sense because it creates incentives. But sensible funding would be more likely to follow if the management structure were sufficiently tackled. Surely it would be better to examine the problem more fundamentally from the Human Resource angle than it already is being. Britain's bad management record is not so much to do with the control of funding as it is to do with bad management. Plenty of large companies in this country are quite simply badly run, because the people running them are poorly trained or have often been over-promoted, or are so absorbed in job security that incentives are continually undermined. And it is much the same with state monopolies. If this problem were seriously tackled, the financial problems might begin to sort themselves out. But in something of a knee-jerk fashion it is always taken for granted that money lies at the root of the problem. Money is simply a method by which human beings regulate their behaviour, yet we assume that by looking at the thing financially the behavioural problems will resolve themselves accordingly. In reality it is the other way round.

The doctor told me about some of the social problems and pressures a good number of his unemployed patients suffer. He loathed the ignorant right-wing attitude that assumes poor people such as them are spongers siphoning every available penny they can from the State. He told me, with a degree of feeling that would be difficult for the most pitiful reactionary to ignore, that he goes into the homes of these people and sees their suffering, listens to their problems, and knows first-hand how alienated many of them feel from the rest of society. He said he would like to help such people. But the tax-cutting, make-what-you-can philosophy did, in his opinion, exclude such people from participating effectively in the mainstream organization of society. He asked, as so many people asked that I met travelling through England, why we cannot obtain the midway point. He would not mind paying a little more tax – again how often I heard this, from one end of the country to the other, like the refrain of a poem – if it meant a better, safer, more just society. Unlike those hugely wealthy hypocrites who say this, he really meant it. Here was no naïve socialist who spent his years at university sitting in the corner of a dingy union bar rolling tatty cigarettes, developing a middle-class idealist's grudge against the ugliness of society, and dreaming about Marxism. Nor was he a liberal sentimentalist. He was a smart young man from a secure background, who admitted he had voted Conservative and as a student had been a vigorous believer in capitalism. But as we lingered at the door and watched the traffic passing at the end of the street, he asked why, as millions of others must do, *why* cannot we achieve simple, level-headed economics with a social responsibility? Probably because there are not enough decent people like him in positions of influence, with a sensible understanding of society, who are close enough to the rough texture of society, to understand what such phraseology even means.

I rode back into Bristol on the upstairs of a double-decker bus. The roads were busy. Some of the shops had crates of fresh fruit and vegetables arranged colourfully along the wide pavements. The video shops had pictures emphasizing guns and fists and chiselled masculine jaws glued to the windows. Groups of children could be seen climbing up and down slides, launching into the air from swings in passing recreation grounds; and above was the sky, the sky high, high above. Every so often, the bus lurched and hooted over to the side of the road and collected clusters of working-class passengers, some of whom might well have been patients of the doctor I had just left behind. There seemed to be a marked amount of coughing coursing throughout those smoky upstairs seats, a background noise I have associated with an assembled body of working-class people since I was young. As I looked at the cheap shops with their hideous facades and their discount notices filing past the windows, as I stared up row after row of Victorian terraced housing running at right-angles to the wide main road where once the trams would have groaned, I reflected on what the doctor had said. In spite of the reforms he was fortunate in that he had a personal interest which he had since been able to cultivate and turn into decent paying work. Because of what he had experienced to be their negative effects, the NHS reforms had, paradoxically, made him broaden his own horizons, and so he was in the process of becoming a part-time GP. But that is not what he, or the government, ever intended, of course. He had wanted to become a doctor since he was a child because he wanted to help people and do something useful with his life. Because he was now expected to perform duties that he did not spend his years at university training to do, for no commensurate rise in income, he was distancing himself from the profession because he was becoming disillusioned. With an ironic shrug of the shoulders he had admitted that he, too, could sell part of his time and his talent in the market-place, for greater remuneration with a reduced amount of stress. He had a wife and family, and various debts accumulated over the years appropriate to his class. He did not see why he should lower his standards. Though he passionately wanted to help human beings and cure disease, he was not prepared to sacrifice his family for the sake of being a doctor. Ultimately, he said he would even be prepared to leave the profession altogether and do something entirely different. I had no doubt that I had listened to the voice of a committed man. I knew I was on the side of the government in that I had no doubt that the running of the National Health Service was in need of a serious review. I knew also that one can pontificate endlessly over such sensitive matters as these, that there is a great deal of emotion bound up with any serious discussion of the subject of the funding of the NHS.

What I was less certain about was to what extent that doctor's decision to become a part-time GP had been a side effect of what the government has been claiming all along is necessary to the more efficient running of the National Health Service – namely, the application of market forces.

Bristol Past, England Present

The bits of Bristol I saw that were very old were interesting enough. I discovered a well-known little alley in the city called Christmas Steps, which surprised me by offering a tiny glimpse of Bristol the medieval seaport. It rather resembled a slab of Lincoln or Canterbury that had been wrenched up and deposited rigidly on a cobbled incline, and is the kind of ancient thoroughfare anywhere would be quite happy to hear itself remembered by. With its gnarled shop fronts and worn flagstones and freshly-painted gas lamps running straight down the middle – the street 'steppered, done and finished, September 1669', at the personal expense of one of Bristol's wealthiest wine merchants – Christmas Steps offered a glimpse of the authentic old Bristol. A small glimpse these days it is true, one which peters out very quickly when you come out onto the streets crowded with tower blocks and traffic at the bottom, but a genuine glimpse nevertheless. Small patches like this can be found elsewhere, but in general Bristol the ancient seaport has long gone, and has been in the process of fading away for many years now. Even the famous Merchant Venturers' Hall, which no old guidebook could fail to gloze over, was blown to pieces during the war. For a long time, anyone thinking about Bristol probably thought of three things – Wills cigarettes, the city's most famous firm, Harvey's Bristol Cream, and Fry's chocolate. I saw something to do with the Harvey company, which is alive and well, down a back street near the university. As for the firm of Wills, cigarettes are no longer manufactured in the city at all, only cigars. The old firm had been absorbed in another great industrial merger, one of the commercial scions of our time, not long before I arrived. Its name has been changed and all cigarette production moved up to Nottingham, though the Wills family, who did not mind ploughing considerable chunks of their fortune back into Bristol, have left a worthy legacy to the city architecturally, one that will live on for many years to come.

That I found Christmas Steps interesting was underlined by the fact that I was drawn back there twice more – perhaps in reality I was trying to escape – on each occasion at night, to eat in an interesting little restaurant I found tucked away down among the duskiness. With a bit of mist gathering at the top of the steep steps blurring the glow of the gas lamps, with long shadows stretching over lumpy gables, with the city reasonably quiet at that hour, with darkness filling in the gaps between buildings hiding who or God knows what, it was possible to imagine something of the seafaring Bristol as it exists in guidebook imagination. After all, if there is one type of environment we probably still expect to find enveloped permanently by subtle swirling fogs – other than the London of the Whitechapel murders, or the city England as portrayed in hackneyed American films – then it must surely be an old English seaport. But though I could see the appeal of these ancient streets, and appreciate the aesthetic congruity of Clifton higher up the hill, I was now growing rather tired of antiquity. And Christmas Steps has none of that marvellous sense of cloudy vagueness during the daylight. As I emerged from the bottom of the alley for the final time, and passed beneath some modern brick architecture struggling feebly to echo the seventeenth-century nook and cranny braced against the incline behind it, a pair of police cars screamed past on the main road, I am sure through traffic lights that were still at red. Their hideous electronic sirens were wailing, their blue lights were flashing, and for a moment the modern Bristol lifting before me had the air of being only another sector of downtown America. Watching the cars disappear out in the direction of the docks made you realize that in broad twentieth-century daylight, you cannot escape the feeling that the emphasis placed upon ancient English thoroughfares such as Christmas Steps, on clusters of sagging timber-framed buildings, is all wrong. All the time, wherever you go, you find yourself walking up and down these oldy-worldy streets, staring in antique and craft shop windows, sitting in cafés or restaurants or pubs jangling with authentic beaten copper jugs playing gentle melodies in warm summer breezes, pandering to this continual idealization of the past, and are led to the cynical conclusion that nobody is interested in what places are like any more, only how they used to be.

During that final afternoon, I found my way through some impressive streets making up the bulk of Bristol's banking and old market quarters, walked across into the city's central shopping area grouped around Broadmead, and there sat on a seat surrounded by the busy crowds. Once again I took out the official Bristol visitor's guide. It was a substantial booklet, and from one end to the other emphasised nothing – almost *nothing* – but the historic aspects of the city. It contained hardly anything but pictures celebrating the glories of the past. I turned the pages at random and found photographs of fluted columns and drawings of Norman castles. I flicked the booklet open again, I promise entirely at random, and saw a photograph of an elderly couple sitting atop a turn-of-the century motor car. Again, and this time a painting of one of Bristol's most famous citizens, John Cabot at the moment of his departure to discover the mainland of North America in 1497. Again, and I saw photographs of Wells Cathedral in Somerset ('the smallest city in England'), the grey ruins of Tintern Abbey miles away in Gwent, and a long cobbled street peppered with reproduction gas lamps. Again, and now I was looking at a picture of Brunel's *SS Great Britain*, and reading about a restored 1937 steam locomotive and an Industrial Museum. Pictures of newly painted barges, a woman dressed in period clothing in a nineteenth-century kitchen, warped timbers, restored alleyways, ancient engravings, Victorian ironwork, absurd indications that among a morass of ferro-concrete and glass you can find a handful of 'original' buildings that have actually survived – in other words, that what has survived is all that is worthy of being given credibility by your emotions or your perceptions. And so it goes, with an occasional reference thrown in, to the city's credit it has got to be said, to a science museum intended to make people more aware of the technology buzzing in the world around them, thank God; and finally a picture of the odd modern building, usually a church. But you have to search very hard indeed for much reference to anything that is associated with the world as it has really developed during the twentieth century. And it is worth remembering that the official visitor's guide for the city of Bristol could have its title changed and be promoting the official outlook of any major town or city in the land.

Throughout the writing of this book, I have felt myself torn constantly between the pros and cons of this emerging late-twentieth-century English cultural atmosphere; between the virtues good and bad of the new post-industrial nostalgia. One half of me appreciates the decent aesthetic qualities inherent to almost anything that is old; the half which enjoys a pleasant afternoon's stroll around it, and a browse among pot-pourri-smelling shops, with my family. But the other half steps back and understands the technological, political, and economic reasons behind the accepted social and aesthetic failures of much of the post-war era – something our official sentimentalists rarely do, least of all in doting guidebooks – the half that is continually aware of the huge amount of goods being sold in these historic shops that are now made in the developing countries of the East. It is this other half of me that questions seriously that a society that devotes so much of its energies to a systematic celebration of its past does so only because it does not, I say again, have a viable concept of the future with which it can feel comfortable or at ease. Why else look backwards unless you have no enthusiasm pulling your attention forwards? It is the underlying manifestation of decline. But then, I suppose it is inevitable that a society that is no longer officially geared to devising and making things should begin to idealize the period in its history when it was considered to be the workshop of the world, and made things all the time. Human beings need to devise and create, and if they can no longer do so via predominantly economic methods, they will find ways of doing so during their pastime and in their dreams. Perhaps there is some hope to be found after all in the fact that a people that still feels the need to extol so thoroughly the virtues of its past is at least feeling the need to extol the virtues of *something*, which is better than not extolling the virtues of anything at all. And here, inevitably, you come back again to our ailing economic performance, our inability to modernize, our badly educated and underskilled workforce – in effect, our lack of a sense of purpose or direction. In this modern nostalgia England, you step outside your medieval tea-room and glance appreciatively up at a string of bow-fronted Dickensian shop fronts. But, if you look hard enough, though of course you don't really have to look very hard at all, you begin to notice the little burglar alarms speckling those pleasant sagging facades made of real lath-and-plaster, making something of a mockery of your aesthetic awareness and feelings of historical romance welling inside. You see the real England that is quietly emerging. Notwithstanding these contradictory observations, it is claimed that in the emerging post-industrial scheme of things we can all happily become dealers in the atmosphere of the past, dealers in knowledge, dealers in other peoples' manufactures, dealers in distribution, dealers in tourism and dealers in leisure; the neat little video cameras and the colourful little burglar alarms protecting us from the headbutting antics of the poor unfortunate savages, packed in between the slabs of pebble-dash and concrete a mile or so beyond, who are no longer required economically to play a part in the emerging scheme of things at all.

At such moments, you step back and begin to understand with a bang the nature of the powerful economic forces that really are at work beneath the surface of the late twentieth century Western world. Forces that are obscured, in this country at least, behind the veneer of dried-flowers hanging in baskets in shop doorways; behind beautifully restored dock buildings; behind the science parks stylishly clad in reflective glass and plastic laminate of the kind I had seen in Birmingham, with business-suited women wearing slender high-heels and sheer stockings weaving between the Japanese communications technology. Forces that are obscured behind restored railway locomotives and little cassette tapes relaying through hidden speakers perfectly the sound of a steam powered past. Forces obscured by the heritage-this and the heritage-that and by the talk of an easy-credit based economy dependant on the buying and selling of huge quantities of imported goods, that mysterious generalization 'invisible earnings' making up for the shortfall in our balance of payments. We are told, in fact, that our emerging post-industrial economy is as inevitable as it is desirable. The future emerging for the Bristol that was expanding all around me that day is the future emerging everywhere. It is a future we are confidently assured, and we can clearly see by using the eyes in our heads, is enabling us not only to deal in our past, but clean up our past and rediscover its aesthetic virtues. (This is the same past that was blown apart by those meddling moral aesthetes and social engineers, and corrupt private sector building companies and political crooks, given a free hand during Harold MacMillan's premiership.) The future that is emerging is a future whereby we can devote more of our energies to the cultivation, presumably, of our sensibilities, now that we are free from the restraint of enforced clumsy labour; enforced, clumsy, dirty manufacturing. It will be a society which is essentially information-based. Its wealth will be generated through what are ambiguously termed desk-based, knowledge-based industries in business parks and new towns and a handful of massive tower blocks being built above the old – as though the manufacture of components in a modern factory were not dependent upon the accumulation of extensive knowledge and experience, and comprehensive research and development!

This, we accept to be the broad face of the England of the future. Except for a minority of highly-skilled, high-technology industries employing limited numbers of people, manufacturing – the serious art of *making* things, outside a bit of part-time embroidery and basket-weaving on adventure holidays – will become a thing of the past. Instead the rapidly industrializing East will become the hot-bed of low-tech manufacturing which the West will neatly exploit. Because the West – the First World – will control the finance, the design, the processing of the essential information that makes the world economy tick, the Third World will in effect become our assembly line. Many of those countries' goods fill our shops and our mail order catalogues and our childrens' toy-boxes already, now that the old industrial heartlands of Britain and the United States are being wound down, their grime stripped away, their aesthetic qualities restored, romanticized, and assessed anew.

This, roughly, is the way things are going according to a number of observers and economic forecasters who from time to time make sweeping statements favourably to something of the effect of what I have written above. But there is in my opinion a very significant knock-on effect that could materialize if this great service-sector scenario were to become a reality on the sort of scale that is talked about; an effect none of the comfortable apologists of the post-industrial scheme of things appears seriously to have considered at all. And that is the social consequences this state of affairs might have on the mind and the spirit of our people, for it is always worth remembering that it is the social consequences that generally mess up the economics. On the other hand, we should not be in the least bit surprised that commentators who have made a life out of economic forecasting, whose upbringing and education and subsequent lifestyle and careers have kept them a special distance from the nuts and bolts of what really goes on, who come nowhere near the workings of industry in a practical capacity, who have little understanding of the aspirations common to people who make and manufacture things, should have a profoundly different kind of aesthetic outlook on life to those that do. That they have little understanding of the way people think whose talents come alive when they are *producing* things, attending to practical problems and giving something constructive back to society, is not so much to do with ignorance as it is to do with the kind of environments and stimulations to which they have been subjected and how they were brought up. You only have to talk to people who manufacture or make things, dozens and dozens of whom I met during this journey both inside boardrooms and out, to understand there is a profound difference in psychology between practical people and many of the thinkers and politicians influencing our affairs. You only have to examine the difference in personality producers exude, as against so many of the dull windbags you come across who simply deal in things or try to organize them. Producers come across as being *interesting* people. Strongly motivated, they often strike you as being enthusiastic about the things they do and the world that surrounds them. They view society as a gigantic mechanism to which they are contributing a useful component, and by doing so this gives them a certain amount of personal satisfaction. It does not matter whether you talk to large-scale pottery or textile manufacturers, or small-scale engineers or manufacturers of over-bath shower screens in the back streets of Rochdale. You perceive in such people a quality of enthusiasm that is almost impossible to put down on paper seriously without being dismissed by that marked quantity of ignorant intellectual observers, who have no comprehension of the workings of industry, as 'sentimental', or 'naïve'. There are plenty of manufacturers and industrialists who are lousy employers, of course, and who would happily make their money in another easier, less responsible way if they could, had they not got bogged down in things the way they have. But they are outweighed by the manufacturers and industrialists who are absorbed by their businesses and their work, and who offer this country the best hope it has got. They are often filled with entrepreneurial flair, bursting with real patriotic feeling, none of your Little England and No Turning Back nonsense. They know instinctively that a nation that is proud of what it makes has its head more firmly on its shoulders than one that isn't.

The frame of mind that does not understand this, like that wider think-tank of boring economists, is, at bottom, constantly justifying its own emotional outlook on the world to itself in everything it thinks and says. Because, as a class, it enjoys a certain amount of intellectual influence and social prestige, it assumes the values it has accumulated at its own spectatorial level of society are automatically the correct ones. It is unlikely it will have much grasp of, or much interest, in science or engineering, for instance. Or that it can begin to comprehend the benefits of sound investment in research and development, and its importance to the growth of a modern civilized people; that it strengthens a society from below, not interventionistically from above. Once you do have an understanding of these things, it profoundly affects the way you contemplate the world that exists around you, because what is wrong with the world becomes depressingly clear. The ordinary people shovelled aside in debates, papers, and policy studies, the people still filling our factories, will not be content to be consigned to a dustbin of low-skilled jobs in a service-based economy, selling sandwiches or delivering laundry, nor should they be expected to. They are generally much happier as human beings when they are producing something, bringing out the personal expression in themselves. It is typical that the sort of middle-class academics who make money from the cultivation of their intellectual abilities, and profoundly influence our affairs instead of honing useful skills out in the market-place of the real world, should have no understanding of this, because it is outside their own rationality or experience, or the ambitions and expectations socially they take for granted as a class. Claiming that we have the wherewithal to design and conceive our manufactures then setting up production lines in the factories of the Third World – as a good number of astute-minded gentlemen are doing in this country already, totally oblivious to the fact they are helping their country to fall slowly on its sword and bringing the day of reckoning ever closer – simply is not good enough. As a philosophy, it is contemptuous and irresponsible in the extreme. It fails to take into account the aspirations of huge numbers of people, from the industrial engineer through to the skilled lathe operator, who happen to be part of our economy, and who unfortunately, will need to be provided with jobs in the blossoming post-industrial Utopia.

Every time I hear someone talking smugly about the elimination of manufacturing as an important commodity of the 'post-industrial' British economy, I see those people I saw in factories in the Potteries and elsewhere being slapped squarely across the face. I see their sensations, their expression, their value as people, being indirectly condemned by naïve economists, social theorists, and inappropriately-educated politicians, who have never performed a proper day's work in their lives, to exist in an economic graveyard, padded out with a low-skilled, poorly-paid, inadequately-educated workforce. And with it I see their sensibilities becoming numbed, which for the future stability of our society I find deeply disturbing, as I suggested back in Liverpool. But we should still remember that, contrary to popular belief, it is industrial manufacturers, and a substantial body of skilled workers, who still earn this country its basic living. We ought also to visit, while we are at it, the end of year shows at some of our design colleges, our art schools, and our universities, if we really believe we needn't bother to manufacture things any longer, that we should dispense with the making of things industrially as a nation, that science isn't important, and that such an intellectually bankrupt situation ought even to be *desirable*, for Christ's sake. I am well aware of the statistics, though I admit it somewhat reluctantly, that point out that manufacturing need not necessarily form the bedrock of a sustainable economy, though I have my doubts even about that. What matters to me, as someone who has yet to come across a substantial body of post-industrial, service-biased apologists with a sound aesthetic awareness, or a practical understanding of what really makes the world and ordinary human beings tick, are, I say again, the social consequences in the medium to longer term – the same term when my own son, and millions of other children like him, will be embarking on their adult lives.

To me it is bad, *spiritually* bad, for a nation to lose the desire to produce things and assume all virtue lies inside an accountant's or a solicitor's or a money dealer's head. A skilled labour force is central to a sophisticated manufacturing economy. And a skilled labour force means better developed minds that are able to tackle the solving of problems, which means a more intelligent people, which means better overall brainpower, which means a nation with greater common sense, which means a stable, more successful, more civilized people. This needs to be shouted from the rooftops by every politician worth his salt. We have got to pull ourselves together before it is too late. An unskilled, increasingly illiterate, subservient workforce will have no means of releasing its emotional energies, or for that matter of being absorbed in anything deeply enough to contain them and enable them to attain maturity. Doped up on asinine television ramming home the prospect that nothing worthwhile can be achieved in life through personal initiative and effort, only by winning it on patronizing quiz shows or through dozy competitions; looking increasingly for stimulation to the bit of tatty excitement offered via its nightly dosage of violent video tomfoolery; swirling around in a vortex of drugs, cheap alcohol, crude thrusting sex, and crude sensations; kept down in a society which no longer possesses the economic framework to invest in them and train them properly, give them decent opportunities or a sense of function in life – a society that does not, in fact, value them constructively at all – then we might be in the process of lighting the fuse to a slow social timebomb. A timebomb that could explode with devastating consequences. But notice how in reality the fuse to that timebomb has already been lit, for a vicious circle is already established whereby the brutalization of masses of ordinary minds, this need for workers who are unskilled and lowly paid by day, masturbating mentally over the sound of machine-gun fire and explosions in their living rooms by night, not requiring to become educated, absorb knowledge, or develop their minds, is becoming an important ingredient to a substantial private sector of the post-industrial economy. What is more, in the post-industrial scheme of things, in this burgeoning reassessment of ourselves from one-, two-, or three-hundred years ago, when one of the chief characteristics of society was its brutality, this body of people is going to grow. Not only is the wheel of irony coming full circle.

Of course, one tires of listening to a handful of snobs who despise the imbecile nature of popular mass culture; who bray endlessly about the crassness and the moronic stupidity of the working classes. One tires of being showered with spittle from a series of raspberries blown continuously by they-that-disapprove, in the same way one tires of reading again and again the barrage of abuse denouncing video culture, youth culture, pop music, satellite dishes, junk food, Spanish holidays, etc, *ad infinitum*. What a pity these people lack the intellectual depth to understand how important this gutter culture is, and will increasingly become, to them retaining their superior social positions as worshippers of a watercolourist's delicate past; just as they fail miserably to understand the economic reasons behind its growth as a social phenomenon at all. Meanwhile, a number of those rapidly-industrializing Third World countries, eager to bring themselves up to First World standards, see the need to produce a well-educated workforce, as the Japanese and the Germans have been busily doing since 1945, if they are to become the hotbed of manufacturing which the developed countries will continue neatly to exploit. If the current post-industrial climate is indeed the way things economically are going to go, then fine; there is not much that can be done about it. But make no mistake, sooner or later the indirect effects of that climate might come back at us like a boomerang, dragging behind them storm clouds we can as yet not even begin to comprehend.

The West is powerful, of course. Iraq knows clearly enough what can happen when the economic stability of the West is threatened. But if we can be bothered to look deeply enough, we might find that the battlefield that is quietly emerging is going to be a very different kind of battlefield indeed. The outcome of that battle, the seeds of which we can see in the economic decline going on all around us, might not be quite so certain, if we happen to be up against societies that for the past fifty years have committed a major proportion of their energies to producing a highly-intelligent workforce with real brainpower.

11

Gloucestershire and the Journey Home

Cheltenham

After such an unpleasant start when I arrived I found that, like J.B. Priestley before me, I was in the end quite reluctant to come away from Bristol, rather as had been the case when I left Newcastle. There was more of the city that I felt I still wanted to see. I did not see much of the old docks, for instance; and I would like to have seen more of Clifton. Bristol did seem like a natural place to conclude the journey, though I still had another week of scheduled travelling to complete. Ahead of me lay Cheltenham, which I had chosen to investigate instead of Bath as a typical modern English spa town, and where I had arranged to meet up again with my wife for the final weekend of the journey, and where we intended to stay with some relatives of ours who run a flourishing company in the centre of the town. Being situated where it is, Cheltenham would also serve as an ideal springboard from which to move on for a few days' contemplation of the ancient honey-coloured stones of the Cotswolds, at the western approach to which it is located. Finally, there would be a short spell amidst the steeples of Oxford, and hopefully some conversation with an historian at the university.

Thinking about all this, and perhaps being distracted by it, as I left the Royal Swallow Hotel and the sunny expanse of College Green behind, and traipsed back across the city for the last time, I became lost. I could not find my way to Temple Meads Station. Laden with heavy bags I found I had walked around in a complete circle when I passed the main entrance to Debenhams for the second time. Becoming increasingly aerated, and with one eye on the train times to Cheltenham, I suddenly stepped into a taxi that appeared alongside me somewhere near a very good new shopping centre I had been into a day or so previously. My last physical memory of Bristol city centre, with the air of the place still touching my face, so to speak – my final memory of big city England during this assignment – was the familiar sound of a Salvation Army Band playing *Good King Wensleslas*, and the incessant blur of rim-lit Christmas shoppers thronging sunlit pavements beneath a cloud of exhaled breath. As I pushed my bags roughly onto the back seat of the car, that jumble of figures swirling this way and that seemed to be a suitable impression to carry away – a final symbolic snapshot, perhaps, one that felt curiously reassuring and yet so quintessentially English, despite the crime statistics and the bad architecture. Then I was away, and the taxi driver was telling me there had been a collision between two trains that morning inside the Severn Tunnel, and I could expect delays when I boarded my own train to Cheltenham.

He was wrong. I did not experience delays, though the train was very full. Most of the passengers were en-route to South Wales. This became evident when the train stopped at Bristol Parkway Station, on the outskirts of the city, and the guard walked through the carriage, informed everybody about the accident in the tunnel and, amidst an all round exhalation of weary breath, said that passengers travelling in that direction and beyond must alight there and board a bus waiting outside the adjacent ticket office. This would take them to the appropriate juncture from which they could resume their journey comfortably by rail. Fortunately I was going the other way. After such an exodus the train, which was an old one that rattled and squeaked and had a bell that rang inside the driver's compartment each time it went past a signal, was nearly empty. I settled back to enjoy the ride as it wound its way slowly through the outskirts of Bristol suburbia, beneath embankments scattered with bent supermarket trolleys and domestic rubbish and clumps of petrified undergrowth, all cheerfully refrigerated beneath a huge canopy of deep blue sky. Then the final band of housing slowly gave way to wideness and green, and the train trundled contentedly along some very straight sections of track, on into the Gloucestershire countryside, until, after about an hour, it began to curve sharply round into the outskirts of Gloucester, a city steeped in historical anecdote, but one that from the vantage point of a train offered the familiar abysmal spectacle of a clutter of trashy housing, weed-infested railway sidings, and vandalized carriages you normally find on the perimeter of modern industrial towns.

And then, after the train doubled back on itself and rattled along for perhaps another ten or fifteen minutes, finally to Cheltenham, the town among the trees, as they say, at the foot of the Cotswold hills. Cheltenham, with its jokes about retired gentlefolk, especially spinsters who used to believe miners drank champagne and kept coal in their baths, and who have today, it is said, moved on to Marbella by way of Bournemouth instead. Cheltenham, with its impeccable Ladies' College, where the descendants of Miss Beale's nineteenth-century girls are not only taught traditional academic subjects but are expected to master the use of computers as well. Cheltenham, with its exclusive Gentleman's College, which by the end of the last century had become the second largest public school in England. Cheltenham, the first garden city, with its plethora of stucco-faced Regency architecture, its crescents and its elegant squares, the biggest and most complete town of its kind ever built, and reminiscent in places of the Brighton and Hove I had only recently left behind. Cheltenham, with its acclaimed explosion of floral display during the summer months, permanently at the top of the Britain in Bloom competition and well-known for it. Cheltenham, which they used to call Poor, Proud and Pretty because of the number of ex-Indian Army colonels who retired there on modest pensions, who were educated and able to speak well, who had exceedingly stiff upper lips, but who were unable really to spend well, like some of their English bourgeois counterparts struggling to keep up appearances back then on working-class incomes did, and in pockets today staunchly continue to do. And Cheltenham

– where I could not believe how far the railway station was located from the town centre proper.

The tone of this last observation aside, there did in fact used to be three stations in Cheltenham, one of which was in the very centre of the town. But two of them have long since disappeared and the one that has been kept, nowhere near as big as you would expect for a place of its size, is about a mile and a half from the shops. A mile and a half might not be very far, but it is a sufficient enough distance to suggest that it might discourage people from arriving in Cheltenham by train. It is also a very frustrating space to have to negotiate when you are carrying cumbersome baggage. When I arrived in Cheltenham I was over an hour early for the time I had arranged to be picked up by my wife. I was hungry so I decided to walk into the town centre to try and find somewhere to eat. But by the time I had struggled with my bags down a wide residential road, where I registered there was a section of pavement designated for cyclist use only when a bell sounded behind me, and reached the periphery of the shops at a place called Montpellier, it was almost time to walk back.

Traversing that length of self-satisfied tree-lined avenue, I entertained the cynical and perhaps rather inequitable thought, reinforced by a conspicuous lack of taxis outside the station (I was told afterwards they were otherwise engaged at the races), that it was perhaps not so much a case of how far the railway station was from the centre of the town, but how far the centre of the town had been kept from the railway station. I could have believed the distance had been calculated to deter visitors, probably because Cheltenham held a high and exclusive opinion of itself. The stout buildings I passed were square-fronted, with balconies and verandas delicately woven with ornamental wrought-iron Hampstead-style canopies. It was plain to see that many had been converted into flats. When I saw them they were all glowing beneath the watchful eye of the late afternoon sun which was now dropping out of sight behind the trees, the windscreens of the cars parked on the drives beginning to mist over as a prelude to frost, a noticeboard in front of one explaining it was a 'home for retired gentlefolk', true to Cheltenham form. In pleasant, leafy, impeccably English provincial spa towns such as Cheltenham, just as in Harrogate or Bath to which it is related and which have a similar social veneer, the feel of the people you see walking the streets is very different to the feel of the people you see walking the streets of Blackburn or Middlesbrough, of that there can be little doubt. You see this reflected in the very bone structure of faces and their proportion to bodies. In fact, I saw enough of Cheltenham in five or ten minutes that afternoon to establish that any high and exclusive opinions the town might hold about itself were neatly reflected in the comfortable, fiscally secure expressions you see walking the streets there, the faint whiff of private schools and genuine leather upholstery hanging in the bitter cold air above their heads. The quality of the shops emphasised it at a glance. They made the salubrious frontages I had seen near the university in Bristol look decidedly down market. Looking along those beaming stucco facades, interpreting the century-and-a-half of English boudoir cultivation and petty-gentry snobbery they implied, equating them to some of the extreme contrasts I had encountered travelling around this country today, I was overwhelmed by the feeling that I ought to be reaching some kind of a generic conclusion about the journey. But if there was a definitive conclusion to be reached about contemporary England at all, and I'm sure there isn't, then I had probably got nearest to it when I was in Basingstoke. I made my way back through the deep dusk to the station car park. My wife's car was now visible, but there was no sign of either her or of my son. I walked up and down the footbridge, went in and out of the booking hall, and then, aching and tired, suddenly recognized a tiny voice shrieking excitedly from the opposite platform.

The Cotswolds and Oxford

We spent the weekend in Cheltenham where we enjoyed much good food, hospitality, and late-night talk. Our relatives were prospering and had recently opened a new shop, not far from one of the others, in effect to take the overflow of customers.

This in the middle of a recession, from people who admit their trade has suffered accordingly. They were talking of selling up soon and having a house built to their own specification in the heart of the Cotswold countryside. Their eldest son attends one of Cheltenham's private schools, and they have a cruiser moored somewhere in the Mediterranean. As at all such moments, late at night at a dinner table, drowsy with wine, pushing cheese and biscuits into my mouth chiefly to fill the gaps between sentences until it was time to speak, staring hypnotically at a candle flame quivering in the lamplight, I seriously wondered why I was motivated to write books when life could conceivably be so much more interesting and less mentally excruciating.

The previous few days had seen the beginning to an extremely cold spell of weather. On the Sunday we drove for miles and miles. We saw magnificent glittering panoramas, watched over from a huge cloudless sky by a sun that seemed to be gawping at the immense frozen distances, at the clusters of rooftops and the gauzy-grey hollows in which huddled the delicate white lace traceries of trees, with almost as much fascination as we were. I couldn't help thinking how typical it was that the weather should finally have changed for the better, and adopted such an intensely biting, atmospheric feel at that late stage of the proceedings. On the Monday I was driven into the Cotswolds. The intention was for me to be deposited in Bourton-on-the-Water, where I would spend the night, before following up a few leads and making my way across to Oxford a day or so later. But when we arrived at Bourton-on-the-Water, early in the afternoon, I was disappointed. There were probably a number of reasons why I should have reacted to the Cotswolds the way I did, not least of which was the tremendous feeling of anti-climax the last few days of travel were beginning to take on. Regardless of that, I have nevertheless thought for a long time that the Cotswolds, where they inform you proudly that some of the hedges have been carbon-dated to be over two-thousand-years-old, not only cover a much smaller area than you expect, but are enormously overrated. They are nothing compared to the Yorkshire Dales, which offer far more than the Cotswolds architecturally, are possessed of a genuine sense of mystery that really does arouse your sense of wonder when you are in some of the more remote valleys, are much bigger, and are much more topographically interesting. As I stood and surveyed Bourton-on-the-Water's much-photographed succession of small stone bridges that afternoon, and tried to remember the name of the river which I had read about a hundred times (the Windrush), I decided the essence of the Cotswold villages was merely the essence of the thatch-roofed villages I had seen in Suffolk, in a different vernacular guise, and in much the same sort of countryside. The most noticeable difference between them was that in the Cotswolds there were actually people walking in relative profusion along some of the streets. Perhaps the stories some of those people would have to tell could be written about another time.

We looked at the usual places that day – at the two Slaughters, at Chipping Campden, at Broadway, and at the wide slippery square of Stow-on-the-Wold, where we ate in a very old café, and struggled to prevent our son from dropping pieces of Lego into his soup. We skirted Cirencester and paced up and down village high streets and attached lanes. We stared up at ancient steeples gleaming full in the sharp sunlight, built on the prosperity of the woollen industry that was once the economic mainstay of the area. We commented on the heavy stone slates sagging with the weight of centuries, and I mentioned how, if they had been situated in some of the mill towns in Yorkshire, they would have been looted and sold for cash by astute builders and roofers for new executive dwellings long ago. We stared across gauzy fields at tiny cottages floating in a pearly-white gossamer haze. We caught sight of twisting lanes and silhouetted figures walking dogs up remote dirt-tracks. We slowed down and gave the pairs of well-groomed women out riding their horses a wide berth. And, of course, even at that time of year, we noted the presence of the ubiquitous American accents, and the United States recommended-accommodation boards tacked to gnarled tree trunks, some of which looked as though they could have been as old as the ancient hedgerows themselves. As we went my wife was driving, and I watched the tracery of distorted trees reflecting on the front of her sunglasses as we glided past clusters of ancient gables and wooden gates glinting with ice, so that I felt like I was participating in one of those surrealistic car commercials you see on television. It was something to do with the contrast between the abiding nature of the Cotswold landscape, and the very real sensation of being carried along in a piece of growling technology that was very much a product of an automated age. Each was as perfect a representation of its own moment as the other, thereby striking an uneasy balance somewhere between the two. We made a thorough but leisurely tour of the entire district, which offered food for the senses and inspiration for any camera or watercolourist's pallette, perhaps even inspiration for poets. The villages and hamlets and clusters of farm buildings suddenly appearing as backlit outlines dripping tears of golden moisture all looked pleasant enough – but I had seen enough.

While inside a shop in one village I suddenly decided what I wanted to do. I went back out and told my wife I thought it was pointless to carry on with the journey any longer, and that I wanted to be sitting in front of my own fire by nightfall. And that was it. Though we lingered for a while in the sub-zero temperatures, I was, nevertheless, determined to reach my final intended destination for the journey. Toward the end of the afternoon, when the mists were gathering again across the distant plains, we left the Cotswolds by the eastern exit – they seemed to finish abruptly once you reached the top of the high street at Burford and joined the dual carriageway there – and drove across to Oxford. We crept through the centre of the city, searching for somewhere to park, noting the familiar scribble of bicycles padlocked to railings, and the row of weighty steeples crowding the wide main street bulkily in the deepening dusk. But we found the accelerating rush-hour intimidating and decided instead not to stop. There the street-lights began flicking on, firstly the same shade of pink as the afternoon sky, along the bottom edge of which the final shreds of day were still hanging; and then, dissolving imperceptibly – as imperceptibly as the moving hands of a clock – to the same fiery orange as where the sun was going down, sending the shifting perspective of Oxford rooftops and chimney stacks and television aerials and leafless trees trailing past us into a dense blue-black silhouette.

Then we began the long drive home. On the way, the mists began to thicken when the sun had disappeared and the landscape became engulfed by a thick wintry fog. The further away from Oxford we drove, the more dense the fog became, so that our speed dropped and dropped, until we began to crawl through a shifting grey murk that swirled in the path of the car's beams so artificially it looked like dry ice being pumped through a flexible tube onto a stage set. There was nothing substantial left around us, nothing but diffused headlights flaring for a moment from the opposite direction, the lurid glow of street lights, frozen verges that appeared then disappeared, and the vague outline of passing gables vanishing into oblivion like ships lost in the mist. I thought how ironic it was, and yet, I suppose, how appropriate, that I should conclude my journey creeping through precisely the same kind of gloomy weather conditions, abandoning the trip as it petered out almost of its own accord, as J.B. Priestley had done nearly sixty years before me. I had never set out with the intention of re-tracing his original footsteps, as Beryl Bainbridge had done ten years before me. I had, in fact, always been anxious to avoid this. But increasingly over the previous three months, as I sat down to contemplate the things I had seen at the end of each day, I had heard the gravelly voice of J.B. Priestley echoing sombrely in the background. I felt it especially after I saw parts of the Tyne, and wondered afterwards what on earth had really changed, apart from a few superficial details, that much since the autumn of 1933.

My Country Left or Right

A number of people have travelled round England since Priestley and written about what they saw and heard and felt and thought. Daniel Defoe and William Cobbett did it long before him in a completely different age. Only a few years before Priestley, H.V. Morton went off in search of England for the first time, as did S.P.B. Mais shortly after him. With their irritating one-sentence, two line paragraphs, both fastened together sentimental passages of words that generally avoided mentioning the real world altogether, though the sober tone, and the style of the prose, to Morton's introduction to his *In Search of England*, which is the only readable part of the book, suggests he might have been more shrewdly aware of what was going on around him than the light-hearted tone of delivery for the other two-hundred-odd pages suggested. During my own journey through England, a newspaper journalist said that Priestley's book not only did its job, which was to give a rounded impression of the England of the day that was both realistic and fair, but that it was also a work of art. He might have added that it bumped up against the economic system of the day, to which all those fine descriptive passages, all those back street experiences and factory tours, were connected. That was the secret to its success, why Priestley's book has endured, and why the nonsense put out by the other people has vanished into oblivion. Priestley has never been taken very seriously by the literary intelligentsia, of course, probably because he was too much an artist, sold too many books, and revealed his feelings too easily to retain credibility among more enlightened circles. Nor was he consistently good enough. But his *English Journey* is still the best, still the most poignant, still the most quoted, still in my opinion one of the best combinations of polemic and description to have been written, still the best and most readable thing he ever wrote, far superior to his novels, which I cannot read. And he pre-empted some of the things said afterwards by other writers who were taken seriously by the literati by at least several years.

In Priestley's day, socialism was the direction in which the will of the English people was pulling itself. The philosophy of capitalism had been largely discredited, and by the end of the war was well on the way to being consigned to the dustbin of political history. Capitalism *does not work* italicized George Orwell confidently in 1941, commenting on how the war had demonstrated that private enterprise, operated solely for private profit, could not deliver the goods. I think Orwell is probably the only English writer who has ever really mattered. But it does not prevent one from concluding, with substantial justification at the beginning of the 1990s, that it has been established that socialism *does not work* either, because it too cannot deliver the goods – or at any rate, could not deliver them in the Soviet

Union and Eastern Europe, where it appeared in its most thorough manifestation, and where it was seen to produce a form of corruption that destroyed countries from the inside out. Socialism, too, as a philosophy has been largely discredited and confined to the dustbin of political history, for the time being anyway, outside the circles of a few cranks and a minority of Communists who persist in living in a vacuum. That socialism *has* been discredited in the West, where it never materialized beyond a few shallow social reforms but where it was conceived and planned, ironically accelerated its decline in the Soviet Bloc, where it did materialize. The truth is that both capitalism and socialism would be capable of working if they were adhered to correctly, if there were no human emotions involved. It is the human beings that cause the difficulty, not the soundness or otherwise of the economics. Elsewhere, Orwell observed that if we really wanted to sort out our problems the economic system applied would hardly matter. That is correct, of course. The trouble is that it is the human race that is not mature enough emotionally to control its primal urges that appears to be at the root of our problems. In the same essay in which he suggested the future of capitalism was in doubt and that socialism was an inevitability, Orwell observed that such a state of affairs was materializing at all because that was what the English people wanted. Sufficient enough pressure was being exerted from below to influence the potential for political change and to force it in a particular direction.

Well, that might have been the case fifty years ago. But for the past thirty or forty, the pull has been the other way, and it was started by the result of the 1951 General Election, the year after Orwell died. As I suggested earlier, my conclusion having grown up in a working-class environment is that the working class has an essentially reactionary caste of mind, and, in spite of much romantic hogwash spouted over generations, probably always has had. (Possibly the only serious thinker to understand this objectively is Enoch Powell.) There are exceptions, of course, sizeable numbers of exceptions, but not enough to influence the strength of the emotional swings that influence societies during different periods in their histories. Probably the clearest indicator to the emotional quality of what could still be regarded ostensibly as the English working class is the feel of *The Sun* and *The Daily Sport*, or more especially their letters' pages, which are perhaps the closest to what would once have been described as genuine proletarian literature that we have yet managed. There is no question that the content of such newspapers, with their cheap sensation and their insipid gimmicks, continues to keep the present set of circumstances carefully balanced. But it is unlikely this is done with the ruthlessness and cunning Marxists and left-wing playwrights popularly like to believe. (It is unlikely because it is doubtful if the editors of these papers are possessed of the necessary level of objective intelligence.) Marxists always delete from their consciousness the uneasy awareness that the gutter press and junk TV, like junk food, might be what the working class actually prefers. When hating capitalists, they forever parry intellectually by claiming that the working-class wants only what it has been conditioned to expect, thereby pinning the blame for everything on the manipulative forces at work at the root of capitalist society. At the same time, they will idealize working-class customs and expression, even its emotional outlook, whilst failing hopelessly to understand that these are a direct result of the fact that the hierarchical structure to which they are opposed exists in society at all. Such naïvety makes no allowance for the gravity of the situation as it stands. For this reason the Left often talks as though the entire capitalist scheme of things is part of a carefully calculated, huge premeditated plot. The Left, especially the extreme Left, likes to believe that politicians and businessmen scheme among themselves the continued suppression and exploitation of the working classes in smoky back rooms, probably somewhere off a corridor in Whitehall. They like to believe this because it answers so many difficult and complicated questions so very quickly and easily. One must never forget that opposing on principle the implication that the present set of social circumstances are unlikely ever to be *able* to be changed is part of the standard ammunition cartridge loaded confidently into any left-winger's verbal machine-gun, especially the gattling-gun of the doctrinaire Marxist. It compensates for their feelings of inadequacy. It compensates too for the deep sense of frustration Western revolutionaries feel, moderate or extreme, civilized or uncivilized, middle class or genuine working class, at their subconscious knowledge that not only are they supported by the system to which they are opposed, but nothing fundamentally is likely ever to be changed.

Behind this kind of thinking lies a persistent stubbornness that fails to consider the realities. It also fails to consider the past hundred-odd years, perhaps even the past two-thousand years, of world history. Socialists have tried and tried, but they have failed to influence the basic psychological shortcomings that lie at the root of the basic human condition; that keep the present set of circumstances intact on a global scale, and that consequently keep human behaviour at the level it is at. Socialists have lost the argument, and it is largely a high-minded illusion these days to believe that they haven't. But then, the failure of socialism connects directly to the mental weaknesses I indicated at the end of the preceding paragraph. All the time they are influencing the perceptions of the sort of people who nowadays still think socialism is a tune worth trumpeting, as they always have, so that they are manipulated continually into a hypocritical acceptance of the benefits they obtain from capitalist culture. The left-wing playwright rails against capitalism, but breathes a sigh of relief when his latest West End work is so successful it earns him the freedom to froth at the mouth for another twelve months, and indulge in the creativity he could not enjoy were he forced to take a mug's job out in the ordinary world. Similarly, the half-baked form of state capitalism that materialized for a few years in this country after the war, masquerading as socialism, was half-baked only because the people responsible for its eventual momentum – a body of the educated English upper-middle class, with a few scholarship boys from the working class thrown in as a token gesture – considered themselves collectivist, but were in reality not much more than a by-product of capitalism imbued with a guilt-complex. They could never bring themselves to let go completely of the tastes and prejudices their upbringing had bred into them, with the level of commitment that would have been necessary to create any chance for genuine progress. The Labour Party might have been primarily an organ of the working class to begin with. But by the time it had managed to achieve any serious political impact, it had degenerated into the sort of shallow liberal reformism that appeared with the post-war Labour government, once the educated classes had got hold of it and injected their own sentiment between the lines – the same sentiment that causes that left-wing playwright to breath his sigh of relief today at the creativity money buys him, and indulge his taste for good food and decent wines. The working-class unions also had a direct interest in the workings of capitalism, particularly during the days of the Empire. The political swing of opinion that was left was at bottom born of the cultural outlook of the pampered liberal conscience that remains with us today. It was essentially a manifestation of the brave reforming impulse that develops in the minds of sensitive, intelligent people who perceive the aesthetic incongruity of the world, who feel uneasy within themselves at the prospect of man's relative inhumanity to man, who believe it is possible to get rid of social injustice, but who are manipulated in their moral behaviour by the automatic assumption that their own secure social positions will remain basically intact. It does not matter what the issues might be. Whether domestic or international, theirs is chiefly a reaction against the basic untidiness of the world. But their motivation is primarily self-centred. Listen to their chuntering long enough, and you soon begin to understand the reason so many of them become agitated by, for instance, the hopeless plight of the underprivileged locked in the crumbling squalor of the inner cities, is not so much that they have any realistic comprehension of what it is actually like to be such a person, as it is that having to drive through such squalid environments deeply offends their aesthetic sensibilities. It goes against the grain of how they feel civilized human beings *ought* to be able to live. But their conception of how civilized human beings ought to be able to live harmoniously is gauged by the standards of their own physical comforts. They fail to understand that to retain the freedoms they presently enjoy – and the intellectual freedoms they have long taken for granted – to finally get rid of poverty, would entail a severe lowering of their own living standards.

You saw this dreary phenomenon assert itself most acutely

during the Gulf War. In squealing for a peaceful solution, both the comfortable socialists sitting around log fires in pine furnished country cottages praying for peace on at least twenty-thousand a year, and those in parties of political opposition who would have pulled their punches rather than get involved in a fight, were stupid enough to transfer their moral and cultural allegiances, but most importantly, their expectations from life, into the mind of a brutal dictator, reared in an entirely different culture. They believed he would have the decency not to allow his people to starve to death if threatened by sanctions because they would not have allowed such a horrible situation to come about *themselves*. That is the crucial point. They took it for granted his values would conform to their own. That was an essentially Western creed, born of a culture that, despite feminist carping, treats women as human beings and can show deep feelings of sentimentality toward animals and the countryside. Much of the Left's political stance was a direct result of this sort of humbug thinking, and of how it had been taught morally to behave. At a crucial moment, the Left would have compromised and stalled for time. And yet the way the Left had been taught morally to behave is a product entirely of Western free-market prosperity. Only the kind of people sheltered by prosperity, who have never comprehended the meaning of the phrase 'freedom from want', never analysed for a moment the economic foundations of their political convictions or their aesthetic outlook, could believe purely diplomatic measures alone would have worked. Did one risk killing a lesser number of people in order to prevent the annihilation of more significant numbers of people in the future, to prevent your own economic stability from suffering, and to retain the balance, or did one not? In a way, the spectacle of a broad section of the Left, and the odd flabby Conservative, innocently believing it was possible to come to an arrangement with Saddam Hussein over Kuwait was reminiscent of Chamberlain waving his white handkerchief as he emerged from the aeroplane in 1938. Chamberlain really believed, in his naïve upper-class way, that Hitler would do the decent thing and keep his word after Munich – because morally, his own schooling had taught him that is what he would have done under the circumstances. Then, as now, it reflected a deep lack of moral courage and an inability to face up to the way the world really works.

It is symptomatic of the conceited air of Western civilization – of the self-indulgence and the self-pity prosperity enables people to cultivate – that such a frame of mind can only truly develop once putting enough food in your belly each day to keep yourself alive is no longer your chief concern. Consequently, while shockwaves from nauseating political complications reverberate throughout the world, and coffee growers are starving in Africa because of their country's debt burden to Western banks and the corruptiveness of their own governments, we can throw up a charity devoted to the welfare of animals that can raise more than twice the amount of revenue of a charity devoted to the welfare of children. We can produce a body of literature that throws itself into tantrums over the aesthetic consequences of modern architecture. The spectacle of civilized people being roused passionately over such ostensibly mundane issues must appear pitiable to an intelligent starving Somalian, who has had enough experience of the internal combustion engine not to take it for granted. It is one of the fundamental flaws of the British Left that it fails to grasp any of this. The prosperous liberal social conscience remains oblivious to the fact that its emotional attitudes, its political predilections, its squirming sensitivities, and the democratic ease with which it can stand up and blow raspberries, are a direct consequence materially of almost everything it opposes. It fails to see its buffered position is a result of millions of people beneath it, in its own country and elsewhere, being nowhere near as prosperous or as enlightened as itself. This cannot be evaded, and we should remember it every time we load big spoonfuls of coffee into our traditional-styled cafetieres. The world behaves one way. A considerable tribe of wealthy, chattering socialists and squashy-minded liberals, some of whom are prominently in the public eye and could be seen lurking in the shadows during Kinnock's closing election campaign rallies, wish to God it would behave another. Meanwhile, their own bank balances continue to fatten under the existing system, giving them an ever-greater freedom to oppose comfortably the nature of the prevailing orthodoxy. All of them hated Mrs Thatcher as a matter of course. All were able to discharge powerful condemnations about social injustice during radio interviews, or criticize the breakdown of community values, during her remarkable reign. But every one of them prospered throughout her premiership, and in particular under Nigel Lawson's review of income tax thresholds for the better-off. In hating Mrs Thatcher they were really hating themselves, for capitalism bought the big guns of the Left the freedom to think socialistically, as it always has.

So they console themselves by claiming *they* would not mind contributing a little more tax to the building of a better, more caring, more tolerant society. The arrogant implication if you read between the lines of these sorts of high-minded claims is that all decent people would automatically do the same – as though everybody else, meanwhile, makes a living in the highly rewarding and satisfying manner that they do! It is very easy to drift ethereally among the clouds like that, to the permanent sound of cuckoos; to despair at the ostensibly selfish motives of millions of ordinary voters – as Kinnock pseudo-suggested during his pitiful resignation and Election defeat speeches – when you are comfortable enough never to have to try and survive in the same mortgage-endowed universe as everybody else. Very easy indeed to wave your fists defiantly in the air on stage at open-air pop concerts, and make vituperative remarks about the country that has given you millions of pounds stashed securely in the bank, along with the social position and the mental space to cultivate your grievances publicly. Very easy indeed when you are a privileged ex-Oxbridge socialist to rail indignantly from the security of a newspaper column about the brutalizing effects of capitalism, when you need not perform a proper day's work in your life, or subject yourself to the rigours of the common market-place, just as you never have and probably never will.

During this journey I was stopped in the street by more than one anti-Establishment clone and asked to either sign petitions or make a small donation to various political causes. Each time I met these people, I thought back to some youngsters I saw travelling to London during the Gulf War on a specially chartered bus to participate in a major public demonstration against the hostilities. NO WAR FOR OIL! such people shrieked and sprayed across walls throughout Britain, failing to notice that it was the same oil that enabled them to travel hundreds of miles economically, to take for granted a standard of living and the relative democratic freedom, to oppose distant wars in the first place. The same people are always violently pro-Pacifist, sliding over the fact that the soldiers fighting on their behalf in the Gulf were also fighting to allow them to retain their comfortable positions as thinking subversives, who generally do not have to worry about where the next meal will come from or whether or not the light will come on the next time they flick a switch, and who would run a mile at the prosect of being put into a situation where they might have a real gun-barrel shoved up their nostril. Such people usually spin the line about the armed forces, like the police, really being defenders of the ruling class and their vested interests. Yes, but does it ever occur to these people that in so doing, the ruling class might also be defending their freedom as political activists opposed to the prevailing orthodoxy as well? That it is possible to see *Living Marxism* on sale in a popular bookseller like W.H. Smith is a case in point. It indicates a democratic freedom the Revolutionary Communist Party that publishes the magazine – a party as diametrically opposed to the prevailing orthodoxy, not to mention the motives of W.H. Smith shareholders, as it is possible to be – would not tolerate for one moment if it were to achieve power, what with the rubbish it talks about establishing dictatorships and the like.

The kind of naïve political thinking I have been discussing is a special characteristic, perhaps an unpleasant by-product, of prosperous capitalist societies like ours with strong hierarchies and strong social traditions. The fact that it has existed in one form or another for as long as it has, but failed to have much impact on the way the rest of society behaves, only serves to underline its remoteness from ordinary thinking and the texture of ordinary emotions. It was inevitable that when placed in a position of political influence during the twenty or thirty years after the war, its outlook torn between understanding what needed to be done and the mental school of conduct, the aesthetic outlook to which at heart it still belonged, it would pull its punches when the pinch finally came. The only reason the working class tolerated it for a few years was because the implication of the promised reforms – nationalization of industry and the creation of a Welfare State – seemed more likely to give the people in the street what they wanted – a better standard of living – than the economic order had hitherto been able to give them. But that, as they say, was before the consumer boom. The shape English society has taken since then, the catalyst being the election of the Conservative government in 1951, is simply too vast a subject to discuss in these pages. For my purposes here it is sufficient to say that, after three decades, the bulk of the working class has had its social aspirations moulded largely by television, by the popular media, and by one aspect of the advertising industry, into one of habitual acquisitiveness; a stupefaction kept in check by the emerging gutter culture I referred to in Bristol and the sort of infantile television programmes we can see every day dominating our television screens. The result is that we are now living in an age when socialism is less likely to become a reality than ever before, and a queasy, brutal form of neo-fascism more likely than ever.

The implication from what I have just written may appear to be that I am assuming socialism is the only serious hope for humankind. I do not believe seriously that it is. If one contemplates the potential for socialism and looks at the types of people that have flocked to man its ranks over the years, the only realistic conclusion that can be reached in the face of enormous odds is that there is little point in trying to cut a concrete cake with a paper knife any longer. It is not even certain that social equality is truly desirable for the human species if it is to survive, which is not necessarily the same as saying if the world is to survive. Socialists who lack the objective level of thinking to understand that should seriously examine their own motives. The politics hardly matter, or at any rate the party politics hardly matter. We live in a rotten, stinking, corrupt world manipulated almost wholly in the interests of the vain and the emotionally immature. You have to assume, if you are possessed of decency and integrity, that you will be crushed and exploited emotionally, directly or inadvertently. You then have to adjust your behaviour by taking nobody at face value and looking permanently back over your shoulder after every move you make. You have to survive. If you have an instinctive commitment toward honesty, if you feel that clutch in the centre of the chest each time you know lies are circulating, remember that the people in positions of influence and authority, to whom you feel you ought to look for guidance, are probably corrupt, useless, or inadequate, and do not have the degree of wisdom or integrity you were naïve enough to imagine they had (in other words, that you have) after all. This is the dilemma faced by decent, genuinely intelligent human beings. They have to learn how to reconcile their thoughts against these things, how to remain afloat economically and conduct their lives safely in the face of unpleasant realities, how to come to terms with the organized dishonesty and stupidity that keeps the world spinning, yet manage to retain peace of mind within themselves.

Like millions of others, I once vaguely believed myself to be socialist. But my political beliefs were, as I have suggested they still are to innumerable socialists, essentially aesthetic in origin. I failed to see that the very things I struggled against were the very things that provided me with the freedom and prosperity to be able to develop the mental space to decide what I thought was wrong with society in the first place. As with people I come across quite frequently, I had nurtured a frivolous comprehension of capitalists and capitalism, though it was always the benefits I perceived in it that held me back from fully embracing socialism. I made no allowance for the benefits the things which I fought against had actually played in moulding my own outlook. By saying these things, I am not saying that I automatically considered myself 'right-wing' and doctrinaire capitalist, because I think the old classifications are no longer adequate. To see this in perspective, you have only to remember there is a very fine line indeed between common sense and that which the Left would normally term 'reactionary'. John Casey pointed out in *The Sunday Telegraph*, when questioning the value of a chunk of the modern English liberal intelligentsia and its infantile political posturing, that 'politics is not a science but an application of practical wisdom'. Travelling around England today has only served to reinforce my belief that this is true.

It is not enough merely to say that one should not feel a sense of guilt about the freedoms and prosperity we enjoy, irrespective of the exploitations or cruelties caused by these things further down the line, and that our priority should be to use what we have achieved in order to change the world into something better. For, bearing in mind that we are living at a crucial moment, it now seems to me that if one considers carefully the development of the human race (or to be more precise, the development of Western civilization) since the Industrial Revolution, if one contemplates the recent political changes in the Soviet Union and Eastern Europe and why they came about, there is only one position that can be seriously adopted politically in a country like ours, or in a part of the world like ours. And that is, it is not really a question of socialism or capitalism, Labour or Conservative, free-market economics or state planning and state control. It is a question of which form of corruption is preferable to the other in the way it influences the living standards of the vast majority of ordinary people, and that is about the best one can hope for. Politics is also, as Hugo Young has written, about managing an imperfect world. And it is worth remembering that Young really meant it is imperfect people that make for an imperfect world.

What we desperately need are not the politics of Left or Right, of Centre-this or Centre-that, but the politics of common sense. But we are less likely to obtain those than we are to obtain socialism. I do not say that as a pessimist, but as a realist. Broadly speaking, the choice politically will always be between various sets of inadequacies, because any power unit will gravitate automatically toward a defence of its own privileges. I said as much in the car as we drove through the fog early that December evening, and I tried to reach one or two conclusions during the closing moments of my journey. But I still found my mind riddled with doubts and contradictions. England has changed enormously since J.B. Priestley made his journey through it towards the end of 1933, but has it really changed all *that* much? Have the basic human impulses at work at the centre of our society and our civilization really changed all that much either? They have not. They have merely been re-distributed, and it is that which really matters. The rest of the underlying forces that have been at work, such as the impact or otherwise on our relative democratic freedoms of recent political legislation, or the fact that the terrible, quite frightening emotional immaturity that lies at the very centre of the world's social affairs is now bound up so strongly with the influence of showbusiness and entertainment, or even the change in the design of traffic bollards for that matter, are mere technicalities. Whatever the tugging this way and that between one economic philosophy and another, or all the newspaper leader writing and think-tank proselytizing in the world, I found myself saying that when one gets down to basics, despite the crime statistics and the bad architecture, and the bullet-shaped vehicle I was being driven in through the fog-bound Oxfordshire countryside, and other minor cosmetic changes, nothing changes much at all really. Not fundamentally anyway. Except, perhaps, the speed and the performance of cars.

But then, as I have already suggested, that is what is so terribly, terribly frightening.

Index

Accrington, 58, 59, 154
A Kind of Loving (Barstow), 24
Albert Dock, 24, 26-28, 48; *see also* Liverpool
'allo 'allo, 250
Alsager, 171
American Express, 260
Andover, 285
Anglian Windows, 221-226; *see also* Norwich
Antiques Roadshow, 174
apple farming, 237-243
Ashley, Laura, 218
Asian community
  Burnley, 60-65
  Bradford, 108-111
Attercliffe, Sheffield, 133
Austen, Jane, 277
Avon Valley, 287

Bainbridge, Beryl, 324
Baker, Kenneth, 67
Balsall Heath, 190-191; *see also* Birmingham
Barlow, Thelma, 118
Barnsley, 284
Basildon, 47, 226, 273
Basingstoke, 1-4, 263, 264, 268, 269-284, 285, 287, 288, 320
  compared to Blackburn, 271-274
  social quality of, 277-284
Bat, 272, 287, 316, 320
Bede, Venerable, 75
Benn, Tony, 80
Bennet, Arnold, 151, 155
Billingham chemical refinery, Cleveland, 91, 94
Binns department store, So. Shields, 85
Birkenhead, 25
Birmingham, 20, 150, 180-205, 206, 207, 229, 234, 260, 294, 308
  architecture of, 184-189
  Balsall Heath, 190-191
  Central Library, 188-189
  Chamberlain Square, 188
  Colmore Row, 187
  a greyhound stadium in, 200-205
  motorway system of, 181-183
  Spaghetti Junction, 183-184
  Paradise Forum, 189-190, 196
  100 Years of British Invention exhibition, 196-200
Birmingham Baptist Inner City Project (BBICP), 190-194
Blackburn, 47, 48-58, 61, 62, 64, 84, 248, 267, 271-274, 276, 278, 320
  compared to Basingstoke, 271-274
  India Mill, Darwen, 53-58
  modern economy of, 49-50
  political complexion of, 278
Blackpool, 255
Bleak House (Dickens), 256
Bletchley, 6
Blinkhorn, Marie, 15
Blue Lamp, The, 10
Body Shop, The, 266

Bolton, 46, 53, 150
Bootle, 28
Bournemouth, 318
Bourton-on-the-Water, 321, 322
Bradford, 105-127, 142, 158, 159, 213, 234, 298
  social complexion of, 108-111
  Little Germany, 116-117, 119
    (compared to Nottingham Lace Market) 142, 145
  Midland Hotel, 111-112
  textile industry of, 120-127
Bradford-on-Avon, 285
Bradford Playhouse and Film Theatre, 117-118
Braine, John, 118, 119, 120
Brazier, Alan, 197-199
Brighouse and Rastrick Brass Band, 11
Brighton, 250-262, 263, 264, 270, 275, 276, 288, 318
  a boarding-house in, 257-259
Brighton Rock (Greene), 256
Bristol, 20, 274, 287, 288-317, 320
  a lodging-house in, 287-291
  Christmas Steps, 303-305
  Clifton, 295, 305, 316
  College Green 292, 294, 316
  environmental quality of, 292-295
  economy of, 296-297
  a General Practitioner in, 297-303
  Merchant Venturers' Hall, 304
  Wills Family, 295, 304
Bristol Economic Development Unit, 297
British Coal, 75
British Rail, 2, 8, 45, 46, 264-268, 285; *see also* Network South East
British Steel Stainless, 128, 133-137
Broadway, 322
Brookside, 23, 43
Bryn, Lancs., 45
Brunel, 274, 306
Buchanan, Colin, 246
Burford, 323
Burnley, 58-65, 66, 93, 191, 267
  old industrial housing, 58-60
  Jinnah Community Centre, Stoneyholme, 60-64
  Reedly Hallow, 58
Burslem, 149, 154-158, 166, 167, 175
Bury St Edmunds, 227, 232
Calder Valley, 112, 113
Cambridge, 83
Canary Wharf, 17, 149, 282
Canterbury, 244-250, 251, 275, 280, 304
Canterbury Heritage Trial, 246
Captain Cook, 92
car crime and joyriding, 34-35, 67-70
Casey, John, 335
Castle, Barbara, 278
Castle Coombe, 283
Casualty, 294
Centre for Policy Studies, 270
Channel Tunnel, 30, 242, 244, 250
Cheltenham, 248, 316, 317, 318-321
Cheshire, 7, 253
Chichester, 265
China, 194
Chipping Campden, 322
Cirencester, 322
Clapham, 263
Clapham Common, 251
class differences, 84–85
Cleese, John, 2
Clifton, 295, 305, 316; *see also* Bristol
Cobbett, William, 324
Cockerell, Sir Christopher, 198
Collins, Phil, 58
Colne, 154, 267
Conservative Party and Conservatism, 7, 16, 35, 277, 278, 281-282
Cookson, Catherine, 70
Coronation Street, 17
Cotswolds, the, 231, 316, 321-323
Country Life Picture Book of Great Britain, The, 211
Coventry, 207-208
Crosby, Bing, 249
Croydon, 251, 270

Dagenham, 47
Daily Sport, The, 327
Daily Telegraph, The, 3, 281
Darlington, 67
Dartford Bridge, 235
Defoe, Daniel, 324
Delors, M., 243
Derby, 147
Derbyshire, 147
Dickens, Charles, 246, 256
Docklands, 17, 18
Dombey and Son (Dickens), 256
Doncaster, 136

Drummond Group PLC, 123
Duchess of York, 275
Dummer, Hants, 275

Easington, Co. Durham, 91
East Kent, 236-244
East Kent Packers, 242
East Malling Research Institute, 240
economy, the
  recent structural changes to, 30-32, 308-314
  difference in philosophy toward north and south, 50-53
Economist, The, 15
Edinburgh, 23, 89
Ely, 207, 208-210
  cathedral, 208-210
Emery, Dick, 257
Engels, Frederick, 9
English governing class, decline of, 170-171
English Journey (Priestley), 176, 325
English nostalgia for the past, 6, 240-243, 305-307
  its link to economic decline, 125-127, 241-242, 307-309
Enterprise Support Programme (ESP), 94-98; *see also* Middlesbrough
Essex Man, 226-227
Euston Station, 5, 6, 53

Farmers Weekly, 237
Felixstowe, 226
Fenton, 155, 159
Fielden, John, MP, 114
Five Towns, the, 151
Forsyth, Bruce, 248

Galbraith, J.K., 250
Gateshead, 71, 73, 74, 80, 82, 90
Gay Times, The, 255
General Election (1992), 6, 242, 282
General Practitioner, a, 297-303; *see also* Bristol
Gibson, Mr, Public Relations Manager, Twyfords, 168, 169, 170, 173, 174
Gladstone Museum, 160-161, 167
Gloucester, 318
Granada Television, 17
Great Ayton, 91, 92, 102, 103
Great North Road, 208
Green Party, 237
Greene, Graham, 232
greyhound racing, 200-205; *see also* Birmingham
Guardian, The, 8
Guildford, 281
Gulf War, 4, 330, 332

Hadleigh, Suffk., 230
Halifax, 120
Hanley, 149, 154-156, 157, 174
Hanley Museum, 174
Harrogate, 320
Larvey, Laurence, 125
Hastings, 253
Hatton, Derek, 24
Heath, Edward, 3, 236
Hebburn, 71, 88
Hebden Bridge, 267
Hepton, Bernard, 118
Heseltine, Michael, 27
Hill, Benny, 269
Hindle Wakes (Houghton), 59
Hislop, Ian, 3
Hitler, 127, 330
Honeyford, Ray, 110
Houghton, Stanley, 59
Hove, 255, 261, 318
Huddersfield, 106-107, 112, 120, 124, 169
Hulme, 13-16; *see also* Manchester
Hundred (100) Years of British Invention exhibition, 196-200; *see also* Birmingham
Huntingdon, 208

Illingworth, Daniel, textile mill, Bradford, 124
India Mill, 53-58; *see also* Blackburn
inflation, 31, 101
inner city decay, 10, 12-16, 35, 41-42, 61-62, 90, 105, 111-112, 156-158, 161-162, 190-191, 194, 204, 293-294, 318, 329
In Search of England (Morton), 325
Iraq, 314

Jackson, Michael, 58
Jarrow, 69, 71, 73, 74, 75, 88
Jay, Peter, 165
Jinnah Community Centre, 60-65; *see also* Burnley
Johnson, Dr, 259

Juliet Bravo, 58
Junor, John, 3

Kaye, Gordon, 118
Kensington, 10, 85, 295
Kersey, 227, 230-234, 235
Kipling, Rudyard, 256
King's Cross Station, 6, 251
Kinnock, Neil, 4, 331, 332
Knapp, Jimmy, 268

Labour Party, 4, 7, 16, 35, 81, 171, 216, 278, 282, 328, 329
Lace Market, 145-147; *see also* Nottingham
Laisterdyke, Bradford, 119
Lambton, Lucinda, 169
Lamont, Norman, 16
Lawson, Nigel, 332
Lavenham, 227, 228-230, 231
Lean, David, 246
Leeds, 105, 181, 269, 293
Leek, 147
Left, the
  naivety of, 327, 329, 333
  hypocrisy of, 81, 328-333
  political failure of, 328-329, 333; *see also* Marxists and Marxism
Leighton Buzzard, 6
Lincoln, 304
Little Germany, 116-117, 119, 142, 145; *see also* Bradford
Liverpool, 11, 20, 22-44, 45, 47, 61, 66, 77, 105, 111, 175, 226, 265
  Adelphi Hotel, 24, 27
  Albert Dock, 24, 26-28, 48
  docks in general, 28-30
  misconceptions of, 39-40
  seen as paradigm of post-industrial urban society 39-40
  Sefton, 28
  Sefton Park, 23, 33-34
  St George's Plateau, 23
  St John's Gardens, 45
  Toxteth, 27, 33-35, (riots) 43-44, 61
Living France, 250
Living Marxism, 250, 333
London, 5-6, 7, 8, 17, 18, 46, 78, 106, 184, 186, 250, 251, 253, 255, 256, 263, 276, 280, 305
Longton, 148, 155, 156, 159, 160-163
Longford, Lord, 42
Los Angeles riots, 3
Lutyens, Sir Edward, 16

MacMillan, Harold, 308
Macrae, Norman, 176
Maidenhead, 274
Mais, S.P.B., 255, 324
Major, John, 4, 282
Malton, N. Yorks, 105
Manchester, 6, 7, 8-22, 47, 275, 293, 294
  Castlefield, 17
  changing city, 20-22
  Piccadilly, 9-10
  Hulme, 13-16
  Deansgate and city centre, 16-17
  Moss Side, 14
  Salford Quays, 18-19
  Trafford Park, 19
Manchester Evening News, 9
manufacturing industry, 220-224, 226, 242, 243
  decline of, 54, 56-57
  English attitude toward, 125-127, 163-165, 196-200, 243
  government neglect of, 121-122
  related to service sector, 31-33
  social importance of, 163, 306-315
Margate, 255
Margin Released (Priestley), 92
Marx, Karl, 9
Marxists and Marxism, 63, 177, 225, 243, 281, 302,
  mental attitude of Marxists, 178, 327; *see also* Left, the
McCartney, Paul, 58
Meadowhall, 128-133; *see also* Sheffield
Meadowhall Estate (The Ridges), 84
Merseyside, *see* Liverpool
Mersey Dock and Harbour Company, 29
MetroCentre, Gateshead, 80, 130
Middlesbrough, 90-103, 134, 234, 320
  Enterprise Support Programme, St Hilda's, 94-98
  jobclub and unemployed, 98-103
  general outline of, 92-94
Militant, 24
Mills, John, 258
Milton Keynes, 7, 275
Modern Review, The, 8
Money Programme, The, 222
Morton, Andrew, 4
Morton, H.V., 208, 232, 324, 325

Mountford, Arnold, CBE, 174
Mousehold Heath, 216

Nairn, Ian, 21, 23, 89
National Dock Labour Scheme, 29
National Health Service, 297-303; *see also* General Practitioner
National Shipbuilders Security, 75
Network South East, 264-268
Newcastle-upon-Tyne, 66-90, 92, 93, 214, 234, 316
  car crime, 67-70
  central part of city, Grainger Street, 88-89
  Metro rail network, 81, 87-88
  municipal housing estates, 70-74
  Ponteland, 78
  shipbuilding and modern economy of, 75-79
Newsnight, 3
North Shields, 71, 80, 81, 83-87, 88
Northern Theatre School, 118, 119
Norwich, 210-226, 227, 229, 275
  a guest-house near, 218-220
  brief history of, 212-213
  Castle Mall shopping centre, 214-215
  Elm Hill, 225
  enigma of, 210-212
  environmental quality of, 214-217
  uPVC window manufacturers in, 221-226
Norwich Society, The, 225
Nottingham, 138-147, 292, 304
  Lace Market, 145-147
  old cobbler's shop in, 145-147

Oldham, 12, 49, 108, 150
Orwell, George, 35, 46, 65, 325, 326
Oxford, 83, 295, 316, 321, 323-324

Pacific Rim, 57
Padiham, Lancs., 50
Palmer, Geoffrey, 279
Palmer Shipbuilding and Iron Company, 75
Panorama, 243
Parsons, Tony, 60
Paxman, Jeremy, 3
Peterlee, 91
Pickering, 105
Pilkington glass factory, 47
political correctness, 8
Portsmouth Harbour, 265
Potteries, The, 7, 148-179
  friendliness of people, 153-154, 176
  pottery factories, 159-160
  a derelict pottery, 161-163
  social quality of, 174-178
Potteries Centre, The, 155-156
Powell, Enoch, 326
Preston, 46
Priestley, J.B., 13, 54, 72, 73, 75, 76, 81, 92, 117, 134, 142, 151, 152, 153, 158, 176, 177, 203, 255, 260, 276, 277, 283, 293, 294, 316, 324, 325, 336
Charles, Prince of Wales, 26, 186, 188, 189

Reader's Digest, 2
Reid, Sir Bob, 268
Revolutionary Communist Party, 333
Richardson, Tony, 118
Richmond, N. Yorks., 66
Ridley, Nicholas, 243
Right, the
  mental attitude of, 36-39, 199-200
Ripon, 283
Robin Hood's Bay, 104-105
Rochdale, 12, 150, 310
Room at the Top (Braine), 118, 119, 124
Rose Grove, Lancs., 267
Royal Doulton, 158, 175
Rushdie, Salman, 110

St Hilda's, 94–98, 103; *see also* Middlesbrough
St Helens, 47
St Mary's Gate, Nottingham, 142, 145; *see also* Lace Market
Salford Quays, 18-19; *see also* Manchester
Salisbury, 285-287
Salvation Army, 191-192
Schlesinger, John, 7
Schwarzenegger, Arnold, 8
Scruton, Roger, 232
Seabrook, Jeremy, 35
Seaham, 91
Shaftesbury, 283
Shakespeare, William, 199
Sheffield, 15, 127-137, 185
  Meadowhall, 128-133
  steel industry, 133-137
Sheriff of Nottingham, 140
Shotton, 91

Silchester, 275
Sinclair, Clive, 196
Slattery, Tony, 3
Snow, Peter, 253
Smith, Horace, 255
social disintegration and some of its causes, 35-43, 312-314
Socialists and socialism, 325-326, 328-329, 330, 331, 334-335; *see also* Left, the *and* Marxists and Marxism
Socialist Worker, 165
Southampton, 27, 263, 264, 266, 269
South Africa, 3, 70
South Downs, 252-253, 264
South Milford, Suffk., 234
South Shields, 71, 75, 79, 81, 82, 85, 86, 87
Soviet Union, 326, 336
Spectator, The, 250
Stafford, 180
Staffordshire Moorlands, 150
Staffordshire Polytechnic, 154
Stephenson, George, 20
Stepney, 47
Steventon, 277
Stockton-on-Tees, 93
Stoke, 150, 154, 155
Stoke-on-Trent, *see* Potteries
Stoneyholme, 60, 63, 65; *see also* Burnley
Stow-on-the-Wold, 322
Stratford-upon-Avon, 272
Straw, Jack, MP, 278
Sun, The, 327
Sunday Telegraph, The, 4, 335
Sunday Times, The, 16, 198
Sunderland, 90
Surrey Occasions Magazine, 11
Sylvac, pottery works, 174

Tati, Jacques, 234
Tadcaster, 269
Tate Gallery, 26
Taylor, A.J.P., 11
Teesside Development Corporation, 93
Terminator, The, 98
Terminator 2, 8
textile industry, 54-58, 106-108, 116, 120-127, 212-213
Thames estuary, 235
Thatcher, Margaret, 4, 20, 24, 30, 220
  blamed for inner city deprivation, 14, 16
  economic philosophy of, 51, 170-171
  economic hopes of, 149
  compared with John Major, 282
  hypocritical left-wing hatred of, 331-332
Todmorden Park, 113-115
Toxteth, 27, 33, 34, 35, (riots) 43-44, 61; *see also* Liverpool
Traditional Homes magazine, 281
Trollope, 36
Tunstall, 149, 150, 155
Turkey, 55
Twyford, Thomas William, 169
Twyfords (Caradon-Twyfords), 168-173, 174, 224
Tyneside, *see* Newcastle-upon-Tyne
Tyne and Wear Metro, *see* Newcastle-upon-Tyne

United Nations, 3
United States of America, 3
uPVC doors and windows, 220-224, 226, 242, 243
  aesthetic consequences of, 220, 222-223
Uttoxeter, 148

Victoria Station, London, 251
Viz magazine, 3
Vranch, Richard, 3

Walsall, 180
Wallsend, 71, 75
Walters, Prof. Alan, 270
Warner, Jack, 10
Washington, Co. Durham, 91
Waterhouse, Keith, 3
Watford, 293
Waugh, Auberon, 8
West Midlands Baptist Association, 192
West, Richard, 257
Wetherby, 269
Whitelaw, Billie, 118
Wigan, 46, 265
Wills Family, 295, 304; *see also* Bristol
Wilmslow, 281
Winchester, 263
Wogan, Terry, 248
Wood and Sons, pottery manufacturers, 165-168, 171
Worstead, Norfk., 213
Worsthorne, Peregrine, 4, 195

Worthing, 264

York, 105, 211, 247, 251
Yorke, Edmund, 168
Yorkshire Dales, 66, 231, 321
Young, Hugo, 242, 336